Advance praise for *Evolution's Iceberg*

"To question the all-creative power of Darwinian evolution is generally considered as a fool's errand, akin to questioning whether the earth is round rather than flat. But in this highly accessible account, abundant scientific evidence is amassed to show a clear mismatch between the theory and the facts. Open-minded readers will surely find it persuasive."

> **Dr Alistair Donald MA PhD BD, former Chaplain of Heriot-Watt University, Edinburgh**

"Evolution's Iceberg is a book with a very clever analytical structure. Guy Douglas has done an excellent job in summarising and demonstrating how the superstructure of some currently favoured thinking is actually holed below the water line. He carefully disarticulates the components that hold that thinking together and provides a case to show that the commonly understood evolutionary paradigm cannot survive."

> **David Galloway MD DSc FRCS FRCP FACS FACP, Honorary Professor of Surgery, University of Glasgow. Former President, Royal College of Physicians and Surgeons of Glasgow**

"In this remarkable and intriguing book, Guy Douglas uses the analogy of the 'unsinkable *Titanic*' creatively to expose the critical deficiencies of modern evolutionary theory with its fundamental tenet of blind 'chance and necessity'. He argues cogently that this is unsustainable, given the breathtaking discoveries of modern molecular biology which point in the very different direction of deliberate design. This is a 'must read' for everyone interested in the origin and sophistication of life as we know it."

> **Dr Alastair Noble, BSc, PhD, former Inspector of Schools, and Assistant Director of Education**

"In this book Guy Douglas presents an insightful parallel between the iceberg that sank the *Titanic*, and the facts of molecular biology on which the reputedly unsinkable theory of evolution founders.

The author examines five critical issues which are widely believed to support evolution, and shows that evolutionary explanations are seriously lacking - holed beneath the waterline: because of the complexity of molecular biology there is no hope that life could have originated through undirected physical and chemical processes, or of substantial new forms arising subsequently, including the supposed evolution of humans from ancestral apes. And it reinforces the evidence that diverse early embryonic development refutes common ancestry, notably of the different classes of vertebrates.

Unfortunately, as Guy Douglas points out, just as it took a long time for most passengers on the *Titanic* to realise that it had struck an iceberg, so most people today are unaware that molecular biology sinks the theory of evolution. Fortunately, this book will help to remedy that, and encourage thinking people to take a fresh look at the evidence."

David W. Swift B.A. (Cantab.), M.Sc., author of *Evolution under the microscope*

Evolution's Iceberg

Evolution's Iceberg

How molecular biology
challenges
the theory of evolution

Guy Douglas

EVOLUTION'S ICEBERG

Copyright © 2024 by Guy Douglas.

ISBN: 978-1-64373-418-7

All rights reserved. Without limiting the rights under copyright reserved above, no part of this publication may be reproduced, stored in a retrieval system, or transmitted, in any form or by any means (electronic, mechanical, photocopying, recording or otherwise), without the prior written permission of the copyright owner of this book.
Revision: 012L

Cover design by James Gentles © 2024.

I am grateful to the James Clerk Maxwell Foundation for permission to reproduce a number of images from their collection.

All Scripture quotations, unless otherwise indicated, are taken from the Holy Bible, New International Version®, NIV®. Copyright ©1973, 1978, 1984, 2011 by Biblica, Inc.™ Used by permission of Zondervan. All rights reserved worldwide. www.zondervan.com
The "NIV" and "New International Version" are trademarks registered in the United States Patent and Trademark Office by Biblica, Inc.™

Published by
Lighthouse Christian Publishing
SAN 257-4330
228 Freedom Parkway
Hoschton, GA 30548
United States of America
www.lighthousechristianpublishing.com

This book is dedicated to my grandchildren:
Emma, Nathanael, Tarron, Jack, Myles, Jacob, Samuel and Evie.

May papa's book offer you a different perspective on the evolutionary story you will have been taught and will have imbibed as you have been growing up. I would encourage you to, as the well known evolutionary biologist and prolific author Richard Dawkins put it, "question everything".

CONTENTS

About the author	1
Prologue	3
Introduction	9

PART 1 - DON'T ROCK THE BOAT!
Critiquing evolution is not anti-science

	1	Science: its limitations	19
	2	Scientists: the new priesthood	41
	3	Evolution: thinking the unthinkable	57

PART 2 - DAMAGE BELOW DECKS!
Five failed predictions of neo-Darwinian theory

		Introduction to part 2	75
	4	Life emerged from chemistry	77
	5	Natural selection has creative power	113
	6	The tree-of-life is recorded in the fossils	153
	7	Similar embryos imply common ancestry	187
	8	The human species evolved from apes	221

PART 3 - SHE'S SINKING!
But few people know this, or that there's a better theory

		Introduction to part 3	267
	9	Why is RMS *Evolution* still afloat?	271
	10	A better theory: Intelligent Design	289
Epilogue		The real tree-of-life	301
Further Reading			305
Appendix A		*Evolution*'s protagonists and their religious views	307

Appendix B The ideology of evolutionism	317
Acknowledgements	321
Notes	323
References	365
Credits and permissions	373
Index	379

About the author

Guy was brought up in 1950s Beith, for a hundred years the most important furniture manufacturing town in Scotland. He earned his BSc (Hons) in electrical and electronic engineering at the University of Glasgow, later gaining a MSc in digital electronics from Heriot Watt University in Edinburgh. With Hewlett Packard, and later Agilent Technologies, his thirty years in the Scottish electronics industry, "Silicon Glen" as it was called, encompassed the design and manufacture of instrumentation used in the testing of telecommunications networks. As someone who enjoyed a career in engineering, the author loves the scientific approach and its accomplishments, is pro-science in its pursuit of truth about the workings of the universe and optimistic about the potential for technology to continue to provide solutions to existing and emerging world problems.

The author therefore comes to the topic of evolution with an engineering bias. Why is this significant? Well, an evolutionary biologist will typically *assume* evolution to be true and then go on to ask "why" questions such as, "**Why** did *Homo sapiens* evolve a large brain?" or "**Why** was colour vision first lost in most mammals and then later regained in some primates?"[1] meaning "What were the evolutionary *benefits* of these adaptations?" The author, however, is more interested in "how" questions, such as, "**How** did *Homo sapiens* evolve upright walking?" or "**How** did a bat evolve echolocation?" by "numerous, successive, slight modifications", to use Darwin's words. The standard "how" answer offered by evolutionary biology is that, given lots of time, novel biological features (such as echolocation and upright walking) will "emerge" as a result of natural selection acting upon random genetic variations.

But the engineer wants to know how, or even whether, this mechanism is capable of generating the new *information* required at the detailed molecular level within living cells. Astonishing discoveries made in molecular biology over the last fifty years or so are not only rendering the "how" questions even more pressing, but are also revealing answers that challenge the received Darwinian wisdom's most consequential claims.

Guy's theological affiliation is to Christianity. Some readers might therefore protest that his Christian worldview will bias his conclusions in relation to evolutionary theory. But this can be countered in two ways. First, many Christians have no problem reconciling the theory of evolution with their religious beliefs. Francis Collins, who led the Human Genome Project, is an example of this view. Such *Evolutionary Creationists* believe that God used the process of evolution to create life (Appendix A explores the spectrum of religious views relating to evolution in more detail). So belief in God does not *automatically* lead to rejection of evolutionary theory.

Second, if the author's theological bias discounts him from critiquing biological evolution, then surely the other side of the same coin is that atheists (such as Richard Dawkins) should be discounted from promoting the theory on account of their (or his) atheistic worldview. Why so? The reason an atheistic *a priori* bias is important when evaluating evolutionary theory is that, for the atheist, some form of naturalistic (meaning unguided, undirected) evolution *must* be true. The atheist believes there is no Creator. Therefore life *must* have happened by a combination of chance and natural law.

For the Christian, however, God may or may not have used an evolutionary process in the course of creating the universe and life. Arguably, the psychology of this situation - a certain ambivalence about the outcome - would suggest that the Christian can take a more objective view of the scientific evidence for and against the theory. ***It's the science that matters***. The author is not an evolutionary biologist, so looks through a porthole or two to assess the claims of that discipline. With an engineering bias, then, the author has been interested in understanding the *how* of evolution for over thirty years. ***How*** does it work? ***Can*** it work? Arguably, as an 'outsider' the author may be able to examine the claims of the theory more dispassionately.

Prologue

On Wednesday 10th April 1912, on the dot of 12 noon, the RMS *Titanic* steamed out of Southampton for the first and, as it turned out, last time. Earlier that morning, more than 900 passengers had boarded *Titanic* eagerly anticipating her maiden voyage. By the evening, the largest man-made moving object the world had ever seen had crossed the English Channel and anchored off Cherbourg where another 250 passengers joined the ship. Travelling overnight, she dropped anchor at 11:30 am near Queenstown (now Cobh) on the southern tip of Ireland. Within two hours, those joining and leaving the ship had brought the full complement on board to nearly 2,200 consisting of thirteen hundred passengers and a crew of almost nine hundred. The Atlantic Ocean and New York beckoned. Weighing anchor, Captain Edward John Smith, affectionately known as 'EJ', steered her out into the open sea. Two thirds of those aboard would never see dry land again.

The transatlantic crossing 'arms race' began almost a century earlier when, in 1819, the first steamship SS *Savannah* sailed from Georgia to Liverpool in 23 days. By 1838, Isambard Kingdom Brunel's *Great Western* reduced the crossing time to 14½ days. The race was on. Brunel had worked out that the bigger the ship, the more efficient and more cost-effective it would be.

In 1906, driven by this enslaving trend, the *Cunard Line* launched two 'state of the art' new ships, the *Lusitania* and *Mauretania*. Lord Inverclyde, chairman of *Cunard*, had persuaded the British government to provide a loan of £2.6 million, an enormous sum at the time, to achieve his objective of dominating the North Atlantic passenger trade using the latest steam turbine technology. *Cunard* was the only shipping line that could now be regarded as fully British and it was facing stiff competition from the *Hamburg-America Line* (German) and the *White Star Line*. The latter had been the subject of a takeover in 1902 by the legendary American financier J.P. Morgan.

Joseph Bruce Ismay, chairman of the *White Star Line*, recognised that his current ships on the North Atlantic route - the *Teutonic*, *Adriatic* and *Oceanic* - would not be able to compete with these new additions to *Cunard's* fleet which had reduced the crossing time to a little under 4½ days. He held an urgent meeting with Lord Pirrie over dinner in the summer of 1907. William James Pirrie, Lord Mayor of Belfast, was chairman of *Harland & Wolff's* shipyard where all recent *White Star Line* ships had been built.

Ismay and Pirrie hatched a plan to outflank *Cunard* by building not two, but three even bigger and more luxurious liners. They chose the names - *Olympic*, *Titanic* and *Gigantic*[1] - to promote an image consistent with their marketing strategy. They were to be the mightiest ships ever built, 882 feet long and displacing 46,000 tons, versus the 788 feet and 32,000 tons of *Lusitania* and *Mauretania*. They decided that it would not be sensible to compete on speed. Their reputation had been built upon operating the biggest, safest, and most luxurious of ships and they concluded that the *White Star Line* could continue to be successful on this battle ground. In any case they could not afford the extra time required to develop turbine engines capable of powering such massive ships. A compromise was agreed. The two main engines driving the port and starboard propellers were to be of the triple expansion reciprocating type. They then added one of the newer turbine engines to drive a third, central propeller.

Meantime, these three almost identical ships were to be the ultimate in luxury, virtually indistinguishable from the very best country house hotels. The *Titanic* boasted electric lighting; a Turkish bath - a leisure suite complete with steam room, hot room, temperate room, cooling room and shampoo room; a swimming pool, squash court and gymnasium; barber shops with hair dryers; separate elevators for first and second class passengers (third class passengers had no option but to climb stairs!); a sumptuous first class lounge and reading room; first, second and third class smoking rooms; a library; first class state rooms in a choice of styles including Louis XV, Renaissance, Georgian, Adam and Queen Anne. The sweeping oak-panelled grand staircase linked the first class reception and dining rooms on Saloon deck with the four decks above and was crowned at Boat Deck level by an ornate dome of opaque glass panels supported by a lattice of iron framing. The second class accommodation was of equivalent standard to first class facilities on most other ships. Even the third class smoking room had oak-panelled walls, teak tables and chairs and a linoleum-covered floor. Many of the third class cabins were fitted with wash basins and running water and the menu offered in the third class dining saloon, included within the price of a ticket, would not look out of place in any reasonable standard of hotel today. All this was carried on nine decks and topped by four huge funnels – although only three were actually needed to vent smoke from the 6 boiler rooms, housing 29 double-ended boilers.

An estimated 100,000 spectators sat on purpose-built grandstands inside the shipyard or stood on the banks of the River Lagan for the auspicious launch occasion. Among the spectators for the launch of *Titanic* on 31st May 1911 were *White Star* chairman J. Bruce Ismay and owner and financier J.P. Morgan, who had travelled from the States especially for the occasion. Both Ismay and Morgan had intended to sail on *Titanic*'s maiden voyage, but the latter cancelled his trip at the last minute, apparently due to ill-health. So it was Ismay who occupied the promenade suite on B Deck which had been designed to Morgan's specifications and intended for his personal use when travelling.

Around 12.15 pm, Lord Pirrie fired the final rocket, the hydraulic triggers were released, and, to the ecstatic cheers of the crowd, *Titanic*'s hull slid down No. 3 slipway into the waiting river below. Once her fitting out and sea trials were complete, *Titanic* left Belfast Lough for good at 8pm on 2nd April 1912 bound for Southampton.

On board were Harland & Wolff's nine-strong Guarantee Group, a team of technical experts whose job was to familiarise the crew with the specifics of this new ship's equipment and to handle any teething problems as they arose. The leader of the Guarantee Group was Thomas Andrews, Lord Pirrie's nephew and *Titanic*'s chief designer. His warmth, humility and ability to lead by example had inspired his colleagues and earned the trust of the shipyard's workers. A perfectionist, he would often be seen carrying a small notebook in which he would log his snagging lists, actions required and ideas he had for improvements or refinements to future designs. When Lord Pirrie retired, Andrews was fully expected to replace him as chairman of the company. It was not to be.

It was now Sunday 14th April 1912, shortly before midnight. Thomas Andrews was poring over the ship's plans in his first class cabin on A Deck. A knock on his door summoned him to the bridge at the urgent request of Captain Smith. Andrews had been so engrossed in his thoughts that he, like most others on the ship, had not noticed anything amiss.

He was to learn that at 11.40 pm, Frederick Fleet, one of two lookouts in *Titanic's* crow's nest, had spotted a strange haze on the horizon which he very quickly realised was an iceberg a mere 500 yards dead ahead. First Officer Murdoch was in charge of the ship at the time. He immediately executed a turn to port and telegraphed a full-astern order to the engine room. *Titanic* was slicing through the water at 22 knots. The steam turbine engine driving the central propeller was not designed to reverse, so only the conventional piston engines driving the port and starboard screws responded to the engine-room command.

During the sea trials in Belfast Lough less than a fortnight previously, the log showed that it took *Titanic* 850 yards in which to complete her emergency stop manoeuvre. Collision with the iceberg had been inevitable from the moment Fleet identified it. EJ Smith

Figure P.1 RMS (Royal Mail Ship) *Titanic* 1912-1912. Side elevation showing the bulkhead arrangements. Collision with the iceberg generated intermittent punctures along the hull, piercing the first five watertight compartments. It was then inevitable that *Titanic* would sink.

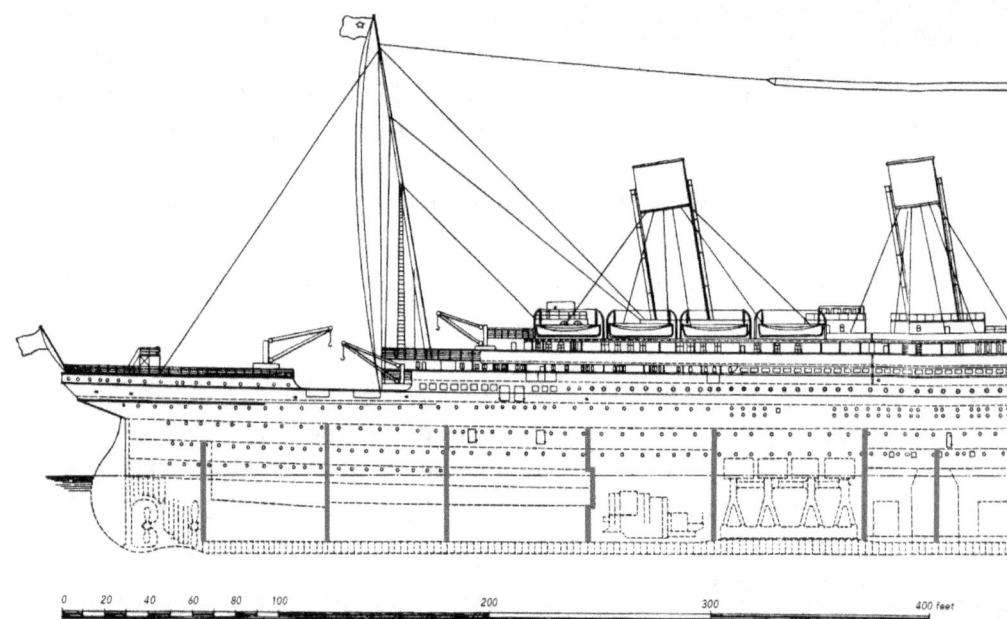

realised there was something wrong immediately, and was on the bridge from his nearby cabin in a few seconds.

Andrews and Smith went below to assess the damage. To their horror they realised water was pouring into five watertight sections as far back from the bow as the most for'ard (No. 6) boiler room.[2] Ten minutes after the collision, water was already ten feet deep in these sections. Andrews' assessment was that the ship could remain afloat for no more than two hours. The first lifeboat was lowered at 12.45 am.

The 'Pride of Belfast', as she had become known, sank at 2.17 am just under 400 miles from the Newfoundland coast.

Only 700 survived of almost 2,200 aboard. Many high society figures lost their lives. The greatest proportion of loss – more than 440 out of about 600 – was among third class passengers. EJ Smith was last seen swimming in the sea carrying an infant to a nearby lifeboat. Thomas Andrews and the entire Guarantee Group also went down with the ship.[3]

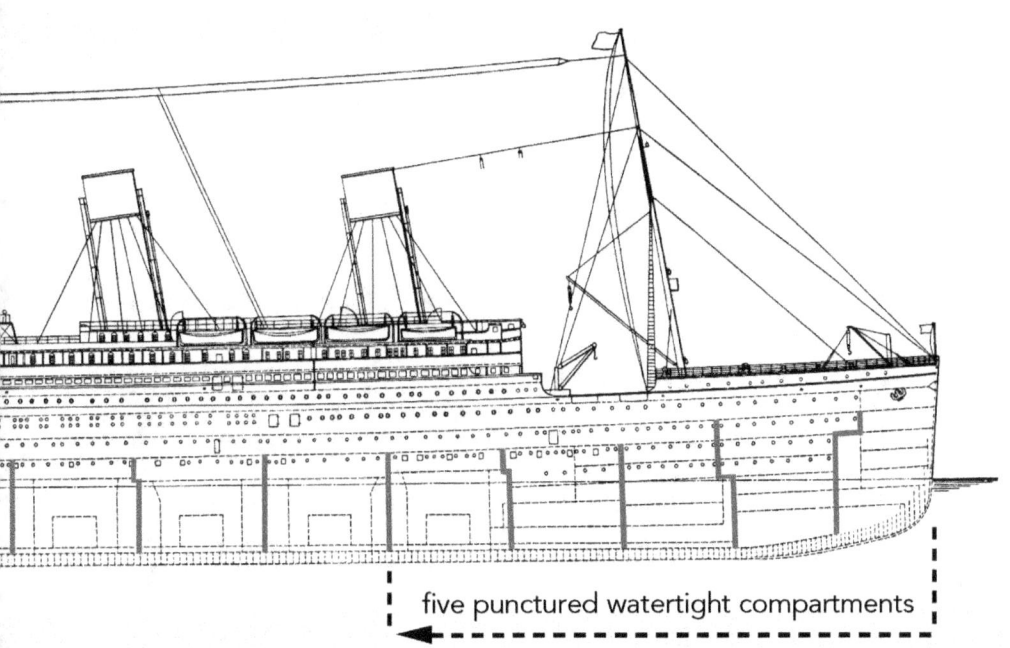

five punctured watertight compartments

Introduction

"Why re-tell the very well-known story of *Titanic* in the prologue of a book about the *Theory of Evolution*?" you may ask.

There are many intriguing aspects to the *Titanic* story. Certainly all those involved in the project, Lord Pirrie, J. Bruce Ismay, J.P. Morgan, the Belfast workers and their families, made sure the whole world knew that this was the biggest, most modern, most luxurious vessel ever to put to sea. This very public tragedy was a disaster of enormous proportions. The accidental loss of 1500 lives in peacetime was devastating on both sides of the Atlantic. The loss to American society of many of her wealthiest people generated massive press interest at the time and long after the event.

But perhaps the twist in the RMS *Titanic* story that has most fascinated succeeding generations and resulted in the creation of hundreds of articles, books, websites and at least six movies, was **the deeply held belief at the time that *Titanic* could not, and therefore would not, sink**. The extent to which people, whether expert in matters of the sea or not, believed that *Titanic* was incapable of sinking is illustrated by this quote from Captain Smith, interviewed in 1907.

> *Shipbuilding is such a perfect art nowadays that absolute disaster, involving the passengers, is inconceivable. Whatever happens, there will be time enough before the vessel sinks to save the lives of every person on board. I will go a bit further.* **I will say that I cannot imagine any condition that would cause the vessel to founder.** *Modern shipbuilding has gone beyond that [emphasis added].*[1]

There is a view that the "unsinkable" narrative developed *after* the sinking, but this is a modern myth.[2] The spirit of the "unsinkable" belief, widely held at the time, is captured brilliantly in the 1997 movie *Titanic*,[3] starring Leonardo DiCaprio and Kate Winslet, who plays the character 'Rose'. As passengers gather on the quay at Southampton, Rose's aristocratic mother poses the question, "So this is the ship they say is unsinkable?" Mr Hockley, Rose's rich American intended, is quick to respond, **"It is unsinkable, God himself could not sink this ship!"**[4]

It is unlikely that Cameron's movie portrays the precise sequence of events in the early hours of 15th April 1912 following the collision with the iceberg - including meetings between the Captain, his senior officers and the Guarantee Group. However, recalling a few scenes from the film will neatly illustrate the likely tensions between belief in *Titanic's* unsinkability and the reality of the perilous situation.

Once the iceberg has been struck, a movie scene ensues in which Thomas Andrews, EJ Smith and his senior officers hastily gather in the chartroom. Andrews briefs the attendees on the extent of the damage. Using an engineer's schematic of the ship, beginning at the bow, he points to each of the first five watertight compartments in turn and makes the key point that all five have been breached. "She could stay afloat with four compartments flooded, but not five." Following a pause he repeated, "Not five", and then, "From this moment, no matter what you do, *Titanic* will founder". J. Bruce Ismay, chairman of the *White Star Line*, had also joined this troubled meeting, anxious for the ship to be underway without further delay. At this point he can contain himself no longer and angrily interjects, **"But this ship can't sink!"** Andrews riposte is swift, **"She's made of iron, sir, I assure you she can, and she will, with mathematical certainty"**.

Shortly, a surreal episode unfolds in which Thomas Andrews, wandering round the first class reception and dining areas, carries a bewildered expression on his face as he observes with disbelief the general passenger reaction to requests from members of the crew to don lifejackets and make their way to muster stations. Andrews is offered a glass of brandy by a passing steward who continues with oblivious dedication to ply other unsuspecting passengers with alcoholic pleasure. Evening entertainment and the party atmosphere continues unabated as if nothing has changed. The paradigm that "…this ship can't sink!" is so deeply held as a core belief, that **the possibility that *Titanic* might actually sink doesn't even begin to register within the consciousness of most passengers.**

Again, in the following scene, Rose's impenetrably upper class mother chastises her maids for chivvying her on with the incongruously ridiculous lifejacket. She orders them to turn on heaters in their suite of rooms and to make a cup of tea upon her imminent return at the can't-come-soon-enough conclusion of this fatuous drill.

There was of course some basis in fact behind the belief that *Titanic* was unsinkable. Huge progress had indeed been made in ship design as indicated in Captain Smith's interview comments. *Titanic* was designed to meet *Board of Trade* guidelines developed in 1890. These required that ships be divided along their length by transverse bulkheads into watertight sections or compartments in order to limit the proportion of a ship that might be flooded in the event of a collision. The guidelines further required that a ship would be able to remain afloat with up to 24% of its length becoming flooded, when constrained within such watertight compartments. In the *Titanic* design, flooding of only the first four compartments would have constituted 23% of the ship's length, whereas the fifth increased the exposure to almost 30%. This was the basis of Andrew's claim in the 1996 movie chartroom scene that *Titanic* would have survived the iceberg collision had only four watertight sections been breached.[5]

A few days after the tragedy on 19th April, an article[6] in an engineering journal suggested that "Responsible persons tend to be satisfied when they have fulfilled either a statutory condition or one which can be definitely interpreted and applied, and are disposed to rest content if such a condition is no more than fulfilled". The article by Professor J.H. Biles then clarifies what often ensues.

> *They then allow their vessels to be called unsinkable,* **but their unsinkability is really only under the conditions named** *[emphasis added].[7]*

The sinking of the *City of Brussels* by collision in the Mersey in 1880 led to a shipbuilding re-think. So for example in 1888, with the *City of Brussels* tragedy still fresh in designers' minds, the steamship *City of New York* was designed to more conservative standards than the Board of Trade required in 1890. A comparison with the *Titanic* bulkhead arrangements is revealing. In the *New York* the bulkheads rose from the keel of the ship 28 feet to the waterline and continued to a further 14 or 15 feet above the waterline, i.e. the bulkheads provided protection against sinking to the extent of at least 50% of the below-waterline bulkhead depth. This contrasted with only 33% on *Titanic* – 10 feet above a waterline bulkhead depth of 30 feet. Putting this another way, the bulkheads only reached to the underside of E Deck on *Titanic*, with a further five decks above this level, compared with only two decks on the *New York*.

So even though RMS *Titanic* met the 1890 Board of Trade recommendations, there had clearly been a degradation in standards since the more conservative *New York* design. Indeed the *New York* might well have survived the iceberg which sank *Titanic*. The reason for this degradation was a capitulation to the view that higher bulkheads would have restricted the movement of passengers around the ship too much, especially inconveniencing to first class passengers. There are surely parallels between how the travelling class in 1912 thought about ship technology generally, with the *Titanic* standing as its most iconic "unsinkable" representative, and how many people think about *Evolution* today. **There is a real sense in which most people today consider the *Theory of Evolution* to be an 'unsinkable ship'.**

In 1912, the notion that an ocean-going liner might sink was unthinkable. The idea did not even enter the consciousness of passengers, crew or the general public. *Harland & Wolff* and the *White Star Line* were so confident that *Titanic* was unsinkable that the decision to carry only enough lifeboat capacity to save less than half the ship's complement was viewed with equanimity.

Similarly today, the *Theory of Evolution* is a generally accepted scientific theory. It is regarded as so foundational, especially within Western culture, that almost no one even thinks to question it – whether in scientific or academic circles, or within the public generally.[8] Just as water is to fish swimming in it, we take it for granted. It is viewed as "fact". The 'unsinkable ship' paradigm is in play and it subconsciously permeates and underpins every strand of our thinking: how we view the universe, the history of the earth and humanity. It began in earnest with Darwin and developed as a hypothesis within biology. But, just as a stone thrown into a pond sends out concentric ripples in all directions, so evolutionary thinking has reached out well beyond biology, influencing and infiltrating so many other disciplines; not only within other branches of science, including cosmology, geology, genetics and palaeontology, just to mention a few; but also within the humanities, such as evolutionary psychology, history, anthropology, sociology, philosophy and theology. Its supremacy is seemingly unassailable, especially in Western society.

Now here's the big 'What-if?'

What if – just as *Titanic* had design flaws that rendered it unsinkable only in a limited sense – what if the science underpinning the *Theory of Evolution* turns out to be valid only in a strictly limited sense?

The thesis of this book is that 19th century Darwinian science, developing as it did in an age that also gave rise to supreme confidence in *Titanic's* unsinkability, has collided with the 'iceberg' of 21st century molecular biology.

The amazing discoveries in the late 20th and especially in the early 21st century – of the exquisite micro-molecular machinery and organisational complexity, together with the hierarchical layers of regulatory control systems inside living cells – have become *Evolution's* 'iceberg'.

We need to ask, "Is it legitimate to have doubts about evolution?" Surely, it is affirmed by the vast majority of people: biologists, scientists generally, and everyone else for that matter. Indeed, in the present climate, anyone who is not an evolutionary biologist and dares to question the veracity of the *Theory* is very likely to be accused of being ignorant, or uneducated, or anti-science, or all three. The tone of such reprimands, as many have experienced, is likely to be patronising, dismissive or even vitriolic. Zoologist Richard Dawkins on one side of the Atlantic and biologist Jerry Coyne on the other are both eloquent and prolific promoters of RMS *Evolution's* 'unsinkable ship' paradigm. The scientific claims of these two prominent members of the officer class aboard RMS *Evolution* will be critically examined throughout this book.

Figure I.1 Richard Dawkins and Jerry Coyne

If a scientist on the inside, a practitioner within the discipline of evolutionary biology, manifests any doubts about the power of natural selection, reviewers of their work are likely to express surprise and disbelief. One insider reviewer of such a doubting author expressed his surprise and indignation.

> What is remarkable is that the author is not someone from the fringes or even outside of evolutionary biology... [He] is one of the founding fathers and pioneers of what is now called the field of molecular evolution... Isn't selection well studied and the well-established driver of adaptive evolutionary change?[9]

Just as a fish when asked about the temperature of the water today by another fish might respond with "What's water?",[10] so the reviewer from within the paradigm of his 'unsinkable ship' doesn't even consider the possibility that there might be a problem with evolution. Integral to the argument of this book is the view that the theory of evolution should be open to scrutiny just like any other scientific theory. To proscribe such analysis would be counter to the spirit of the scientific enterprise.

In **Part 1: DON'T ROCK THE BOAT! - Critiquing evolution is not anti-science,** we'll begin by exploring questions like:
- What is "science"?
- What is "evolution"?
- Has "science" ever got things wrong?
- Is "science" in conflict with "religion"?
- Has "science" become the ultimate authority?
- Can a (real) scientist believe in God?
- Do all scientific disciplines speak with equal authority?

In **Part 2: DAMAGE BELOW DECKS! - Five failed predictions of neo-Darwinism,** we'll go down 'below decks' on RMS *Evolution* now that it has collided with the 'molecular biology iceberg' and inspect the damage inside five putatively watertight compartments; five different strands of evidence claimed to support the theory:
- The origin of life.
- The power of natural selection to invent.
- The fossil record.
- Embryology and genetics.
- Human evolution.

The implication of the findings in Part 2 is that evolution is no more than a modern creation myth. So in **Part 3: SHE'S SINKING! - But few people know this, or that there's a better theory,** we'll ask why it is that most 'smart' people still believe the grand claims of evolution to be true and why our academic, media and educational institutions still fervently promote the orthodox paradigm while failing to present the counter-evidence. We'll also explore a theory that better explains the origin of biological information - Intelligent Design.

There are metaphysical, or worldview, repercussions emanating from this conclusion about the science. The Epilogue briefly explores the implications of the conclusion for belief in God. And two appendices outline, respectively, the religious views of the key protagonists involved in the debate, and the ideological implications of evolutionism.

Perhaps you've never even thought about questioning the evolutionary narrative you've been brought up with. Perhaps you've only ever come across evidence that *supports* the theory. This book will explore the counter-evidence, by no means exhaustively, with a particular emphasis upon areas impacted by findings in molecular biology.

Maybe it's time to think the unthinkable, sink the unsinkable.

Part 1

DON'T ROCK THE BOAT!

Critiquing evolution is not anti-science

Bruce Ismay – White Star Line Chairman

"But this ship can't sink!"

Chapter 1
Science: its limitations

I know no finer illustration of the most important message taught by the history of science: the subtle and inevitable hold that theory exerts upon data and observation. Reality does not speak to us objectively, and no scientist can be free from constraints of psyche and society. The greatest impediment to scientific innovation is usually a conceptual lock, not a factual lack.[1]

Stephen Jay Gould (1941-2002)

We begin with a brief exploration of the achievements of science and then ask:
- Does science sometimes get things wrong?
- What is "science"?
- Do all sciences speak with equal authority?

Scientific achievements are impressive

Just as passengers boarding RMS *Titanic* could not fail to be impressed by its sheer size, elegance and sophistication, similarly *science* is generally held in very high esteem in today's society. Its achievements are impressive, indeed life-changing, and its innovations are everywhere to be seen in use around us: from microwave ovens and mobile smartphones to microprocessors and magnetic resonance imaging; from spaceflight and satnav to solar panels and surgical organ transplants.

Consider mind-boggling feats of engineering, such as launching the *Voyager* spacecraft on trajectories taking it to the edge of the solar system and beyond, with power and communication technology still functioning so as to be able to send back spellbinding images of each distant planet in turn, together with its unique rings and moons.

Perhaps even more extraordinary are some down to earth achievements. In the last two hundred years in the developed world – and in recent decades even in the developing world – dramatic improvements have been made in reducing childhood deaths from infectious diseases. In relation to this, Harvard professor of psychology

Steven Pinker reminds us that "[t]he fruits of science are not just pharmaceuticals such as vaccines, antibiotics, antiretrovirals, and deworming pills". Millions of lives have also been saved worldwide by the adoption of relatively simple ideas that are cheap to implement. Pinker catalogues some of these obvious-in-retrospect innovations: "... boiling, filtering or adding bleach to water; washing hands; giving iodine supplements to pregnant women; breast feeding and cuddling infants;[2] defecating in latrines rather than in fields, streets, and waterways; protecting children with insecticide-impregnated bed nets; and treating diarrhoea with a solution of salt and sugar in clean water".[3]

Traditional farming methods would not have been able to meet the challenge of feeding a fast-growing world population. Probably *the* most significant contribution to mitigating this pending disaster has been attributed to the work of two German chemists. In 1909 Fritz Haber became the first to discover a commercially feasible way of fixing nitrogen, meaning to convert nitrogen in the atmosphere into ammonia which could then become the basis of a synthetic fertiliser. Carl Bosch, chief research engineer at BASF,[4] then converted Haber's tabletop apparatus into an industry[5] which has revolutionised world food production. The Haber-Bosch breakthrough is estimated to have saved the lives of 2.7 billion people.[6]

Infant mortality rates have plummeted in the last hundred years, first in the West and more recently in the rest of the world. In a similar way, life expectancy has surged over the same period.

Meantime, thanks to computer technology and the worldwide communications network – the largest machine made by humanity so far – a majority of the world population has almost instantaneous access to a vast amount of knowledge and information via the internet (about half the adults in the world own a smartphone)[7] resulting in huge educational benefits.

Without doubt, science and technology have brought enormous improvements in health, longevity, quality of life and standard of living, as well as insights into the workings of the universe. This is much to be celebrated.

The possibility that *Titanic* might sink would not have occurred to most of its passengers and, given the unassailable and well deserved prestige of science not only in academia but also among the general public, the majority of us today largely accept without question pronouncements made by high profile members of the science community. So is it legitimate to call into question – as is about to happen in Part 2 – an established scientific theory?

Does science sometimes get things wrong?

Well, yes, it does. Let's take a look at a few examples. The first examples that occur to the author as an engineer are two well known engineering disasters – in addition to RMS *Titanic* of course!

SPACE SHUTTLE 'CHALLENGER'. On 28th January 1986, 73 seconds after launch, the *Challenger* space shuttle exploded killing all seven on board, including the first non-professional astronaut, Christa McAuliffe, a New Hampshire school teacher. The disaster, which resulted in the Shuttle programme being grounded for two and a half years pending redesign, was caused by the failure of both primary and secondary O-rings on the right solid rocket booster. The problems with the O-rings had been known. Roger Boisjoly, a mechanical engineer working for Morton Thiokol, the company that designed the solid rocket boosters, wrote a memo in July 1985 expressing his concerns. In January 1985 he discovered that one of the primary O-rings in a recovered booster had been breached and that the secondary ring had been damaged. He suspected that the rubber material was becoming brittle at low temperature.

On the evening before the fateful launch, the forecast had indicated a launch temperature of -1°C. Boisjoly with the support of another engineer recommended a "no-go" decision in the conference call with NASA. But management expediency won the day.[8] **The problem** with the O-rings had been known – but **was ignored and information** about it **suppressed**.

THE CHERNOBYL DISASTER. It would seem 1986 was a bad year for engineering disasters. At 1:23 am on 26th April, Unit 4 at the Chernobyl nuclear power plant in eastern Ukraine exploded, leaving an opening through which it could freely "spit" radiation into the atmosphere.[9] The consequences were enormous and are still unfolding today. In 2005 United Nations agencies estimated that 4,000 people may die in the future of radiation-related causes. More recent estimates have been significantly higher. In the first five years after the disaster, cases of cancer among local children increased by 90%. Over 140,000 square kilometres of territory was severely contaminated by radiation: 19%,

5% and 1% of the populations of Belarus, Ukraine and Russia, respectively – a total of over 4 million people – had to be resettled.[10] Plutonium-239, with a half-life of 24,000 years, will render the area around the plant unsafe for human habitation for at least another 20,000 years.[11] The nuclear plume was detectable in Germany, France, northern Italy and as far away as northern North America.

The immediate cause of the accident was a complicated series of tests – run erratically over a three-day period spanning several different shifts of operators of mixed experience and ability – that went badly wrong. The Russian RBMK[12] design was inherently less stable under adverse conditions and less securely contained than the Pressurised Water Reactor (PWR) design more common in the West.

It turns out that there had been a near accident at a similar reactor installation near Leningrad in 1975, when its reactor was nearly destroyed. As the Russian historian Serhii Plokhy recorded, "The details of that accident were withheld from the personnel of other nuclear plants".[13]

Amazingly, even after Chernobyl operators had seen with their own eyes lumps of burning (highly radioactive) graphite lying on the ground – which could only have come from the reactor core – it still did not occur to them that the reactor had in fact exploded. This state of denial was induced by a **reverential belief in the superiority and infallibility of Soviet science**[14] **and an unshakeable conviction that it was not possible for a nuclear reactor to explode**.[15] Plokhy also attributed initial denial to "**Mass blindness**. Many see what has happened but do not believe it… **The myth of the reactor's safety was shared by everyone in the industry, from top to bottom.**"[16]

… and mainstream science too …

To be clear, **there is no anti-science agenda in play here**; simply a recognition that all scientific claims to knowledge are provisional and may require to be revised in the light of new evidence.

PHLOGISTON OR OXYGEN?[17] Joseph Priestley (1733-1804) developed the phlogiston theory of combustion. This stated that anything that could burn or support combustion contained a substance called *phlogiston*: that during burning, phlogiston was given off and lost into the atmosphere. In a later experiment – heating red oxide of mercury –

he isolated a gas which he thought was air from which phlogiston had been removed. He called it dephlogisticated air. What he had actually discovered was oxygen. Antoine Lavoisier (1743-94) has been credited with sorting out Priestley's error. Yet throughout the rest of his life, **Priestley never abandoned his phlogiston theory.** He was never able to accept Lavoisier's insight that the gas was a distinct species, one of the two main constituents of the atmosphere.

Figure 1.1
Joseph Priestley

THEY LAUGHED AT WEGENER.[18] In 1912, Alfred Wegener (1880-1930) published a book in his native German language which in the 1924 English translation was entitled *Origin of Continents and Oceans*. Up to the early 1900s it had been widely believed by geologists that the general shape and position of continents had remained unchanged since the time when the Earth's crust had solidified many millions of years in the past. Wegener's hypothesis was that continents had moved and were still on the move, slowly drifting. He put forward lots of evidence including the intriguing fact that if you

Figure 1.2
Alfred Wegener

make cardboard cut-outs of the continents from a map of the world, the west coast of Africa and of Europe fit surprisingly well into the east coast of South and North America respectively. **Experts laughed** at Wegener. As Robert Youngson puts it, "**To do otherwise would be to throw aside some of their most cherished beliefs** about the structure of the earth [emphasis added]".[19] Despite decades of opposition, by around 1960 the science of plate tectonics had been accepted and it now forms an integral part of our understanding of the geological history of the Earth. The idea that continents 'float' on regions of molten magma 10 to 40 miles below sea level explains, for example, the positions and patterns of volcanoes and earthquake zones throughout the world. Sadly Wegener died not knowing that his theory would become mainstream.

BRETZ'S "OUTRAGEOUS HYPOTHESIS".[20] Continuing with the geology theme, Charles Lyell (1797-1875), building on the work of John Playfair (1748-1819) and James Hutton who died the year Lyell was born, vigorously promoted what came to be known as *uniformitarianism*. This was the idea often summed up by the phrase "the present is the key to the past" in which all geological features formed during the history of the Earth could be explained only in terms of processes in operation today – and operating with the same *degree* or *intensity* as today – including the action of rivers, tides, volcanoes and earthquakes.[21] Lyell was the winner in an ideological battle between *uniformitarians*, like himself, and *catastrophists* such as Adam Sedgwick (1785-1873), who believed the evidence pointed to the earth having undergone several catastrophic geological episodes.

Figure 1.3 J. Harlen Bretz.

Fast forward to the 1920s, by which time Lyell's uniformitarianism was taken to be axiomatic. J. Harlen Bretz[22] (1882-1981) had been surveying the geology of the Channeled Scabland near Spokane in the Pacific Northwest of the USA. Certain features of the terrain, especially the pattern of the coulees (dry trench-like valleys with vertical walls and flat floors), led him to believe that a monstrous flood had occurred. The flood would have been around 100 miles wide (160 km) with water depths of over 100 metres in places. This theory seemed ridiculous to the scientific community of the time whose Lyell-ian **dogmatic adherence to uniformitarianism** required that all such geological features, such as today's Columbia River Scablands, be explained by small amounts of water, slowly shaping the surroundings over aeons.

Bretz was verbally ambushed by his colleagues at a meeting of the Geological Society in Washington, D.C. in 1927.[23] For decades, his hypothesis was roundly rejected by most other geologists **until a new generation of practitioners revisited the field data**. By the 1960s it was finally accepted that during the most recent ice age a huge lake – Lake Missoula – had formed. When its ice dam failed catastrophically it is estimated to have discharged its contents at the rate of 17 million cubic metres/second, equivalent to 15 times the combined flow of all the rivers in the world. In places the discharging water reached depths of 230 metres and the flow reached speeds of 65 and even 85 miles/hour (30-40 m/s), eroding 200 cubic kilometres of silt, sediment and basalt.[24]

THE LOBOTOMY.[25] In 1949, Egas Moniz was awarded the Nobel Prize for his invention of a surgical treatment for mental illness. A lobotomy involved drilling a hole into each side of the skull. A lobotomy knife was then used to remove cores from the frontal lobes of the brain on each side and the holes sealed. This was said to cure anxiety, delusions, paranoia, mania and depression. Patients, so it was claimed, became more calm, content and easier to manage. Within four decades of the Nobel Prize being awarded, 40,000 lobotomies had been performed throughout the world. The accelerated use of the procedure – despite the lack of supporting evidence and notwithstanding the concerns of many colleagues – was primarily thanks to the **zealotry** of the charismatic surgeon, Walter Freeman (1895-1972).

Figure 1.4
Egas Moniz.

Many rich and famous people became persuaded of this invasive treatment's effectiveness including Joseph Kennedy. The father of President John F. Kennedy, he decided to have his daughter, Rosemary, lobotomised. Rosemary had suffered from mild developmental delay and was an embarrassment to the Kennedy family. She emerged from the surgery physically and mentally disabled and was consigned to a psychiatric hospital for the rest of her life.

Finally, by the early 2000s, lobotomies were no longer seen as a tool for institutional control, but rather as the subject of horror movies. This is an example of the harm that can be caused by **an untested, uncritiqued scientific theory** and of **how even highly educated people can be duped**.

PEPTIC ULCERS MUST BE CAUSED BY LIFESTYLE.[26] It had been a long established belief that stress and lifestyle were the cause of peptic ulcers. In 1982 two Australian researchers Barry Marshall and Robin Warren concluded that a bacterium, *Helicobacter pylori* colonises the human stomach and causes peptic ulcer and other gastric diseases. But the medical orthodoxy stated that bacteria couldn't possibly survive in the stomach's acidic environment. **Despite experiencing scepticism bordering upon ridicule**, Marshall and Warren persisted, continuing to assemble evidence for their claim. This culminated astonishingly in Marshall deliberately infecting himself with the bacillus and contracting acute gastric illness in the process. The two researchers were finally honoured with a Nobel Prize in 2005 for their breakthrough which had **overturned the received wisdom**.

"STEADY STATE" OR "BIG BANG". The ancient Greek philosopher, Aristotle, believed the universe was eternal – having no beginning and no end. Following the rediscovery and veneration of Greek philosophy from as early as the 12th century, but certainly by the 18th, the eternal universe idea became the predominant one in science. Einstein agreed with that view and ensured that his general relativity equations were consistent with such an unchanging, non-expanding universe.

However, in 1927, Georges Lemaître (1894-1966), a Belgian Diocesan priest, mathematician and astronomer, had rediscovered the work of the Russian mathematician Alexander Friedmann (1888-1925). In 1922 Friedmann had used Einstein's equations to model universes that expanded. Lemaître's paper went further than Friedmann, grounded in his own astronomical observations, and he was first to derive what are now known as Hubble's Law and Hubble's Constant, two years before Edwin Hubble (1889-1953) published his own work. Hubble's observations confirmed Lemaître's theory that galaxies are moving away from us and that the further away they are, the faster they are moving. This strengthened the argument that the universe had a beginning – a *Big Bang*.

The famous astronomer, Sir Fred Hoyle (1915-2001), was a *Big Bang* sceptic. So, in 1948 he, together with Hermann Bondi and Thomas Gold, formulated *Steady State* theory as an alternative, motivated in part by a desire to do away with the need for a beginning (or a possible end) to the universe.[27] Their idea was that as galaxies spread out, new galaxies formed in the empty space that was left, much as, in a flowing river, individual molecules of water flow away but the river's appearance remains the same.

Big Bang theory was finally victorious when one of its predictions was confirmed in 1964 by radio astronomers Arno Penzias and Robert Wilson who detected a particular spectral contour of radiation which has become known as the *Cosmic Microwave Background* radiation. But Sir Fred Hoyle died in 2001 still uncertain about Big Bang theory.

This illustrates how **a dearly held theory which is fundamental to our understanding** (of the universe, in this case) **can be overturned and replaced** by a quite different paradigm.

Even *incomplete* theories are a type of "wrong", as in these last two:

EUCLID HAD ONLY PART OF THE STORY.[28] Euclid, who lived around 300BC, was one of the world's most outstandingly great men. Euclidian geometry has been taught using his book, known simply as "Euclid", for over 2,000 years, perhaps the best selling mathematical textbook of all time. His theorems concluded, for example, that parallel lines, however long, will never meet, and that the internal angles of a triangle will always add up to 180 degrees. However, as Nicolai Lobachevsky's ideas - later developed by the better known Georg Riemann - demonstrated in the first half of the 19th century, Euclid's conclusions were only valid on a plane - a flat surface. If we think of the surface of a sphere, such as the Earth, lines of longitude *are* perfectly parallel at the equator, yet *meet* at both North and South Poles. Similarly, if we draw a triangle on the surface of a sphere, the sum of the internal angles is always greater than 180°, the larger the triangle, the greater the sum of the angles! For most routine calculations involving short distances on the Earth - for example a civil engineer designing triangular sections in the construction of a bridge - Euclid will do just fine. But, for airlines planning trans-oceanic routes, the shortest distance between two points is not a straight Euclidian line, but rather the arc of the great circle passing through these points. So **Euclid's geometry was correct, but incomplete**, in the sense of applying only to a surface of zero curvature - which is actually the least commonly encountered case.

NEWTON HAD ONLY PART OF A DIFFERENT STORY.[29] As with Euclidian geometry which was "wrong" in the sense of being "incomplete", so with Sir Isaac Newton's law of gravitation. Newton (1642-1727) developed an equation relating the gravitational force experienced by a body in the presence of another one being proportional to the product of their respective masses divided by the square of the distance between them. For most practical purposes it is valid. Indeed, this equation together with Newton's laws of motion is sufficient to calculate the velocity required to be achieved by, say, a space station, in order for it to remain in a given orbit around the Earth. However, Newton believed space was Euclidian (flat) – as we've just been discussing – and did not affect motion. He also believed in absolute time – time that flowed at a constant rate independent of the observer. Again for most practical purposes these assumptions work just fine. But it was Einstein's general theory of relativity that overturned both of these ideas 240 years after Newton.

Building on Riemannian geometry (see above) and James Clerk Maxwell's work on electromagnetic radiation, Einstein's theory posits that space is neither flat nor uniform. Rather space is distorted by the presence of massive objects such as the Sun and its planets, including the Earth. Think of the uniformly flat surface of a snooker table,[30] but made of a soft spongy material. Now imagine placing several larger-than-snooker-size balls of different sizes and weights in different positions on the table's spongy surface. Each ball will now sit at the bottom of a hollow dish-shape: the heavier the ball, the deeper the dish. Suppose we now cue a *normal* snooker ball from near one corner of the table hoping to send it to the opposite corner. What path will it follow? Well, clearly, it won't move in a perfectly straight line but will spiral in towards each of the larger ball shapes in its path.

Figure 1.5 Isaac Newton

And Einstein predicted that even light, travelling in 'straight' lines, will follow the contours of these 'hollows' in space distorted by the presence of massive stars and planets. The total solar eclipse on 20th May 1919 was an opportunity to test Einstein's prediction that light would be deflected by the Sun's mass distorting space. The effect was confirmed by Arthur Eddington and team when they detected the predicted change in the apparent position of stars being viewed close to the eclipsed Sun. Similarly, Einstein demonstrated that time does not flow at an absolute rate, but rather depends on how fast the observer is moving and the strength of the gravitational field experienced by the observer. **Newton's laws**, while useful for most practical purposes, **cannot be extrapolated to the large scale**.

WHAT CAN WE LEARN FROM SUCH SCIENTIFIC ERRORS?

This necessarily limited selection of instances in which science or engineering was mistaken indicates that despite the popular ubiquitous image of the dispassionate, objective, white-laboratory-coated scientist, it turns out that the history of science exhibits many of the faults, failings and foibles of most other human enterprises. Physical chemist and philosopher Michael Polanyi (1891-1976) admitted this.

> To acknowledge a person as a scientist - and even as a very great scientist - is merely to acknowledge him [sic] as competent in science, which admits the possibility that he [sic] was, or is, in many ways mistaken.[31]

The engineering disasters cited above - Space Shuttle and Chernobyl - have design shortcomings at their root. In each case the problems were known by at least some of those 'on the ground', those most closely involved with designing, implementing or operating the engineered artefact. But two other very human factors were at work in these examples to a greater or lesser extent: a **fear** of informing those further up the hierarchy of known or suspected problems, and management **expediency** overriding engineering judgment.

With the Chernobyl tragedy, in the immediate aftermath of the reactor explosion, the response amongst the operators was a comprehensive **denial** that anything was seriously wrong at all. Their mindset was that "reactors do not explode" and "**Soviet science is infallible**". Here then an echo of the "But this ship can't sink!" paradigm.

When we consider the lobotomy blunder, we find an example of a procedure being implemented that was **not evidence-based.** Instead it was driven by **obsession**, or by an almost cultish movement that was **in vogue at the time**. Perhaps another motive was to preserve the profit and reputations of those who promoted it.

The remaining examples exhibit what historian of science, Thomas Kuhn, describes as **"normal science" when it is in need of what he calls a "paradigm shift".**

> Closely examined ... that enterprise [normal science] seems an attempt to force nature into the preformed and relatively inflexible box that the [current] paradigm supplies.[32]

"Normal science" then, operates within a shared framework of assumptions and agreed practices, which Kuhn labels the "current" or "ruling paradigm". So in the classic illusion, Fig. 1.6, do you see an old woman looking down to the left or a young woman looking away from us?

Kuhn points out that the commonly held view that science develops incrementally in a linear way is erroneous: "... the textbook tendency to make the development of science linear hides a process that lies at the heart of the most significant episodes of scientific development". Looking at the same ink on the page in the figure we can 'see' something quite different from our first understanding, but it requires a conscious 'switch' of interpretation.

Kuhn has more to say about the potential for textbooks to mislead.

Figure 1.6
Old or young woman?

> Because they aim quickly to acquaint the student with what the contemporary scientific community thinks it knows, textbooks treat the various experiments, concepts, laws and theories of the current normal science as separately and as nearly seriatim [point by point] as possible... But that is not the way a science develops.[33]

As the anomalies uncovered during the course of *normal science* accumulate, the *ruling paradigm* is ultimately called into question, "... after persistent failure to solve a noteworthy puzzle has given rise to crisis". And usually the crisis is identified and addressed by a small number of individuals in the first instance.

> Any new interpretation of nature, whether a discovery or a theory, emerges first in the mind of one or a few individuals. It is they who first learn to see science and the world differently ... Invariably their attention has been intensely concentrated upon the crisis-provoking-problems ...[34]

So for example, the 'crisis' of parallel lines at the equator meeting at the poles, finally calls Euclid's two thousand year old paradigm into question. Likewise Newton's assumption that space was flat and unaffected by the presence of huge masses was in need of a paradigm shift, a revolution if you like, in order for science to make progress. Often, scientists betray their human frailties when they never make that paradigm shift. **Pride prevents them from ever accepting the new way of seeing the world**: Priestley never gave up his phlogiston theory; Hoyle was reluctant to accept Big Bang theory; Wegener's plate tectonics theory was rejected for decades by scientific orthodoxy, and

Bretz's catastrophic flood theory was only vindicated after one generation of geologists had given way to another. It took almost two and half decades for medical science to accept bacterial causation of peptic ulcers.

IT IS OFTEN ARGUED THAT SCIENCE IS SELF-CORRECTING.
But how many years had to elapse before many of these old paradigms were overturned and corrected? Forty, fifty, eighty and even hundreds of years in some cases. The quantum physicist, Max Planck (1858-1947), expressed the perhaps surprising view that science only makes progress one funeral at a time.

> ... a new scientific truth does not triumph by convincing its opponents and making them see the light, but rather because its opponents eventually die, and a new generation grows up that is familiar with it.[35]

Physicist William Thomson, better known as Lord Kelvin, made this famous claim in 1900, "There is nothing new to be discovered in physics now. All that remains is more and more precise measurement". And he was not alone in his misplaced confidence. In 1894, Nobel Laureate Albert Michelson wrote in a similar vein.

> The more important laws and facts of physical science have now been discovered, and these are now so firmly established that the possibility of their ever being supplanted in consequence of future discoveries is exceedingly remote ... Our future discoveries must be looked for in the sixth place of decimals.[36]

Within five years however, Albert Einstein's theory of *Special Relativity* had been published, followed within another ten years by *General Relativity*; and in the 1920s Erwin Schrödinger, Werner Heisenberg and Max Born developed *quantum mechanics* – all of which discredit Kelvin's and Michelson's, by then embarrassing, pronouncements.

One of the salient lessons we should derive from these observations is that **what science**, as Kuhn put it, **"thinks it knows" today, may in fact be overturned** by a new paradigm sooner or later.

As we progress through subsequent chapters and apply these learnings to the theory of evolution, we'll discover that:
- Darwinian evolution is an incomplete theory (similar to the Euclid and Newton examples above). Actually we'll come to realise that the theory can explain only a small fraction of what is claimed for it.

- Even well educated people – in both the sciences and the humanities – have a reverential belief in the explanatory power of the theory, a belief which is misplaced (as in the Chernobyl and lobotomy examples).
- There is a blindness to, denial of, or suppression of counter-evidence (as in the Space Shuttle, Chernobyl and Bretz examples).
- Critics fear for their careers if they voice their reservations and are likely to be ridiculed if they do so (as in the Space Shuttle, Chernobyl, Wegener, Bretz and Marshall & Warren examples).
- There is a reluctance to accept that the theory is in crisis and in need of a paradigm shift (as in the Priestley and Hoyle examples).

The theory of evolution, then, just like any other healthy branch of science, **should also be regarded as provisional, and should therefore be open to legitimate critique.**

What is "science"?

A common public perception is that although "science" encompasses many different disciplines – such as physics, cosmology, geology, biology – they can all be embraced within a single definition and all use very similar methodologies. This view seems to justify the stereotypical labelling of anyone who doubts, say, evolutionary theory (the appropriate example in our context) as "anti-science". But is this common public perception entirely warranted? Here, according to Wikipedia, is a definition of science.

> *Science ... is a systematic enterprise that builds and organizes knowledge in the form of **testable** explanations and predictions about the universe [emphasis added].*[37]

The mathematician John Lennox points out that not all branches of science are in fact *testable*: "Contrary to popular impression, there is no one agreed scientific method ... precise definition is very illusive ... consider the following attempt by Michael Ruse [internationally acclaimed philosopher of science]. He holds that science 'by definition deals only with the natural, the repeatable, that which is governed by law'".[38]

As Lennox elucidates, this definition would rule out all of what are sometimes called the "historical sciences"[39] such as cosmology, geology, palaeontology (the study of fossils) and the historical claims of evolutionary biology, on the grounds of (non-) "repeatability". So for example, scientists did not observe the *Big Bang* as it occurred; nor can we repeat it in the laboratory – or anything approaching the gargantuan, unattainable energies involved.

Contrary to the popular view, it turns out that historians and philosophers of science do not agree about how to define science. Scientists in different fields use different methods, here described by philosopher of science Stephen Meyer.

> *Some sciences perform laboratory experiments. Some do not. Some sciences name, classify, and organize natural objects; some sciences seek to discover natural laws; others seek to reconstruct past events ... Some provide mathematical descriptions of natural phenomena ... Some explain general or repeatable phenomena by reference to natural laws or general theories. Some study unique or particular events and seek to explain them by reference to (past) causal events ... Some sciences test their theories by making predictions; some test their theories by assessing their explanatory power. Some ... involve direct verification; some employ more indirect methods of testing.*[40]

So let's explore the relationship amongst different scientific disciplines a little further.

Do all sciences speak with equal authority?

In George Orwell's novel, *Animal Farm*, the ruling species – the pigs – hypocritically proclaim that all animals are equal, but that some are more equal than others![41] The question for us here – absent the whiff of sarcasm – is: "are some sciences *less* equal than others?" Thomas Kuhn points out that

> *... practitioners of widely separated fields, say astronomy and taxonomic botany, are educated by exposure to quite different achievements described in very different books. And even men who, being in closely related fields, begin by studying the same books and achievements may acquire rather different paradigms in the course of professional specialization.*[42]

Biomedical engineer, Rob Stadler,[43] partitions questions to which we may be seeking answers into three categories:[44]

   a. Those science cannot answer.
   b. Those science can answer with high confidence.
   c. Those science can attempt to answer with low confidence.

He assigns questions such as, "What is the meaning of life?" and "Should I ask her to marry me?" to category (a). For the questions science can attempt to answer he then identifies six criteria to help us

Table 1.1

	Criteria of High-Confidence Science	Criteria of Low-Confidence Science
1	Repeatable	Not repeatable
2	Directly measurable and accurate results	Indirectly measured, extrapolated, or inaccurate results
3	Prospective, interventional study	Retrospective, observational study
4	Careful to avoid bias	Clear opportunities for bias
5	Careful to avoid assumptions	Many assumptions required
6	Sober judgment of results	Overstated confidence or scope of results

decide which can be answered with high- and which with low-confidence. These are reproduced in Table 1.1.[45]

Stadler's **first** criterion is the concept of **repeatability**. He takes, as an example, lifting a bowling ball to a known height, starting a stopwatch simultaneously with the ball being dropped and timing how long it takes the ball to reach the ground. This is an example of an experiment that can be repeated as many times as desired. There are a number of variables that will need to be controlled: the exact height of the ball, air density, temperature, and so on. If the variables are properly controlled we would expect the results to be repeatable and we should have high confidence in them.

The time taken for the ball to fall to the ground can be **read out directly** from the stopwatch so we'd expect accurate results. This meets the **second** criterion for high-confidence.

In relation to the **third** criterion, this is an **interventional** study; we are carrying out an experiment that has been designed in advance and is capable of being repeated.

Stadler points out that "Everyone has bias. Everyone."[46] (And that, of course, includes the present author and anyone reading this book.) Indeed the scientific errors discussed above are replete with examples of this: Hoyle's ideological bias against an explanation that implied the universe had a beginning; the bias of 'experts' in the community of geologists against Wegener's and Betz's respective hypotheses; Priestley's **bias** in favour of his phlogiston theory; and so on. This is the **fourth** criterion. In the case of dropping a ball from a known height, there are fewer opportunities for bias, and these can be offset thanks to repeatability: other practitioners, having a whole range of beliefs, experiences and goals, could repeat the experiment independently.

It's important to explicitly identify and assess the effect of any **assumptions**, the **fifth** criterion, such as whether the effects of air resistance and the polish used on the ball are negligible. In ancient Greece, Aristotle's armchair assumption was that a heavy ball would fall faster than a lighter one, but Galileo is credited with using a (repeatable) experiment to demonstrate that the acceleration due to gravity was in fact independent of the object's weight.[47]

The **sixth** criterion is **sober judgment of results**. In drawing conclusions from the bowling ball experiment it would be important to list its limitations: that the results have been obtained at a specific geographical location (the Earth's gravitational force varies by 0.7% depending on the location),[48] with a specific air density, and under specific temperature and wind conditions.

So in conclusion, the question, "How fast does a bowling ball fall to the ground?" can be answered by high-confidence science. Stadler contrasts that question – which *can* be answered with high confidence – with this one, "How did King Tutankhamun die?" He describes a study published in 2010 that brought advanced technology to bear, including computed tomographic imaging (CT scan) and DNA genetic analysis.[49] Table 1.2[50] illustrates that the low-confidence criteria are more appropriate for this question. So what are the key points we should take away from Stadler's work?

A. Not all scientific disciplines are able to make claims with equal confidence.
B. Even within a given discipline, depending on the question asked, not all criteria may be able to be met with high confidence.
C. The sciences addressing historical questions are more likely to fail to meet the high-confidence criteria.

Clearly a spectrum of confidence is involved, depending on which criteria can be answered with high- and which with low-confidence. So

Table 1.2

	Criteria of Low-Confidence Science	How did King Tutankhamun die?
1	Not repeatable	While data collection could be repeated, his death was a one-off historical event.
2	Indirectly measured, extrapolated, or inaccurate results	We can't interview any witnesses to his death and they didn't provide any documentation. Any reports we do have may not make sense in terms of modern medicine. The evidence we do have – DNA, bone malformations, leg fracture, etc. indirectly relate to cause of death.
3	Retrospective, observational study	The study makes observations about the distant past. Retrospective observational studies are not able to control variables and therefore can only *suggest associations*, not conclude causality.
4	Clear opportunities for bias	The results are subjective, the interpretation of the observed findings is highly dependent on personal bias.
5	Many assumptions are required	Some assumptions may have strong archaeological support and others may not. Example assumptions are: • The body is actually that of King Tut. • The body was not damaged by the burial or excavation processes. • Malaria was associated with his death (evidence of malaria was found). • DNA can survive 3,300 years, and contamination did not occur.
6	Overstated confidence in results	To their credit, the authors admit a lack of confidence in their conclusion.

in relation to point (C) above, Stadler indicates that science could provide a higher confidence answer to the question, "How did Michael Jackson die?"; a lower confidence answer to the question, "How did King Tut die?"; and a very low confidence answer to the question, "How did this fossilised dinosaur die?"[51] He concludes that

> [t]he real problem is when low-confidence science is inappropriately portrayed as high-confidence science.[52]

Using a not dissimilar approach, Thaxton et al.[53] discriminate between what they call "operation" science and "origin" science. Their examples of operation science include: the recurring motion of the planets around the sun, the swinging of a pendulum, the parabolic trajectory of a cannonball, a single cell turning by stages into a fully formed organism, the recurrent cubic structure of table salt crystallising out of water solution, and the migration pattern of a Monarch butterfly.[54] Each of these repeatable examples meet Stadler's high confidence criteria, in which theories can be tested and falsified if necessary. So, for example, Aristotle's theory in relation to a thrown projectile was that its trajectory was a straight line until it ran out of forward impetus and that the object then dropped vertically to the ground.[55] Empirical observation, of course, has since falsified his rectilinear theory in favour of the true, parabolic one. In contrast, one-off origin science events that are believed to have occurred in the past, such as the *Big Bang*, or the emergence of the first life from non-living chemicals, "…cannot be falsified by empirical test if they are false, as can theories of operation science."[56] **The important distinction between high confidence "operation" science and lower confidence "origin" or "historical" science should be borne in mind** as we proceed, especially in Part 2.

WHAT ABOUT THE PEER REVIEW PROCESS?

But you might be thinking, "Surely peer-reviewed, published scientific papers have been scrutinised to remove bias, acknowledge assumptions, and manifest sober judgment of results?" Biochemist Rupert Sheldrake reveals that the reality is somewhat different.

> Published data have to pass through three selective filters. The first filtration of data occurs when experimenters decide to publish some results rather than others; the second when editors of journals consider only certain kinds of results eligible for publication; and the third in **the peer-review process, which ensures that expected results are more likely to be approved for publication than unexpected results** … How much does this practice affect the sciences? No one knows [emphasis added].[57]

After discussing some examples of fraud in science ultimately exposed by brave whistleblowers – which there isn't space to go into here[58] – Sheldrake concludes that

> [s]cientists usually assume fraud is rare and unimportant because science is self-correcting. Ironically, this complacent belief produces an environment in which deception can flourish.[59]

So if a researcher, or research group, wishes to publish a paper that attempts to challenge an existing paradigm – because they believe the large number of anomalies or instances of counter-evidence have brought the current paradigm into crisis – the peer review process is very likely to cause the paper to be rejected, since the reviewers will very likely be uncompromising adherents of the current paradigm. It would seem, therefore that **bias and unacknowledged assumptions may be inherent to the peer review process**.

Lower lifeboat 1!

Here's a summary of Chapter 1.

- Few doubt that amazing progress has been made thanks to science, especially visible in the wonders of technology all around us that have improved our life expectancy and quality of life worldwide.
- Science is fallible after all. Despite the high esteem bestowed upon scientists by society, they are nevertheless human, and science is not immune to human nature's flaws.
- Scientists can be blind to, and completely discount, evidence before their eyes when it runs counter to the current ruling paradigm.
- There is very strong peer pressure, or groupthink, to conform to the ruling orthodoxy. This can result in fear of revealing or disclosing counter-evidence in the first place, or rejection of such evidence when subjected to a peer review process.
- Seemingly well established, unquestioned scientific paradigms, or ways of thinking about the world, *can* be overturned, or at least significantly modified, by a new paradigm decades or even hundreds of years later, when anomalies and counter-evidence bring the ruling paradigm into crisis.
- When counter-evidence does force the current paradigm into crisis, a conscious 'switch' in interpretation of the data is essential in order to escape the power of Gould's "conceptual lock" (opening quote to the chapter).

- Not all branches of science speak with equal authority. Science is not a monolithic set of disciplines. Where a particular field of study fails to include one or more of the following: interventional repeatable experiments designed in advance, parameters that are directly measurable, evaluation of researcher bias, full identification of assumptions, a sober statement of its conclusions, such a study or discipline must be considered lower confidence than those that *can* meet these criteria.
- Even Stephen Jay Gould admitted that **the "origin" or "historical" sciences - which would include** cosmology, historical geology, **evolutionary biology** and, of course his own field, palaeontology - **cannot speak with the same authority as "operation" sciences such as physics, chemistry**, and the medical and engineering sciences.[60]
- The ever-present danger is that low-confidence science may be inappropriately portrayed as high-confidence science.
- **All scientific theories are provisional** and may need to be revisited in the light of new evidence. **The theory of evolution**, therefore, just like any other healthy branch of science **should be open to legitimate critique in the light of new evidence from, for example, molecular biology**.

So, has science become a new pseudo-religion in Western society with an ideology of its own? And if we generally accept the authority of science, do we have to reject traditional religion? These themes will be explored in Chapter 2.

Chapter 2
Scientists: the new priesthood

Truth can be determined only by the judgement of experts... Everything is decided by very small groups of men,[1] in fact, by single experts... Scientific activities are controlled by universities, academies and scientific societies, but such control is as far removed from popular control as it possibly could be.[2]

George Sarton

This chapter begins with an introduction to the idea that science has become the predominant source of truth and that some scientists have become a kind of 'priesthood'. We then ask three questions to explore whether such a view can be justified:
- Is science the only source of truth?
- Are science and religion in conflict?
- What's the real conflict?

Are some scientists the new priests?

Karl Marx once described religion as the "opium of the people".[3] Could it be that society, at least in the Western world, has become subliminally addicted to *Science* as its one true source of knowledge, enlightenment and meaning? Michael Polanyi admitted that

> ... a complex historical movement has ... led ... to the establishment in our time of the scientific method as the supreme interpreter of human affairs.[4]

Biochemist Rupert Sheldrake describes the power and intellectual appeal of science in society today.

> Since the late nineteenth century, science has dominated and transformed the earth. It has touched everyone's lives through technology and modern medicine. Its intellectual prestige is almost unchallenged. Its influence is greater than almost any other system of thought in all of human history ... it also has a strong intellectual appeal.[5]

Sheldrake goes on to discuss the concept of a kind of "scientific priesthood" and traces the idea back to Francis Bacon (1561-1626),

"[Bacon] foresaw the power of organised science more than anyone else".[6] Sheldrake has described Bacon's uncanny prediction.

> Bacon envisaged that the scientific priesthood would ... be linked to the state through patronage, forming a kind of established church of science.[7]

Sheldrake concludes that "... he was prophetic ... There is no separation of science and state. [Some] **scientists play the role of an established priesthood**, influencing government policies on the arts of warfare, industry, agriculture, medicine, education and research [emphasis added]".

By the 1950s, the power and reputation of institutional science had reached an unprecedented level. In a similar sense in which the Roman Catholic Church of the late Middle Ages had unquestioned power vested in a small number of people, or even just one person,[8] it could be argued that science today has effectively assumed that priestly mantle. And today the media, including the broadcast media, of which the BBC is probably the most influential, certainly in the UK, continue to promote this high view of science through presenters whom Sheldrake might describe as its "high priests". The well known zoologist Richard Dawkins was the first holder of the Charles Simonyi Chair in the Public Understanding of Science at the University of Oxford. He would almost certainly be a candidate for the "priesthood" function described by Bacon and Sheldrake, especially in that educationally empowering role.

Yet palaeontologist Niles Eldredge (1943-) was refreshingly honest in his book *The Monkey Business* when he pointed out that "Many scientists really do seem to believe they have a special access to the truth ... they expect to be believed ... especially, by the public at large. Throwing down scientific thunderbolts from Olympian heights, scientists come across as authoritarian truth givers whose word must be taken unquestioned. That all evidence shows the behavior of scientists clearly to be no different from the ways in which other people behave is somehow overlooked in all this".[9]

So despite the propensity for many (not all) high-profile scientists to adopt a priestly manner, whether consciously or otherwise, Eldredge and Sheldrake admit that **the behaviour of scientists is actually no different to those of people in other spheres of the human enterprise**.

Is science the only source of truth?
The celebrated philosopher Bertrand Russell (1872-1970) manifests this stereotypical view.

> Whatever knowledge is attainable, must be attained by scientific methods; and what science cannot discover, mankind cannot know.[10]

The excessive belief in the power and omniscience of scientific knowledge is properly referred to as *scientism*. Yet **Russell's claim is self-defeating logically**: what "scientific method" can we employ to provide evidence for his statement? None: which implies that it is not a statement *of* science, but rather a claim *about* science and, according to its own logic, we therefore cannot know it to be true. In fact, Nobel Laureate Sir Peter Medawar, a biologist and scientist, is more in tune with the limitations of science when he points out that "There is no quicker way for a scientist to bring discredit upon his profession than roundly to declare ... that science knows, or soon will know, the answers to all questions worth asking, and that questions which do not admit a scientific answer are in some way non-questions or 'pseudo-questions' that only simpletons ask and only the gullible profess to be able to answer". Medawar lists some specifics.

> The existence of a limit to science is, however, made clear by its inability to answer elementary childlike questions having to do with first and last things - questions such as: "How did everything begin?"; "What are we all here for?"; "What is the point of living?"[11]

When Peter Atkins, a chemistry professor and outspoken atheist, challenged William Lane Craig to deny that "science can account for everything", Craig obliged. He listed five categories of belief which are rational to hold, but which science is incompetent to prove: logical and mathematical proofs; metaphysical truths, such as belief in the existence of other minds and the reality of the external world; ethical beliefs about statements of value; aesthetic judgments such as beauty and goodness; and most remarkably, science itself: science cannot be justified by the scientific method.[12]

Are science and religion in conflict?
In quoting Ricky Gervais, who is an entertainer not a scientist, Sheldrake comments that he "borrows the authority of science to support his atheism". Gervais has a high view of science.

> **Science seeks truth**. And it **does not discriminate**. For better or worse it finds things out. Science is humble. It knows what it knows and it **knows**

what it doesn't know. It bases its conclusions and beliefs on hard evidence - evidence that is constantly updated and upgraded. *It doesn't get offended when new facts come along.* It embraces the body of knowledge. *It doesn't hold onto medieval practices* because they are a tradition [emphasis added].[13]

Hopefully the reader will have recognised by this point that contrary examples - of every single one of the putatively positive characteristics (highlighted in his quote) that Ricky Gervais attributes to science - are legion. As Rupert Sheldrake makes clear, "**Gervais's idealised view of science is hopelessly naïve** in the context of the history and sociology of science. It portrays scientists as open-minded seekers of truth, not ordinary people competing for funds and prestige, constrained by peer group pressures and hemmed in by prejudices and taboos [emphasis added]".[14]

Since this book is primarily about the scientific evidence for and against evolutionary theory, why do we need to address the question of conflict between science and religion? (The focus here will be on the relationship between science and Christianity.) Ricky Gervais' barbed put-downs: "medieval practices" and "traditions", follow in the wake of the experience of recent years when the so-called *New Atheists* have attacked religions in general, and Christianity in particular, wielding *science* as a weapon and claiming that science renders religion obsolete. Given the naïve views Gervais holds about the scientific enterprise - and he is by no means alone - the New Atheists were surely justified in thinking that weaponising science will advance their cause.

So for example, Richard Dawkins published *The God Delusion*[15] in 2006. In its preface, he states his aim, "If this book works as I intend, religious readers who open it will be atheists when they put it down".[16] With similar intent, Sam Harris published *The End of Faith* in 2005, followed a year later by *Letter to a Christian Nation*. Daniel Dennett's book *Darwin's Dangerous Idea* was first published in 1995. Richard Carrier's publication, *Why I am not a Christian?* also uses science, especially the theory of evolution, to discredit Christianity.[17]

This conflict hypothesis can be traced back to two books, *History of the Conflict Between Religion and Science*,[18] by John William Draper and *History of the Warfare of Science with Theology in Christendom*[19] by Andrew Dickson White. These were first published in 1873 and 1895 respectively. Draper is uncompromising.

> Then has it come to this, that ... **Christianity and Science are** recognised by their respective adherents as being **absolutely incompatible**; they cannot exist together; one must yield to the other, mankind must make its choice – it cannot have both [emphasis added].[20]

Indeed the view that a choice must be made between science and religion is widespread within Western society; that if you accept scientific explanations, then you *must* reject religious ones; that anyone entering a church must switch off the rational part of her or his brain for the duration of a worship service. Coming more up to date, in *The End of Christianity*, edited by John W. Loftus in 2011, David Eller, a Professor of Anthropology at the Community College of Denver, echoes Draper's sentiments in his chapter entitled, *Is Religion compatible with Science?*

> ... science can only proceed when it is liberated from the specific claims and the general mindset of religion. This was true in Galileo's time, and it is true today.[21]

Eller's mention of Galileo is no doubt intended to trigger in the modern mind the story of science triumphing over a superstitious and regressive Roman Catholic Church. It's one of the icons of those who hold to the "conflict" view today. And it's part of a wider narrative that Europe descended into the so-called *Dark Ages* as the Roman Empire collapsed. Voltaire (1694-1778) described the era as one when "barbarism, superstition, [and] ignorance covered the face of the world."[22] The sociologist Rodney Stark points out that the very concept of the *Dark Ages* is a myth invented by eighteenth century intellectuals – Jean-Jacques Rousseau (1712-1778) and Edward Gibbon (1737-1794) in addition to Voltaire and others – who were determined to slander Christianity. Stark continues, "Nevertheless, serious historians have known for decades that these claims are a *complete fraud* [emphasis in original]".[23] Atheist historian Tim O'Neill agrees, "The concept of "the Dark Ages" ... [is] a commonly held and popularly believed set of ideas that has its origin in polemicists of the eighteenth and nineteenth centuries but which has been rejected by more recent historians".[24]

The conflict narrative goes on to hold that modern science finally emerged from "the Dark Ages" in the 17th century when we began to put aside superstition and irrationality, such that the so-called "Scientific Revolution" could be born. But more recently some historians have demonstrated that what today we would call "science" was alive and well long before Copernicus and Galileo. So, for example in relation to the "Copernican Revolution", Stark has more to say.

> Just as there was no "Dark Ages", there was no "Scientific Revolution". Rather, the notion of a Scientific Revolution was invented to discredit the medieval Church by claiming that science burst forth in full bloom ... only when a weakened Christianity no longer could suppress it.[25]

Figure 2.1
Nicolaus Copernicus

The start of the so-called Scientific Revolution is usually attributed to **Nicolaus Copernicus** (1473-1543), but Stark points out that the idea that the earth orbits the sun did not come to him out of the blue. Rather, Copernicus learned the fundamentals from his professors in the universities of Bologna, Padua and Ferrara. Stark goes on to list and describe **thirteen pious men - who would be called scientists today - living prior to Copernicus**, between 1175 and 1464, who introduced "controlled scientific experiment into Western thought."[26] These scholars made important contributions to optics, astronomy (recognising its distinction from astrology), botany, geography, chemistry and mathematics. They knew that the earth and all the heavenly bodies were spheres and that space was a frictionless vacuum. Roger Bacon (ca. 1214-94) - not to be confused with the later Francis Bacon (1561-1626) - predicted future inventions such as microscopes, telescopes and flying machines. William of Ockham (ca. 1285-1394)[27] anticipated Newton's *First Law of Motion* by proposing that once God had set heavenly bodies in motion, they would, facing no friction, remain in motion thereafter.[28]

Isaac Newton (1642-1727) famously remarked, "If I have seen further it is by standing on the shoulders of giants".[29] It is often assumed that he was simply professing humility. However, his statement was in fact a tribute to many others. In addition to those earlier thinkers just mentioned, Stark lists **over fifty natural philosophers (the scientists of their day)** who lived between the publication of Copernicus's *De Revolutionibus* in 1543 and Newton's death in 1727 **on whose "shoulders" Newton was able to "stand"**. Stark shares another insight.

2 – Scientists: the new priesthood

Just as a group of eighteenth century philosophers invented the notion of the "Dark Ages" to discredit Christianity, they labeled their own era the "Enlightenment" on the grounds that religious darkness had finally been dispelled by secular humanism ... Thus did Voltaire, Rousseau, Locke, Hume, and others wrap themselves in the achievements of the "Scientific Revolution" as they celebrated the victory of secularism, eventuating in the Marquis of Laplace's claim that God was now an unnecessary hypothesis.[30]

Stark makes clear[31] that none of these champions of the Enlightenment - Voltaire, Rousseau, etc. - played *any* part in the ongoing *scientific* enterprise. And of those who did (the fifty or more scientists mentioned above), 13 were members of the clergy. Stark then identified 60% as being *devout*, by which he meant there was clear evidence of especially deep religious involvement; 38% as *conventional*, meaning there was no evidence of scepticism but their piety did not stand out as other than satisfactory to their associates. He labelled only 2% - one person - as *skeptic*.[32] The *skeptic* was Edmond Halley after whom the famous comet was named.

Figure 2.2
Edmond Halley

The *devout* category included Newton, who wrote far more on theology than on physics. Johannes Kepler (1571-1630) similarly described his own motivation.

The chief aim of all investigations of the external world should be to discover the rational order which has been imposed on it by God, and which he revealed to us in mathematics.[33]

The famous phrase, "thinking God's thoughts after him" was also his. It was Kepler who analysed Tycho Brahe's (1546-1601) meticulous observations of the orbit of Mars and deduced that planetary orbits were elliptical rather than circular-with-epicycles as in Ptolemy's model.

Similarly, many other distinguished scientists[34] believed in God: Galileo (1564-1642), Pascal (1623-62), Boyle (1627-91), Faraday (1791-1867), Babbage (1791-1871), Mendel (1822-84), Pasteur (1822-95), Kelvin (1824-1927) and Maxwell (1831-79). Nick Spencer, Research Director at *Theos*, points out that Robert Boyle, "one of the greatest scientists of the age ... left funds for a lecture series intended 'for the defence of the Christian religion against atheists and other unbelievers'".[35] James Clerk Maxwell, whose work on light and the

Figure 2.3 Michael Faraday, Charles Babbage and James Clerk Maxwell.

electromagnetic spectrum Einstein regarded as indispensably foundational to his own relativity breakthroughs, had these words inscribed (in Latin) over the archway of the Cavendish Laboratory in Cambridge, "Great are the works of the Lord; they are pondered by all who delight in them".[36]

Now there is a view that if all these men (and they were all men) had been scientists today, they would not have been believers in God. But, there are several problems with this view.

SCIENCE FLOURISHED ONLY IN CHRISTIAN EUROPE. While certain technologies and elements of science developed in ancient Greece, in China and in the early Islamic world, ongoing scientific development was not sustained in these cultures until much more recent times. The British philosopher and mathematician Alfred North Whitehead concluded in 1925 that "… the images of God and creation found in non-European faiths, especially those in Asia, are too impersonal or too irrational to have sustained science". It has been noted that some Greek philosophers regarded the cosmos, and inanimate objects more generally, as living things and therefore attributed, for example, the movement of heavenly bodies to appetites, not to inanimate forces.[37]

BIBLICAL TEACHING SUPPORTS SCIENTIFIC ENDEAVOUR. For philosophers and theologians, the Judaeo-Christian doctrine of Adam's fall from grace affected his *intellectual* abilities as well as his moral ones. Nick Spencer puts it this way, "Contrary to the popular view of Enlightenment rationalism powering its way towards scientific success by having raised its eyes to the glories of the human intellect, [Peter] Harrison, suggests that

> *... the birth of modern experimental science was not attended with a new awareness of the powers and capacities of human reason, but rather the opposite - a consciousness of the manifold deficiencies of the intellect, of the misery of the human condition, and of the limited scope of scientific achievement."*[38]

In other words, because these theists believed in fallen humanity, they realised that empirical science - carrying out experiments to test an idea - was essential to overcoming humanity's fallible intellectual faculties. In the prior Aristotelean paradigm, if an idea seemed plausible from the comfort of an armchair, experimental testing was assumed to be unnecessary.[39] Spencer continues, "The Fellows of the Royal Society were doing nothing less than forging a new Eden" and in this way the natural philosopher became "not only religiously motivated, but religiously empowered... Christianity served as science's apt and able midwife".[40] Author Francis Schaeffer agreed, "it was the biblical mentality which gave birth to modern science".[41] And as C.S. Lewis succinctly put it, "Men became scientific because they expected Law in Nature and they expected Law in Nature because they believed in a Legislator".[42] These early scientists wanted to investigate and discover *how* God had ordered the universe.[43]

MANY SCIENTISTS TODAY ARE THEISTS. John Lennox cites a survey carried out in 1996 and reported in *Nature*. It was a repeat of a survey done in 1916. One thousand scientists selected at random were asked whether they believed in both a God who answered prayer and in personal immortality. As Lennox points out this is much more specific than simply belief in some kind of divine being.[44] The results are in Table 2.1.

Though we are now some twenty years into the 21st century, the surprise here is just how little the "Yes" vote changed over the course of the 20th century, contrary to the popular view. Lennox further points

Response to the 'belief' question	1916	1996
Yes	41.8%	39.6%
No	41.5%	45.5%
Agnostic	16.7%	14.9%

Table 2.1

out that between 1901 and 2000, over 60% of Nobel Laureates were Christians.[45] So the notion that science and God don't mix and that those who believe in God are ignorant is simply not true.

FAMOUS SCIENTISTS DIDN'T SEE ANY CONFLICT. Even if the speculative view turned out to be correct that Newton, Kepler, Faraday, Clerk Maxwell, *et al.*, would be atheists if they were scientists today, the key point is that *they* did not see any conflict between their belief in God and the scientific work in which they were engaged. Newton, for example, having discovered that the gravitational attraction between two heavenly bodies is proportional to the product of their respective masses and inversely proportional to the square of the distance between them, simply marvelled at *how* God had designed the universe.

WHAT ABOUT THE 'GALILEO AFFAIR'?

The modern myth about Galileo has it that he was effectively an atheist martyr for science, that he secured a victory over the medieval church which taught that the sun orbited the earth – because the Bible said so – while Galileo had proved that the earth orbited the sun, and that apparently he was then tortured and imprisoned for the rest of his life, all because of his science.

The real outworking of events was much more complex and nuanced than the popular understanding. The myth has been unmasked in detail elsewhere[46] so only a few brief points will be made here.

1. It is true that the almost sixty-nine year old Galileo was called before the Roman Inquisition and charged with heresy. The heretical aspect of his teaching was the claim that the earth is not stationary, but rather *moves* (around the sun).[47] When he was found guilty, however, he was not tortured, but rather held in very comfortable house arrest, still free to pursue his scientific studies, and died there of natural causes less than nine years later.

Figure 2.4
Galileo Galilei.

2. The dominant geocentric paradigm at the time – that the sun, stars and planets circled the earth – was that of Aristotle (384-322 BC) supported by a mathematical model developed by Ptolemy (ca.

100-170 AD). Aristotle's paradigm had been adopted by the medieval church as being agreeable to scripture. By the time of Copernicus, of course, the paradigm was in crisis because it did not fit with the latest empirical observations of the movement of planets. The surprise here is that many *Jesuit* astronomers agreed with Galileo that the heliocentric model was better. Meantime, also surprisingly, other *secular* philosophers were enraged that he had dared to challenge Aristotle and tried to influence church authorities to oppose him. Meantime the historical context was tricky. The unfolding of the Galileo affair occurred shortly after the Reformation[48] when the Roman Church's Counter-Reformation was in full swing, bringing with it a crackdown on intellectual freedom.

3. Galileo's duplicitous ego was probably his own worst enemy. He had a habit of denouncing in vitriolic terms those who disagreed with him. This style got him into trouble with Pope Urban VIII (reigned 1623-44) – who had previously supported him – when he published his *Dialogue Concerning the Two Chief World Systems* in 1632 in which he, albeit by indirect subterfuge, portrayed the Pope as a simpleton. Despite this the Pope used his power to protect Galileo from any *serious* punishment at the hands of the Inquisition.

4. In the midst of all this, there is no doubt that **Galileo was a devout Christian throughout his life.**[49] To put it another way, when Galileo came to the view that the sun, rather than the earth, was the centre of the solar system, he didn't ever relinquish his belief in God. According to Stark, he "often expressed his faith to his daughter and friends after his trial was over".[50]

What's the real conflict?

While there is a commonly held view that there's something uneasy in the relationship between science and religion, not only are a significant proportion of scientists Christians, but Christianity was also the intellectual framework that provided motivation and sustaining power to the pursuit of experimental science over the last millennium or more, certainly up until the 20th century.

However, there is a *genuine* conflict. The aphorism, "there's no smoke without fire" is apt here. The conflict is between *materialism* (or *naturalism*) and *theism*. *Materialism* is the belief that nothing in the universe exists except matter and energy and that greater complexity such as life and consciousness have all emerged from atoms, molecules and their interactions over billions of years. *Naturalism*, is very similar, being the view that everything arises as a result of natural causes. (All materialists are naturalists, but some naturalists hold that mind and consciousness exist apart from matter.) The enigmatic astronomer Carl Sagan expressed this philosophical outlook succinctly when he opened his 1980 series *Cosmos* with these words, "The Cosmos is all there is or ever was or ever will be".

The scientific method is sometimes characterised as *methodological naturalism*. The biologist Jonathan Wells explains, "science is limited to materialistic explanations because repeatable experiments can be done only on material objects and physical forces". Wells, however, then describes what tends to happen *in practice*.

> In principle, methodological naturalism is not a claim about reality, but [rather] a limitation on the method. It does not rule out the existence of a non-material realm. But in practice many scientists **assume** that if they search long enough they **will** find a materialistic explanation for whatever they are investigating [emphasis added].

Pulling this together, Wells concludes that "This **assumption** ... is not just a statement about method. It is equivalent to materialistic philosophy, which regards material objects and physical forces as the only realities [emphasis added]".[51]

So this assumption – that a materialistic explanation will eventually be found – is just that, a generally undeclared assumption (recall that declaring assumptions is one of Stadler's six criteria for high confidence science). How did this come about? It has been adopted implicitly by modern science as a result of the Laplacean picture[52] known as *determinism*. Pierre-Simon Laplace's (1749-1827) hypothesis can be summarised in this way: if we know the present state of everything in the universe precisely, then in principle we can calculate the precise state of the universe at some later defined time based on known laws of motion.[53] Newtonian mechanics does not require that the universe is a closed causal system, nor does determinism *per se*. Nevertheless, following the spirit of Laplace, a closed-universe *assumption* is now the norm. The philosopher Alvin Plantinga put it

Figure 2.5
Pierre-Simon Laplace.

this way.

> *Although this addition is not at all implied by the physics (as I said, it's a philosophical or theological assumption), it was and is widely accepted, and indeed so widely accepted that it is often completely overlooked in contexts where it is crucial. That the universe is indeed closed, once more, is not testified to by classical science nor a consequence of it.*[54]

We get a glimpse of this philosophy working when scientists sometimes handle the laws of science as if they were <u>pre</u>scriptive, meaning events <u>must</u> unfold in a certain way. Whereas scientific laws are strictly <u>de</u>scriptive: we observe the behaviour of, say, a ball falling, then infer – in this case – a mathematical model to describe that behaviour, and finally test the model by further experiment. This law *describes* the acceleration of a body in a gravitational field. And consider this: the law doesn't even *explain* gravity, in the sense that we don't know what "gravity" actually is.[55] Similarly, we know that kinetic energy can be converted into potential energy, that chemical energy can be converted into electrical energy and so on, but we don't know what "energy" actually is.

In most applications of scientific enquiry, the tacit assumption of philosophical materialism is of no consequence whatever, such as in the case of modelling the gravitational attraction between two masses. In the subject matter of this book, **however, when considering the origin and development of life, it will be important to bear in mind the ubiquitous *assumption* of philosophical materialism within the scientific community.**

If you were unsure about the dominance of materialism as a philosophy within scientific orthodoxy, this statement by the eminent evolutionary biologist and geneticist Richard Lewontin – breathtakingly revealing in its honesty – may well remove any remaining doubt.

> *Our willingness to accept scientific claims that are against common sense is the key to an understanding of the real struggle between science and the supernatural. We take the side of science **in spite** of the patent absurdity of some of its constructs ... **in spite** of the tolerance of the scientific community for unsubstantiated just-so stories, because we have a prior commitment ... to materialism. It is not that the methods and institutions of science somehow compel us to accept a material explanation of the phenomenal world but, on the contrary, that we are forced by our **a priori** adherence to material causes to create an apparatus of investigation and a set of concepts that produce material explanations, no matter how counter-intuitive, no matter how mystifying to the*

uninitiated. Moreover, that materialism is absolute, for we cannot allow a Divine Foot in the door [emphasis in original].[56]

(As an aside here, Plantinga takes the discussion one step further. He concludes, surprisingly perhaps, that naturalism is a self-defeating philosophy that does not support scientific enquiry.)[57]

Lower lifeboat 2!

Here's a summary of Chapter 2.

- There is a sense in which the authority attributed to "science" has elevated it to the status of a pseudo-religion: the putative one true source of *all* knowledge in Western society.
- Some high-profile scientists have effectively become the priesthood of this new creed, whose pronouncements are widely regarded as incontestable in the same sense in which statements made by priests in the medieval church were beyond dispute.
- "Scientism", the notion that science is the only source of truth, is expressed succinctly by one of these new "high priests", the chemist Peter Atkins, "There is no reason to suppose that science cannot deal with every aspect of existence".[58]
- But Atkins' claim is not a scientifically demonstrable assertion. Rather it is a philosophical claim *about* science, and Atkins is no more credible in this sphere than any other layperson.
- Atkins also claims that "Science and religion cannot be reconciled".[59] But, contrary to this popularly held view, there is no inherent conflict between Christianity and the scientific pursuit of knowledge.
- Instead, historical evidence supports the view that the scientific enterprise took off and was sustained only in medieval Europe precisely because (what today we would call) scientists "… expected law in nature because they believed in a lawgiver".[60]
- There is a conflict, however. But it's not between Christianity and science. Rather it's between *theism* and *philosophical materialism*. These are both belief systems, the former believes a God exists who created the universe, is independent of it, but can act supernaturally within it. The latter takes the view that the universe is a closed system and that everything *must* be explained in terms of interactions between matter and energy, as candidly articulated by Lewontin (pp. 53-54).
- The media primarily give publicity to 'high priests' of science who adhere to this materialistic worldview.

- Most of the public and even scientists themselves don't realise the pervasiveness of this bias. They believe that "science" is a neutral investigative tool. Indeed, if they think about it at all, they simply believe that's the way science has to be, blissfully unaware that much of mainstream science adheres to a specific ideology – philosophical materialism.
- In most spheres of science this would be of no importance, but when we're considering hypotheses relating to how all living things came into being, then we'd be wise to keep this in mind going forward.
- After all, what if materialism is not true? What if it misrepresents reality, as so many scientists, philosophers, artists and other scholars attest?
- There is a tendency for the public to believe – similar to Lord Kelvin and Albert Michelson at the turn of the 19th century, and reinforced in today's world by the media and the scientific priesthood – that our current state of scientific knowledge and understanding of the universe is entirely settled, 'unsinkable' science.
- But, just as ships "made of iron" are not "unsinkable", so even apparently well-established theories universally accepted within the current scientific consensus may turn out to be incomplete or simply wrong in the light of new discoveries and understandings.
- This principle applies as much to the theory of evolution as to any other set of scientific theories. Arguably the ideological baggage incumbent in the theory may be protecting the science from proper critique and scrutiny.

So what is "evolution"? Does "evolution" always mean the same thing? What did Darwin claim? Is it watertight? These topics and more will be addressed in the next chapter.

Chapter 3

Evolution: thinking the unthinkable

It is absolutely safe to say that if you meet somebody who claims not to believe in evolution, that person is ignorant, stupid or insane (or wicked, but I'd rather not consider that).[1]

Richard Dawkins

In Chapter 3 we'll begin by exploring whether the theory of evolution is "operation" or "historical" science. Then we'll ask:
- What was Darwin's contribution?
- What is neo-Darwinism?
- Does "evolution" have different meanings?
- Were initial objections religious ones?
- Do evolutionists invoke 'god' arguments?

Evolution: high or low confidence science?

Clearly, with the above quote, the eminent zoologist Richard Dawkins wishes to keep the RMS *Evolution* on a steady course and would counsel against anyone daring to think the 'ship' might be unsafe. In a similarly admonishing vein, he has declared

> *... never take seriously anybody who says, "I cannot believe that so-and-so could have evolved by gradual selection".[2]*

In case we didn't get the message, in 2010, he had this to say, "Evolution is a fact. Beyond reasonable doubt, beyond serious doubt, beyond sane, informed, intelligent doubt, beyond doubt evolution is a fact."[3] And he is not alone in vociferously affirming the "fact" of evolution. From the other side of the Atlantic acclaimed biologist Jerry Coyne has assured us that

> *... evolution is as solidly established as any scientific fact ... and scientists need no more convincing.[4]*

The views of popularisers of evolution – including Dawkins and Coyne – will make frequent appearances throughout this book. Here's another Dawkins' assertion, "Today the theory of evolution is about as much open to doubt as the theory that the earth goes round the sun …".[5] There are a couple of aspects worthy of note in the comparison he makes here.

First, let's for a moment transpose the two theories in the quote, to read thus: "Today the theory that the earth goes round the sun is about as much open to doubt as the theory of evolution". Have you ever come across a physicist seeking to reassure us of the heliocentric view in this way?

Second, using Stadler's criteria (Table 1.1), we note that Dawkins is attempting to equate evolution, which is a non-repeatable, extrapolated, low-confidence science with a repeatable, directly measurable, high-confidence one.[6] And this is the reason astrophysicists haven't felt the need to justify their earth-orbiting-the-sun theory in the way that Dawkins has done for evolution.

Dawkins repeats this category of error in *A Devil's Chaplain*. In responding "… to the allegation that our 'faith' in … scientific truth is just that – faith …" he begins with his minimal response: "… science gets results". He follows this with, "If you are flying to an international congress of anthropologists or literary critics, the reason you will probably get there – the reason you don't plummet into a ploughed field – is that a lot of Western scientifically trained engineers have got their sums right". He goes on, "Science boosts its claim to truth by its spectacular ability to make matter and energy jump through hoops on command, and to predict what will happen and when … [including] the power to slingshot rockets around Jupiter to reach Saturn, or intercept and repair the Hubble telescope …".[7]

Each of the examples Dawkins cites are from the engineering sciences, which you will recall from Chapter 1, are likely to tick all the high-confidence science criteria (and even then, as we noted, spacecraft and indeed aircraft do occasionally crash). He doesn't say for example, "Western science, by getting its sums right, has demonstrated that life arose from non-living chemicals", or that, "Western science, by getting its sums right, has demonstrated that fishlike creatures have evolved into amphibians and that amphibians have evolved into reptiles …".

As a historical science, then, **the theory of evolution's grand claims tick all the low-confidence-science criteria.** Perhaps evolutionists do grasp the key point here: that "science" is not a monolithic set of disciplines and that invoking comparisons between lower-confidence evolutionary biology and branches of science that are higher-confidence and do "get results", is beneficial to their cause. It would seem, perhaps, that the credibility of evolutionary theory gets a 'free ride' from the demonstrable achievements of the physical, or "operation" sciences.

Another curious feature of statements such as the opening quote to the chapter, is their sense of the logical error known as the 'genetic fallacy': that's to say, rather than engage with the arguments, why not simply ridicule the person making them. The philosopher David Hume (1711-1776) was not impressed when the genetic fallacy was used instead of making an argument. As he put it in the voice of one of his dialoguing characters, "Who could imagine ... that [one of the other debaters] ... would attempt to refute his antagonists by affixing a nickname to them; and ... have recourse to invective and declamation instead of reasoning?"[8]

Surely the truth of a scientific theory ought to be judged in terms of the evidence and counter-evidence? Does the touchy nature of such declarations indicate that the writer is well aware that there are evidential shortcomings? In Part 2, you will be able to come to your own conclusion. Alternatively, is there something else going on here? Do prominent evolutionists perceive a threat to their deeply held ideological predisposition? We'll come back to that question in Part 3.

But first we need to 'clear the decks' a little bit and ask, "What is 'evolution'?" It is variously labelled by its proponents as "the truth", "reality", "a historical fact", "an extremely probable idea", "a well-substantiated hypothesis", "a well-substantiated theory", "a former theory", "a common-sense fact", "a fact, not a theory", "a fact, theory and path".[9] We begin by exploring Darwin's achievements.

What was Darwin's contribution?

Charles Darwin (1809-1882) in his time was perhaps one of the greatest naturalists the world had ever seen,[10] Fig. 3.1. His innovative work on earthworms and barnacles, including his discovery of their hermaphrodite sexuality, for example, was legendary.

However, it was not his work on earthworms or barnacles that gave rise to his becoming a household name. In November 1859, Darwin published – to give it its full title – *On the Origin of Species By Means of Natural Selection, or the Preservation of Favoured Races in the Struggle for Life* (hereafter, *Origin of Species* or simply *The Origin*). Darwin has been uniquely credited with establishing the first truly "scientific"[11] explanation of the origin and evolution of all species that have ever lived. The customary narrative is captured well in this short magazine article.

> *The story behind the discovery of evolution is among the best-known tales in the history of science. In 1831, Charles Darwin set off for South America on a five-year voyage. During a stopover in the Galápagos Islands – an isolated cluster of islands off the coast of Ecuador – he observed that the size of finches' bills varied from island to island. Darwin concluded that all of the finches had originated from the same ancestor, and had then gone on to adapt new characteristics to suit their different environments. In 1859, Darwin published his book 'On the Origin of Species' and the theory of evolution was born.*[12]

Figure 3.1 Charles Darwin's statue in London's Natural History Museum.

As Sir Fred Hoyle and Chandra Wickramasinghe put it, "In popular opinion, scientific ideas about biological evolution changed decisively with the publication of Darwin's *Origin of Species* in 1859".[13] The impression is given that Darwin made a major breakthrough independently and entirely against the tide of his contemporaries' views. However, as is often the case, what was actually going on in his time has been obscured by the popular version.

In Darwin's time, the ruling paradigm was that of the Swedish naturalist Carolus Linnaeus (Carl von Linne, 1707-78). Building upon the work of others, he published a comprehensive plant classification system in 1737. A.N. Wilson in his biography of Darwin explained that

> *Linnaeus's system implied a fixity of species: else how could it be possible to distinguish one from another. His main purpose, however, was to classify, not to theorize, and if the effect of his work was to strengthen, among many naturalists, the notion of fixity of species, this was not his primary intention.*[14]

So although it had not been Linnaeus's intention, many other (what today we would call) scientists, such as the geologist Charles Lyell, understood "fixity of species" to be the orthodox view in the early 1800s. On this view, it was widely believed that species do not change over time, that they had been created as we see them today and even in the geographical settings in which we find them today. And Charles Lyell, who did not accept this orthodoxy, was one of those who had a major influence upon the development of Darwin's ideas.

But Darwin was not the first to claim that life had evolved. His grandfather, Erasmus Darwin, published *Zoonomia* in 1794, which espoused the idea that species evolved from one to another. When Darwin studied medicine at the University of Edinburgh, Robert Jameson, Professor of Natural History from 1804 to 1854, and Robert Edmond Grant (1793-1874) also sowed seeds through their geology and zoology talks respectively. These lectures encompassed evolutionary thinking and had a significant influence upon Darwin. Similarly, Jean-Baptiste Lamarck (1744-1829) and Giambattista Brocchi (1772-1826) had already developed evolutionary ideas.[15] Lamarck's thesis was that animals *acquired* new characteristics during their lifetimes and then passed them on to their offspring on a cumulative basis. His classic example was that of a giraffe reaching up to eat leaves on higher tree branches and stretching its neck in the process. He postulated that this acquired characteristic – a longer neck – would then be passed on to the next generation. Lamarckian ideas were later largely rejected by Darwin and others in favour of *natural selection*, though, as it turns out, they are making a bit of a comeback today.

Then in 1844 an anonymous publication appeared, *Vestiges of the Natural History of Creation*, which pre-empted many of Darwin's themes. After some time it came to light that the author was an Edinburgh journalist, publisher and bookseller, Robert Chambers (1802-71). Wilson maintains that

> ... [Chambers] scooped Darwin. What Darwin must have seen, as he anxiously read 'Vestiges', was the basic unoriginality of his own mind. Chambers, anonymously, but with tremendous pace and brio, spelt out a natural origin for species in a framework of material causation.[16]

Nor was Darwin the first to identify *natural selection* specifically as a causal mechanism involved in species changing over time. L.C. Eiseley, on the occasion of the centennial jubilee of the *Origin of Species* in 1959, gave an account of other references to *natural selection* prior to

1859. Most significantly, he cites Edward Blyth (1810-1873) who published essays in 1835-37 in the *Magazine of Natural History*. He "believed that nature was operating a system of selection of species which was analogous to a human breeder selecting particular dogs or pigeons".[17] Eiseley reveals that

> [a]s one leafs through Blyth's small papers ... one is amazed by the ideas which reappear in [Darwin's] trial essays of 1842 and 1844 and which Darwin never altered throughout his life.[18]

In 1837 Blyth asked the crucial question, "May not, then, a large portion of what are considered species have descended from a common parentage?" But he drew back from answering in the affirmative. His answer was "No", taking the view that *natural selection* was a conservative process. That is to say, once a species had adapted to its environment, why should it change significantly, as would have been necessary if all species had evolved from a common ancestral stock?[19] So for Blyth, *natural selection* was very limited in its ability to effect change in a species.

It was Charles Darwin – nearly outflanked by Alfred Russel Wallace (1823-1913) with almost exactly the same idea as Darwin – who answered "Yes" to the question posed by Blyth.

Darwin, then, was not the one who first expounded the concept of *natural selection*, but he was the first to make the grand claim that *natural selection* acting upon random variations within species could explain the origin of *all* species from one, or from a small number of original creatures; that the "... same principle that accounts for the shape of a finch's beak also accounts for the difference between a bee and an elephant".[20] In Chapter 5, we'll explore this claim in detail and find that the evidence doesn't hold water and instead points in a different direction.

While there is no doubt that Darwin was a great naturalist, it would appear that – contrary to the view that he was of a shy and retiring, even humble, disposition – there was another side to his personality that was ambitious and which jealously guarded the ownership of "his theory".[21] As a result he was remiss in not giving credit to most of those mentioned above (one exception is Lyell) and to others whose ideas he had incorporated into his famous work.[22] But, as we'll see in Parts 2 and 3, history is likely to show that Blyth's view was closer to the truth – that *natural selection* is very limited in its ability to effect change – and that Darwin was almost certainly wrong in his grand claim.

What is neo-Darwinism?
In a nutshell, Charles Darwin's core theory was that:
- Variations arise at random within species.
- Due to their particular variations, some members of the species will be better adapted to the environment than others.
- The better adapted individuals will have more offspring.
- The offspring will inherit the successful adaptations.
- As a consequence the population will change over time.

But Darwin didn't know what the source of variations is. By the 1920s there had been a rediscovery of the work of the Augustinian friar Gregor Mendel (1822-84) in what is now the Czech Republic. Mendel published a paper in 1866, *Experiments in Plant Hybridisation*, which was largely ignored by the scientific community at the time. In it he described experiments with garden peas. He discovered, for example, that when he crossed green and yellow varieties, the hybrids were all yellow. But in the second generation the yellow to green ratio was 3:1. So he concluded that some traits are what he called "dominant" (in this case "yellow") and others "recessive" (the "green" trait). In this way he established the basis of genetic inheritance and the science of genetics. Whereas Darwin thought that inheritance involved a subsequently inseparable *blending*[23] of characteristics, like mixing red and yellow paint to yield orange, Mendel discovered the idea of discrete genes which come in alternative varieties, known as alleles. Two alleles are inherited, one from each parent. If different alleles are inherited from each parent, one will be dominant and the other recessive. Only if both alleles inherited are of the recessive trait will that trait be expressed in the phenotype (physical characteristics) of the offspring - green peas, for example.

In 1903, Hugo de Vries (1848-1935) coined the term "mutation" to indicate a random change occurring in a gene. The combination of *mutations* and *natural selection* gave birth to *neo-Darwinism*: a melding of Darwinian evolution with Mendelian genetics. By the 1930s, neo-Darwinism had been promoted by the statistician and geneticist Ronald A. Fisher (1890-1962), evolutionary biologist Ernst Mayr (1904-2005), biologist and geneticist Theodosius Dobzhansky (1900-75) and palaeontologist George Gaylord Simpson (1902-84), among others.

Does "evolution" have different meanings?

So we return to the question, "What does 'evolution' mean?" Our initial reaction might be, "We all know what "evolution" means!" but it turns out the word can have several importantly different meanings. Here's how one high-school biology textbook describes *"The theory of evolution"* for the purposes of educating the next generation.

> As the earth cooled ... chemical reactions might have produced compounds like amino acids and enzymes which could make other reactions take place. If these chemicals somehow came together inside a membrane, they would form the first single-celled creatures, such as bacteria ... The first single-celled creatures might have given rise to many-celled creatures if the cells stuck together after cell division ... As a result the creatures would become more complicated and different forms would arise ... Some might swim in the surface waters like shrimps or burrow in the sand like worms ... Over a period of 400 million years it is thought that some fish-like creatures developed legs and lungs and so became amphibia, like newts. Some amphibian ancestors could have developed scales and the ability to lay eggs on land and so become reptiles. One group of ancient reptiles might have given rise to the birds by developing feathers and wings and another group, by developing fur and producing milk, could have become the mammals.[24]

Notice, in passing, the number of times "if", "might", "would", "could", "somehow" and "it is thought that" appear in this narrative, indicating its speculative nature. Although Darwin's evolutionary account only begins after one or a small number of species had already come into existence, modern textbooks such as this one typically construct an all-encompassing story of unguided evolution. The story begins with inanimate chemicals generating the first living cell. This in turn evolves, producing every species alive today. And this is the most commonly understood meaning of "evolution". **In the rest of this book we'll use the shorter label** *"Evolution"* **(with a capital and italicised) to designate this unguided "particles-to-people" meaning.**

We now come to the problem of equivocation or doublespeak. Unlike in physics where terms like "momentum" and "kinetic energy" are precisely defined,[25] and there is no ambiguity, "evolution" is often used to mean different things even by the same author within the same discussion. For instance, not even the fiercest critic of Darwinism doubts that all the varieties of dogs existing today descended from wolves over many hundreds of years, or that bacteria have developed resistance to antibiotics over time, or that finch beaks on the Galápagos islands became more robust during periods of drought.

Yet, while there is no doubt that these species have changed over time, the varieties of dogs are all still dogs, the bacteria are still bacteria, and the finches are still finches. So when antibiotic resistance in bacteria is described as "evolution" we're being invited to agree that this kind of small-scale change can be extrapolated (a low-confidence-science criterion remember), to bacteria-to-Beethoven evolution. This is known as equivocation – the logical fallacy that involves shifting from one meaning of a word to another within the same argument. Such small-scale change is often more precisely labelled "microevolution".

Why is it important to draw out these distinctions? **The problem here is that evidence that *does* support the idea that species "change over time"** – microevolution – **is often used by evolutionary biologists to support the much grander claim of "particles-to-people"** *Evolution*.

Table 3.1 illustrates some of the different meanings we'll encounter and the more specific terms that will be used in this book going forward. As an example of how equivocation can mislead the reader, here's a sentence from Jerry Coyne's, *Why Evolution Is True*.

> Although the idea of evolution itself was not original to Darwin, the copious evidence he mustered in its favour convinced most scientists and many educated readers that life had indeed changed over time.[26]

Here is the same sentence, annotated within square brackets with appropriate definitions as per Table 3.1: "Although the idea of evolution [*Evolution*] itself was not original to Darwin, the copious evidence he mustered in its favour convinced most scientists and many educated readers that life had indeed changed over time [microevolution]". Coyne, intentionally or otherwise, conflates the meanings of "microevolution" and "*Evolution*".

Many advocates of neo-Darwinism claim that there is no difference between microevolution (finch-beak, small-scale evolution) and macroevolution (new body plans, such as birds or mammals evolving from reptilians). Macroevolution, they argue, simply uses the same process that drives microevolution, but operates over vast periods of time. But those who are critical of *Evolution*, while agreeing that small-scale change occurs over time, posit that any such change is limited and sooner or later runs out of steam long before macroevolution can take place. In Part 2 we'll explore this question and discover the limitations of the microevolutionary process.

Meaning	Term used in this book
Sometimes "evolution" is used to mean natural selection acting upon mutations – reputed to be the **mechanism** or cause of evolution. When copying errors (mutations) occur in an organism's DNA those organisms best adapted to their environment will produce most offspring. Thus natural selection filters out the less well adapted individuals.	mutations plus natural selection
Sometimes "evolution" is used to mean **small-scale change over time**. For example, the size and shape of finch beaks has been observed to change over a period of a few years as the climate has changed.	microevolution
Sometimes "evolution" is used to mean the **evolution of new body plans**. For example, amphibians emerging from a fish-like ancestor or birds emerging from a reptile-like ancestor.	macroevolution
Sometimes "evolution" is used to mean **bacteria-to-Beethoven** evolution: the idea that all modern life forms emerged and developed gradually from the first single-celled organism. It is often depicted as a tree with branches spreading out from its trunk.	universal common descent
Sometimes "evolution" is used to mean **particles-to-people** evolution: universal common descent plus "chemical evolution" – the emergence of single-celled life from non-living chemicals. "*Evolution*" (with a capital and italicised) will be used for this meaning.	*Evolution*

Table 3.1 The word "evolution" can be used by evolutionary biologists to mean different things as listed above. The corresponding terms to be used in this book are also given. **In each case purely natural, unguided, undirected, processes are assumed to be at work.**

Here's Jerry Coyne once more as he defines what he calls "the modern theory of evolution" (annotated with shifting meanings).

*Life on Earth evolved gradually beginning with one primitive species – perhaps a self-replicating molecule – that lived more than 3.5 billion years ago [*Evolution*]; it then branched out over time [universal common descent], throwing off many new and diverse species [macroevolution]; and the mechanism for most (but not all) of evolutionary change is natural selection [mutations plus natural selection].*[27]

Were initial objections religious ones?

In Chapter 2 we explored the iconic story – in wide circulation today – in which Galileo is universally regarded as a martyr for science in opposition to the Roman Catholic Church of the time. We discovered that this representation is a myth and a distortion of the much more complex real history surrounding the events.

Another icon of science supposedly triumphing over religion, this time specifically relating to Darwinism, is the tale of the clash between the anthropologist, Thomas Henry Huxley (1825-95) and Samuel Wilberforce (1805-73), Bishop of Oxford, dubbed "Soapy Sam". The story goes that in a debate hosted by the British Association for the Advancement of Science held in Oxford's Natural History Museum on 30th June 1860, Huxley, the competent scientist, demolished the scientifically ignorant churchman. Rehearsing the modern myth, the outspoken atheist Christopher Hitchens (1949-2011),[28] described the encounter in scathing terms: "[Huxley] in front of a large audience cleaned Wilberforce's clock, ate his lunch, used him as a mop for the floor, and all that".[29]

Once again, historians have uncovered a more nuanced account. First, Wilberforce was no ignoramus. He had a first-class degree in mathematics and kept up his scientific interests while pursuing his ecclesiastical calling. Samuel was the son of William Wilberforce, whose tireless campaign over decades led to the abolition of slavery in the British Empire. Prior to the debate he had consulted with Sir Richard Owen (1804-92), founder of the famous London Natural History Museum, and published a hostile review of *The Origin* in the *Quarterly Review*. Contrary to the popular myth that his opposition was of a religious nature, his objections to Darwin's theory were, in fact, purely on scientific grounds. Where he blundered in the debate was that, after setting out his scientific objections, rather than sitting down "covered with honour",[30] as Wilson put it, in his excitement and over-confidence, he turned to Huxley and inquired, "Was it through his grandfather or his grandmother that he traced his descent from an ape?" This frivolous 'snob remark', in the context of a serious scientific discussion, allowed Huxley to take advantage as the argument descended into ridicule and rebuttal infused with political undertones. The result is that while William Wilberforce is judged by history as a hero, his son is perceived as a loser.[31] Nevertheless, reports *at the time* were kinder to the Bishop. The *Athenaeum's*[32] report "gave the impression that honours were about even, saying that, 'Wilberforce and Huxley have each found foemen worthy of their steel'".[33]

What were Soapy Sam's scientific objections to *The Origin*? Darwin made much of drawing an analogy between artificial selective breeding of pigeons (and other domesticated species) and natural selection, "daily and hourly" scrutinising species over epochs of time. So the Bishop's first objection was that, in Wilson's words, "... domestic breeders do not, in fact, create new species – they merely modify existing species – and the wild descendants of domesticated types, rather than continuing to develop, in fact revert to the original type. If anything therefore, the behaviour of animals under domestication disproved rather than proved the Darwinian thesis".[34] Second, the geological evidence lacked the host of transitional forms that ought to be observed according to Darwin's theory of gradualism. Darwin admitted that Wilberforce's review was

> ... uncommonly clever; it picks out with skill all the most conjectural parts, and brings forward well all the difficulties. It quizzes me most splendidly.[35]

It will be argued – in Chapters 5 and 6 respectively – that neither of these two points has been satisfactorily answered to this day.

In addition to Samuel Wilberforce and Richard Owen, Darwin had other contemporary critics. Lord Kelvin was unconvinced by the science. In reviews of the first edition, Cambridge Professor of Geology Adam Sedgwick, and Professor of Zoology and Geology at Harvard Louis Agassiz (1807-73) had rejected the idea of evolution outright. Fleeming Jenkin, a Scottish engineer who had worked with another well-known Scot, James Clerk Maxwell, some of whose breakthrough work we encountered earlier, wrote a review of the fourth edition of *The Origin* in 1867 in the *North British Review*. He made the salient point that "A given animal or plant appears to be contained as it were within a sphere of variation; one individual lies near the surface, another individual, of the same species, near another part of the surface; the average animal at the centre ...".[36] In other words, he's arguing that **species do vary, but within a strict "sphere" of limited size**. Asa Gray (1820-88), Professor of Natural History at Harvard, with whom Darwin had communicated regularly over the years, still remained convinced that evolution needed a guiding intelligence. The biologist Sir George Jackson Mivart (1827-1900) developed a remarkably apposite critique of Darwin's theory, including these objections:

3 – Evolution: thinking the unthinkable

> *That Natural Selection is incompetent to account for the incipient stages of useful structures... That there are grounds for thinking that specific differences may be developed suddenly instead of gradually. That the opinion that species have definite though very different limits to their variability is still tenable. That certain fossil transitional forms are absent which might have been expected to be present ...*[37]

There were, of course, *some* dissenters from Darwin's thesis in *The Origin* on *religious* grounds. Indeed Thomas Huxley, who became known as Darwin's Bulldog, made it his business to reduce the influence of enemies of the theory by implying that *any* objections were for reasons of religious bigotry. It turned out to be a very useful and effective device at closing down intellectual opposition. The tactic is still in use today.

Robert Fitzroy was one casualty of this ploy. Rear Admiral Fitzroy had been the Captain of the famous *Beagle* voyage around the world in which the young Darwin was able to pursue his studies of nature in meticulous detail, including the study of wildlife on the iconic Galápagos Islands. It was Robert Fitzroy who made a 'religious' contribution later in the Oxford debate. A.N. Wilson writes that Fitzroy "wanted to put on record that he regretted giving Darwin the chance to sail around the world, thereby beginning the train of thought which undermined the word of God".[38] Fitzroy was no fool. He was a Fellow of the Royal Society and following retirement from the Royal Navy was chief of the meteorological society of the Board of Trade. But unfortunately, his speech created the impression that his main concern was – not that Darwin was wrong – but that he might be right!

Nevertheless, it should be noted that the main early objections to the theory were on purely scientific grounds. Today these issues are even more acutely germane. In Part 2, we will explore them (and others) in detail.

Do evolutionists invoke 'god' arguments?

Now here's an odd thing. While there were a small number of objectors to the theory on purely religious grounds, it's actually Darwin and his contemporary defenders today who typically bring God into the argument! Lots of god-wouldn't-have-done-it-that-way examples can be found in Coyne's *Evolution Is True*. Here are a few of them. In the five quotations that follow, emphasis has been added.

> *These hernias are bad ... **No intelligent designer** would have given us this tortuous testicular journey.*[39]

> There is **no reason why a celestial designer**, fashioning organisms from scratch like an architect designs buildings, should make new species by remodeling the features of existing ones.[40]
>
> Wouldn't it be **odd if a creator** helped an ostrich balance itself by giving it appendages that just happen to look exactly like reduced wings ...[41]
>
> **Why would a creator** put a pathway for making vitamin C in all these species, and then inactivate it?[42]
>
> ... we never see adaptations that benefit the species at the expense of the individual - something that we might have expected **if organisms were designed by a beneficent creator**.[43]

Unsurprisingly, Dawkins had already been offering his take on what God would not do. Here's one of his.

> It is as though cheetahs had been **designed by one deity** and antelopes by **a rival deity**. Alternatively, **if there is only one Creator** who made the tiger and the lamb, the cheetah and the gazelle, **what is He playing at? Is He a sadist** who enjoys spectator sports? ... [emphasis added].[44]

But these are theological arguments, not scientific ones.[45] Or to put it another way, shouldn't we expect scientists to be concentrating on the *how* of evolution rather than *why*? That's to say, working out in detail *how* testicles, wings and cheetahs, and even a pathway for making vitamin C, evolved. But apparently not. Coyne claims that

> ... the onus is not on evolutionary biologists to sketch out a precise step-by-step scenario documenting exactly how a complex character evolved.[46]

This is an astonishing statement. It prompts questions like, "So, whose job is it?" and "What *do* evolutionary biologists do, then?" Apparently there's not even a detectable sense of obligation on the part of biologists to make an attempt at a plausible evolutionary scenario. A.N. Wilson was surprised too, "It is hard to think of any other branch of modern science - quantum theory, for example, or discoveries in electro-magnetism, neuroscience or astronomy - whose proponents spend as much time talking about errors of theology as of the truth of their own area of expertise".[47] Quite so.

Lower lifeboat 3!
Here's a summary of Chapter 3.

- As a historical science, the *grand claims* of the theory of evolution tick most of the low-confidence-science criteria.
- Charles Darwin is often portrayed as the one who independently discovered the principle of natural selection, but he was very protective of his theory and largely failed to give credit to a number of others.
- Edward Blyth, for example, had already identified natural selection as an active mechanism in biology.
- Yet, while Darwin made the grand claim that, thanks to natural selection, all extant species had evolved from "one or a small number" of original creatures, Blyth concluded that natural selection was strictly limited in its ability to effect change.
- History gave Darwin the ideological victory, but does evidence accumulated since support Darwin or Blyth?
- The Oxford debate between Thomas Henry Huxley (dubbed Darwin's bulldog) and Bishop Samuel Wilberforce (Soapy Sam) has become an iconic instance of the alleged triumph of science over religion, on a par with the Galileo affair.
- Yet, Soapy Sam's objections to Darwin's theory were actually on scientific grounds, not religious ones as the popular myth would have us believe.
- Some promoters of evolutionary theory both in Darwin's time (such as Huxley) and today have found it convenient to claim that opponents of the theory do so on purely religious grounds. This tactic diverts attention from genuine questions about the science.
- Yet oddly, it's many of today's evolutionists who most often use theological (God-wouldn't-have-done-it-that-way) arguments to justify their conclusions.
- Darwin didn't know what the source of variation is that natural selection operates upon. *Neo-Darwinism*, also known as *The Modern Synthesis*, identifies that source of variation as genetic mutations (copying errors in the genes).
- The word "evolution" is often used to mean different things by evolutionary biologists at different times. Such *equivocation* can mislead students of the subject and the public at large, because evidence that supports one meaning, say "change over time", may

be used later – even within the same sentence – to support a particles-to-people evolutionary claim (which the cited evidence does not automatically support).
- It's going to be important to discriminate amongst these various meanings as we come across them (see Table 3.1).
- Going forward in our investigation, *"Evolution"* will be our shorthand designation for unguided particles-to-people evolution.

Popularisers of *Evolution* such as Richard Dawkins and Jerry Coyne maintain that the evidence comprehensively supports the theory of evolution and are very dismissive of anyone who questions that view. Is there a hint here that they may be well aware that evolutionary biology, a historical science, ticks most of Stadler's low-confidence science criteria boxes. After all, if the evidence is robust, then why should there be any objection to it being scrutinised? Isn't that a core feature of the scientific enterprise?

At the risk of being labelled "ignorant, stupid or insane" then (see the opening quote to the chapter), are we ready to survey some 'watertight compartments' of evidence below deck? **Let's think the unthinkable,** explore some of *Evolution*'s predictions **and**, taking advice from one of the "New Ten Commandments" Dawkins cites in *The God Delusion*, "**question everything**" [emphasis added].[48]

Part 2

DAMAGE BELOW DECKS!

Five failed predictions of neo-Darwinian theory

Edward J. Smith – Captain of *Titanic*

"I will say that I cannot imagine any condition that would cause the vessel to founder."

Introduction to part 2

Probably the most deeply held values concern predictions: they should be accurate; quantitative predictions are preferable to qualitative ones; whatever the margin of permissible error, it should be consistently satisfied in a given field;[1]

Thomas Kuhn

Reminder of the big 'What-if?'

Just as *Titanic* had design flaws that rendered it unsinkable only in a limited sense, what if the science underpinning the *Theory of Evolution* turns out to be valid only in a strictly limited sense? What if 19th century Darwinian science, developing as it did in an age that also gave rise to supreme confidence in *Titanic's* unsinkability, has collided with the 'iceberg' of 21st century molecular biology. The amazing discoveries in the late 20th and especially in the early 21st century – of the exquisite micro-molecular machinery and organisational complexity, together with the hierarchical layers of regulatory control systems inside living cells – have become *Evolution*'s 'iceberg'.

RMS *Titanic* was unsinkable in a limited sense: specifically if up to four watertight sections were breached, but would sink as a "mathematical certainty" if five or more compartments became flooded. In relation to particles-to-people *Evolution* then, let's be clear: few doubt that the basic neo-Darwinian mechanism – natural selection acting on variations – is a real phenomenon that can explain adaptation; why polar bears are white rather than brown or black for example, or why finch beaks on the Galápagos Islands have varied in size by way of adapting to changing climatic conditions.[2] As we've discovered in Chapter 3, this kind of change is often labelled *microevolution*. However, as we'll see in Chapter 5, such adaptations may not be due to the origination of *new* genes, but rather to the *corruption* of already existing ones. And, in any case, what about the origin of *beaks* and *fur*, never mind finches and bears themselves? The grand claim of the *Theory* is this: that this very same mechanism can account for the mindless, unguided origin and evolution of the entirety of life in all its complexity and diversity – *macroevolution*. Ernst Mayr, one of the great proponents of neo-Darwinism, asserted that

> *... all evolution is due to the accumulation of small genetic changes guided by natural selection and that transpecific evolution is **nothing but***

an extrapolation and magnification of the events which take place within population genetics [emphasis added].[3]

In other words, Mayr is claiming that natural selection acting upon mutations repeated over and over again, happening over millions of years, is all that is needed to explain the macroevolution textbook claim above.

It is in relation to *macroevolution* that a growing number of scientists and others are recognising that RMS *Evolution* has collided with the molecular biology 'iceberg' and that the grand claim of the *Theory of Evolution* cannot be sustained by the evidence. Or to put it in the active voice, the extraordinary discoveries made by molecular biologists in the last thirty years or so, using technology that was not available in Darwin's time, have now tested the *Theory* and found weaknesses which demonstrate that natural selection acting upon random genetic mutations is incapable of producing macro-evolutionary outcomes. Just like the too-low bulkheads in *Titanic*, the weaknesses were there all along. Chapters 4 to 8 aim to justify this conclusion.

In the opening quote above, Thomas Kuhn emphasises how important it is to the credibility of a field of science that its predictions are met and seen to be met. Influential thinker Steven Pinker agrees, "... the acid test of empirical rationality is *prediction*. Science proceeds by testing the predictions of hypotheses [emphasis in original]".[4] Pinker also warns against the genetic fallacy - ignoring a critique because of who the critic is or represents, rather than addressing the critic's argument, "... all ideas have to come from somewhere, and their birthplace has no bearing on their merit".[5] And again, "You're not allowed to forcibly shut people up who disagree with you".[6]

Jerry Coyne agrees, "All scientific truth is provisional, subject to modifications in light of new evidence ... it is possible that despite thousands of observations that support Darwinism, new data might show it to be wrong. I think this is unlikely, but scientists, unlike zealots, can't afford to become arrogant about what they accept as true".[7]

So let's venture below deck, explore the internals of five 'watertight compartments' and examine five predictions of evolutionary theory.

Chapter 4

FAILED PREDICTION #1

Life emerged from chemistry

… it is possible to interpret the early emergence of life on Earth as a hint… that simple life may be inevitable, given the right conditions.[1]

Brian Cox (1968-)

We begin with a prediction in the watertight compartment at the 'sharp end' of RMS *Evolution* – nearest to the bow below the fo'c's'le: **that basic cellular life emerged from inanimate matter through mindless unguided processes.**

Our first survey will recognise that as a prediction:
- It's widely believed to be true.

Then we'll descend below decks seeking answers to these questions:
- Is "simple" life simple?
- Is origin-of-life chemistry easy?
- Is origin-of-life chemistry plausible?
- Is matter, energy and lots of time enough?

It's widely believed to be true

The popular television documentary presenter and professor of physics Brian Cox encapsulates in the above quote the widely held belief in academia, the media and the general public, that living *biochemistry* emerged from non-living *geochemistry*.

Strictly speaking, Darwin's theory of natural selection only begins to take effect once simple life exists, or at least, some kind of self-replicating system. In *The Origin*, he envisaged today's huge diversity of life evolving from "a few forms" or from "one".[2] However, in a letter to his friend Joseph Hooker he speculated, albeit privately at the time, "… if (& oh what a big if) we could conceive in some warm little pond with all sorts of ammonia & phosphoric salts ... that a protein compound was chemically formed, ready to undergo still more complex changes ...".[3]

Clearly, then, Darwin anticipated the largely universal assumption today that *Evolution* is generally understood to begin with *chemical evolution* also known as *abiogenesis:* that the first living cell emerged of its own accord from just the right mix of interacting inanimate matter. In his book, *Human Universe*, Cox articulates the perceived inevitability of abiogenesis in a little more detail.

> *The most vivid example of emergent complexity ... the origin of life on Earth has a sense of inevitability about it, because its basic processes are chemical reactions that will proceed given the right conditions. These conditions were present in the oceans of Earth 3.8 billion years ago, possibly earlier, and they led to the emergence of single-celled organisms.*[4]

That life is "inevitable" somewhere in the universe is generally believed because the observable universe is so large (some estimates suggest one trillion galaxies each with perhaps 100 billion stars)[5] and has been in existence for so long (the current estimate is 13.8 billion years).[6]

Cox tells the story of a conference organised by a young astronomer called Frank Drake in November 1961 which illustrates the early optimism in relation to this putative inevitability.[7] It was the first meeting of SETI (the Search for Extraterrestrial Intelligence) and it focused on the question, "How many intelligent civilisations exist in [our] Milky Way galaxy that we could in principle communicate with?" Drake developed what has become known eponymously as The Drake Equation:[8]

$$N = R_* \times f_p \times n_e \times f_l \times f_i \times f_c \times L \text{ where,}$$

N	the number of civilisations in our galaxy with which radio communication might be possible.
R_*	the average rate of star formation in our galaxy.
f_p	the fraction of those stars that have planets.
n_e	the average number of planets that can potentially support life per star that has planets.
f_l	the fraction of those planets that actually develop life at some point.

4 – FAILED PREDICTION #1: Life emerged from chemistry

f_i the fraction of those planets that actually go on to develop intelligent life (civilisations).

f_c the fraction of civilisations that develop a technology that releases detectable signs of their existence into space.

L   the length of time for which such civilisations release detectable signals into space.

The meeting reached a consensus and concluded that we could potentially communicate with as many as 10,000 civilisations – in our galaxy alone! It should be noted that, at best, only estimates of the first three terms in *The Drake Equation* can be informed by *measurable* data. Remembering Stadler's criteria from Chapter 1, the other four terms (at least) would tend to tick all the low-confidence science categories of unrepeatable, indirectly measurable, observational rather than interventional, and would be open to bias and overstatement together with reliance upon unverifiable assumptions.

This early SETI conclusion is equivalent to saying that 1 in every 20 million solar systems in the Milky Way will have evolved not just simple life, but advanced civilisations capable of transmitting radio signals that testify to their existence. At the time of writing, more than sixty years on, no such signals have been detected.[9]

Cox asserts that there is evidence pointing to the emergence of life on Earth 3.8 billion years ago; that's to say, almost immediately after the end of the so-called *Late Heavy Bombardment* when comets and meteorites were thought to have been pounding the Earth and surely obliterating any origin-of-life attempts there might have been prior to its end.

Then, following the logic of *The Drake Equation*, together with the belief that life arose very soon after meteorite bombardment quietened down, Cox says "… we might venture that the probability of life arising on a planet that could support it – the term f_l in the Drake Equation – is close to 100 per cent".[10] Now he goes on to admit that this is highly speculative. But note the thrust of his belief here: that given the right conditions, abiogenesis, the emergence of life from inanimate matter, is **not only inevitable** but it's **also easy**.

In 2019, Brian Cox presented a documentary series, *Planets*, screened on BBC television, in which he reiterated the above views, including the idea that "there may have been and may still be life on Mars".[11] In one of the episodes of the series, Dr Ashwin Vasavada, an engineer working in NASA's Jet Propulsion Laboratory, offers this opinion.

> *For me personally, I find it might actually be more surprising if we never found evidence of life on Mars. Everything we've found suggests that Mars was such a friendly, supportive place for life in its early history and there should be a lot of planets like that around other stars, lots of life in the universe. So maybe we're getting to the point where it'll be more surprising if we never find other life.*[12]

Biotechnologist Matti Leisola points out that watching such documentaries, "one gets the impression that it was relatively easy for blind natural forces to make complex molecules, animals and plants".[13]

Back in his book *Human Universe*, Cox clearly agrees with Vasavada's confidence when he makes this bold assertion, "The laws of nature self-evidently allow life to exist, and no matter how improbable, life must have arisen an infinite number of times".[14] This statement exhibits more than one logical faux-pas.

1. "... **no matter how improbable**, life must have arisen ...": what if the probability is so low that it is barely distinguishable from zero? Clearly Cox's *assumption* is that the probability is nowhere near zero. Later in this chapter we'll discover that such an assumption has no justification.
2. "... **life must have arisen** ...": this is based on Cox's *assumption* that life arose and evolved by purely unguided natural processes. He later articulates this as, "All we know for sure is that it happened here [on Earth]."[15] This statement commits the logical fallacy of assuming the answer. **Whereas all we actually know for sure is that life *exists* here.**
3. "... **an infinite number of times.**" Now to be fair to Cox, he prefaces the sentence in question with "if the universe is infinite in extent ... we are not alone". Now it is not known whether the universe is finite or infinite, but the observable universe is certainly finite, so it would seem to be overstating the case to suggest that "life must have arisen an infinite number of times".[16]
4. Finally, just because, "**The laws of nature self-evidently allow life to exist** ...", it does not follow logically that the laws *caused* life to arise. There's a hint of the reification fallacy in this sentence. That's to say Cox attributes agency to an abstract concept: "laws" don't create anything. For instance, the law that 2+2 = 4 will not put £4 into anyone's bank account.[17]

4 – FAILED PREDICTION #1: Life emerged from chemistry

We should recognise in these claims the effects of unexamined assumptions, bias and overstatement, leading to, as Stadler warned, "low-confidence science being presented as high-confidence science".

Brian Cox, of course, is not alone in his view that spontaneous life was inevitable. Geologist David Rothery, for example, gives the impression that the presence of liquid water on a planet renders the inception of life all but inevitable: "... part of the northern hemisphere [of Mars] was once occupied by a shallow sea. That being so, it would be rather surprising if primitive life had not developed ...".[18]

Biochemist Nick Lane, in *Life Ascending: the Ten Great Inventions of Evolution*, tantalisingly states the goal of his first chapter, "I want to show that the origin of life is not the great mystery it is sometimes made out to be, but that life emerges, perhaps almost inevitably, from the turning of our globe".[19]

And in 2005, in response to the *Edge* Question[20] put to over one hundred eminent intellectuals, "What do you believe is true, even though you cannot prove it?", many included similar beliefs to that articulated by Stephen Petranek, the then editor-in-chief of *Discover* magazine: "I believe that life is common throughout the universe and that we will find another Earth-like planet within a decade".[21]

Richard Dawkins, too, thinks that life has arisen numerous times in the universe. He estimates that there are a billion billion planets in the universe.[22] Dawkins is being cautious at this point because this is a very conservative estimate. But he then goes on to say

> [n]ow, suppose the origin of life, the spontaneous arising of something equivalent to DNA, really was quite a staggeringly improbable event. Suppose it was so improbable as to occur on only one in a billion planets ... even with such absurdly long odds, life will still have arisen on a billion planets – of which Earth, of course, is one.[23]

We'll see later in this chapter that Dawkins belief that life arises on one planet in a billion – while longer odds than the early SETI estimates of 1 in 20 million solar systems with technologically advanced civilisations – far from being "absurdly long odds", actually underestimates the odds by many orders of magnitude.[24]

The popular view, then, is that the spontaneous origin-of-life is inevitable and even relatively easy. Because the universe is so huge, life has arisen perhaps billions of times over its lifetime. And of course movies and drama series such as *Star Wars* and *Star Trek* are all based on the belief that "alien" life is ubiquitous in the universe.

Is there a solid scientific basis for this widely held view? We proceed by questioning **three assumptions** inherent in the "inevitable and easy'" narrative:
- A "simple" or "primitive" **living cell really is simple**.
- **Origin-of-Life chemistry is** sufficiently **undemanding**.
- The chemical interactions of **matter and energy are all that is needed** to explain the emergence of life many times over, given that the universe is so vast and so long-lived.

Is "simple" life simple?

My guess is that ... the origin of life probably wasn't all that improbable.[25]

Richard Dawkins

Viewing a living cell with the best microscopes available at the time - achieving magnifications of several hundred times - Darwin's contemporaries were able to decipher not much more than that cells had a cell wall, a nucleus, and protoplasm - the seemingly uniform matter, always on the move, filling the space between the nucleus and the cell wall. In 1868, the biologist Ernst Haeckel (1834-1919), who functioned as a kind of 'Darwin's bulldog' in Germany, described cells as

> ... organisms which ... consist entirely of shapeless, simple homogeneous matter ... nothing more than a shapeless mobile, little lump of mucus or slime ... Simpler or more imperfect organisms we cannot possibly conceive.[26]

In a 2018 paper authored by more than thirty multidisciplinary scientists, Edward Steele *et al.* admitted the falsity of this view and that it should have been challenged some sixty years ago. The notion that the earliest living cells were "exceedingly simple structures", they point out, "should of course have been critically examined and rejected after the discovery of the exceedingly complex molecular structures involved in proteins and in DNA".[27]

Contrast Haeckel's bold, yet prematurely confident assessment above[28] with this word picture written in 1985 - little more than a century later - by biochemist Michael Denton: "To grasp the reality of life as it has been revealed by molecular biology, we must magnify a cell a thousand million times until it is twenty kilometres in diameter and resembles a giant airship large enough to cover a great city like London or New York. What we would then see would be an object of unparalleled complexity and adaptive design. On the surface of the

4 – FAILED PREDICTION #1: Life emerged from chemistry

cell we would see millions of openings, like the port holes of a vast space ship, opening and closing to allow a continual stream of materials to flow in and out. If we were to enter one of these openings we would find ourselves in a world of supreme technology and bewildering complexity. We would see endless highly organised corridors and conduits branching in every direction away from the perimeter of the cell, some leading to the central memory bank in the nucleus and others to assembly plants and processing units".[29] These conduits would be buzzing with a huge range of materials and assemblages being shuttled along inwards to the nucleus or out towards the processing plants near the perimeter. Mind boggling control and organisation is involved. See Fig. 4.1.

Denton goes on to describe the significance of proteins which will be important in our story shortly: "We would notice that the simplest of the functional components of the cell, the protein molecules, were astonishingly complex pieces of molecular machinery, each one consisting of [at least] three thousand atoms arranged in highly organised 3-D spatial conformation".[30] Similarly in 1998, Bruce Alberts, president emeritus of the National Academy of Sciences at the time, described by Alvin Plantinga as "no friend of Intelligent Design"[31] expresses the new realisation that life is extraordinarily complex.

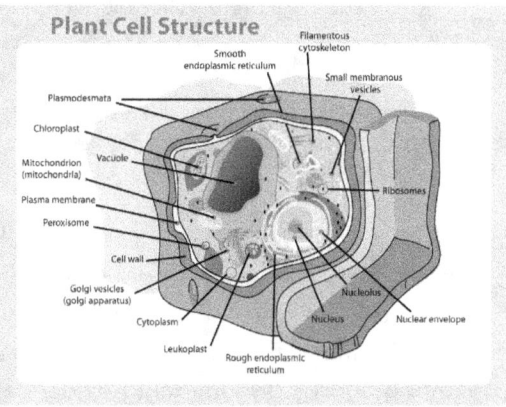

Figure 4.1 (Above) a bacterial cell. (Below) a plant cell. These are examples of *prokaryotic* (no nucleus) and *eukaryotic* cells respectively.

> ... the chemistry that makes life possible is much more elaborate than anything we students had ever considered. Proteins make up most of the dry mass of the cell. But instead of a cell dominated by randomly colliding individual protein molecules, we now know that nearly every major

> process in a cell is carried out by assemblies of 10 or more protein molecules ... each of these protein assemblies interacts with several other large complexes of proteins. Indeed, the entire cell can be viewed as a factory that contains an elaborate network of interlocking assembly lines, each of which is composed of a set of large protein machines.[32]

Marcos Eberlin, a chemist specialising in mass-spectrometry, describes cells as "... cybernetic, multi molecular cities full of high-tech machines, power plants, and even nano-robots".[33] In summary, far from "simple" life being simple, the complexity of the simplest living cell, capable of replicating itself, is greater than the complexity of RMS *Titanic* to the same extent that *Titanic* is more complex than one of its rivets.[34] A three minute animation[35] by Stephen Meyer, well worth watching, gives a sense of this complexity.

Is origin-of-life chemistry easy?

Here are two divergent opinions from scientists, neither of whom is an expert in origin-of-life chemistry, although both have surveyed the evidence emerging from the multi-disciplinary field over extended periods of time.

> I am not a chemist, and I must rely on chemists to get their sums right. Different chemists prefer different pet theories, and there is no shortage of theories.[36]
>
> Richard Dawkins

> ... no known scientific principle suggests an inbuilt drive from matter to life. No known law of physics or chemistry favors the emergence of the living state over other states. Physics and chemistry are, as far as we can tell, 'life blind'.[37]
>
> Physicist Paul Davies

In his quote above, Dawkins alludes to the fact we've come across previously that many different disciplines have knowledge and insights that can be brought to bear on *Evolution*, and that includes chemical evolution. Different branches of science can bring to the table confirming and/or disconfirming evidence. Dawkins admits that, as a biologist, he has little contribution to make to the problem of explaining the origin of the first life from non-living matter. He simply passes the buck to the chemistry department, confident in the belief that there *will* be a solution. Clearly, Paul Davies, a physicist is not so sure. He sees the stark discontinuity between "life blind" chemicals and "the living state".

WHAT'S THE MAGNITUDE OF THE CHALLENGE? Fig. 4.2 gives a sense of the problems that need to be solved if chemical evolution –

4 - FAILED PREDICTION #1: Life emerged from chemistry

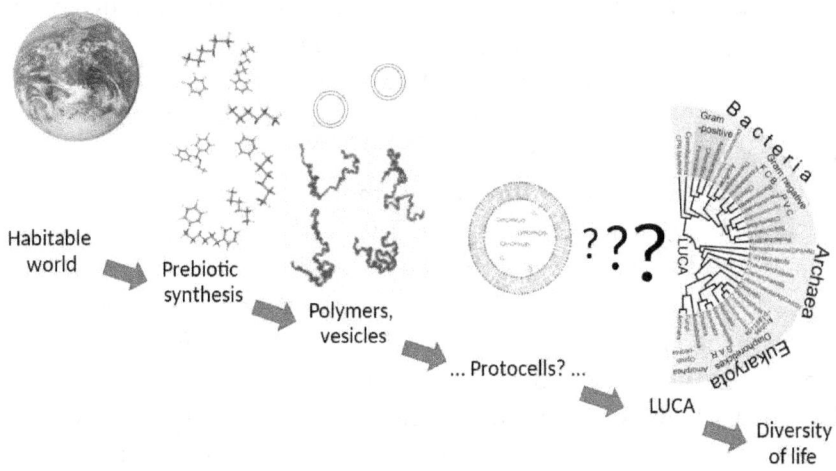

Figure 4.2 The chemical evolution challenge and its major stages.

abiogenesis - really happened. The first requirement is a habitable world[38] (top left in Fig. 4.2) acting as host to basic chemicals such as nitrogen, methane, ammonia and of course water, either as water vapour in the atmosphere of the early Earth or, as we'll see shortly, in deep ocean hydrothermal vents. Next a "primordial soup" of amino acids, sugars and other organic molecules would need to have formed (prebiotic synthesis). These simple organic molecules would then need to have combined into very large molecules (polymers) such as proteins and DNA, and into large assemblages of polymers (vesicles). The next stage is envisaged as the formation of a "protocell" in which a cell wall (membrane) encloses the polymerised organic molecules. The final requirement is the emergence of a highly structured, fully functioning cell with hierarchical layers of command and control to orchestrate the efforts of microscopic machines and processing plants built out of protein assemblies (listed as LUCA,[39] the Last Universal Common Ancestor, in Fig. 4.2. See more detail in Fig. 4.1). All life is then presumed to have evolved from LUCA.

WHAT EVIDENCE SUPPORTS CHEMICAL EVOLUTION? Developing their ideas from Darwin's "warm little pond" speculation, the Russian biochemist Alexander Oparin (1894-1980) and the British evolutionist J.B.S. Haldane (1892-1964) independently suggested in the 1920s that life must have originated in a primeval soup of organic molecules.[40]

Then in 1953, building on especially Oparin's assumptions about the composition of Earth's early atmosphere, Stanley Miller (1930-2007), under the supervision of Nobel-prize-winning chemist Harold Urey (1893-1981), carried out an experiment which was heralded as groundbreaking.

The classic **Miller-Urey experiment** used electrical spark discharges to simulate lightning and induce chemical reactions within a mixture of water vapour, ammonia, methane and hydrogen. A condenser and trap then captured the resulting products, see Fig. 4.3. After several days and weeks the brown sludge was found to include a number of different amino acids, such as glycine and alanine, some of the building blocks of proteins, which are in turn essential to the workings of even simple cellular life. Almost overnight the Miller-Urey experiment became an iconic symbol of optimism to origin-of-life researchers. One contemporary researcher, Nick Lane, ventured that

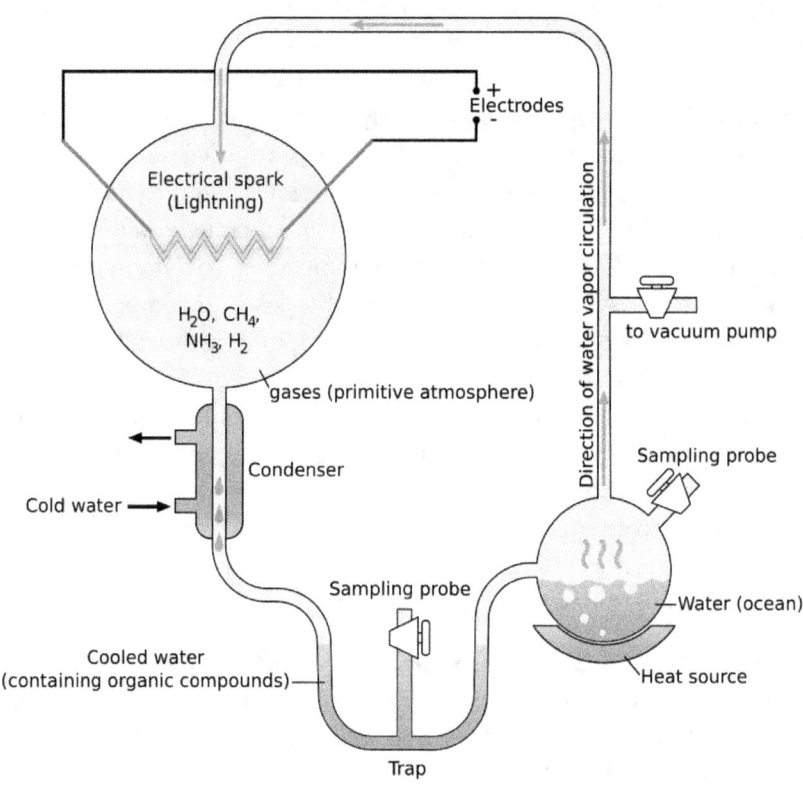

Figure 4.3 Miller-Urey experiment.

4 – FAILED PREDICTION #1: Life emerged from chemistry

> ... the basic building blocks of life all congealed out of the mix. It was as if they were waiting to be bidden into existence. Suddenly the origin of life looked easy ... the story made the cover of Time magazine – an unprecedented splash of publicity for a scientific experiment.[41]

However, the experiment, along with these conclusions, has since been challenged. First, 98% of the sludge was made up of tar and carboxylic acids with amino acids constituting only 2% of the yield;[42] at best only thirteen of the twenty amino acids essential to life were positively identified, mingling with around thirty non-proteinous amino acids.[43] Second, and of more fundamental import, it is now believed that the primordial Earth never had what chemists call a "reducing" atmosphere. It had never been rich in methane, ammonia and hydrogen. Instead, it is believed to have consisted mainly of nitrogen and carbon dioxide with a few other trace elements, and when you try applying spark discharges to that mix, Lane admits that there's "scarcely an amino acid in sight".[44]

Despite the dismal reality, the Miller-Urey experiment still appears as an icon in many scientific textbooks,[45] and in this way promotes the misleading message to unsuspecting students that chemists have all but solved the origin-of-life problem.

Another theory was formulated by the Scottish organic chemist Alexander Cairns-Smith (1931-2016): that life originated using **clay crystals** as a template and this allowed long organic molecules to polymerise. Others have suggested mineral crystalline surfaces such as iron pyrites (fool's gold) as a matrix for linking amino acids together to form proteins.[46]

Meanwhile in the late 1970s, to avoid the 'wrong' atmosphere problem, the focus of research moved to **hydrothermal vents** found at deep ocean ridges in all the major oceans. Some of these vents, known as "black smokers", grow as high as 90 metres above the ocean floor and belch a black 'smoke' of acidic metal sulphides at temperatures up to 400°C, welling up from the magma below into the waters of the deep ocean. These 'chimneys' play host to an abundance of life – giant versions of mussels, clams, tube-worms and shrimps that feed on a mat of bacteria. The bacteria are able to form organic matter by reacting carbon dioxide with hydrogen that they've extracted from the smokers' hydrogen sulphide gas. Günter Wächtershäuser (born 1938), German chemist and patent lawyer, came up with an origin-of-life scheme using chemical compounds produced by the black smokers: hydrogen sulphide, carbon monoxide and iron pyrites (one of the sulphur based minerals that constitute the black smoker chimneys). Despite Wächtershäuser's ebullient revolutionary approach there are serious misgivings with his proposal, primarily the difficulty of concentration levels being so low that the polymerisation of the large biological molecules essential to life, such as RNA and DNA, would never happen.[47]

But there's a second type of hydrothermal vent which usually occurs some distance away from mid-ocean ridges. These form as water enters and reacts chemically with newly formed ocean-floor, producing so-called "serpentine" rock. These vents are quite different from the black smokers. Instead of being acidic they are alkaline, indeed they are often labelled "**alkaline vents**". They're not nearly so hot and instead of a dirty black colour they are a much gentler mottled (serpentine) green. They can still grow nearly as tall as black smokers, see Fig. 4.4. The attraction of alkaline vents is, first, that the much acclaimed reducing mixture of (Miller-Urey) gases emanate from them: mostly hydrogen with traces of methane, ammonia and hydrogen sulphide. And second, it has been found that the serpentine rock forms "complex structures, riddled with tiny bubbles and compartments"[48] similar in size to a living cell (no more than one tenth of a millimetre in diameter). Origin-of-life researcher Mike Russell proposed that the tiny bubbles could solve the concentration problem, allowing the constituent gases and their organic molecule products to

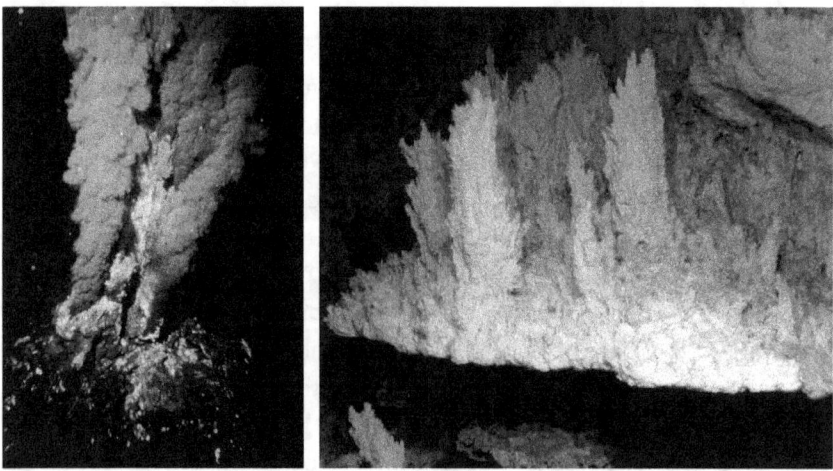

Figure 4.4 Deep sea hydrothermal vents.
(Left) a Black Smoker. (Right) an Alkaline Vent.

concentrate while their crystalline fool's-gold walls would help catalyse the polymerisation of the required large organic molecules.

Another process that has gained prominence in recent decades, thanks to Russell's work with American biochemist Bill Martin, is that of **"proton gradients"**[49] which occur naturally as the gases from an alkaline vent react with the acidic ocean waters. The energy flowing from a proton gradient – much like water flowing downhill, driving a turbine and generating electricity – is able to jump start the chemical reaction between hydrogen and carbon dioxide, which are otherwise hesitant to tango. But Lane points out that there's a problem.

> Of course a natural proton gradient is only of use if life is able to harness the gradient, and later on generate its own gradient... Today it requires numerous proteins specified by genes, and there is **no reason to suppose that such a complex system could have evolved in the first place without proteins and genes** – genes composed of DNA. And so we have an interesting loop. Life could not leave the vents until it had learnt how to harness its own [proton] gradient, but it could only harness its own gradient using genes and DNA [emphasis added].[50]

Lane goes on to conclude, "It seems inescapable: life must have evolved a surprising degree of sophistication in its rocky hatchery".[51] But this conclusion simply *assumes* that purposeless, unguided chemical evolution is actually plausible.

The so-called **RNA World** theory has gained popularity in recent decades. The contributions claimed for this idea are that RNA is simpler than DNA and that RNA has slight protein behavioural properties. This theory will be discussed in the next chapter.

Is origin-of-life chemistry plausible?

In 1984 three scientists – biochemist Charles Thaxton, materials engineering professor Walter Bradley and geochemist Roger Olsen – published *The Mystery of Life's Origin: Reassessing Current Theories*. Their thesis was that within little more than 30 years of the Miller-Urey experiment (and coincidentally, also in 1953, Crick and Watson's famous discovery of the chemical structure of DNA), origin-of-life research was in crisis. Their message was that current approaches to the origin-of-life were hopeless failures. What were their interdisciplinary findings?

THE 'WRONG' ATMOSPHERE PROBLEM.[52] They point out that the constituent gases in the Miller-Urey experiment were almost certainly chosen not because the early earth atmosphere was known to consist of these, but because the experimenters knew these ingredients would be needed to produce the desired organic molecules.

INVESTIGATOR INTERFERENCE. They agree with other commentators who articulate the problem well, "These experiments ... claim abiotic synthesis for what has in fact been produced and designed by intelligent and very much biotic man".[53] In other words the investigator has designed the scheme in advance and altered the conditions and constraints applied to the chemistry in their experimental setup in order to achieve the desired results. Simulation of prebiotic conditions here is therefore an illusion.

THE THERMODYNAMIC PROBLEM. Life requires both a highly *ordered* state and one of high *energy density*.[54] Yet the universe exhibits two fundamental tendencies in opposite directions to these requirements: a tendency towards *disorder* and a tendency towards states of *low energy*.

First, then, there's a propensity for ordered things to become disordered (this will come as no surprise to parents despairing of teenagers' bedrooms). As an example of this proclivity, if you return to drink what was a hot cup of coffee an hour ago, its tepid temperature, now identical to that of the surrounding room, would confirm the universal tendency towards uniformity. To put it another way, if you returned to your cup in another hour and the aromatic smelling coffee was beautifully hot, you would conclude that someone had heated it up in the microwave and would reject the highly improbable theory that the liquid in the cup had spontaneously risen in temperature relative to the rest of the room. This phenomenon has been encapsulated in Boltzmann's Second *Law of Thermodynamics* which holds that "entropy" – a measure of disorder or randomness – always increases. Something increasing sounds like a good thing, but counterintuitively entropy is not a measure of *order* in the universe but rather of *disorder*.[55] Now someone might point out that the words "in a closed system" were missing from the above description of the 2nd Law. Steven Pinker, for example, affirms that

> **Organisms are open systems**: *they capture energy from the sun, food or ocean vents to carve out temperature pockets of order in their bodies ... while they dump heat and waste into the environment, increasing disorder in the world as a whole [emphasis added]*.[56]

4 – FAILED PREDICTION #1: Life emerged from chemistry

We note that Pinker refers to "organisms" – which are already alive by definition (highly ordered and with high energy density). There is no dispute here. Indeed, Peter Molton has defined life as "regions of order which use energy to maintain their organisation against the disruptive force of entropy".[57] Living organisms have sophisticated mechanisms for harnessing the energy from the sun or from food. Elsewhere Pinker admits that "… even if we were fitted with perfectly tuned biological hardware, the march of entropy would degrade it … Violently thrashing molecules constantly collide with the machinery of our cells, including the very machinery that staves off entropy by correcting errors and repairing damage. As damage to the various damage-control systems accumulates, the risk of collapse increases exponentially …".[58]

But in the prebiotic world of lifeless chemicals, we have no sophisticated error-correcting protein machines on hand to stave off the "molecules constantly colliding" with our just-formed fragile life-friendly chemistry. **The addition of energy *per se* does not automatically lead to a reduction in entropy.** Exploding a stick of dynamite under a pile of bricks will not build a house, for example.

Now just as water flows downhill unaided, some chemical reactions are close to being 'downhill' ones. Given the input gases in the Miller-Urey experiment, for example, an undirected energy injection from an electrical spark is all that's necessary to initiate the 'downhill' reactions that produce some of the essential-for-life amino acids, along with a lot of other life-useless compounds. This is the prebiotic synthesis stage in Fig. 4.2. The polymerisation reactions in the next stage, however, are not thermodynamically favourable. Thaxton *et al.* do "get their sums right".[59] They calculate the reduction in entropy required and demonstrate that "While the *maintenance* of living systems is easily rationalised in terms of thermodynamics, the *origin* of such living systems is quite another matter [emphasis in original]".[60] Some form of "mechanism of coupling"[61] – such as sophisticated molecular machinery in living cells – is required to appropriately direct "the energy flow through the system".[62] Mathematician and philosopher of science David Berlinski concludes that the question inevitably returns to its old familiar haunts: **"how did living creatures acquire the mechanisms [sophisticated molecular machines] needed to exploit all that free energy? [emphasis added]"**.[63]

Second, the tendency towards low energy density. Thinking of icebergs, as the ambient temperature drops to around zero degrees, water condenses to form ice. Now the crystalline structure of ice is a more *ordered* state – lower entropy – than liquid water, but it is also a state of lower *energy density* (the molecules are in much slower motion). Meantime the entropy (disorder) of the *overall* system has increased. Why? Because as the condensation process takes place, heat energy is given off into the atmosphere increasing its entropy. But recall that **life needs both *high energy density* and a *highly ordered state*.**

In 2020, more than thirty-five years after the original, *The Mystery of Life's Origin* was re-published, this time with the subtitle *The Continuing Controversy*.[64] Remarkably, now more than 65 years after Miller-Urey, none of the original text by Bradley, Olsen and Thaxton needed to be edited. Their critiques had not been invalidated by subsequent origin-of-life workers. Half a dozen new chapters had been added by other authors. Their supplementary material brought the new release right up to date.

One of these authors, the physicist Brian Miller, has more to say on the energy problem in relation to protocells and deep sea hydrothermal vents. It would appear that the energy density needed to maintain a cellular organism is about 2 milliwatts per gram.[65] Can alkaline vents get anywhere near this level of energy density? Miller says no: "However, experimental simulations of vents under ideal conditions only generate … 1 nanowatt per gram", less than a millionth of what is needed. "As a result, alkaline vents could never supply even the smallest fraction of the power needed … Other scenarios perform no better."[66]

Astrophysicist Guillermo Gonzalez concurs: "…while some biological precursors might be made in hydrothermal vents and others might be made on the surface via concentration by evaporation or [ultraviolet] radiation, no single setting is compatible with all the required precursors".[67]

THE CONFIGURATION ENTROPY PROBLEM. This rather esoteric label, used by Thaxton *et al.*, refers to the fact that, even if we have all the right amino acids readily available, there are many ways in which they can join together into a chain (polymerise) to form a protein which are neither determined nor constrained by the chemistry. The thermodynamic issues mentioned above are already problematic. But order or low entropy – as in the ordered structure of hydrogen and oxygen atoms in an ice crystal – is not enough. Biologically useful polymers need a source of *information*, so that in this example amino acids are assembled in the correct order to produce a protein that fulfils some useful function. We'll explore the *information* topic in depth shortly.

HUGE HURDLES TO BE OVERCOME IN THE CHEMISTRY. Also writing in the re-release of *Mystery* is synthetic organic chemist James Tour. He and his chemical engineering team have developed nano-vehicles[68] – molecular-sized nano-cars and nano-trucks – that can move across the surface of, for example, a living cell. One objective is to be able to 'drill' through a bacterial cell wall with a view to improving the effectiveness of antibiotics. The ultra-tiny nano-vehicles typically have a chassis built of fused aromatic rings, fitted with fullerene (hollow cage of carbon atoms) wheels and a molecular motor. Clearly, Tour has direct experience of what is needed to build molecular machines such as those required by basic living systems.

In recent years he has taken a strong interest in origin-of-life chemistry and has become one of its most outspoken critics. As we've already noted, the chemistry on its own does not seem to 'want' to do what life requires of it to get going. In order to get chemistry moving in a life-friendly direction – not all the way to a living cell, Tour affirms that no one has ever got anywhere near doing that – there are a number of fundamental requirements.[69]

- It is essential to start with *purified* reagents (earlier reactions may have produced non-life-friendly chemical compounds that would interfere with the desired outcome).
- Reagents need to be added in the right order. They can't all be there at the start.
- Certain reaction products must be removed so they don't create interfering cross-reactions that would otherwise build up in the system, use up the starting materials and inhibit the desired reactions.
- The parameters of temperature, pressure, solvent, light intensity, pH and atmospheric gas concentration have to be carefully controlled in order to build complex molecular structures. For example some reagents must be heated to high temperatures and then cooled down quickly.
- If particular reactions are allowed to keep going, without being stopped at the right time, incorrect polymerisation will occur and

useless products will be assembled. It's almost impossible to remove a moiety (the latest small addition to a larger molecule) once it has been added. If this happens, the synthesis will need to recommence from the first step.
- Yields of the desired product are very low, so there's a strong likelihood of running out of material and having to work through the process repeatedly from the beginning having acquired more starting materials.
- Characterisation of what's been built so far: in a living cell there are proteins called enzymes that check what structure has been built and, if there's an error, other enzymes deconstruct the faulty product for re-use.

In prebiotic conditions, unlike in the chemistry lab, there is no targeted goal and it's hard to imagine that any of these requirements can be met. Even to move a few steps towards life you have to (intelligently) design the process. It has to be choreographed.

PROTOCELL EXPERIMENTS - A CRITIQUE. A protocell (Stage 4 in Fig. 4.2) is envisaged as a self-organised, collection of lipids (oily compounds) forming a spherical outer membrane. It's seen as a stepping-stone to a fully functioning cell. Tour, among others, is sceptical of this research work too. His view is that most "so-called protocell assembly experiments on origin-of-life research"[70] can be summed up as:
- Purchase some lipid chemicals in high purity, generally from a chemical company.
- Add those lipids to water and observe a small amount of it form the simple and expected thermodynamically driven assembly of those lipids into synthetic bilayer vesicles upon agitation. In other words there's no surprise that this should happen.
- Other molecules will sometimes be added to get engulfed by the vesicle as it forms.
- Publish a paper claiming that the synthetic vesicle is a protocell and suggestive of many forms of cellular life.
- Engage with the media to ramp up the hype.
- Watch the layperson being misled; not just the layperson, many academic professors have also been misinformed.

He goes on to point out that these experiments use just one type of lipid, whereas researchers have found that cell membranes are constructed out of thousands of different lipid structures and different internal versus external surface structures; protein-lipid complexes form passive transport sites and active pumps for the passage of ions and molecules through bilayer membranes. Many of these act as highly specific controlled gateways only letting certain molecules and materials pass through the cell wall. And all of this fails to take into account the possible combinations of interactions within a cell. Considering only protein-to-protein interactions, Peter Tompa of Johns Hopkins University, estimated that for a single yeast cell, that number is $10^{79,000,000,000}$, which is a one followed by 79 billion zeroes, an unimaginably huge number. The vast majority of these interactions would be destructive or, at best, not useful.

Science writer Ed Regis makes it all sound very easy, "Life began with little bags of garbage, random assortments of molecules doing some crude kind of metabolism... The garbage bags grow and occasionally split into two, and the ones that grow and split faster win".[71] Tour sums up his exasperation with such 'just so' stories.

> ..."little bags of garbage" are precisely what origin-of-life researchers have been making. Those "little bags of garbage" have no more resemblance to living cells than a big bag of garbage resembles a horse.[72]

In more measured tones perhaps, Australian molecular immunologist Edward Steele and his thirty-two colleagues nevertheless agree, "Modern ideas of abiogenesis in hydrothermal vents or elsewhere on the primitive Earth have developed into sophisticated conjectures with little or no evidential support".[73]

Perhaps unsurprisingly, these, along with some high profile scientists before them, have also concluded that life arising on Earth by purely natural processes is implausible. They have turned to the vastness of the universe in search of a solution.

PANSPERMIA. In 1973 Francis Crick, the co-discoverer of the chemical structure of DNA, and chemist Leslie Orgel **concluded that the spontaneous generation of life on earth was so improbable as to be implausible**. In response they developed their theory of 'Directed Panspermia', proposing that life was seeded on earth from elsewhere in the universe by an extraterrestrial intelligence.

Then in 1984, Sir Fred Hoyle and Chandra Wickramasinghe published their book, *Evolution From Space: A Theory of Cosmic Creationism*,[74] which expounded their version of Panspermia. They recognised that Darwinian natural selection cannot operate until a self-replicating system is in existence, which implies that the first such system must have arisen by random trial and error. They then estimated the probability that enough protein molecules to support a single-cell life-form might arise spontaneously. The number they calculated was one chance in $10^{40,000}$ (that's a one followed by 40,000 zeroes).[75] This result compelled them to conclude that it was **absurd to believe abiogenesis** had occurred **on Earth** and that this amounted to a disproof of the terrestrial chemical evolutionary theory.[76]

From the time of Aristotle, it had been widely believed that life in the form of maggots, for example, could arise *spontaneously* from dead flesh. But in 1859 (same year as *The Origin* was published) Louis Pasteur demonstrated conclusively that, if flies were prevented from laying eggs on dead organic material, no life emerged. Hoyle and Wickramasinghe remark with astonishment, "Yet by a remarkable piece of mental gymnastics biologists were still happy to believe that life started on the Earth through spontaneous processes".[77] And indeed they still do today.

Nick Lane clings to the terrestrial origin hypothesis dismissing Panspermia, 'Directed' or otherwise.

> *The usual reason for seeking salvation elsewhere in the universe is time: there has not been enough time, on earth, for the stupefying complexity of life to evolve. But who says? The Nobel laureate, Christian de Duve ... argues ... that the determinism of chemistry means that life had to emerge quickly ... chemical reactions must happen rapidly or not at all ... [otherwise] reactants will simply dissipate or break down in the meantime ...* **The origin of life was certainly a matter of chemistry**, *so ... the basic reactions of life must have taken place spontaneously and quickly [emphasis added].*[78]

Hoyle's and Wickramasinghe's alternative theory was that chemical evolution had occurred elsewhere within the vast expanses of the universe. Genetic material was then able to make its way through space to Earth, propelled by radiation pressure.

> *Genes are to be regarded as cosmic. They arrive at the Earth as DNA or RNA, either as fully-fledged cells, or as viruses ... or ... fragments of genetic material. The genes are ready to function when they arrive.*[79]

The issue with Panspermia theory is that it doesn't solve the dilemma of origins, it simply pushes the problem off to some other where and some other time in the universe. And we'll see why that doesn't work shortly. But there are several difficulties with Lane's defence of a terrestrial origin.

First, Hoyle's and Wickramasinghe's cogent scrutiny of origins considers not only chemical evolution, but also includes a devastating critique of the power of the neo-Darwinian mechanism - mutations plus natural selection - to evolve new genes capable of producing novel features in species (in Chapter 5 we'll examine this in more detail). They believe that all such new genetic material - leading to more and more complex species - arrived fully functional from space.

Second, there's the question of chemical determinism. As we've discovered there are good reasons to doubt that chemistry will automatically and inevitably move in a life-friendly direction given the right conditions. But there's a real irony here. The theoretical and quantum physicist David Bohm notes that "... just when physics and chemistry are abandoning mechanistic (aka *deterministic*) interpretations for *probabilistic* [aka quantum] ones, biology is adopting them".[80]

Third, even if the chemistry-of-life problem were to be solved - and as we've seen no one is anywhere near doing that - Lane's assertion, echoing that of Dawkins earlier, that the "origin of life was certainly a matter of chemistry" simply assumes that chemistry **alone** can solve the mystery of life's origin. But can it? That's the question we now need to address.

Is matter, energy and lots of time enough?

Life is nothing other than physics and chemistry, mere electricity.[81]

Astronomer Esko Valtaoja

Any event that is not absolutely impossible ... becomes probable if enough time passes.[82]

Zoologist George Gaylord Simpson

THE FUNDAMENTAL PROBLEM IS: *INFORMATION*.
According to Esko Valtaoja (1951-), then, all you need is physics, chemistry and electricity (not 'love' with apologies to the *Beatles*!). Is he correct? And is Gaylord Simpson (1902-84) right in thinking there has been enough time since the *Big Bang* for life to have arisen?

Let's assume here, against the evidence, that Lane's and de Duve's optimism is justified and that, within hydrothermal vents or elsewhere, the required reactions amongst high concentrations of the right basic chemicals will have been catalysed to "spontaneously and quickly" produce the building blocks of life, such as amino acids (needed for proteins) and nucleotides (needed for DNA). Will deterministic processes solve the rest of the origin-of-life problem? Hoyle and Wickramasinghe are sceptical.

> *How could such a highly organised structure as a human, or a mouse, horse, or flower for that matter, have emerged from a largely disordered situation that existed [on the early] Earth? ... **Nobody can deny that information would be needed to make a flower or a human, but exactly how much information?**[83] ... There is a huge gulf in this respect between inorganic systems and even the most humble forms of life, which means that much explaining remains to be done [emphasis added].*[84]

Shortly we're going to explore why we need proteins and just how rare functionally useful proteins are. But first ...

WHAT IS INFORMATION? At a TED talk in 2016, Riccardo Sabatini offered one form of answer when he addressed the question, "How much information is needed to assemble a human baby in 3-D?" The size of file needed, he said, to specify the unique position of each atom (of carbon, nitrogen, hydrogen, etc.) would not only fill one thumb drive, but "... will actually fill an entire *Titanic* full of thumb drives multiplied 2,000 times".[85] He then paid tribute to each pregnant woman who, he added, "is assembling the biggest amount of information that you will ever encounter. Forget big data, forget anything you have heard of. This is the biggest amount of information that exists".

However, as he then pointed out, the information has been stored in a much smarter way in our DNA, the human genome, a copy of which is encapsulated within almost every cell in the human body. So clearly it's *physically* much more compact than 2,000 *Titanics*. But what's even smarter is that the information is stored as a set of *instructions* – much like a computer program or app – rather than by specifying the location of each constituent atom. These instructions (in DNA's own alphabet, see Chapter 5) are 3 billion letters long. How can we get a sense of how much information this is? Well, if we were to print out the entire human genome on paper – Sabatini demonstrated by wheeling in 180 bound volumes loaded onto five trolleys – it requires a total of 262,000 pages of printed text weighing 450 kilograms. Notice that **the information itself is not a *physical* entity**. It's stored in one way when printed out on paper and it's stored in a different way within the chemical structure of DNA. But the stored information is identical in both cases. We can write alphanumeric

4 – FAILED PREDICTION #1: Life emerged from chemistry

characters on a sheet of paper in any order. The order is not determined by the chemistry of paper and ink. Similarly, genetic instructions can be stored in any order within DNA. The order is not constrained by DNA's chemical structure. *Information*, then, is distinct from matter and energy.

HOW CAN WE QUANTIFY INFORMATION? The human genome is likely to contain more information than that of a bacterium,[86] but how can we quantify it?

Around midnight (the exact timing aboard ship is disputed) on Sunday 14th April 1912, as RMS *Titanic* was sinking, the radio operator began transmitting the two internationally recognised Morse distress signals alternately: "CQD" and "SOS". In the former, "CQ" may have stood for "sécu" from the French *sécurité*. Another possibility is shorthand for "seek you". It had been traditionally used in land telegraph emergencies, and the Marconi International Marine Communication Company had added "D" for "distress". It was shortly after the *Titanic* disaster that "SOS" became the single standard maritime distress call in the interests of consistency. It is likely that SOS was derived from the phrase "Save our Souls" or "Save our Ship". Strictly speaking the Morse code distress call is a sequence of three dots followed *immediately* by three dashes and three more dots:

• • • ▬ ▬ ▬ • • •

The full sequence would then be repeated at brief intervals. Transmitting "SOS" as individual letters, however, would have required the operator to introduce a pause after each letter. Over the years a number of these run-together letters have become standard. For example KN means "start of transmission". The reasons why these symbols were chosen may be lost. What is important is that SOS is a single morse symbol, not S-O-S.

Now imagine a wireless operator aboard another ship who began to receive what turned out to be RMS *Titanic's* distress signal. There are 26 morse code letters and 10 numbers, one for each letter of the alphabet and one each for digits zero to nine (see Fig. 4.5). In addition there are a few procedural symbols, like SOS, but we will ignore the rest of these for the sake of clarity here. Exactly 18 of the letters and numbers begin with a dash. So after the first dot has been received, the operator was able to eliminate half of the symbols. Now, if there

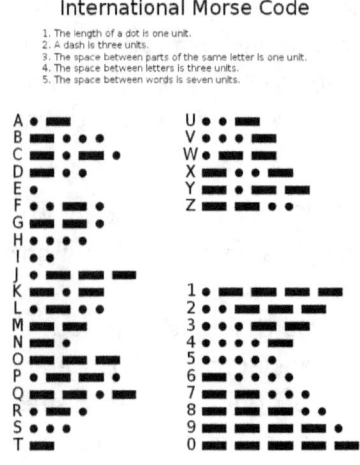

Figure 4.5 Morse Code.

had been a pause after that first dot, the operator would have interpreted it as the letter "E". But the next dot followed without a pause. Only 10 sequences begin with two or more dots, so another 8 characters had now been eliminated. A pause here would have signified the letter "I". But again, the third dot followed immediately. There were then only 6 possibilities (apart from the distress signal): "H", "S", "V", "3", "4" and "5". Then the first dash arrived. If there had been a pause after that dash, there would have been only one possibility, the letter "V". But no pause, straight onto the next dash. From this point onwards, an experienced radio operator would have known what was coming, because all of the alphabet and numerals had now been eliminated. It *must* be the distress call. And sure enough the third dash followed immediately by three dots completed the first "SOS" sequence.

An American communications engineer, Claude Shannon, has become known as the father of information theory and his work has become integral to any "information" discussion. Working at Bell Laboratories in New Jersey during and after the Second World War, he was interested in determining the maximum rate at which information could be communicated over, for example, a radio channel of known bandwidth when the signal level may be low relative to the background noise. As part of this work he defined a measure of information as the amount of uncertainty eliminated by the content of that information. So as each Morse code dot, dash and pause from *Titanic's* radio was received by a wireless operator in another ship, the uncertainty of the message steadily reduced. Or to put it another way, the content of the message became more certain as each new symbol arrived. Shannon expressed this progressively reducing uncertainty mathematically as:

$$\text{Information, } I = -n\log_2(p)$$

where n is the number of symbols in the sequence of interest and p is the probability of each symbol occurring. The logarithm to the base 2

4 – FAILED PREDICTION #1: Life emerged from chemistry

results in the information (I) being measured in bits (binary digits). In other words it represents the minimum number of yes/no decisions needed to obtain certainty about the message content. Shannon's information measure is based on the idea that the more improbable an event – the less likely it is – the greater the amount of information that has been communicated by that event occurring.

When we toss a coin, for example, there are two possibilities, a head or a tail, equivalent to a single yes/no decision. The probability of the outcome being a head is therefore $1/2$. From Shannon's equation this corresponds to 1 bit of information. The probability of getting five heads in a row is $(1/2) \times (1/2) \times (1/2) \times (1/2) \times (1/2)$, or $(1/32)$ which translates to 5 bits. Dice, however, offer six possible outcomes each throw. The probability then of throwing two sixes in a row is $(1/6) \times (1/6)$, or $(1/36)$. This translates to 5.17 Shannon bits of information. So two dice throws are more than equivalent to 5 coin tosses.

Now consider these three strings of text:
1. SOSSOSSOSSOSSOSSOSSOSSOSSOSSOS
2. misnfs tzxyco htkpudrbv gkelaofwq
3. five failed darwinian predictions

All three strings have 33 characters drawn from the English alphabet, including the 'space' character. The first string exhibits **order**, the distress signal repeated over and over again. If a radio operator in another nearby ship detects the first "SOS", then no new information is added by the repeated transmissions. The operator would have literally "got the message". This string also therefore exhibits what is called **redundancy**. Indeed, we noted earlier that once the radio operator has heard three dots and two dashes, all without intermediate pauses, the remaining dash and three dots are also now redundant in the strict sense of not adding any *new* information. The remnant of the distress signal string could have been predicted by the operator. Because of its redundancy, string (1) can be labelled as **compressible** – into two instructions: first type "SOS"; then repeat ten times.

The second string consists of characters selected at random. It is not *compressible*, in the sense that no shorter set of instructions exists that would specify its precise content. The second string is therefore categorised as **complex**.

The third string also has no *redundancy* and is also therefore *complex*. From the point of view of Shannon information content, however, strings (2) and (3) are identical: the probability of each character in its respective string is ($1/27$) and there are 33 of them (including spaces) and this equates to I = 157 bits for both strings. But **the third string is not only complex**, it also has meaning. It conveys a message that can be understood. This property of containing meaning or having a specific function has been defined as **specified complexity**. (Now of course the third string could also be *compressible* and exhibit *redundancy*, see note,[87] but the key point is that it conveys meaning or function.) Now let's apply this approach to one of life's most important building blocks – proteins.

WHAT ARE PROTEINS? Proteins of different kinds form our hair, skin, nails and muscles. Haemoglobin is a protein that transfers oxygen from our lungs to all our body tissues and organs. Insulin controls the sugar level in our blood. Individual proteins and protein assemblies are required to read and translate the information contained in DNA. More than one hundred proteins are involved in cell mitosis (the division of a

Figure 4.6 Carbon (C), hydrogen (H), oxygen (O) and nitrogen (N) atoms combine to form glycine, the simplest amino acid. Like all amino acids it begins with a carboxyl group, –COOH and ends with an amino group, –NH_2. Each peptide bond forms by the removal of one water molecule (H_2O). Combining several amino acids with peptide bonds is how polypeptides are formed.

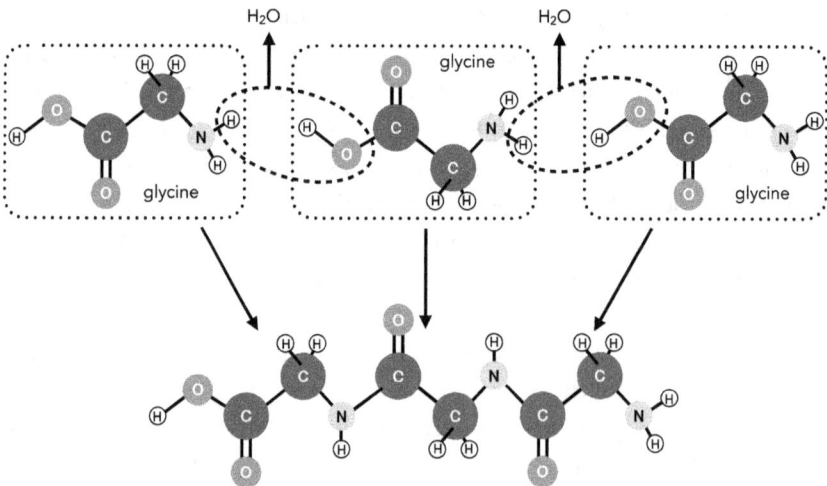

A polypeptide beginning to form

4 – FAILED PREDICTION #1: Life emerged from chemistry

cell into two 'daughter' cells). The *E. coli* single-cell bacterium may contain two million proteins at any one time.[88] Proteins called enzymes facilitate chemical reactions in tiny fractions of a second that would otherwise take years to complete, if at all. Leisola summarises enzymes as "…biochemical machines crucial to life. These proteins catalyze all the reactions in the cell. They recognize, cut, glue, transport, oxidize, move, and change parts of molecules. But how do you get enzymes, or any kind of protein in the first place?"[89] Eberlin is even more unequivocal, "Life on Earth could not wait for enzymes to show up. No enzymes, no fast reactions, no life".[90]

Just as there are 26 *letters* in the English alphabet, there are 20 different *amino acids* – the 'characters' – in the protein 'alphabet'. And **just as letters of the alphabet can be sequenced in any order, similarly, the twenty biologically useful amino acids can combine in any order**. Chemistry neither determines nor constrains the sequence. However, just as a precise sequence of letters is required for an English sentence to convey a coherent message, similarly, **for biologically active proteins the sequence must be very specific.**

Each protein, then, consists of a specific chain of amino acid residues – on average 300 of them[91] – connected together chemically by what are called peptide bonds. This is why proteins are sometimes described as polypeptides. Fig. 4.6 shows the simplest amino acid, glycine, and how peptide bonds form. Other amino acids, such as leucine and serine, have a similar core with more complex side chains. Once the chain has formed, other protein machines called chaperones may be required to facilitate the folding of the chain into a distinct 3-dimensional shape, often with an active site which has a precise structural configuration. Fig. 4.7 gives a sense of the 3-dimensional shape of a folded protein.

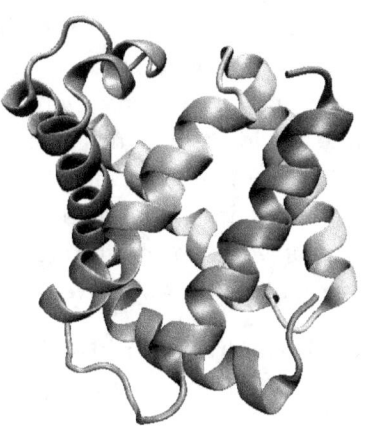

Figure 4.7 The small 153-amino acid protein myoglobin, the primary carrier and storage centre of oxygen in muscle.

In the 1930s the molecular structure of keratin, the protein key to the structure of hair, was identified using a technique called X-ray crystallography. The British scientist, William Astbury, found that keratin consisted of a simple repetitive pattern of amino acids,[92] not unlike the first "SOS" string above and not dissimilar to lifeless crystalline structures like salt (sodium chloride). Extrapolating (note!) from this finding, Astbury then predicted that all proteins would exhibit only *order* and not *complexity*, never mind *specified complexity*. But keratin turned out to be the exception rather than the rule. Biochemist Fred Sanger discovered in the 1950s that insulin has a highly irregular, non-repeating pattern[93] and subsequent discoveries confirmed the almost universal ubiquity of *specified complexity* amongst proteins. By the 1960s, as more and more was being revealed about the structure of proteins, a few mathematicians and engineers, such as MIT's Murray Eden,[94] were beginning to pay attention and to ask questions of evolutionary biologists. This culminated in a 1966 symposium at the Wistar Institute in Philadelphia, chaired by the British Nobel Prize-winner, Sir Peter Medawar. The mathematicians described their concern as the "combinatorial problem": the longer a chain of amino acid residues is that constitutes a given protein, the greater the number of possible permutations of different amino acids within the chain; the number of permutations grows exponentially with each addition to the chain.

No one would be unduly surprised if the string "SOS" were to appear randomly on a Scrabble board. But if the phrase "five failed darwinian predictions" were to be discovered on the same board, no one would attribute this event to chance.

The mathematicians' concerns gave rise to two questions, "How many of these permutations will actually be functional?" and, "Does the universe have the resources to find a specific protein, say myoglobin (Fig. 4.7)?" We begin with the latter question.

CAN THE UNIVERSE BUILD EVEN ONE <u>SPECIFIC</u> PROTEIN?

To solve this scene-setting puzzle two issues need to be addressed:

1. How difficult is the problem of 'finding' a specific protein?

The difficulty of the problem equates to determining the information content of a protein. We're going to evaluate this for a small protein like myoglobin, let's call it 150 amino acid residues long. (In the bacterium *E. coli*, the great majority of life-essential proteins have longer sequences than this.)[95] We have a choice of 20 amino acids for each link in the chain. Once we have the first two links, the number of

4 – FAILED PREDICTION #1: Life emerged from chemistry

possible permutations is 20 x 20 = 400. The third link brings the tally to 20 x 20 x 20, or 8,000 possibilities (remember, the sequence is not determined by the chemistry and sequence is crucial). So for a protein of 150 amino acids the number of possible permutations is 20 times itself 150 times, or 20^{150}. It's easier to think in powers of ten, so this is equivalent to about 10^{195}. That's to say, the probability, or "difficulty", of finding a particular protein by trial-and-error is one chance in a 1 followed by one hundred and ninety-five zeroes – a number that would take nearly five lines of text to write out in full here.

2. Is the universe we observe vast enough and has it existed for long enough to 'find' our protein?

Those who are sceptical that life can arise spontaneously might say, "the appearance of the first living organism is an extremely improbable [event]". Philosopher and historian Richard Carrier's response to this view is, "... so is winning the lottery, and yet lotteries are routinely won. Why? Because the odds of winning a lottery depend not just on how unlikely a win it is – like, let's say, a one in a billion chance – but on how often the game is played ... the only way life could arise by accident is if the universe tried countless times and only very rarely succeeded. Lo and behold, we observe that is exactly what happened: the universe has been mixing chemicals for over twelve billion years in over a billion-trillion star systems. That is exactly what we would have to see if life arose by accident".[96] Sounds impressive, but is Carrier right? Do his sums compute?

Now, let's say after dinner one evening aboard RMS *Titanic* six of the passengers amuse themselves throwing dice. Each of the passengers simultaneously rolls their die. What is the probability of at least one six being thrown? The answer is not 1, as we might think, but less than two-thirds.[97] Similarly, given the answer to (1) above, even after 10^{195} trials, we cannot be certain of building a specific protein, the probability is still only about two-thirds. Carrier seems optimistic that the universe can deliver the necessary number of trials. Is he right?

The mathematician William Dembski has analysed this question along these lines:[98] let's be absurdly generous and assume that every atom in the observable universe could become a microscopic factory, each with access to a plentiful supply of the twenty amino acids vital for life, and that each microscopic factory is somehow capable of carrying out one trial after another of building 150 amino-acid-long polypeptides. Let's further assume that, not only can it carry out such a trial every second the universe has been in existence, but even every tiny fraction of a second. Dembski used the Planck time, the smallest time interval known to physics, named after the quantum physicist, Max Planck. This makes around 10^{43} trial opportunities available *every* second. The number of seconds that have elapsed since the *Big Bang* 13.8 billion years ago is less than 10^{18}. Estimates of the number of atoms in the universe vary.[99] The most common is 10^{80} atoms. So the number of trials available throughout the observable universe since its inception (known as the *probabilistic resources* of the universe) is:

No. of atoms x No. of seconds x No. of Planck opportunities:
10^{80} x 10^{18} x 10^{43} = 10^{141} (we simply add the exponents).

Recall that even after 10^{195} trials, we cannot be certain of producing a single specific protein. Evidently, we are short by a factor of at least 10^{54} (the exponent is 195 minus 141). That's to say, the universe's probabilistic resources, and Carrier's assumptions about them, are deficient by a factor of at least 1,000,000,000,000,000,000,000,000, 000,000,000,000,000,000,000,000,000,000 trials![100] The universe, even with these extraordinarily generous assumptions, has simply not been able to sample anywhere near enough of the possible permutations. Despite apocryphal stories[101] assuring us that a universe full of monkeys bashing away on typewriters for aeons will eventually produce the works of Shakespeare, it turns out that the universe we know can only achieve 468 Shannon bits (10^{141}) – not even two lines of text on this page – whereas just a single sonnet contains a massive 2293 bits (10^{690}) of information. It was this argument that persuaded philosopher Antony Flew to abandon his lifelong atheism: "I was particularly impressed with [the Israeli scientist] Gerry Schroeder's point-by-point refutation of what I call the 'monkey theorem' ... If the theorem won't work for a single sonnet, then it's simply absurd to suggest that the more elaborate feat of the origin of life could have been achieved by chance".[102]

We now turn to the other question arising from the Wistar symposium. It was known that proteins could tolerate *some* level of sequence variation, but how much?

CAN THE UNIVERSE BUILD EVEN ONE **FUNCTIONAL** PROTEIN?

When the engineers' and mathematicians' concerns were raised at the Wistar symposium, evolutionary biologists took comfort in the fact that proteins were known to tolerate a substitute amino acid (a different one of the twenty) at some positions along their chains. This meant that *several* sequence permutations were likely to be functional, not just a single *unique* sequence. And this offered comfort to the biologists because they could assume that functional proteins were not as rare as some had thought. It would not be too difficult, they assumed, to find a polypeptide that would function, at least to some extent.

That gives rise to the question, how *rare* are polypeptide chains that will *both* fold into a 3-D shape *and* do something useful in a living cell? In other words, how rare are *functional* proteins? Here's an analogy to illustrate the idea of 'rarity' using the English, rather than the protein, alphabet. When looking up the word "prediction" in an electronic dictionary and upon entering the first four letters, "pred", my dictionary offered 88 words. So the dictionary 'knew' of only 88 words beginning "pred" that were 'functional'. Given that six letters had yet to be entered, the number of all *possible* permutations still remaining at that point was 26^6, or nearly 309 million. The rarity of words beginning with "pred" in this dictionary was therefore 88 in 309,000,000 or about 1 in 3.5 million.

In 1966 the question of the *rarity* of functional protein sequences could not be answered. But molecular biology has progressed enormously since then and, just in the last twenty years, that question has been answered. Douglas Axe trained as a chemical engineer. Later, working in protein chemistry at the University of Cambridge, he became interested in the question of how proteins could have evolved by a Darwinian mechanism. Following theoretical and experimental work he published papers in the *Journal of Molecular Biology* (2000) and in *BIO-Complexity* (2010) in which he estimated the proportion of proteins of 150 amino acid residues long that would perform a function (meaning folding *and* having an active site).[103] The answer was 1 in 10^{74}. In other words only one protein in a hundred trillion, trillion, trillion, trillion, trillion, trillion would be useful. This means that functional proteins are incredibly rare: as isolated as finding one specific hydrogen atom on the surface of a sphere of hydrogen atoms the size of the observable universe.[104]

Coming back down to earth for a moment, could the Earth have 'found' a single functional protein over its 4.6 billion year history? Denton points out that

> it can easily be shown that no more than 10^{40} possible proteins could ever have existed on earth since its formation.[105]

Axe's work therefore demonstrates that the Earth could not have discovered a single protein, since the number of trials available to it has been short by a factor of $10^{74-40} = 10^{34}$, or ten billion trillion trillion. And in Chapter 5 we will discover that even given the existence of a functional protein, there has been insufficient time on Earth to evolve a very closely related protein whose amino acid sequence differs in only a small number of locations.

Returning to the universe, then, and considering only Axe's rarity conclusion alongside the observable universe's probabilistic resources of 10^{141}, the universe would struggle to discover as few as *two* functional proteins: 1 in $10^{74} \times 10^{74} = 1$ in 10^{148}. However, there are two more obstacles in the way of successful polypeptide assembly that we should now take into consideration.

First,[106] almost all of the amino acids come in two varieties, or optical isomers, as they are called. The topology of one isomer is left-handed, the other its right-handed mirror-image. Amino acids produced by Miller-Urey or hydrothermal-vent-type experiments produce equal proportions of both isomers. Life-friendly proteins, however, will only tolerate left-handed versions. This means another informational improbability will affect the assembly of our 150 long polypeptide: $(1/2)^{150}$ which is roughly equivalent to 1 chance in 10^{45}.

Second,[107] the chemical connection between amino acids needs to be via a peptide bond. Else the protein will not fold properly. But there are other ways in which the amino acids *could* bind together and, left to themselves, peptide bonds form only about 50% of the time. So, we now have a further 1 chance in 10^{45} to factor in. Pulling together, then, Axe's rarity of finding a functional protein with these other two obstacles,[108] the probability of forming just one *functional* protein is $10^{74+45+45} = 10^{164}$. If we now recall that **the universe**, with lavishly generous assumptions, can only achieve 10^{141} trials then, astonishingly, it **is very unlikely to generate even a single functional protein**. In 1984 Hoyle and Wickramasinghe anticipated this result.

> *Darwinian evolution is most unlikely to get even one polypeptide* [protein] *right, let alone the thousands on which living cells depend for their*

survival ... yet no one seems prepared to blow the whistle decisively on the theory.[109]

Even basic life needs much more than a *single* functional protein. The simplest bacterial cell is estimated to require at least 250 *different* protein designs.[110] One suggestion by evolutionary biologists has been that perhaps all functional proteins are clustered close together in the space of all sequence possibilities. But further work by Axe has shown that to be an unrequited hope. Proteins turn out to exhibit an enormously diverse range of amino acid residue sequences and fold into very different 3-dimensional shapes.[111]

Another proposed escape route is the idea that perhaps proteins were much *shorter* in the first life and therefore more likely to be 'found' by trial and error. But this harks back to the repetitive pattern assumption. The majority of proteins, including those shorter than 150 amino acid residues in length, exhibit *specified complexity*.[112]

Yet another attempt to side-step the issue is the "lucky accident" approach, a metaphorical shrug of the shoulders: "Maybe we got lucky and the universe found a functional protein after only a few million attempts rather than at least 10^{164}". The problem with this is that we need to get lucky not just once. The probabilities that reflect reality have to be defied at least 250 times.

Steele and his co-authors reached a similar conclusion, "The transformation of an ensemble of appropriately chosen biological monomers (e.g. amino acids, nucleotides) into a primitive living cell capable of further evolution appears to require overcoming an information hurdle of superastronomical proportions, an event that could not have happened within the time frame of the Earth except, we believe, as a miracle. All laboratory experiments attempting to simulate such an event have so far led to dismal failure".[113]

The advocates of so-called *self-organization* have recognised problems with the neo-Darwinian mechanism. They are seeking alternative laws of nature to explain the origin and evolution of life. They cite examples such as crystalline structures, snowflakes and vortices; in other words, behaviours that emerge in nature from the interplay of large quantities of atoms or molecules that might not have been predicted from the properties of individual particles (see Chapter 10). But, while law-like algorithms *can* produce *order* and arguably even *complexity*, it seems implausible in principle that such explanations can generate information and *specified complexity*.

Indeed, it has been argued that the very idea of "self-organization" is incoherent.[114]

Imagine someone who had never heard of it before stumbling upon Mount Rushmore, Fig. 4.8, and embarking on an investigation into its cause. Our explorer, however, is only willing to consider causes that would be classed as 'natural' processes, such as wind and water erosion, earthquakes, volcanic eruptions, temperature and pressure variation and so on. Will the real cause ever be identified?

If we found counters arranged on a Scrabble board that read, "five failed darwinian predictions" we would immediately infer intelligent causation (even without the capital "D"!). By the same logic, the extreme rarity of functional proteins, relative to the known universe's ability to 'find' even one, similarly points towards intelligent causation.

Figure 4.8 Mount Rushmore, South Dakota. Gutzon Borglum designed the sculpture of U.S. Presidents, George Washington, Thomas Jefferson, Theodore Roosevelt and Abraham Lincoln, completed in 1941.

Lower lifeboat 4!

Here's a summary of Chapter 4.

Late on the night of 14th April 1912 lookout Frederick Fleet came to the sickening realisation that a menacing iceberg was dead ahead and that RMS *Titanic* was on a collision course with it. In a similar way:

- A few scientists tangentially connected with origin-of-life research paid a visit to RMS *Evolution*'s crow's nest to get a better view of the big picture.
- What they saw looming on the horizon was the 'iceberg' of mathematics and molecular biology. MIT engineering professor Murray Eden sounded a warning bell at a symposium in 1966. Fred Hoyle and Chandra Wickramasinghe raised the alarm in 1984. But it was too late.
- Towards the end of the 1990s, RMS *Evolution* collided with that iceberg. Origin-of-life researchers had been steaming straight ahead trying to solve the chemistry problem. They thought that it was only and all about chemistry. If they could just find the right conditions that could plausibly have been available in a prebiotic world, then the chemicals essential to life such as proteins and DNA (see Chapter 5) would arise spontaneously.
- Yet in seventy years of intensive work, origin-of-life chemical research has made no progress of any significance. We are no nearer to simulating the origination of anything approaching a living cell under laboratory conditions, never mind those that simulate a prebiotic environment.
- Instead, as we've converged on the iceberg and begun to understand the over 90% that's 'under the water', the mind-boggling layers of organisation and complexity in the workings of a cell, the target for origin-of-life research has moved further away, towards - arguably *beyond* – the horizon.
- While concentrating on the "just chemistry" question, **researchers have failed to grapple with the real problem...**
- **Information**: what makes DNA and proteins (and some other biomolecules) unique amongst chemicals is not just their respective chemical structures, but the fact that they carry or express functional information, language, a code: what's known as *specified complexity*.

- Hoyle's and Wickramasinghe's 1984 alarm bell was that "Although relevant mathematical results only became known in recent years, they are not particularly difficult to derive, and it is something of a mystery to understand why they were not derived long ago. Possibly the reason was that the results are not particularly helpful to Darwinian theory".[115]
- The crucial work of Douglas Axe in the early 2000s made the mathematical argument even more robust. It demonstrated the **extraordinary extreme rarity** of amino acid sequences required to make almost every functional protein.
- Axe's, and other similar, results[116] amount to a proof that **the observable universe is incapable of making a single functional protein by natural processes, never mind the hundreds of other designs needed for even the simplest living cell.**
- Contrary to Dawkins' view that "The origin of life ... had to happen *only* once",[117] it would seem that it couldn't happen, *even* once.[118]
- As Tan and Stadler conclude, "all observable evidence provides no hope that natural processes can produce life".[119]

Meantime the vast majority of the academic community, together with other intellectuals – whether scientifically trained or not – in collusion with educators and the media, believe that life arising by naturalistic processes in the universe is "inevitable" and even "easy" and that scientists, if they have not solved the problem yet, soon will.

Yet, while these folks are busy rearranging deckchairs on RMS *Evolution*, oblivious to the damage down below, her for'ard origin-of-life 'watertight compartment' has been fatally breached and with "mathematical certainty" will overflow its bulkhead.

That overflow will compound the problems for all compartments aft of this one. This is the first failed prediction of neo-Darwinian *Evolution* and, arguably, we need go no further. **The first link in the anchor chain is broken. Particles-to-people *Evolution* can't get started.** RMS *Evolution* is powering forward into the ice.

Chapter 5

FAILED PREDICTION #2

Natural selection has creative power

In artificial selection it is the breeder rather than nature who sorts out which variants are "good" or "bad" ... Since domestication of wild species took place only in the relatively short period since humans became civilized, Darwin knew that it wouldn't be much of a stretch to accept that **natural selection could create** *much greater diversity over a much longer time [emphasis added].*[1]

Jerry Coyne (1949-)

Having discovered the irreparable damage to the 'watertight compartment' nearest to the bow of RMS *Evolution*, we now venture below deck once more to check out the status of the second compartment. Is the prediction that "natural selection has creative power" still 'holding water'? As we drop down through successively lower decks we'll survey these topics:

- It *is* predicted to have creative power.
- Dawkins' "Mount Improbable".
- How DNA stores information.
- The chicken-and-egg problem.
- Junk DNA.
- Computer simulations.
- Classic illustrations of natural selection.
- Artificial selection.
- Downhill evolution.
- Can deep time save the show?
- The limits of mutation and selection.
- Irreducible complexity.
- The 'bad design' argument.

It *is* predicted to have creative power

Most of us would agree with Richard Dawkins that "The complexity of living organisms" and their "apparent design ... cries out for an explanation".[2] Darwin claimed and today's neo-Darwinists claim that the whole point about natural selection is that it has the power to produce biological complexity, complexity that – and everyone agrees with this – *looks as if* it had been designed. Jerry Coyne is explicit, "[Natural] Selection ... explains **apparent design** in nature by a purely materialistic process that doesn't require creation or guidance by supernatural forces [emphasis added]".[3] And in Coyne's quote at the head of the chapter, he clearly sees **natural selection** as **a creative agent**. For Dawkins, natural selection is of fundamental importance, "Patrick Matthew and Edward Blyth ... discovered natural selection before Darwin did ... but ... they didn't understand how *important* it is ... they didn't see it as a *general* phenomenon with universal significance – with the power to drive the evolution of all living things in the direction of positive improvement [emphasis in original]".[4] Mark Pallen in *The Rough Guide to Evolution* trumpets the power and creativity of natural selection.

> *Although it stretches the imagination, descent with modification* **powered by natural selection ... and its creative power** *makes biology much grander and more interesting than the fixed laws and repetitive planetary orbits of physics [emphasis added].*[5]

Evolutionists seem to agree, then, that natural selection exhibits powerful creative agency. Ken Miller, professor of biology at Brown University, puts it this way, "It works ... because of the **great blind power of natural selection to innovate**, to test, and to discard what fails in favour of what succeeds [emphasis added]".[6]

What, then, about information content? Recall that in Chapter 4 we came across the concept of complex specified information. Dawkins recognises the importance of information, "The difference between life and non-life is a matter not of substance but of information. **Living things contain prodigious quantities of information**. Most of the information is digitally coded in DNA ... [emphasis added]".[7] The prominent intellectual Steven Pinker, in *Enlightenment Now*, also adds the "information" dimension to natural selection's capabilities, assuring us that "**Information ... gets accumulated in a genome in the course of evolution** [emphasis added]".[8] He gives no justification for this claim, but to be fair, his book is not primarily a treatise on evolution. Nevertheless he is quite correct that natural selection *needs to* have the ability to cumulatively produce information if novel biological form is to evolve. So we'll be asking the question, "**Is** there evidence that supports the claim that **natural selection** is **capable of creating specified complexity: information?**"

Dawkins' "Mount Improbable"

First, what is natural selection? Let's hear from Darwin himself.

> ... natural selection is daily and hourly scrutinising, throughout the world, every variation, even the slightest; rejecting that which is bad, preserving and adding up all that is good; silently and insensibly working, whenever opportunity offers, at the improvement of each organic being ...⁹ ... thus the standard of perfection will have been rendered higher.¹⁰

In Darwin's account we see the idea of successive improvements secured in ratchet-fashion, natural selection preserving each improvement and building one upon another in search of perfection. Dawkins uses an analogy of a mountain with a steep cliff on one side and a gentle slope on the other. Fig. 5.1 is a simple representation of this idea. While he agrees that a huge jump in information content – from a single-celled bacterium at the bottom of the cliff to that of, say, a horse at the top – is highly improbable, he postulates that round the other side of the mountain a gentle slope exists that will allow the summit to nevertheless be reached via tiny, much less improbable steps, one at a time.

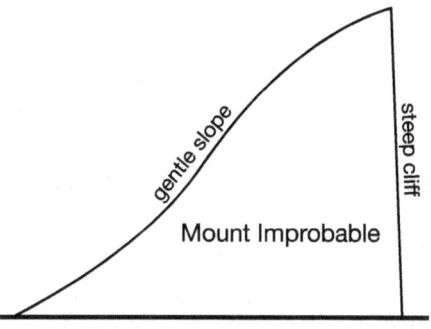

Figure 5.1 Mount Improbable.

> Natural selection is an improbability pump ... It systematically seizes the minority of random changes that have what it takes to survive, and accumulates them, step by tiny step over unimaginable timescales, until **evolution** eventually **climbs mountains of improbability** and diversity, peaks whose height and range **seem to know no limit**, the metaphorical mountain I have called "**Mount Improbable**" [emphasis added].¹¹

And by this process **he believes that "Descendants can depart indefinitely from the ancestral form**, and each departure becomes a potential ancestor to future variants [emphasis added]".¹² Is Dawkins right that indefinite departure from an ancestral form is possible? Is it true that there is a gradual way of achieving complexity?

Shortly, we'll examine some computer simulations and then some well known examples in nature used to illustrate natural selection. But first we'll need some background in how DNA stores information. We already know from Chapter 4 that the genome *does* store complex specified information, but not *how* it does it. If you are already familiar with this topic, you can simply skip the next section.

How DNA stores information

In 1953, the American zoologist James Watson and the British physicist Francis Crick discovered the structure of deoxyribonucleic acid (DNA) at what had been Maxwell's Cavendish Laboratory. They celebrated in a local Cambridge pub on the breakthrough day, proclaiming – to anyone who was listening – that they had found the secret of life. While, for some years much had already been known about the chemical constituents of DNA, its three-dimensional structure, which was key to understanding its role in the cell, had not been understood until that day. Crick and Watson's finding owed a huge debt to the skilful and painstaking X-ray crystallography work of Rosalind Franklin and others under the supervision of Lawrence Bragg. Bragg had pioneered the approach of firing an X-ray beam at a crystalline structure – in this case DNA – detecting the diffraction pattern of the scattered X-rays, and making deductions about its 3-D structure.

So we now know that DNA has a form similar to a spiral staircase, except that *both* sides of the staircase are spiral in shape – hence the famous "double helix" description, see Fig. 5.2. These helical 'backbones', as they are called, support the rungs of the staircase. The two anti-parallel backbones – each running in the opposite direction to the other – consist of deoxyribose sugars linked together by phosphate molecules. Each rung in the staircase is made up of two nitrogenous bases, each strongly bonded to the sugar on its respective backbone and then joined together in the middle by weaker hydrogen bonds.

There are four nitrogenous bases: Adenine (A) and Guanine (G) are double-ring pyrimidines and Thymine (T) and Cytosine (C) are single-ring purines. One of Watson's breakthrough insights was that, because of the single-ring / double-ring nature of the bases, each rung of the staircase had to be made up of one of each ring type so that all the rungs would have very similar physical dimensions. So it turns out that A can only bond to T, and G only to C. What this means, then, is

5 – FAILED PREDICTION #2: Natural selection has creative power

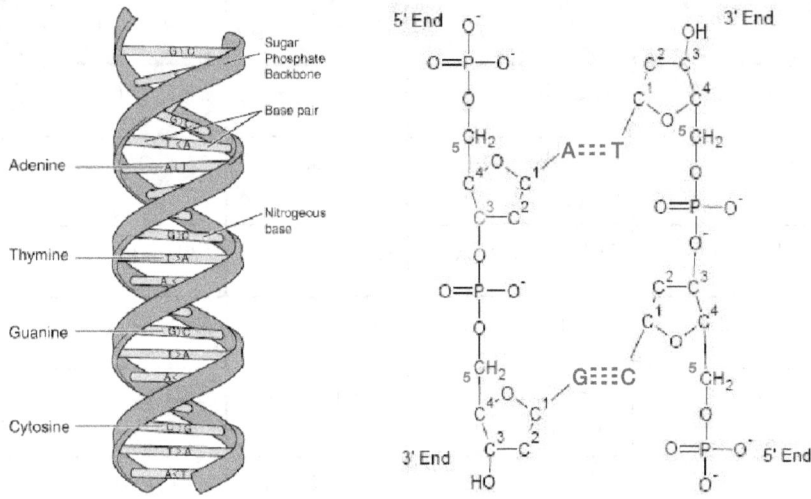

Figure 5.2 (Left) the DNA double helix connected by the A, G, C and T 'rungs of the ladder'. (Right) the sugar (pentagons) and phosphate (PO_4) chemical structure of the two anti-parallel 'backbones'. Two hydrogen bonds connect Adenine to Thymine, three connect Guanine to Cytosine.

that there are only four possible 'rung' combinations: AT, TA, GC and CG.

That's a summary of the chemistry. But what is key here is that constraints of the chemistry can be satisfied by **rungs of the staircase being in any order**. So as we move along a strand of DNA, an AT rung could be followed by another AT, or by a TA, GC or CG rung. To put it another way, **the chemistry does not determine the sequence of bases along the length of the DNA**. There is no particular law-like chemical affinity that pre-determines how the sequence of bases will be constructed in DNA. And **this is precisely why DNA can act as a store of information**. In computer memory, information is stored using a binary code: zeroes and ones. DNA uses a quaternary code, a four-letter alphabet: A, C, G and T, but the principle is identical. The full, coiled-up string of DNA – the genome – protected within the nucleus of human cells runs to three billion nucleotide bases, or letters. Recall from Chapter 4 that this would print out onto 262,000 pages of text using DNA's four-letter alphabet. As we discovered in Chapter 4, even to transition from non-living chemicals to the simplest bacterial genome, with only a few million base pairs, a huge infusion of information is required.

Amino Acid	Codon Triplet	Amino Acid	Codon Triplet
Phenylalanine	UUU, UUC	Histidine	CAU, CAC
Leucine	UUA, UUG, CUU, CUC, CUA, CUG	Glutamine	CAA, CAG
Isoleucine	AUU, AUC, AUA	Asparagine	AAU, AAC
Methionine	AUG (START)	Lysine	AAA, AAG
Valine	GUU, GUC, GUA, GUG	Aspartic acid	GAU, GAC
Serine	UCU, UCC, UCA, UCG, AGU, AGC	Glutamic acid	GAA, GAG
Proline	CCU, CCC, CCA, CCG	Cysteine	UGU, UGC
Threonine	ACU, ACC, ACA, ACG	Tryptophan	UGG
Alanine	GCU, GCC, GCA, GCG	Arginine	CGU, CGC, CGA, CGG, AGA, AGG
Tyrosene	UAU, UAC	Glycine	GGU, GGC, GGA, GGG
STOP	UAA, UAG, UGA		

Table 5.1 The genetic code translates from DNA/RNA's (four-base) 'alphabet' into the protein (20-amino-acid) 'alphabet'. The table identifies, from an RNA perspective, which codon triplets specify which amino acids. RNA substitutes uracil (U) for DNA's thymine (T).

How is the information used in a living cell? When a cell divides into two, each 'daughter' cell needs a copy of its DNA. The beautiful symmetry of the dual-stranded structure facilitates that replication with a low error rate. Protein machines break the hydrogen bonds in the middle of each rung and the two helical backbones separate, each with their respective 'half' of the rungs. This process results in two copies of the same information, each ready for the addition of newly formed complementary nucleotides complete with their sugar and phosphate helical backbones and bases chemically matched to the original half-genomes. Each step in this replication process is driven by a suite of protein machines reminiscent of a robotic car production assembly line.

DNA also stores the information used by the cell to produce its protein machines (Fig. 5.3). Typically the sequence of bases carrying the information that specifies a particular protein is called a gene. The process here is that a complex protein machine called *RNA polymerase*, beginning at the start of the gene, works its way along it, transcribing ('reading' and copying) the gene's content onto a string of RNA (ribonucleic acid). RNA is chemically similar to DNA with two key differences in this context: first, it has only one strand instead of two, and second, the purine Uracil (U) replaces Thymine (T). Although U is chemically slightly different from T, it represents exactly the same information. The RNA string, now messenger RNA (mRNA) moves out of the nucleus and into a large and complex protein (and RNA) machine called a ribosome which uses the information contained in mRNA to assemble the specified sequence of amino acids and thus form the required protein. The ribosome needs the services of a range of RNA-based molecules called transfer RNA (tRNA). Each tRNA

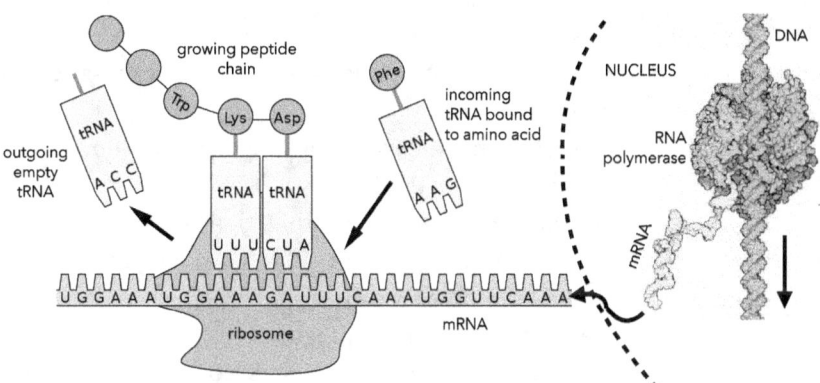

Figure 5.3 Protein production begins (right) by RNA polymerase, a complex protein machine, transcribing the DNA code of a gene onto messenger RNA (mRNA) within the nucleus. The mRNA string then leaves the nucleus and enters a ribosome (also a complex protein machine) where transfer RNA (tRNA) molecules translate each 3-letter mRNA codon into the 20-symbol amino acid alphabet. For example the codon AAA translates to a Lysine amino acid, see Table 5.1. In this way a long peptide chain of amino acids forms which then folds into the final protein shape sometimes aided by a chaperone (yet another complex protein machine).

assembly is shaped a little bit like a key, which is very appropriate because its function is to translate the DNA alphabet, A-C-G-T, (A-C-G-U in RNA) into the protein alphabet – the 20 amino acids we met in Chapter 4. Similar to Morse code which uses strings of dots and dashes to correspond to letters and numbers, a specific string of bases in DNA, called a codon, translates to a specific amino acid. Each DNA codon consists of three bases, just like a three letter word. Why three? A single base (A, C, G or T) could specify only one of four amino acids, while two could uniquely identify 4 x 4 = 16. With three bases, each codon *could* specify up to 64 amino acids. Since there are only 20, other meanings can be included, e.g. the codon "UAA" means "Stop reading here." In addition, a given amino acid may be specified by more than one codon triplet. This renders the system more robust in relation to copying errors. Table 5.1 shows which codon specifies which amino acid or instruction.

The chicken-and-egg problem

The coding that specifies complex molecular machines – proteins – resides within the DNA. Yet numerous molecular machines are needed for each stage of protein manufacture – copying and translating the DNA information, assembling the specified string of amino acids, and folding into the correct 3-D shape. **This is a classic chicken-and-egg problem**. It raises two questions:
1. **How could this system have evolved in tiny one-at-a-time steps**, by mutation and natural selection?
2. **How could the genetic code itself** – that translates from the 4-character DNA alphabet into the 20-character amino acid alphabet – **have evolved on a step-by-step basis?**

One attempt to answer the first question is to postulate an intermediate **RNA world**. RNA appears to have some basic catalytic functionality (like proteins) as well as the ability to carry information (like DNA). One hypothesis, then, is that RNA came first and fulfilled both roles. However, in terms of the chemistry, RNA is only slightly simpler than DNA, and its chemical structure is less stable. In any case, we're still left with the fundamental problem: can natural selection accumulate information (within RNA in this scenario) that specifies functional proteins?

A new issue arises at this point and it's to do with another failed mini-prediction of *Evolution*.

Junk DNA

Evolutionary theory had predicted that our bodies would be littered with worthless, superfluous organs, known as *vestigial* organs. And while at one time more than a hundred organs within the human body were believed to be vestigial, most are now known to have an important function, including our tonsils and appendix.[13] In a similar way the theory predicts that the trial-and-error approach of natural selection will result in the accumulation of large quantities of leftover, useless strings of DNA. More recent discoveries have demonstrated the failure of this mini-prediction too. At least 80%, and counting, of the genome is now known to be functional.

In the 1970s, as research into DNA and proteins developed, it was realised that perhaps only 2% of the genome coded for proteins. What, then, of the other 98%? Gene duplication is one type of mutation in which a second copy, or even multiple copies of a gene might be generated in error, a bit like copying and pasting this sentence one or more times. Additionally, genes that *did* have a use at one time in an organism's evolutionary past may have become disused. Evolutionary theory predicts that such DNA copying errors and seemingly redundant genes – consequently labelled *pseudogenes* – have been accumulating over millions of years and that the genome has thus become cluttered with unused detritus over aeons. The term *junk DNA* was therefore coined to tag the putatively unused 98% of the genome. In 1980 Francis Crick and Leslie Orgel wrote that "Much DNA in higher organisms is little better than junk" and "it would be folly in such cases to hunt obsessively for"[14] its function. In 2003 Dawkins maintained that "Genomes are littered with nonfunctional pseudogenes, faulty duplicates of functional genes that do nothing ... And there's lots more DNA that doesn't even deserve the name pseudogene".[15] Ken Miller had already spelled it out in 1994: "... the human genome is littered with pseudogenes, gene fragments, 'orphaned' genes, 'junk' DNA, and so many repeated copies of pointless DNA sequences that it cannot be attributed to anything that resembles intelligent design".[16]

Following the completion of the Human Genome Project (HGP) in 2003, the ENCODE,[17] FANTOM[18] and other projects set out – despite Crick and Orgel's advice that they would be wasting their time – to establish a comprehensive encyclopaedia of functional elements, including gene promoters, gene regulatory networks and determinants of chromosome structure and function.[19] These projects have determined – contrary to the evolutionary prediction – that a very high percentage of the non-protein-coding regions of the genome does, in fact, have a function.[20] By 2010, the former leader of the HGP, Francis Collins, having previously advocated the *junk DNA* label, admitted that "discoveries of the past decade, little known to most of the public, have completely overturned much of what used to be taught in high school biology. **If you thought the DNA molecule comprised thousands of genes but far more 'junk DNA', think again** [emphasis added]".[21] The term "pseudogene" is becoming redundant. Yet as late as 2010, Dawkins was still rehearsing the myth of junk DNA together with his take on theology, "It stretches even [creationists'] ingenuity to make up a convincing reason why an intelligent designer should have created a pseudogene … unless he was deliberately setting out to fool us".[22]

So when we take a look inside this particular locker below deck we find a mini-failed prediction. It's an example of what has been called "Darwin-of-the-Gaps":[23] we don't know what the function of "X" is, so we'll assume it has none, because the theory of evolution predicts the existence of large amounts of non-functional left-over baggage. This theme will pop up again.

What's fascinating about this volte-face is that the actual evidence, now that it has been investigated, points towards a design explanation. Indeed, **the hypothesis that the information in DNA has been designed would predict that most of the DNA content would be functional**. Arguably, adherence to the 'wrong' theory has delayed research into genome function, as well as into the purpose of so-called vestigial organs.

Another fascinating layer of additional DNA complexity that recent research has uncovered is that **some nucleotide base sequences** have palindromic properties. They **can be 'read' in both directions**, specifying one protein when read in a 'forward' direction and a different protein in the reverse direction. *BioEssays* Editor-in-Chief Andrew Moore explains, "One of the intriguing things about DNA sequences is that a single sequence can "encode" more than one piece of information depending on what is "reading" it and in which direction – viral genomes are classic examples in which genes read in one direction to produce a given protein overlap with one or more genes read in the opposite direction to produce different proteins. It's a bit like making simple messages with reverse-pair words (a so-called emordnilap). For example: REEDSTOPSFLOW, which, by an imaginary reading device, could be divided into REED STOPS FLOW. Read backwards, it would give WOLF SPOTS DEER."[24]

DNA has often been compared to computer software. Bill Gates, who should know something about computer code, expressed his astonishment in this way, "**DNA is like a computer program but far, far more advanced than any software ever created** [emphasis added]".[25]

Computer simulations

In *The Blind Watchmaker*, Dawkins recalls the scenario of monkeys bashing away on typewriters and eventually producing all the works of Shakespeare. Inspired by this, he, along with a colleague, developed a computer program to simulate what he called "cumulative selection" using a phrase from *Hamlet*. Effectively he wanted to illustrate the power of natural selection. He describes how he entered the following random string of characters into his suitably programmed computer:[26]

WDLMNLT DTJBKWIRZREZLMQCO P

He indicated that the program then 'breeds' 'offspring', he doesn't specify how many, from this starting phrase.[27] The software introduces occasional random copying errors, "mutations", into each of the "progeny". It then compares each "daughter" phrase with the Shakespearian sentence, METHINKS IT IS LIKE A WEASEL and selects the phrase which "however slightly, most resembles the target phrase". The next cycle of the program then breeds from the newly selected phrase, repeating the process until the target is reached. Following various runs with different random starting phrases, he found that the target was reached after somewhere between 41 and 64 "generations".

Now what's wrong with the "METHINKS" analogy? Even if we ignore the obvious designed contrivances – the very existence of a starting phrase, having exactly the correct length (28 characters), the keyboard being restricted to 26 (capital) letters and a space bar, and the fact that the computer provides the all-important replicating system – there are two fundamental problems.

First, natural selection is a blind process and therefore has zero sense of a "target". The title of Dawkins' book after all is *The Blind Watchmaker*. Dawkins knows this perfectly well, illustrated on another occasion when he reminds us, "… for nature, of course, has no understanding or awareness of anything at all".[28] Yet his program 'knows' not only that there *is* a target, but also exactly *what* that target is.

Second, remembering *Mount Improbable*, the gentle step-by-step journey to the summit requires that each step delivers a *functional* improvement, "however slight". **Natural selection can only go to work on something that already exists and has at least *some* functionality.** So, given that natural selection knows no target, has no teleological foresight, in what sense is a phrase that has, say, every seventh character correct, an improvement – the 7th, 14th, 21st and 28th letters in this phrase match the target:

WDLMNLK DTJBKSIRZREZAMQCO PL

There is no sense in which this new phrase contains more information, not even in a Shannon sense, because the number of characters is unchanged from the original gobbledygook, but, more importantly, not in a *specified complexity* sense either. The new gibberish is just as meaningless as the old. In Dawkins' simulation, it typically takes until at least the 10th generation before a single word is recognisable, such as "A" with a space either side. So the analogy fails in its own terms.

However, Dawkins' idea of using a language analogy is highly appropriate to the A-C-G-T alphabet of DNA and to the 20-amino-acid alphabet of proteins. But, given what we know from Chapter 4 – that *functional* proteins are extremely rare (only 1 in 10^{74}), his METHINKS analogy – which assumes that as many as 1 in 27 mutations are beneficial – comes close to amounting to a proof that there is no gentle slope to the summit of *Mount Improbable*. Perhaps a better geological analogy would be Monument Valley (Fig. 5.4) with large regions of featureless wilderness in between isolated near vertical pinnacles, slightly rounded near the top, to represent the limited tolerance proteins have for amino acid substitutions, and the all-round sheer drop representing catastrophic loss of protein function as soon as that tolerance is exceeded.

Yet Dawkins, Professor for the Public Understanding of Science at Oxford (1995-2008), taught almost exactly this misleading analogy to a generation of young people in episode three of the 1991 *Faraday Christmas Lectures*, this time using the target phrase "More giddy my desires than a monkey" from *As You Like It*. In *The God Delusion* (2006) he uses two other analogies – a faulty bank vault combination lock and "Hunt the Slipper"[29] – both of which exhibit precisely the same rudimentary flaws.

Figure 5.4 Monument Valley. A better analogy than *Mount Improbable*. Proteins are isolated from one another in 'sequence space' with limited tolerance for variation (steep cliffs on all sides). Even this image is highly optimistic. To be representative of real protein isolation, the monuments should be much, much further part.

A number of other computer programs have been developed, all aiming to simulate natural selection at work and all claiming that (apparent) design can be produced without intelligence. It's beyond the scope of this book to review each one in detail, but software engineer Winston Ewart's investigation[30] into *Ev* by Thomas Schneider, *Steiner Trees* by Dave Thomas, *Avida* by Richard Lenski *et al.*, and others, demonstrates that each attempt misrepresents the real biological world in some way. He concludes, "In some cases there is an explicit target, and evolution has information about how far away it is from the target [similar to METHINKS]. In other cases, aspects of the solution are preprogrammed into the simulation. In still other cases, the problem itself was carefully chosen to have properties amenable to evolution. Whatever the individual case, the simulations work because of the teleological [having foresight] fine-tuning by the programmer".[31]

Classic illustrations of natural selection

We now examine some examples from nature, examples that are widely used to imply that natural selection has creative power.

THE PEPPERED MOTH.[32] is presented as a classic example of natural selection at work, Fig. 5.5. In the 1800s, according to the textbooks, as the industrial revolution progressed apace, the population of moths in England shifted from predominantly light-coloured to a darker-

Figure 5.5 The peppered moth. Dark coloured (more melanic) moths would be camouflaged against tree bark blackened by soot.

coloured variety. This was thought to be due to trees, whose bark had previously been covered in light-coloured lichens, becoming blackened by soot, such that dark-coloured moths were now better camouflaged in the presence of bird predators. To test this hypothesis, the British biologist Bernard Kettlewell, in the 1950s, bred populations of light and dark-coloured moths. He then released mixed populations into two separate woods, one in the Birmingham area and the other in Dorset. The tree trunks in the former industrialised environment were darkened by soot, while the barks of the latter tended to be lighter in colour. The outcome of Kettlewell's experiment was that the proportion of dark coloured moths increased in the wood near Birmingham while light coloured moths began to dominate the Dorset population.

GALÁPAGOS FINCHES.[33] Darwin famously visited the Galápagos Islands during his round-the-world voyage on HMS *Beagle*. Finch beaks have since become of legendary importance to the evolutionary story, see Fig. 5.6. During the 1970s ecologists Rosemary and Peter Grant traced the lineages of finches over several generations. They observed that, during a major period of drought, finches which survived were those with larger body weight and increased beak size, and deduced that, in the relative

Figure 5.6 Galápagos Finches.

absence of softer fruits, these large-beaked birds were better able to crack the harder nuts that were still available. They then estimated that if droughts were to occur every ten years, a new species of finch would arise within a couple of centuries. However, they also observed that when rainfall was plentiful, natural selection resulted in the smaller finches dominating once more.

ENDLER'S GUPPIES.[34] Female guppies living in mountain streams near Trinidad are attracted to colourful male guppies. Unfortunately, colourful males are easily identified by predatory fish. Biologist John Endler conducted a range of experiments with various mixes of populations in different ponds. So for example, when he introduced predatory fish into a pond containing brightly coloured males, the male population soon changed from exhibiting lots of colourful spots to fewer drab ones.

MOTHS, FINCHES AND GUPPIES. So let's take stock of what's going on here. Moths, it turns out, do not naturally rest on the trunks of trees, but rather on the underside of branches or leaves, so there is a view that Kettlewell's peppered moth experiments may in fact have been rigged by pinning dark and light coloured moths onto tree trunks.[35] However, that aside, if we take the experimental results at face value, what has been demonstrated is a change in gene frequencies – an increased proportion of the more melanic moths relative to the light coloured ones, against the background of sooty tree trunks and vice versa where the tree trunks were lighter in colour. Was any new information created? No, **the genes for light and dark coloured moths were both already present at the beginning** of the experiment.

Likewise the genes for brightly coloured and then more drab male guppies were present before Endler began his experiments. Similarly with the finches. The Grants even observed a full cycle in which natural selection resulted in the resurgence of the small, pointy beaks over against the larger ones that had been prevalent when dry climate conditions prevailed. Yet Dawkins claims that

> ... when there is a systematic increase or decrease in the frequency with which we see a particular gene in a gene pool, that is precisely and exactly what is meant by evolution.[36]

Did you spot the equivocation logical fallacy (Chapter 3)? By claiming that "evolution" is **no more than** "systematic increases in gene frequencies", we are being tempted into accepting examples such as finches, moths and guppies as evidence for macroevolution and perhaps even universal common descent. Instead, **these classics are all good examples of microevolution**, small-scale changes over time, which is not controversial (see Table 3.1). No new genetic information has been produced. No novel biological features have been created.

In addition, recent developments in technology have allowed much more rapid sequencing of the genomes of a wide range of organisms. Biochemist Michael Behe recounts that the molecular level genetic changes that produce different finch beaks have now been identified. The ALX1 gene codes for a protein of 326 amino-acid residues that appears with very similar sequence in the genome of mammals, fish and birds. Of the 326 positions in the Galápagos finches, it turns out that only two amino-acid changes cause the difference between the pointiest and bluntest beaked finches, one at position 112, the other at position 208. The gene in the blunt beaked finch appears to be the mutated one because it differs from the ALX1 gene in most other animals. And here's the crunch: computer simulations predict that these mutations *impair* the function of the protein coded by ALX1.

So here's an interesting phenomenon. **A loss of information** – loss, because it damages protein function by making it less specific – is nevertheless selected by natural selection, because it **improves survival rate** under dry climate conditions. This is important because it demonstrates, in this case, that **not only has natural selection not accumulated any new information** – "climbed a mountain of improbability" in Dawkins' parlance – **it has resulted in a loss of specificity**. On Dawkins' *Mount Improbable*, natural selection has facilitated **a downhill move**.

AFRICAN CICHLID (pronounced 'sick-lid') **FISH**. There are eight levels of taxonomic classification: Domain, Kingdom, Phylum, Class, Order, Family, Genus and the more familiar Species, see Table 5.2. Species of the *Cichlidae* family of fish are found in India, Madagascar and Central & South America. However, it's the species which populate the great African Lakes – Lake Victoria, Lake Malawi and Lake Tanganyika – that are of interest here. Each of the lakes has its own unique set of four to five hundred species. They vary in colour right across the rainbow spectrum, some with intricate patterns. Some are just a few centimetres long, others grow to nearly two metres. Some feed on other fish, some on snails, insects or algae or are bottom feeders.

	Cichlid Fish	Dogs
Domain	Eukaryota	Eukaryota
Kingdom	Animalia	Animalia
Phylum	Chordata	Chordata
Class	Actinopterygii	Mammalia
Order	Perciformes	Carnivora
Family	Cichlidae	Canidae
Genus	Various	Canis
Species	Various	Canis familiaris

Table 5.2 The taxonomic classifications of cichlid fish and the domestic dog. Taxonomists classify organisms into groups based on common anatomical features (morphology). Species that share one or more features in common are grouped within one genus. Likewise genera sharing similar features are grouped within one family, etc. all the way up to Domain.

At different times in the past water levels have varied greatly in all three lakes, but Lake Victoria is the shallowest and appears to have dried out completely a number of times.

The last time it dried out is estimated to be around seventeen thousand years ago. This means those species must have evolved in situ since then. This is often viewed as a dramatic example of evolution in almost real time.[37] Behe describes it this way:

> The huge number of brand-new cichlid species in Lake Victoria has been widely hailed as the most spectacular example of evolution in relatively modern times and spoken of in breathless terms everywhere from popular articles, to student textbooks, to professional publications.[38]

Yet ichthyologist George Barlow, in his book *The Cichlid Fishes*, commented that "what seems to be major changes in appearance have evolved with little variation of the basic plan".[39] And crucially, although Lakes Malawi and Tanganyika are much older than Lake Victoria, estimated to be a few million and ten million years respectively, their species have not generated any wider variety than the latter achieved in less than 17,000 years. They are all still members of the same *Cichlidae* family. And Behe goes on, "… the independently evolved lineages of each lake often resemble each other closely, clearly **demonstrating the limited range of variation, which apparently can appear very rapidly – and then just as quickly stagnate** [emphasis added]".[40] We've already seen exactly the same pattern of adherence-to-type in moths, finches and guppies. We observe no changes above the classification level of Family (Table 5.2). Behe continues, "… drawing the limit of unguided, Darwinian evolution at the family level seems quite compelling". After reviewing examples of birds (finches and honeycreepers), fish (cichlids), insects (fruit flies and beetles), reptiles (anoles) and plants (silverswords and lobelias), all exhibiting the same pattern across different classification levels of class, phylum and even kingdom, Behe concludes that "we have stumbled across a fundamental principle in operation".[41]

> ... minor random variations around a designed blueprint are possible and can be helpful, but are severely limited in scope. **For new basic designs such as those at the biological level of family and above, additional information is necessary**, information that is beyond the ability of mindless processes to provide [emphasis added].[42]

Artificial Selection

We continue our survey of the second 'watertight compartment' in RMS *Evolution*.

> ... when undergraduates first open a copy of the Origin of Species, they expect to find a text that vigorously shakes the intellectual foundations of European civilization to the core, and are therefore surprised and disappointed to find themselves reading page after page about pigeons.[43]
>
> Nick Spencer

Darwin made much of what he saw as the analogy between *natural* selection and *artificial* selection. He noted what pigeon breeders (in The Origin) and breeders of dogs, cats, horses, cattle, etc. (in The Variation of Animals and Plants under Domestication) had achieved. Here's Dawkins on artificial selection: "[It] is not just an analogy for natural selection. It constitutes a true *experimental* – as opposed to observational – test of the hypothesis that selection causes evolutionary change [emphasis in original]".[44] Dawkins, Coyne and Nick Lane have all enthused about the potential evolutionary mileage to be made from dog varieties. Dawkins argues that if artificial selection, starting with probably a Eurasian wolf[45] a few hundred years ago, can produce about 200 varieties of dog breeds "from Great Danes to Yorkies, from Scotties to Airedales, from ridgeback to dachshunds, from whippets to St Bernards", with "truly dramatic changes in anatomy and behaviour", then give natural selection ten or a hundred million years and "just think what might be achieved".[46] Lane joins in, "All our modern breeds of dog ... evolved from a wolf, admittedly with help from us, in a [few thousand years]".[47]

What are we to make of the ubiquitous dog analogy? First, as Lane obligingly confesses – "admittedly with help from us" – artificial selection is just that, artificial, in the sense of being guided by the target the breeder has in mind. And here we have an echo of Dawkins' METHINKS analogy: the target had been embedded in the computer simulation software by the (human) programmer. So, contra Dawkins, dog breeding is not an experiment in *natural* selection (notice that the word "natural" is conveniently omitted in the second sentence of his quote in the previous paragraph). One might ask how much evolution was observed in wolves by *natural* selection during the same few centuries?

Second, Dawkins, Coyne and others, seem to think that those who disagree with them believe in the *fixity* or *immutability* of species: that God created all species exactly as they are today and with the exact geographical distribution we observe today. As we saw in Chapter 3, Charles Lyell promoted this myth and certainly no serious critic of *Evolution* takes that view today. The amazing differences achieved by dog, cat, cattle, etc. breeders is evidence that change *within* species *does* occur and this comes as no surprise to anyone.

Third, animal breeding – artificial selection – demonstrates that **there are limits to how much change can be achieved**. The undeniable fact is that **all of the different varieties of dog are still dogs even after intensive selection** directed by the breeders. They are all recognisably of the dog species: *Canis familiaris*, their genus and species taxonomic classifications respectively (Table 5.2). Arguably this is counter-evidence to the Dawkins claim that descendants can depart, "indefinitely from [their] ancestral form".

Fourth, do we see evidence of creative power here? **No novel biological features have materialised**. All the dogs have four legs, two ears, two eyes, a tail and the all important nose, just like the ancestral wolf.

Fifth, recent genome sequencing has allowed some assessment to be made of the mutations that have educed the various dog breeds. Here are just a few of those enumerated by Behe:[48]

- Degradation of a my-ostatin gene results in increased muscle mass (e.g. the bulldog).
- Yellow coat colour: loss of function in the mel-anocortin 1 receptor; black coat: deletion of a glycine residue from β-defensin.
- Short muzzle is associated with mutations in the genes THBS2 and SMOC2, which probably lessen their activity, and with a point mutation in BMP3 that likely damages the protein.

- Short tails are associated with a protein loss of function coded by a single copy of the mutated T gene. Two copies of the mutated gene (i.e. if both parents have the mutation) are lethal to a dog before birth.
- The friendliness of dogs towards humans, relative to wolves, is associated with the disruption of genes GTF2I and GTF2IRD1. Bridgett von Holdt et al. point out that "Deletion of this region in humans is linked to Williams-Beuren syndrome ... a multisystem congenital disorder characterized by hypersocial behavior".[49]

Behe summarises the situation, "... **the great majority of dog mutations unwittingly selected by us humans are very likely to be damaging, degrading or outright loss of [function] ones** [emphasis added]".[50] See Fig. 5.7.[51]

Finally, **has any new genetic information accumulated? No.** As the last point clarified, most mutations are *down Mount Improbable*'s hill. Each breed has only a subset of the wolf's genomic information, so in each descendent line there has been a loss of information. Bulldogs no longer have all the genetic information needed to produce wolves and neither do Black Labradors. Yet the information to produce these two dramatically different varieties was already present in the wolf. Crossing a Bulldog and a Black Labrador – a Bullador – might result in a restoration of at least some of the lost information in their offspring. If all dog varieties were allowed to freely interbreed, a reversion to the wolf type with a recovery of most of its genetic information would be likely to ensue.

Figure 5.7 Genetically inherited problems with the bulldog breed include hip dysplasia, pelvic torsion, heart valve problems, jaw structure dental problems, rolled inward eyelids, breathing and choking difficulties due to tongue and airway structure and mange skin disease.

Downhill evolution

If *Evolution* is true, **natural selection should have the power to generate new information. Instead the overwhelming trend demonstrated by the evidence is a downhill loss-of-information scenario.** That's not to deny that such <u>de</u>volution may often be beneficial for an organism in the short term. Here are some examples.

THE POLAR BEAR. Darwin didn't make reference to this example, but he surely could have used it to advantage in arguing the case for his theory. Clearly, polar bears are much better adapted, through natural selection, to icy polar regions than their brown and black cousins. Their better camouflage makes them more successful predators and other adaptations help them to cope with their higher-fat diet of, mainly, seals. But again, genetic sequencing has now uncovered detail about the mutations in their DNA that have produced these adaptations. Scientists have discovered multiple mutations in the gene APOB, which is involved in fat metabolism. Computer analysis of the mutations concluded that they are very likely to damage the function of the protein that APOB codes for. Meantime, mutations to the gene LYST, thought to be responsible for the loss of brown/black fur pigmentation, were similarly found to be almost certainly damaging.[52] Here is natural selection doing its work – the mutations were beneficial, in the sense that the polar bear became better able to survive in white-out arctic regions – yet we see a loss of information, information that had previously been present in the genome.

ANTIBIOTIC RESISTANCE.[53] When penicillin was first introduced it was regarded as a "miracle drug". Jerry Coyne explains, "In 1941, the drug could wipe out every strain of [*Staphylococcus aureus*] in the world. Now, seventy-years later, more than 95% of staph strains are resistant to penicillin ... This is natural selection, pure and simple ... about the best example we have of selection in action".[54] Since then other antibiotics have been discovered including erythromycin and tetracycline. Dawkins chips in, "New antibiotics have been coming out at frequent intervals since then, and bacteria have evolved resistance to just about every one of them".[55]

How does antibiotic resistance come about? Two main mechanisms are at work:
1. Penicillin works by interfering with a bacterium's molecular machine involved in building its cell wall. It turned out that *some*

bacteria – even before penicillin was used as an antibiotic – already had resistance to it, contrary to Coyne's assertion that it could wipe out "every strain". They had an enzyme called "penicillinase" which chemically cuts penicillin like a pair of scissors and thus disables it. Clearly these bacteria were able to survive and thrive in the presence of penicillin in the host bloodstream.

2. Some antibiotics succeed by obstructing the activity of significant cellular machinery such as RNA polymerase (transcribes DNA information) or the ribosome protein assembly apparatus. The antibiotic would achieve this by binding to the active site on these key bacterial protein machines and in this way prevent the bacterium from growing or even reproducing. In the cases where bacteria have evolved resistance they have usually done so by a single point mutation in their DNA, perhaps resulting in one amino acid change in a protein sequence. Such a mutation works by changing the shape of the active site slightly such that the antibiotic no longer 'recognises' the binding sight and becomes ineffective.

So what can we conclude about the power and creativity of natural selection? In the first case no new functionality was created by natural selection, penicillinase already existed within the bacterial population. In the second scenario, survival in the presence of an antibiotic is obviously better than death, so degrading the specificity of a protein, such that it's a little less effective at its intended function, is a winning tactic – natural selection will select for it. But this is a kind of 'scorched earth' strategy rather than an 'arms race' approach. The former is about degrading existing infrastructure, the latter would require the creation of an entirely new capability. Experiments have shown that when the antibiotic is removed from the environment, the non-resistant strain soon out-competes the mutant. There is no evidence from antibiotic resistance that novel bacterial functionality has evolved.[56] (The discussion of Lenski's experiment below also supports this view.) The British bacteriologist Alan Linton has pointed out that "Throughout 150 years of the science of bacteriology, there is no evidence that one species of bacteria has changed into another".[57]

BLIND CAVE FISH AND FLIGHTLESS BIRDS. Coyne, Dawkins and others promote another commonly believed source of evidence for

Evolution: fish and other creatures that have lost their sight and birds that have atrophied wings all had ancestors that were able to see and fly respectively. Here's Dawkins: "Vestigial eyes are evidence of evolution ... why would a divine creator nevertheless furnish [a blind fish, salamander, shrimp, etc.] with dummy eyes, clearly related to eyes but non-functional".[58] And again, "... all flightless birds, including [ostriches, emus, rheas, penguins and flightless cormorants] which lost their wings a very long time ago, are clearly descended from ancestors that used them to fly. No reasonable observer ... who thinks about it should find it very hard - why not impossible? - to doubt the fact of evolution".[59]

We note in passing his equivocation in the use of the word "evolution". And that theology also inescapably creeps into the argument once more. Now certainly natural selection is at work in these situations. Blind fish swimming near the surface would be selected against since they would neither be able to see predators nor their prey. However, in an environment devoid of light, eyes are not only useless, but, since even fish with functional eyes might easily damage them in collision with the walls of their cave home, they could become an entry point for infection and be a disadvantage.

What this evidence demonstrates is that there are **many more ways of breaking a complex system than there are of creating a functional one** in the first place. A car can be disabled by cutting the fuel line anywhere along its length, removing any of the wheels, electrically isolating the fuel injection system, throwing away the key, disconnecting ignition system wiring under the dashboard or in the engine compartment, and in a multitude of other ways. Indeed, when different blind varieties of the same species have been hybridised, some have been found to produce seeing offspring - because their respective parents' vision systems had been disabled by *different* mutations.[60] What's odd about the vestigial line of argument often pursued by advocates of *Evolution*, is that the only view it defeats is a belief in the 'fixity of species', that mutations don't happen and species do not change. To reiterate, while some contemporaries of Darwin may have adhered to this thesis in the 19th century, none of the key critics of neo-Darwinism today have ever expressed that view.

Once again, information has been lost, not gained. The movement is downhill. The vestigial eye/wing argument tells us nothing about how vision and flight systems could have evolved in the first place, but rather leaves that question entirely unanswered.

Promoters of evolution argue that examples of atavism such as the claimed occasional recurrence of "vestigial" hen's[61] teeth[62] and human tails[63] are evidence of evolutionary common descent. However, there are good reasons to doubt the claims and their support for common ancestry (see notes).

SICKLE-CELL ANAEMIA.[64] When a mutation in the gene that codes for haemoglobin replaces a glutamine amino acid by valine (see Table 5.1) at a single specific point in its sequence, someone inheriting the mutation from *both* parents develops sickle-cell anaemia. This results in a life expectancy of around 45 years due to the misshapen red blood cells tending to distort and block the sufferer's smallest blood vessels. In regions of the world where malaria is prevalent, however, inheriting one copy of the mutated gene can be beneficial. The mutation gives them resistance to the malarial parasite *Plasmodium falciparum*. Why? The single-cell parasite invades red blood cells, but since half of the human host's blood cells are misshapen, the parasite is unable to feed properly and the distorted cells are detected when circulating through the spleen. The parasite is then destroyed along with the mutated cell. Meantime the host may live a life that is relatively symptom free and have more offspring on average than those who have inherited either two mutations (sickle-cell anaemia disease) or none (so no resistance to malaria). This is natural selection in action. But again, we can conclude that information has been lost from the human genome – it's a scorched earth, downhill story. In addition to sickle-cell anaemia, Behe documents thalassemia[65] and a number of other debilitating inherited diseases which also give some protection against malaria. But they are all single point mutations that break genes in some way, especially the genes coding for haemoglobin.

Can deep time save the ship?

Time, aeons of it, was regarded by Darwin and is regarded by his disciples today as the factor that saves the evolutionary show; with reference to dogs, Dawkins contends, "If so much change can be achieved in just a few centuries or even decades, just think what might be achieved in ten or a hundred million years".[66]

Since we don't have time machines to let us somehow view macroevolution in operation either in the past or into the future,

Richard Lenski and his team at Michigan State University have found one way of exploring what neo-Darwinism might be capable of at the macro level. And that's why Dawkins describes his team's experiment as an example of evolution "before our very eyes".[67] Humans have very long generation times, twenty years or more, and a relatively small population. Lenski's brilliantly conceived and designed experiment used *Escherichia coli* (*E. coli*) a very common bacterium, which produces **six or seven generations every day with huge population sizes**. In this way the equivalent of millions of years of, say, mammal evolution can be simulated in decades.

In 1988 Lenski's team filled twelve identical flasks with a (primarily) glucose solution – food for the bacteria – before adding a small population of cloned genetically identical *E. coli* to each warm flask. The 12 populations were then destined to evolve separately. During the course of the first day the population of bacteria in each flask grew dramatically – 6 or 7 generations – until they ran out of glucose. The next day one hundredth of the population of each flask was transferred into its own brand new flask suitably stocked with nutrient, and this process was repeated daily. Periodically the team would freeze a sample of the bacteria so that it would be possible to make genetic comparisons across 'evolutionary time'.

What were their findings? More than thirty years on, each starting flask of bacteria had exceeded 65,000 generations, which is equivalent to well over a million years of human evolution. The total number of bacteria that had existed in Lenski's experiment thus far is nearly one hundred trillion (10^{14}). This is **about a hundred times greater than the one trillion primates** estimated to have lived in the last 10 million years **that evolutionists think led to humans**.[68]

After fifty thousand generations the growth rate of the descendants was 70% greater than the original cells. But most of this acceleration had occurred early on and then reached a plateau. The growth rate was already 37% higher after only two thousand generations.

These outcomes would *appear* to be evolutionary improvements at the level of the phenotype (the form and capability of the organism), but as Behe makes clear, "The crucial point is this: **in order to properly assess what random mutation can do, we must evaluate evolution at the molecular level. Basing our judgment only on superficial effects can badly mislead us** [emphasis added]".

By the early 2000s the technology to rapidly sequence genomes had arrived on the scene and Lenski's team took full advantage. They sequenced representative cultures after 500, 1000, 1500, 2000, 5000, 10,000, 15,000, 20,000, 30,000, 40,000, and 50,000 generations. Behe summarises the findings.

> *Remarkably, they discovered fifty-nine genes that had changed their activity levels, either increased or (mostly) decreased them, all in the same direction in eight of the twelve mutant strains. This was presented by some evolution popularisers as reflecting the repeated independent selection of multiple precise mutations. In fact, as the authors directly stated in their paper, all those changes are due to the alteration of a single regulatory gene (dubbed spoT) for a protein that controls something called the "stringent response" – a process that normally signals other genes that already are attuned to it that there's an emergency due to the onset of starvation and to change their activity according to a preset plan.*[69]

And there's more. It turns out that although they all had accrued point mutations in their spoT gene, **the mutations were in different places in each strain**. This, Behe points out, is the **"hallmark of a mutation that degrades or eliminates the activity of the protein it alters** [emphasis added]".[70] If we contrast degrading actions with constructive ones in the context of RMS *Titanic* we might reason as follows: as she was sinking, what could we have done to keep the ship afloat for as long as possible? We could have thrown all the loose fittings, furniture and provisions overboard to reduce the weight, then the funnels, superstructure and engines too if we could. But once these had gone over the side, they would be lost forever. What we would really have preferred to have done was to increase the height of the bulkheads to prevent overspill and dramatically expand the capacity of the pumps. But these innovations would have required major redesign effort.

Returning to *E. coli*, after 50,000 generations of "relentless mutation and selection", Behe concludes, "… **it's very likely that all the identified beneficial mutations worked by degrading or outright breaking the respective ancestor genes. And the havoc wreaked by random mutations was frozen in place by natural selection** [emphasis added]."[71]

Then in one strain of the bacterium, something dramatic happened after about 33,000 generations. The researchers came in that morning to observe that its flask had become very cloudy, an indication that the population density had increased by leaps and bounds. It was discovered that the bacterium had 'learned' how to eat citrate – a sugar derived from citrus fruit – as well as its staple glucose (for technical reasons the nutrient fed to the bacteria included lots more citrate than glucose). So now the mutant bug rapidly outgrew its cousins. Had the bacterium evolved a novel function? No. *E. coli* was already known to be able to eat citrate, but only in the absence of oxygen. At the molecular level what had happened was that a mutation had copied a section of DNA "serendipitously placing a different control region from a nearby gene next to the [duplicated] gene, allowing it to work when oxygen *is* present".[72] A normally-off 'switch' has mutated to be normally-on: no information gain here.[73]

This was hailed in the press at the time as a giant step en route to becoming a new species, but as Behe points out, "In thirty thousand generations Lake Victoria cichlids produced hundreds of new species. The bacterium has yet to produce one."[74] But the real take-home here is that, "Whatever **the bug's** fate from here," this full-time citrate-eating bacterium, **had already "irrevocably lost the services of perhaps a dozen genes** [emphasis added]".[75] More worryingly, in six of the twelve strains, including the citrate binge eater, their mutation rate had increased by 150 times. Lenski discovered that this was because of a single mutation – one extra nucleotide had been inserted into a gene that normally codes for a protein involved in DNA repair. As a consequence, damaging mutations in these strains are likely to accumulate more quickly going forward.

In the *Mount Improbable* metaphor **what we are seeing here is downhill movement – loss of information.**

The limits of mutation and selection

We can already see the evidence of sea water welling up from damage below, but we have two more decks to survey.

As discussed, we're unable to observe what *actually* happened thousands, never mind millions, of years ago. So the key to investigating the limits of neo-Darwinism lies in studying huge populations of organisms with short generation times. Behe has reviewed a couple of **situations which trump Lenski's experiment in terms of population sizes.** We also consider whether a new protein can evolve from an already-existing very similar one.

THE PARASITE THAT CAUSES MALARIA. The first example is the flip side of the sickle-cell anaemia trench warfare story: the malarial parasite's acquired resistance to various medical treatments.

Atovaquone has been one such treatment. Clinical studies found that one in a trillion (10^{12}) cells of *P. falciparum* had spontaneous resistance due to "a single amino acid mutation ... at position 268 in one protein".[76] The result is that resistance to atovaquone is found in about every third person with malaria. However, resistance to another drug – chloroquine – has appeared no more than ten times in the last fifty years. It occurs in only about every billionth person with the disease, in other words in typically one person in the world at any given time.[77] Why the difference? The parasite uses a protein called PfCRT as a pump. It has been identified that, **not just one, but a minimum of two amino acid mutations**, specifically at positions 76 and 220 respectively in PfCRT, **both need to occur simultaneously** to confer resistance, such that the parasite survives in the presence of chloroquine. Is the mutated protein pump an improvement? Does it represent the evolution of novel functionality? Apparently not. When chloroquine is no longer present, the resistant mutant strain of the parasite is soon swamped by the resurgence of the original organism, so it would seem that the mutations that conferred chloroquine resistance actually degrade the performance of the pump. Meantime, although *P. falciparum* has evolved resistance to these and other modern attempts to treat malaria within a few decades, it has completely failed over thousands of years to out-manoeuvre the sickle-cell single-point mutation in its human host.

HUMAN IMMUNODEFICIENCY VIRUS (HIV). A review of HIV yields similar results. The virus mutates about ten thousand times faster than a cell, such as the malarial parasite, because the virus doesn't have error correcting capability. Behe indicates that "on average each new copy of the virus contains one change ... from its parent. HIV mutates at the evolutionary speed limit – Darwinian evolution just can't go faster".[78] **Again populations are huge with about 10^{20} copies of the virus** in the last few decades. This, together with the super-fast mutation rate, means that every possible combination of up to six simultaneous point mutations is likely to have occurred in that time. Yet a hundred million trillion viruses later, **"there have been no significant basic biochemical changes in the virus at all** ... HIV continues to do exactly the same thing, to bind the same way [to the same target protein on the surface of human immune system cells] [emphasis added]".[79] It hasn't even developed the ability to enter other kinds of cells.

5 – FAILED PREDICTION #2: Natural selection has creative power

NEW PROTEINS FROM OLD. Protein biochemists Ann Gauger and Douglas Axe, among others,[80] reached similar conclusions via a different route.[81] As we saw in Chapter 4, Axe had already investigated what he describes as "the large-scale problem" for protein evolution: can Darwinian evolution innovate an entirely new protein fold together with its novel functionality? As we discovered, the probability was so low that the answer was effectively "no", not even with access to the probabilistic resources of the observable universe over its lifetime.

But **what about the evolution of a novel protein from an already existing very similar one?** Often enzymes cluster into families which exhibit very similar amino acid sequences and structures, but which fulfil very different chemical catalytic functions. **It is widely believed by evolutionary biologists that such evolution has been routine** throughout the history of life on earth.

Through a combination of experimental and theoretical work, Gauger and Axe set out to test this hypothesis, what they described as "the small-scale problem". Could one protein evolve from the other by gene duplication[82] followed by further mutation and selection? They identified two enzymes in *E. coli* bacteria which met the similarity criteria in terms of amino acid sequence and 3-D structure, but whose metabolic functions were quite different, Kbl_2 and $BioF_2$. Each was involved in the metabolism of quite different products (threonine and biotin respectively). Through painstaking work they were able to identify seven nucleotide mutations that would be required (as an absolute minimum), to evolve the function of $BioF_2$ starting with the sequence of a functional Kbl_2 enzyme. They then applied commonly used population modelling to estimate what's known as the "waiting time" for these seven specific mutations to occur. The result was that **one million trillion trillion (10^{30}) generations would need to unfold.** Yet at 1,000 generations per year, **Earth's history has only had time for ten trillion (10^{13}) generations**. Gauger and Axe concluded that **Darwinian evolution can't explain the dissimilarities**, and that's what matters.

> ... we argue here that the Darwinian explanation ... appears to be inadequate. Its deficiencies become evident when the focus moves from similarities to **dissimilarities**, and in particular to functionally important dissimilarities – to innovations. The extent to which Darwinian evolution can explain enzymatic innovation seems, on careful inspection, to be very limited [emphasis in original].[83]

The conclusions from these three recent pieces of research cast significant doubt over the ability of the Darwinian process to innovate. Even fairly simple novel functionality seems to require the coordinated arrival of at least half a dozen mutations. But **natural selection can't endure the "waiting time" for such a large number of simultaneous mutations to occur**. Instead it seizes upon the much earlier arrival of typically no more than two coordinated point mutations that result in survival, even if some degradation of function ensues.

LIMITATIONS – WITH MATHEMATICAL CERTAINTY.

Chloroquine resistance required two simultaneous mutations. Knowing how long it took the malarial parasite to acquire chloroquine resistance, Behe could do some sums. He multiplied the number of parasites in someone who is very ill by the number of people who get malaria every year and by the number of years chloroquine has been in use. The odds of it acquiring resistance came out at one in a hundred billion billion (10^{20}).

What if evolution needed to produce a change that required four coordinated mutations, twice the chloroquine resistance complexity? The probability would be 1 in 10^{20} x 1 in 10^{20} = 1 in 10^{40}. Now, bacteria are by far the most populous organism on earth and yet it is estimated that no more than 10^{40} cells have existed in the entire four-billion-year history of life on Earth. Behe concludes that a cluster of 4 coordinated mutations

> is a reasonable first place to draw a tentative line marking the edge of evolution for all of life on earth. We would not expect such an event to happen in all of the organisms that have ever lived over the entire history of life on this planet. So **if we did find features that would have required [such a cluster of 4] or more, then we can infer that they likely did not arise by a Darwinian process** [emphasis added].[84]

Irreducible Complexity

As the flooding waters rise inexorably, there's one more deck below that we need to check out. The photograph in Fig. 5.8 could be mistaken for the workings of an industrial machine of some kind. But, no. Astonishingly, these interlocking gears belong to a plant-hopper. Their meshed cogs coordinate the movement of the insect's hind legs so that it launches itself into the air with huge acceleration in a synchronised way, while maintaining good control over direction of travel. The plant-hopper was there long before humans invented gear wheels and clockwork mechanisms. Michael Behe has defined "design" as "the purposeful arrangement of parts."[85] When we see parts, components, words or symbols arranged in a purposeful way we immediately infer that *design* by an intelligent mind is the best explanation for what we have observed. As we take in the characteristics of Mount Rushmore or RMS *Titanic*, we immediately recognise the outworking of purposeful design. The plant-hopper's gears similarly echo that instantaneously evoked sense that foresight has been in play.

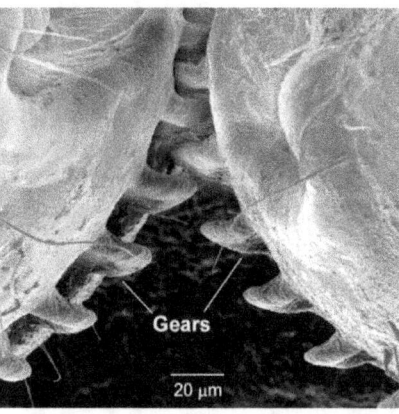

Figure 5.8 Gears synchronise the hind legs of the plant-hopper insect. The scale bar represents 2 one-thousandths of a centimetre.

Behe coined the term *Irreducible Complexity* in his 1996 book, *Darwin's Black Box*.[86] He introduced the concept using the human-designed mousetrap as an illustration, Fig. 5.9. The mousetrap consists of a base, a hammer, which traps and kills the mouse, a spring, a holding bar and a catch (plus a few staples). Each of these parts has been carefully designed so that the whole will function as a coherent unit. The shape and dimensions of each of the components must be held within strict limits, the spring needs to be of the right strength, and so on, for the mousetrap to function. **If any one of these five component parts is removed, it's not just that the trap won't catch so many mice. It won't catch any.** The metaphor of *Mount Improbable*'s cliff face comes to mind. All of the parts must be present and correct for the mousetrap to work at all. Remove one part and we have zero functionality. In *The Origin*, Darwin put out this challenge:

Figure 5.9 Remove any one component of the mousetrap and we catch **zero** mice, not fewer mice.

> If it could be demonstrated that any complex organ existed which could not possibly have been formed by numerous, successive, slight modifications, my theory would absolutely break down.[87]

This is Darwin affirming that his mechanism (mutations plus natural selection in today's synthesis) absolutely requires that *Mount Improbable* has a gentle slope to the summit: "numerous, successive, slight modifications", with each step along the way being both functional and resulting in survival benefit. Clearly the mousetrap would defeat Darwin's challenge. The question then is, "Are there any molecular machines in living organisms that are similarly *irreducibly complex*?"

THE BACTERIAL FLAGELLUM. Three huge propellers driven by twin triple expansion reciprocating steam engines and a single central steam turbine engine powered RMS *Titanic* across the Atlantic ocean. Bacteria in search of food, such as *E. coli*, need to move around in their liquid environment too. They do this using a long whip-like propeller: the filament, connected via a universal joint: the hook, to a motor mounted between the inner and outer membranes of the bacterial cell, Fig. 5.10. The motor is uncannily like a human-designed electric motor. But it's only five millionths of a centimetre in length. It has a rotor, a stator and a drive shaft with its bushings and bearings. Some flagella can rotate at 100,000 rpm and change direction within a quarter of a turn, propelling the bacterium through a watery medium at about twenty lengths per second. This little nano-machine, the like of which Darwin had never encountered, is built from around forty different proteins, including signalling proteins to turn the motor on and off, each of which, as we know from Chapter 4, exhibits specified complexity in its own right.

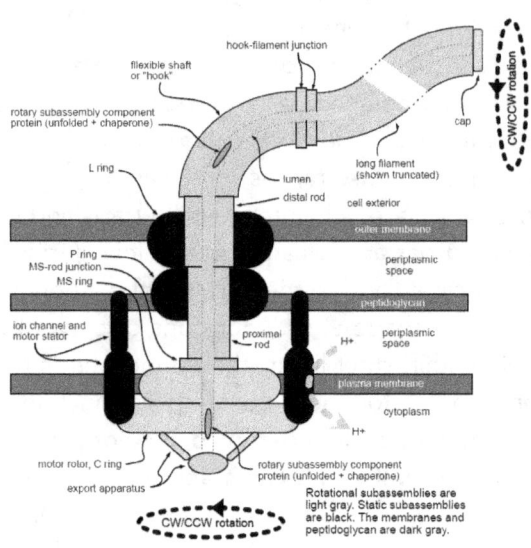

Figure 5.10 Schematic of a common flagellar motor used to propel *E. coli*, for example, in search of food.

Behe's contention is that the flagellar motor is an example of irreducible complexity. **If any single component, the rotor, the hook,**

5 – FAILED PREDICTION #2: Natural selection has creative power

etc. were removed, the system would fail completely. The bacterium would be unable to move and find nutrition. Behe had checked the literature to see if anyone had worked out how this motor could have evolved step-by-improving-functional-step. The answer was: no one.

In 2005 a highly publicised trial took place in Dover, Pennsylvania: Kitzmiller vs Dover Area School District. The School District had placed a biology book in their library which promoted the Intelligent Design (ID) view and had encouraged school pupils to read it. Some parents had objected to this and the American Civil Liberties Union (ACLU) led the legal challenge in court (this theme will be taken up in Part 3). Behe reluctantly appeared as a witness at the trial to support the technical case for ID. The bacterial flagellum was on the agenda. Biology professor Ken Miller of Brown University disagreed with Behe and appeared as a witness for the ACLU. Miller argued that a simpler nano-machine, the Type III Secretory System (T3SS) - constructed from around ten different proteins - evolved first. The bacterium then co-opted the T3SS on the way to evolving the flagellum (the needle-like T3SS is used by pathogenic bacteria such as salmonella to inject toxins into the cells of their host). However, since the trial (the court found for the ACLU), several lines of evidence have emerged which strongly indicate - even with evolutionary assumptions - that **the flagellar motor (FM) must have evolved first and the T3SS independently much later**:

1. Mutation density studies: the genes that build the FM exhibit more mutations than those for the T3SS and this indicates that the FM is older.
2. Phylogenetic distribution: the FM occurs widely across many bacterial species, whereas the T3SS is only found in a small subset of bacteria. Again this suggests that the FM has become more widespread because it has been around longer.
3. The plasmid problem: the genes for building the T3SS are found only in plasmids (mobile units that transfer genetic material from one species to another) and not in the core circular bacterial chromosome itself. This core would have been in place earlier than plasmids.
4. The age of eukaryotic cells: the T3SS injects toxins into eukaryotic cells - the cells of higher level organisms such as plants and animals. Yet prokaryotic cells (bacteria) are widely believed to have evolved hundreds of millions of years earlier, so the FM

would have been required long before the T3SS would have been of any use.

In any case, no evolutionary account exists of how the constituent proteins needed for the T3SS evolved, never mind the additional proteins required for the FM. RMS *Titanic* had to be assembled in a specific order: the keel was laid down followed by the framing structures before decks and superstructure could be added. Similarly a bacterium needs to build its FM in the right order. This raises the further question of how the assembly instructions for the FM, encoded in the bacterial core DNA, could have evolved on a step-by-step basis.

The flagellar motor case delivers a double jeopardy for *Evolution*. First, it **demonstrates that neo-Darwinism fails to explain the step-by-step evolution of such nano-systems** - the flagellar motor is only one example of countless complex molecular machines and systems being found in living cells. Microbiologist James Shapiro agrees that not one has been adequately explained, "In fact, there are no detailed Darwinian accounts for the evolution of any fundamental biochemical or cellular system, only a variety of wishful speculations".[88] In relation to the flagellum, Behe concludes, "even though we are told that biology must be seen through the lens of evolution, no scientist has ever published a model to account for the gradual evolution of this extraordinary molecular machine".[89] Nearly twenty-five years since he first published the FM example - ample opportunity for rebuttal - this is still the case. Darwin's challenge has been met, so in his own words, on these grounds alone, his theory will "absolutely breakdown".[83]

And second, **it presents evidence for intelligent design, because it manifests the purposeful arrangement of parts** and the presence of complex specified information. When we come across such information in the form of text in a document or code in a piece of software or in a radio signal, our uniform experience is that the ultimate source of that information is a mind.

In *Darwin's Black Box*, Behe describes and analyses other examples of irreducible complexity such as the intricacies and interdependencies of the blood clotting cascade. Over twenty different proteins are involved in this process in which it's just as important to prevent clotting occurring when it's not required, and to remove a clot once it is no longer necessary, as it is to quickly activate clotting when it is required. His first example, however, relates to vision. This brings us back to the eye.

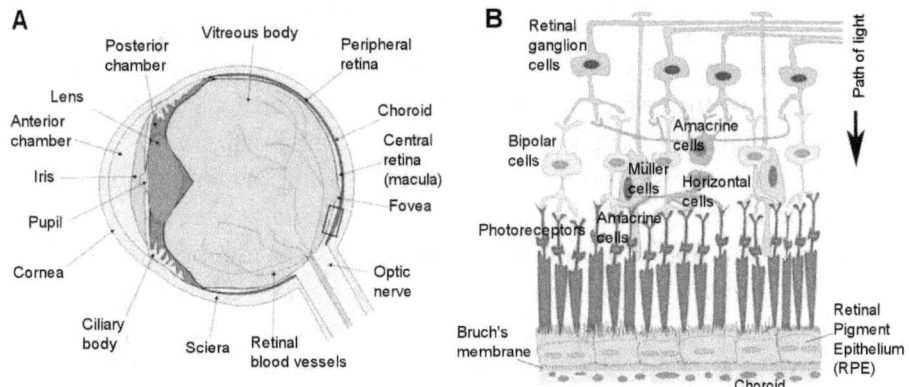

Figure 5.11 (A) Eye anatomy. (B) Rather than 'wired backwards' the photoreceptors need an intimate connection with the RPE.

THE EYE. The evolution of our vertebrate eye has attracted much attention over the last one hundred and fifty years. In Darwin's time the anatomy of the eye (Fig. 5.11(A)) was well understood, and, noting that other organisms had simpler vision systems, he argued that our eye could have evolved through a series of steps from the jellyfish's light sensitive spot, through the marine limpet's cupped, and the marine snail's lensed eyes respectively. In more recent times, Coyne,[90] Dawkins[91] and Lane[92] have all lauded the work of a paper[93] which appeared in the *Proceedings of the Royal Society* in 1994. Here's Dawkins' praise for the paper, "The principle of how [evolution of the eye] might have happened, and the speed with which it might have been accomplished, has been beautifully demonstrated in a computer model by a pair of Swedish biologists called Dan Nilsson and Susanne Pelger".[94] Like Darwin, the Swedes envisaged that the eye could have evolved by natural selection from a flat "patch of light sensitive epithelium" which gradually morphed into a deepened hemispherical pit with a narrowed aperture culminating in the addition of a lens. They calculated that, changing only 1% at a time, the improved morphology could be achieved in 1,829 steps. They then estimated this would require 364,000 generations and, assuming simple sea creatures with generation times of around one year, they concluded that eyes could evolve in less than four hundred thousand years.

Are Dawkins, Coyne and Lane, among others, right to celebrate this "demonstration" of eye evolution? Dawkins claims that Nilsson and Pelger created a *computer* model. This assertion might create the impression that the Swedes simulated molecular biological reality, and modelled mutations at the genetic level within DNA. On reading the paper, however, we discover that they neither developed a *computer* model,[95] nor modelled genetic mutations. The core of Nilsson's and Pelger's paper is purely an exercise in mathematics and optical physics. It demonstrated that an almost linear improvement in spatial resolution[96] of an initially existing light sensitive spot will occur **provided the geometry mutates as required** - the deepening of the pit, the narrowing of the aperture and the appearance of a lens. There is no great surprise here. Crucially, the paper says nothing about biology, never mind molecular biology. **The paper evades the fact that new genes are required** to produce the required novel morphology within a developing embryo. Secondly, as Swift also points out, the equation used by Nilsson and Pelger to estimate the number of generations required **assumes *artificial* selection** - the action of a breeder - **not *natural* selection.**[97]

So the claim that Nilsson and Pelger demonstrated how the eye evolved and how quickly, is simply untrue. Berlinski sums up the situation with penetrating accuracy, "Far from demonstrating the emergence of a complicated biological structure, what they succeeded in showing was simply that an imaginary population of [pre-existing] light-sensitive cells could be flogged relentlessly up a simple adaptive peak, a point never at issue because never in doubt".[98]

In any case, as Axe explains, the various physical elements of the eye represent sub-systems which together form a coherent whole within a complete visual system.[99] Fig. 5.12 illustrates the extraordinary complexity via a hierarchical structured breakdown of the full visual system. It begins with five sub-systems - eyes, optic nerve system, visual processing system, eye movement system and tear system - and successively breaks them down into their components and sub-components culminating in proteins and amino acids.

Returning to Behe, he **questions the notion of beginning by assuming the existence of a light-sensitive spot** (never mind, as discussed, that an optic nerve system and a visual processing system are also required, however "simple" the organism). The spot is an irreducibly complex system in its own right: the arrival of a photon triggers a whole sequence of around a dozen chemical interactions involving molecules such as 11-*cis*-retinal and proteins such as rhodopsin and transducin, climaxing within tiny fractions of a second in an electric current reaching the brain via the optic nerve. Behe

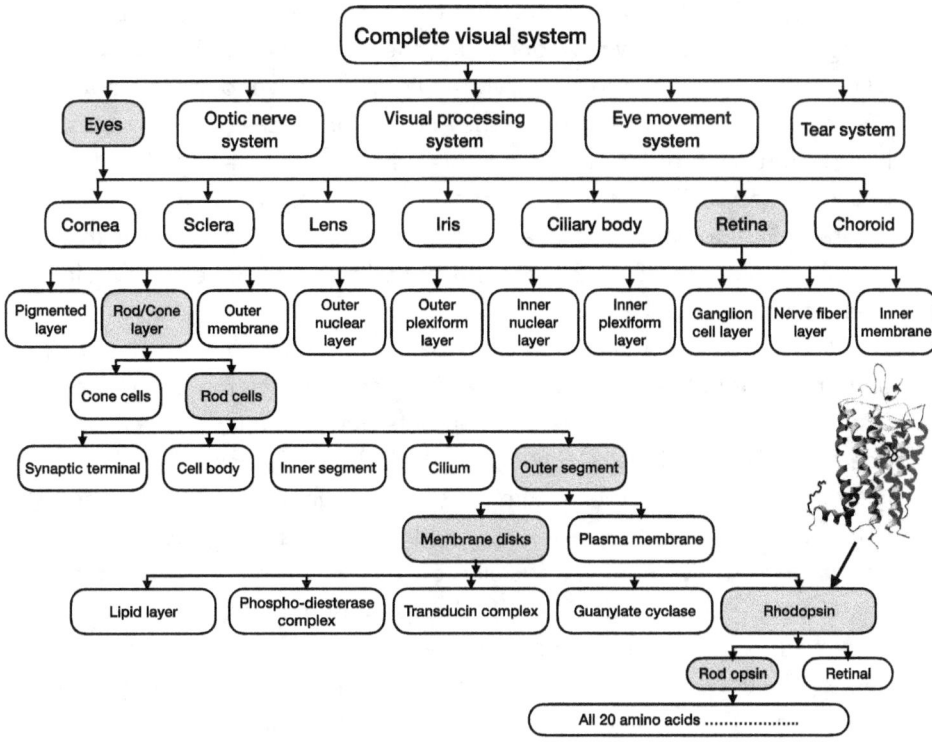

Figure 5.12 A breakdown of the visual system to sub-system level all the way down to molecular level following just one branch of the hierarchy.

describes the detail,[100] which includes how the whole system is reset (also non-trivial) ready for the next cycle. He concludes, "Now that the black box of vision has been opened, it is no longer enough for an evolutionary explanation of that power to consider only the anatomical structures of whole eyes, as Darwin did in the nineteenth century ... Each of the anatomical steps that Darwin thought were so simple actually involves staggeringly complicated biochemical processes that cannot be papered over with rhetoric ... **Until recently ... evolutionary biologists could be unconcerned with the molecular details** of life because so little was known about them. Now the black box of the cell has been opened, and **the infinitesimal world that stands revealed must be explained** [emphasis added]".[101]

The "bad design" argument

This brings us to an all-pervasive argument frequently rehearsed by evolutionary biologists. According to them, the eye is badly designed:

"... the eye's 'photocells' are pointing backwards, away from the scene being looked at. The 'wires' connecting the photocells to the brain run all over the surface of the retina, so the light rays have to pass through a carpet of massed wires before they hit the photocells ... it's not just bad design, it's the design of a complete idiot",[102] opines Dawkins. He describes the backward installation of the retina as an "error" and that natural selection has nevertheless made the best of it. He suggests that if such a design (Fig. 5.11(B)) were proposed by an engineer he should be sent back to the drawing board.

Those who have designed an apparatus that has to work, not just on paper, but in the real world, know that the specification of a device inevitably entails conflicting requirements. RMS *Titanic*, for instance, needed to be luxurious, which, due to the extra weight associated with luxury, compromised the maximum speed attainable relative to her competitors. And decisively in relation to her catastrophic sinking, freedom of movement, especially of the first and second class passengers, was judged to be a higher priority than improving safety by elevating the watertight compartment bulkheads and by installing enough lifeboats to accommodate all of the passengers. It could be argued that *Titanic* was badly designed. But bad design, even when true, doesn't imply no design.[103]

It turns out, contra Dawkins, that the "engineer" had a good reason for the "photocells" being "wired backwards". One of the design constraints is that the photoreceptors (rods and cones) need to be intimately connected with a rich blood supply. This is provided by the (opaque) retinal pigment epithelium (RPE) which forms the back of the retina. In addition to providing nutrients, just one other example of its interactions is that the protein attachment chemical, retinal, is constantly exchanged between photoreceptors and the RPE as part of the reset cycle mentioned above (re-isomerizing *trans*-retinal into 11-*cis*-retinal).[104] If it were not for this facility, recovery from temporary blindness following exposure to bright light would take much longer.[105] Dawkins' "carpet of massed wires" misrepresents the fact that the nerves connected to each photoreceptor are, in fact, designed to behave as waveguides, just like fibre optic cables. Finally, the so-called "blind spot" caused by the nerves making their way through the RPE to the brain is compensated for by having two eyes, since their respective blind spots don't coincide on the field of view.

The "Bad Design" labelling is a bad argument. It is both an *argument from ignorance*: we don't (yet) know of any good reasons why it was designed this way; and its a *Darwin-of-the-gaps* argument once more: this seems badly designed, therefore evolution must have done it (because that's what we'd expect of evolution).

Lower lifeboat 5!

Here's a summary of Chapter 5.

Through our education system and the media we've all been repeatedly assured that natural selection has the power to create all of the living world we see around us, including ourselves. Dawkins expresses it this way, "Darwin discovered the alternative to chance and design ... The answer is cumulative natural selection. Provided that a smoothly cumulative gradient exists - not a difficult condition to realise - natural selection is likely to find it, and will propel evolution up the slopes of *Mount Improbable* to apparently limitless heights of perfection".[106] In this chapter, however, we've discovered that each of the points in this statement can now be challenged:

- **"Cumulative natural selection"**. Computer simulations, by Dawkins and others, intended to illustrate how this process works misrepresent its power and fail in their own terms. They invoke foresight in some way: that natural selection somehow 'knows' its target and how far away it currently is from it.
- **"Provided that a smoothly cumulative gradient exists"**. Actually it turns out that a smooth gradient is in fact a "difficult condition to realise". The irreducible complexity of molecular machines - the bacterial flagellum is just one example - and the finding that even the "small-scale problem" of evolving a new protein, needing only seven nucleotide mutations relative to another in the same family, are both beyond the reach of natural selection.
- **"Find it, and ... propel evolution up the slopes"**. Natural selection can only operate upon something that already exists. It's not a creative agent in itself (though such reification is often attributed to it by popularisers). In order to move *up Mount Improbable*, it's randomly occurring mutations that must "find" something that is functional. But, the proportion of configurations at the molecular level that produce *any function at all* is so extraordinarily tiny as to be vanishingly small.

- **"Limitless"**. The classic textbook examples of melanic moths, finch beaks, cichlid fish and, more recently, Lenski's *E. coli* experiments, are good illustrations of microevolution (change within species), but provide no evidence that macroevolution (at family level and above) could have occurred. Likewise, artificial selection – intensive breeding of dogs, cattle, etc. – strongly suggests that there are limits to the amount of change achievable by selection, whether natural or artificial.

And there's more:
- Now that molecular biologists are able to sequence genomes with relative ease compared to even twenty years ago, we know that mutations in finch beaks, various dog breeds, polar bears, blind cave fish and flightless birds, antibiotic resistance, sickle cell anaemia, Lenski's *E. coli* and more, almost all exhibit *lost* or *damaged* function.
- And while *damaging* mutations *can* be beneficial (because they improve the survival rate of bacteria in the presence of an antibiotic, or of polar bears in icy arctic regions, or of blind fish in dark underwater caves, etc.), the problem is that natural selection then 'freezes' such loss-of-information mutations in place and that functionality is most likely lost forever.
- The evidence therefore points strongly in the direction of devolution: sliding down *Mount Improbable*, not climbing up it. Behe summarises, "Life hasn't evolved. Overwhelmingly it has devolved".[107]
- The reason for this is clear. There are far more ways of breaking something that currently works than there are of configuring a system to work in the first place.
- So mutations occurring at random are far more likely to *damage* or completely *disable* an existing gene function *long before* new functionality can be "found".

Our survey, then, of RMS *Evolution*'s second 'watertight compartment' – the prediction that *natural selection has creative power* – has revealed a gaping hole punctured in the hull by the molecular biology iceberg. The icy sea water is flooding in and will overflow into 'watertight compartments' further aft.

Chapter 6

FAILED PREDICTION #3

The tree-of-life is recorded in the fossils

Since there are fossil remains of ancient life, we should be able to find some evidence of evolutionary change in the fossil record ... we should be able to see species changing over time, forming lineages showing "descent with modification" ... We should be able to find examples of species that link together major groups... like birds with reptiles and fish with amphibians. Moreover these ... "transitional forms" ... should occur in layers of rock that date to the time when groups are supposed to have diverged.[1]

Jerry Coyne

RMS *Titanic's* emergency investigation team proceeded with urgency to check for damage in the third watertight compartment. In this chapter we'll investigate the following topics, one 'deck' at a time:
- Fossils: the prediction.
- Darwin knew about a problem down below.
- Darwin's problem hasn't gone away.
- More damage: Punctuated Equilibria.
- Explosion in the Cambrian.
- What about Darwin's escape route?
- An orchard – not a tree.
- The information 'hole' again.
- Other explosions.
- Lost at sea: Extinctions.
- Ice warnings… and stories of intermediates.

Fossils: the prediction

The only diagram Darwin included in *The Origin* depicted a branching tree to illustrate the idea that all of life had descended from one or from a small number of original organisms by "descent with modification", driven by natural selection. This iconic image has come to be known as the "Tree-of-Life". Fig. 6.1 illustrates German biologist

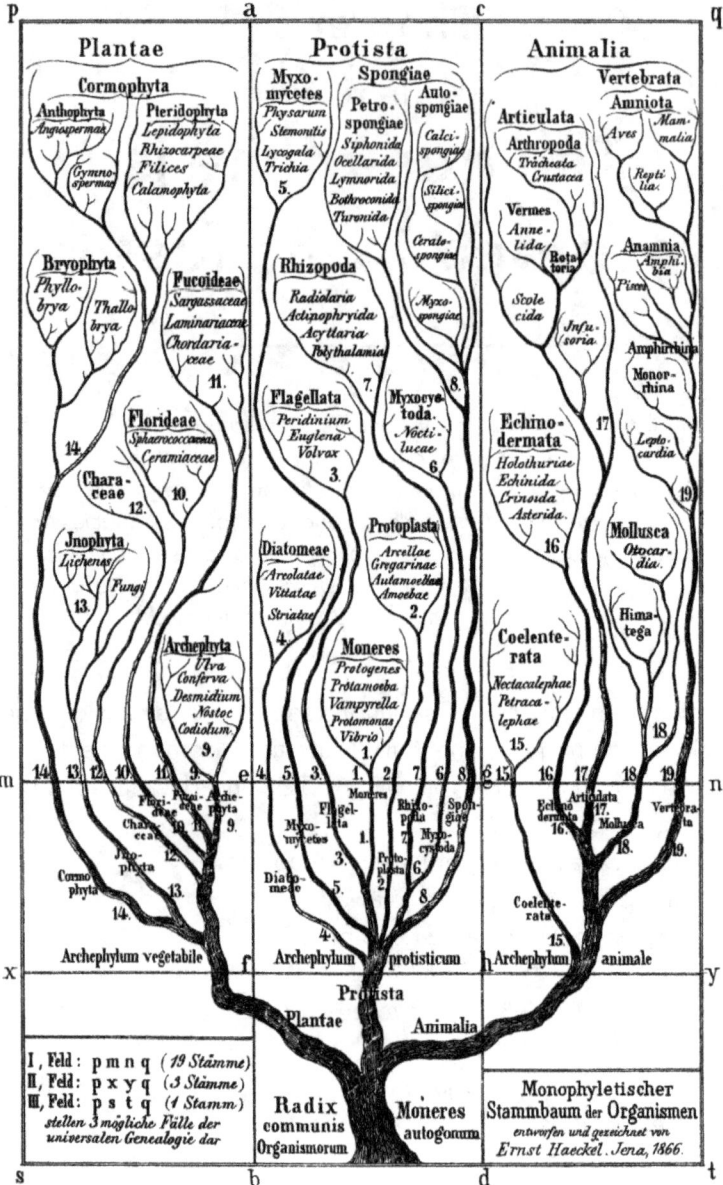

Figure 6.1 The "Tree-of-Life" as depicted by Ernst Haeckel, a German biologist, in his *Generelle Morphologie der Organismen* (1866).

Ernst Haeckel's rendering of it. In the quote above, Jerry Coyne articulates the prediction that, if evolutionary theory is true, we should be able to see evidence of this "tree" in the fossil "record". That we should see a progression from older to younger rock layers beginning with a very small number of species which differentiate gradually in small steps into what could then be classified as new species, differentiating further such that a new genus can be identified, further still as new families evolve (e.g. the cat family, the dog family), eventually through order, class and phylum (body plan) as per the taxonomic classifications in Table 5.2. So what we should see in the fossil record is species gradually diversifying over long periods of time into higher levels of classification as the information to build these higher levels accumulates through mutation and natural selection. What are some examples of different body plans or phyla (the plural of phylum)? There are over thirty of them in the animal kingdom. Here are just three examples:

- *chordates* – includes vertebrates such as fish, reptiles, birds and mammals such as humans.
- *arthropods* – includes insects, spiders and crabs.
- *molluscs* – includes mussels, scallops, clams and octopus.

In Darwin's words, "As natural selection acts solely by accumulating slight, successive, favourable variations, it can produce no great or sudden modification; it can act only by very short and slow steps. Hence the canon of 'Natura non facit saltum' [nature doesn't make jumps]".[2]

As we go below deck in RMS *Evolution*'s third 'watertight compartment' we'll survey the hull once more to see whether any damage has been sustained here.

Darwin knew about a problem down below

Almost before we descend below 'B' deck, there are ominous signs of water rising up the stairwell. Darwin knew that his prediction was in trouble, "… why, if species have descended from other species by insensibly fine gradations, do we not everywhere see innumerable transitional forms?"[3] And, "As on the theory of natural selection an interminable number of intermediate forms must have existed … **Why does not every collection of fossil remains afford plain evidence of the gradation and [change][4] of the forms of life? We meet no such evidence, and this is the most obvious and forcible of the many objections which may be urged against my theory** [emphasis added]."[5]

Darwin's mentor in geology had been Charles Lyell, almost twelve years his senior. When still only twenty-two Darwin first read Lyell's newly published *Principles of Geology* in 1832 while circumnavigating the globe onboard HMS *Beagle*. Consolidating the gains made by James Hutton and John Playfair before him, Lyell strongly promoted his *uniformitarian* views over against *catastrophism*. He adopted three "rules" of uniformitarianism, often summarised as "the present is the key to the past":[6]

- Geologists must assume that the basic laws of nature (such as gravity) had not changed over time.
- No causes other than those that we can now see acting should be employed in explanations.
- Such causes (earthquakes, volcanoes, floods and so on) have not varied in degree or intensity over geological time either.

The second and especially the third rules were controversial at the time and are even refuted by some geologists today.[7] Lyell's objective was to supplant the hitherto hegemony of those geologists - such as Georges Cuvier (1769-1832), Louis Agassiz, William Buckland (1784-1856) and Adam Sedgwick - who believed the earth had been shaped by relative inactivity interrupted by one or more catastrophic events in its past, such as Noah's flood.[8] History demonstrates that he was entirely successful. Lyell and Hutton are regarded as the founding fathers of modern geology, and uniformitarian orthodoxy over against catastrophism has become the ruling paradigm among geologists today.

Were Lyell's rules based on empirical geological reality? The distinguished Harvard palaeontologist, Stephen Jay Gould (1941-2002), didn't think so. Gould was an atheistic evolutionist, not dissimilar to Dawkins in his evolutionary zeal, yet he was candid about Lyell's authoritarian approach, "I ... find it deliciously ironic that cardboard history touts Lyell's victory as the triumph of fieldwork, while [in fact] catastrophists were the true champions of a geological record read as directly seen. **Lyell**, by contrast **urged that theory** - the substantive uniformities of rate and state - **be imposed upon the literal record to interpolate within it what theory expected but imperfect data did not provide** [emphasis added]".[9] In a letter to one of his reviewers, Lyell reveals that his objective was to "free the science from Moses"[10] - clearly a theological predilection. We note here Lyell's recourse to several of Stadler's low-confidence science criteria, including *extrapolation*, many opportunities for *bias* and many *assumptions* required.

6 – FAILED PREDICTION #3: The tree-of-life is recorded in the fossils

Following Lyell's lead, Darwin believed that layers of fossil-bearing rock had accumulated over vast ages of time and he assumed that the geological record was imperfect, that there were gaps, long periods when fossils were not captured in layers of sediment, and that soft bodied organisms would not have fossilised.[11] **This assumed imperfection of the fossil record, was Darwin's get out, together with the undeniable fact that palaeontology was in its infancy during his lifetime** and many of the world's rock layers were still to disclose their fossil secrets. Darwin's hope was that, as the decades unfolded, much more extensive explorations of the world's fossils would reveal slow gradual evolution in the rocks – in confirmation of his theory.

Darwin's problem hasn't gone away

In the last one hundred and fifty years palaeontology has made huge strides. In Darwin's time the number of professional palaeontologists could be counted on two hands. By 1985, however, Denton could estimate that "probably 99.9% of all paleontological work has been carried out since 1860".[12] Many millions more fossils have been discovered and analysed all over the world. So, has the big picture changed? Have the alleged gaps been filled in? Do we now have "innumerable transitional forms"?

In the 1970s a few refreshingly honest palaeontologists began to 'come out' in relation to fossil reality. **Gould described the persistence of the "extreme rarity of transitional forms in the fossil record ... as the trade secret of paleontology** [emphasis added]". He went on to say that

> [t]he evolutionary trees that adorn our textbooks **have data only at the tips and nodes of their branches; the rest is inference**, however reasonable, not the evidence of fossils. Yet Darwin was so wedded to gradualism that he wagered his entire theory on a denial of this literal record ... Darwin's argument [the incompleteness of the fossil record] still persists as the favoured escape of most paleontologists from the embarrassment of a record that seems to show so little of evolution directly ... I wish only to point out that it was never "seen" in the rocks [emphasis added].[13]

Gould explicitly articulates the discordance between the fossil record and Darwin's gradualism:

> The history of most fossil species includes **two features particularly inconsistent with gradualism**:
> - **Stasis**. Most species exhibit no directional change during their tenure on earth. They appear in the fossil record looking much the same as when

they disappear; morphological change is usually limited and directionless.

- **Sudden appearance**. *In any local area, a species does not arise gradually by the steady transformation of its ancestors; it appears all at once and 'fully formed' [emphasis added].*[14]

The palaeontologist Niles Eldredge who was a curator at the American Museum of Natural History, found common cause with Gould. He describes how, in their fossil studies of trilobites, clams and snails, they discovered that "most gradual change … in the fossil record seems to be more

- a to-ing and fro-ing – a sort of oscillation within a spectrum of possible states.

Typically a lineage will get larger for a while, then start to get smaller. Indeed, modification in average size of organisms within a lineage remains the most common form of gradual change reported from the fossil record in the paleontological literature".[15] As an example of the "to-ing and fro-ing", when studying fossil trilobites in successive rock strata, he observed that the number of columns of eyes first increased from fifteen to seventeen and then reduced once more to typically fifteen. He confesses, "I was not prepared for the inertial stolidity of my fossils. They didn't seem to want to change".[16] In 1979 the American palaeontologist Steven Stanley agreed, "**The known fossil record** fails to document a single example of phyletic evolution accomplishing a major morphologic transition and hence **offers no evidence that the gradualistic model can be valid** [emphasis added]".[17]

Given Darwin's prediction about the fossil record and his expectations about future findings subsequently re-energised by the neo-Darwinian genetic synthesis of the 1930s, **the pressure upon palaeontologists to deliver results, to 'find evolution' in the rocks was immense**. Eldredge admits that

> … we [palaeontologists] have preferred a collective tacit acceptance of the story of gradual adaptive change, a story that strengthened and became even more entrenched as the synthesis took hold. **We … have said that the history of life supports that interpretation, all the while knowing that it does not** [emphasis added].[18]

Gould echoed these sentiments, "Paleontologists have paid an enormous price for Darwin's argument. We fancy ourselves as the only true students of life's history, yet to preserve our favored account of evolution by natural selection **we view our data as so bad that we**

almost never see the very process we profess to study [emphasis added]".[19]

The message is clear: when new species arrive within the fossil record they appear suddenly and without any gradual evolutionary ancestry leading up to them in earlier rock layers (sudden appearance), and they continue relatively unchanged in subsequent rock layers (stasis). No new biological features evolve – Eldredge's trilobites appear fully formed, complete with, for example, complex eyes already present. **There is no evidence of the steady, *Mount Improbable*-style, accrual of biological information, only the tinkering of microevolution**. In 1953, there had already been some support for this 'heretical', yet honest, view from one of the architects of the neo-Darwinian synthesis, George Gaylord Simpson. Eldredge recounts how, in stressing that "… the fossil record virtually demanded *some* notion of rapid change, Simpson was reversing the old tendency to *ignore* the facts in favour of the theory [emphasis in original]". Eldredge continued, "And he was also conceding that **gradual evolution just does not get anywhere in producing the truly new** [emphasis added]".[20]

More damage: Punctuated Equilibria

Here's the dilemma. Eldredge recognised and admitted that "stasis… was a general phenomenon in the fossil record, that new species typically appear rather abruptly in the fossil record, and that they commonly overlap in time with their apparent ancestor …"[21] For him the choice was "between two unappetising alternatives: either you stick to conventional theory despite the rather poor fit of the fossils, or you focus on the empirics and say that saltation [jumping] looks like a reasonable model of the evolutionary process – in which case you must embrace a set of rather dubious biological propositions".[22] In other words the fossil record does not exhibit the slow gradual evolution as predicted by the theory; Eldredge's choice was therefore to ignore the fossil evidence and defer to the theory, or to embrace the possibility of rapid evolutionary jumps, which was anathema to Darwinian theory.[23]

So as not to be impaled upon the horns of either of these "unappetising alternatives", Eldredge and Gould sought to offer some evolutionary explanation of rock reality. In 1972, they proposed their theory of *punctuated equilibria*[24] (singular "equilibrium"), sometimes irreverently nicknamed "Punk Eek".[25] This hypothesis co-opted the idea of *allopatric* speciation, a process already posited by evolutionary biologists. The concept here is that rather than a new species evolving *gradually* in the *same* local geographical area as its ancestor (known as *sympatric* speciation), instead a small subset of the ancestral population would have migrated to a new locality and, separated by a mountain range or some other geological feature (a river, or island, perhaps), would there *rapidly* evolve one or more novel biological characteristics by way of adaptation to their new environment. The newly evolved descendent species might then return to the original geographical location but would be sufficiently different as to be recognised as a new species. Eldredge explains, "At its simplest, punctuated equilibria entails the recognition of stasis and the realisation that patterns of change in the fossil record are best explained by allopatric speciation … stasis had become something of a professional embarrassment to be politely ignored, so alien did it seem to what evolution ought to look like in the fossil record".[26]

Eldredge and Gould introduced a second strand to punctuated equilibrium theory: *species selection*. The conventional view of natural selection is that it operates at the level of individuals *within* species: if an *individual* acquires a new beneficial mutation, it will be favoured by natural selection relative to other individuals of the species, and the mutant's offspring will come to dominate the population. We saw this happening in Lenski's *E. coli* project. *Species selection* is the hypothesis that natural selection would also operate at the *species* level, favouring one species over several other competing species. Then with a combination of allopatric speciation, and species selection, Eldredge and Gould claimed to be able to explain the sudden appearance of a new species (punctuated) followed by long periods of stasis (equilibrium). They even claimed that Punk Eek could explain rapid macroevolution - the emergence of novel animal body plans. Fig. 6.2 illustrates Eldredge and Gould's modified tree-of-life. It still assumes a single branching tree of universal common descent, but the branches split off so quickly that they are effectively horizontal in geological time.

While there was some positive reaction - a sense of relief from many other palaeontologists that their 'trade secret' was now out in the open - Eldredge and Gould's *punctuated equilibria* theory evoked some strongly negative, even hostile, reactions. It had stirred up a hornet's nest.[27] Their claim to explain rapid macroevolution led some critics to assume - mistakenly according to Eldredge and Gould - that

6 – FAILED PREDICTION #3: The tree-of-life is recorded in the fossils

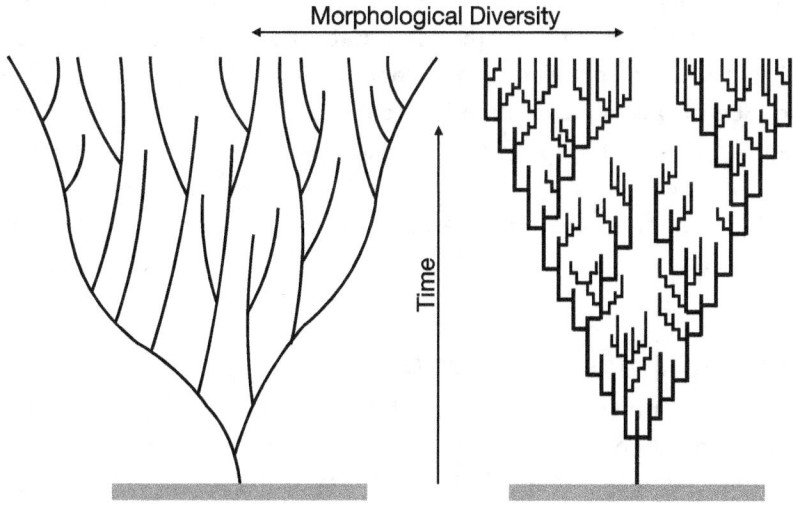

Figure 6.2 A comparison of the "Tree-of-Life" as envisaged by *Punctuated Equilibria* theory (right) and the conventional gradualist evolutionary tree (left).

they were resurrecting Richard Goldschmidt's discredited "hopeful monster" idea. Goldschmidt had published *The Material Basis of Evolution* in 1940. He knew about the jumpiness of the fossil record. His explanation was that macro-mutations were the force behind the appearance of novel biological features. The idea was that a "normal" parent might spontaneously have given birth to an entirely novel "anatomical package", as a result of a macro-mutation (a saltation). He postulated that a reptile, for example, might have given birth to a fully mammalian offspring in one generation. The prime-movers of neo-Darwinism, Dobzhansky, Mayr and Simpson were quick to vigorously oppose Goldschmidt's anti-gradualistic theory.[28]

At best, however, *punctuated equilibria* helps to explain sudden appearances at the species level, but offers no new mechanism in addition to mutations plus natural selection that could explain the evolution of novel body plans (phyla), or even new biological features such as flight feathers or the eye.

Setting aside the controversies surrounding the detail of *punctuated equilibria* and the rights and wrongs of the ire directed at them following their 1972 and subsequent publications, the key question for us here is, "**Why** did Eldredge and Gould see **the need for**

a new theory?" Clearly, it was because they, Stanley, Simpson and others bravely revealed that **the fossil data did not exhibit the pattern anticipated and predicted by Darwinism. There was and is no evidence of gradual *Evolution* in the rocks** - the inside story that had been suppressed for so long. As Denton put it, "... the fossil record is about as discontinuous as it was when Darwin was writing the *Origin*. The intermediates have remained as elusive as ever and their absence remains, a century later, one of the most striking characteristics of the fossil record".[29]

Explosion in the Cambrian

The story - almost certainly apocryphal - is told of Charles Doolittle Walcott, the then director of the Smithsonian Institution, making his return journey at the end of his 1909 fossil prospecting field season. Snow was already falling, so the story goes, and Mrs Walcott's horse slid on the trail and turned up a slab of rock that immediately attracted her husband's attention. Fossilised in the slab were a number of unusual, even strange, creatures. Mrs Walcott, if we go with this embellishment of the story, had discovered what came to be known as the *Cambrian explosion* on Mount Wapta in the Canadian Rockies, 3000 feet above the town of Field. What *is* certainly known is that in 1911 Charles Walcott made this extraordinary find in the Burgess Shale. What had he (or they) found?

Some 65,000 fossil specimens were collected over a period of several years by Walcott's team. According to Stephen Meyer, it was "perhaps the most dramatic discovery in the history of paleontology, a rich trove of middle Cambrian-era fossils, including many previously unknown animal forms, preserved in exquisite detail, suggesting an event of greater suddenness than had been known even in Darwin's time and detailing a greater diversity of biological form and architecture than had hitherto been imagined".[30] Fig. 6.3 places the Cambrian period, named after particular rock strata in Wales, within the context of the overall orthodox geological timescale. From around 3.8 billion years ago until about 570 mya (million years ago) only single-celled organisms had existed, according to evidence in Precambrian rock layers. The Cambrian period spanned 541-485 mya.

By Darwin's time, discontinuity in the fossil record was well known to palaeontologists such as Sedgwick and Agassiz, not as the exception, but as the rule. Indeed, in 1811, it was the Englishman

6 – FAILED PREDICTION #3: The tree-of-life is recorded in the fossils

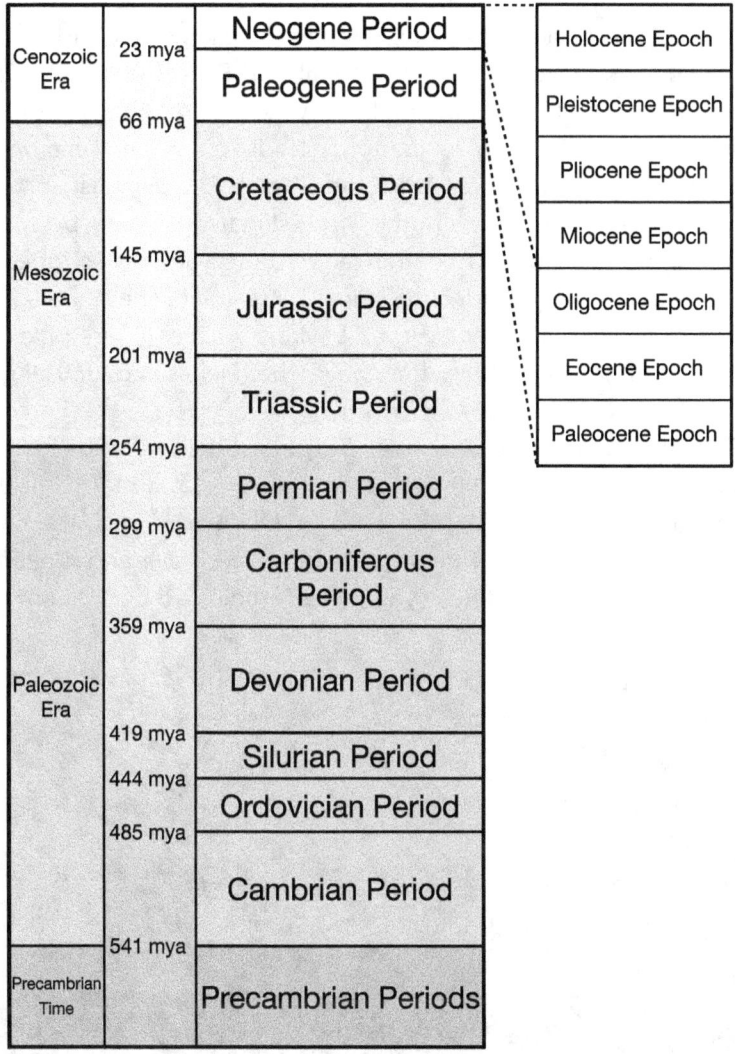

Figure 6.3 The conventional geological timescale with its eras, periods and epochs; mya = "million years ago". The Cenozoic era is sometimes divided into two alternative periods: the Quaternary (2.6 million years) comprising the Holocene and Pleistocene epochs, and the Tertiary (63.4 million years) with its five epochs from the Pliocene through to the Paleocene.

William Smith, while excavating channels for Britain's system of canals, who recognised that rock strata could be distinguished by this very discontinuity – certain fossils that were specific to each layer. For example, starfish and sea-scorpions first appear in what has been called the Ordovician Period; coral reefs, ray-finned and lobe-finned fish in the Silurian; the first amphibians in the Devonian Period; and so on. The sudden appearance in the Cambrian Period of brachiopods (shelly marine creatures) and trilobites was already known. Both of these animals exhibit highly complex body plans and anatomies. Trilobites, now extinct, were arthropods – crab-like animals, some as large as 70 centimetres in length. The distinctive trilobite body had three longitudinal lobes: a central raised lobe with flatter lobes on either side and a body divided into three parts: head, chest and tail, up to thirty segments in all, see Fig. 6.4. Many species of trilobite had compound fully-lensed eyes, that gave them all-round 360-degree vision.[31]

Doolittle's excavation of the Burgess Shale announced the heretofore unknown sudden appearance in the Cambrian Period of such enigmatic and bizarre animals as *Hallucigenia* – even the name suggests its surprising and mysterious form – *Marrella* and *Opabinia*, see Fig. 6.4. The latter had five eyes, fifteen articulated body segments,

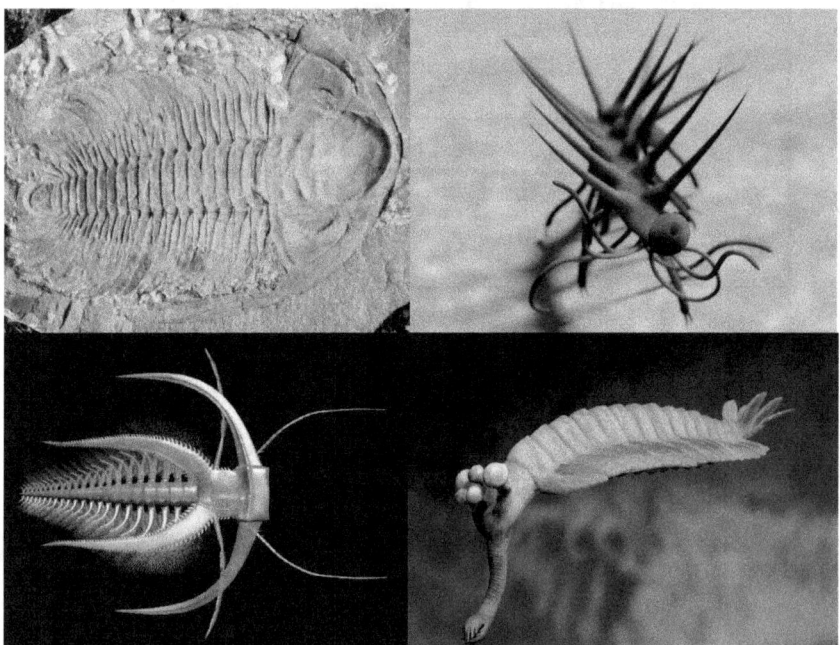

Figure 6.4 The sudden appearance in the Cambrian period of creatures with a surprising number of vastly different body plans (phyla). Four examples shown here, clockwise from top left: a fossil Trilobite and reconstructions of *Hallucigenia*, *Opabinia* and *Marrella*.

twenty-eight gills, an intricate nervous system and a claw on the end of a long trunk-like proboscis.[32]

How should all these novel specimens be classified in terms of phyla, class, etc.? A true disciple of Darwin, Walcott's presupposition was that, especially the earliest fossils such as these, would "fall into a limited number of large and well known groups, and that life's history generally moves toward increasing complexity and diversity".[33] Walcott therefore, in Gould's word, "shoehorned"[34] all of the Burgess finds into a small number of existing phyla.

Then in the 1960s, British palaeontologists Harry Whittington, Simon Conway Morris and Derek Briggs revisited the Burgess Shale. They found that grouping some of the animals within well-established taxonomic categories (as Walcott had done), even the higher ones such as class or phylum strained the limits of these classifications. So, for example, Walcott had classified *Opabinia* as an arthropod. To do so he felt he had to alter – today we would say "photoshop" – his drawing of the organism. In Whittington's words, "Several [of his drawings] are heavily retouched to the point of falsification of certain features …".[35] Gould attests to Walcott's tunnel vision[36] – he simply 'knew' that *Opabinia* was an arthropod, so he 'found' only two eyes. Whittington found five. Walcott found no antennae, mandibles or maxillae (specific characteristics of arthropods), so concluded, "If these appendages were large they have been broken off; if small they may be concealed beneath the crushed and flattened large posterior section of the head". Gould describes this as "a lovely example of apparently unconscious bias in science … He never even mentioned the obvious third alternative – that you don't see them because they don't exist". Walcott's paradigm thinking prevented him from 'seeing' what was actually there. Today *Opabinia* has been allocated to its own phylum because it bears "no known relationship to modern groups".[37] Another Burgess Shale animal, *Anomalocaris*, literally "odd shrimp", which grew up to two feet in length, has been allocated its own phylum.[38] Meantime, to this day, it hasn't been decided how to classify *Nectocaris*.[39]

The main pulse of the Cambrian explosion occurred over a period of only about five million years between 530 and 525 mya[40] which represents little more than 0.1% of the age of the Earth. In this geologically almost instantaneous interval we see the first appearance of twenty of around twenty-six animal phyla[41] known in the fossil

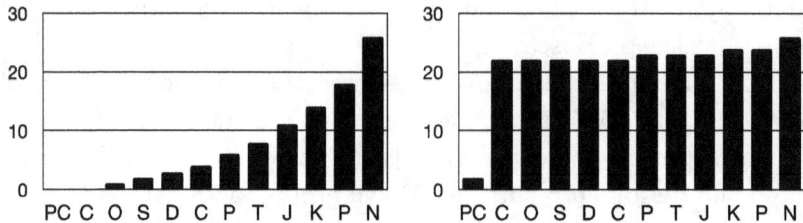

Figure 6.5 These two charts represent the cumulative number of animal phyla in relation to geological time from the Precambrian (PC) through the Cambrian (C), Ordovician (O), etc. to the Neogene (N) period. The chart on the left represents what Darwinian theory would predict should have happened. The chart on the right illustrates the actual abrupt appearance of twenty phyla in the Cambrian period with very few others appearing later.

record, including: cnidarians (corals and jellyfish), molluscs (squid and clams), echinoderms (sea stars and sea urchins), arthropods (trilobites and insects) and chordates (to which all vertebrates including human beings belong).[42] Fig. 6.5 illustrates the *expected* (according to Darwinian assumptions) and *actual* appearance of novel body plans (phyla) over geological time.

Let's remind ourselves of the Darwinian expectations. Richard Dawkins articulates the theory well, "What had been distinct species within one genus become, in the fullness of time, distinct genera within one family. Later, families will be found to have diverged to the point where taxonomists (specialists in classification) prefer to call them orders, then classes, then phyla".[43] This is what might be described as the "bottom-up" prediction: species gradually diversifying over long periods of time into higher and higher levels of classification, ultimately evolving new phyla. Biologists describe this expected pattern as *diversity* (small-scale species and genera differences) first, leading in time to *disparity* (differences in body-plan).[44] What do we actually see? The Cambrian explosion is a classic example of the sudden appearance of a large number of entirely new animal forms with novel body plans and the absence of any fossils of transitional species leading up to them. Meyer summarises the issue – which relates to the general fossil picture not just the Cambrian explosion – with this quote from three palaeontologists.

> Douglas Erwin, James Valentine, and Jack Sepkoski note in their study of skeletonized marine invertebrates: "The fossil record suggests that the major pulse of diversification of phyla occurs before that of classes, classes

> *before that of orders, orders before that of families ... the higher taxa do not seem to have diverged through an accumulation of lower taxa".*[45]

So what the rocks actually express is – disparity (radical differences) first, then diversity (small-scale diversification). It's the very opposite of Darwin's prediction and not what we'd expect from the gradualist mutations plus natural selection mechanism.

Echoing Walcott's discoveries, Chinese palaeontologists Xian-Guang Hou, J. Y. Chen and Gui-Qing Zhou employed farm workers in the mid-1980s to help them unearth fossil remains near the town of Chengjiang in Kunming Province. In the Maotianshan Shale they discovered Cambrian-era fossils in even older sedimentary strata than the Burgess finds, many of them even more exquisitely preserved. This has become known as the *Chengjiang explosion*. It only reinforced exactly the same disparity-first-diversity-later pattern of the Burgess. The finds included more chordates with their digestive tract and spine-like notochord, some with a relatively large brain. Even small jawless fish were found. Previously such vertebrates were not thought to have appeared until about 475 mya in the Ordovician period.[46]

What about Darwin's escape route?

Walcott was aware that no fossils of transitional species leading up to the Cambrian explosion had been found. The more recent Chengjiang find confirms this discontinuity. Was there a reasonable explanation for it in Walcott's time? There were three possibilities:

1. As palaeontology work continued, the missing transitional fossils would be found.
2. The fossil record is incomplete. Representatives of transitional species simply failed to fossilise.
3. There were no transitional species.

As we know, Darwin regarded (1) and (2) as possibilities but had to reject (3) for his theory to be true. Likewise, Dawkins, ever the Darwinian gradualist, agreed with his mentor.

> *... the mere fact that there are few, if any, fossils of most animal phyla before the Cambrian should not stampede us into assuming that those phyla evolved extremely rapidly ... all those Cambrian fossils **must have had** continuously evolving antecedents. Those **antecedents had to be there**, but they have not been discovered. Whatever the reason, and whatever the timescale, they **failed to fossilise, but they must have been there** [emphasis added].*[47]

1. The missing transitional fossils will eventually be found. Walcott did not believe – as Darwin did in his time – that more fossil hunting on the continents would find the missing fossils.[48] He concluded that such searches, if not exhaustive, had been sufficiently extensive to find the intermediates if they had been there. Nevertheless, he still favoured option (1), but turned to the oceans for his version of what's called the "artefact hypothesis" (that our sampling of the fossil record so far has 'missed' the intermediates).[49] Although his Cambrian Burgess find was high in the Rockies of British Columbia, Walcott believed these strata may have been separated from their Precambrian precursors by geological uplift and that the transitional fossils would be found in deep ocean sediments.

Coincidentally within a year of Walcott's team first uncovering their mysterious creatures, Wegener was working on his plate tectonic theory. As we know from Chapter 1, his work was ignored for about 40 years. But thanks to him, it is now believed the ocean floors are less than 180 million years old – much too young to yield Precambrian fossils. This scuppers Walcott's hypothesis, which, as Gould clarifies, "rested, as [he] knew only too well, upon the most treacherous kind of argument that a scientist can ever use – negative evidence [the assumption that absence of evidence of transitional fossils is not evidence of their absence]".[50]

It has been argued that fauna first found in the Ediacaran Hills of southeastern Australia, and subsequently in similar layers in Namibia, Newfoundland, north-western Russia and England, could have been ancestral to the phyla of the Cambrian explosion. The Ediacaran, sometimes labelled Vendian, strata have been dated to 570-565 mya in the Precambrian period. However, there is uncertainty as to whether these fossils are even of the kingdom Animalia. Their classifications are hotly debated and the consensus is that the Cambrian animals are not descended from these. A comment in an article in *Nature* argues that if the Ediacaran fauna "were animals, they bore little or no resemblance to any other creatures, either fossil or extant".[51]

2. Transitional fossils failed to fossilise. It has been suggested that the reason we do not find precursors in the Precambrian rocks is that they were most likely soft-bodied. If they were too soft, too small or both – so the argument goes – they may not have fossilised. However, other evidence gives the lie to this justification. Setting aside the observation that arthropods which appeared suddenly in the Cambrian – trilobites,

Marrella, Fuxianhuia protensa, Waptia, Anomalocaris – all had hard exoskeletons or body parts and any precursors that had existed would have been unlikely to survive as purely soft bodied creatures, nevertheless, **fossils of soft bodied animals do occur in the fossil record.** The Chengjiang discoveries included "many ... well-preserved animals ... including soft-bodied members of phyla such as Cnidaria (corals and jellyfish), Ctenophora (comb jellies), Annelida (a type of "ringed" segmented worm) ...", as well as, "soft tissues and organs such as eyes, intestines, stomachs ... mouths and nerves ... the contents of the guts of several animals".[52] Similarly, the Burgess Shale preserved many soft-bodied creatures and structures, including worms, sea-anemone-like animals and jelly-fish-like animals.[53] In addition, fossils of blue-green algae, single-celled algae, and cells with a nucleus (eukaryotes) are well known in the Precambrian strata. Such single-celled organisms are not only small, but also lack hard parts. Late Precambrian rocks have also preserved adult sponges (mostly soft bodied) but also, astonishingly, even embryonic sponges.[54] It follows, then, that **the argument from poor fossilisation of soft-bodied creatures as an explanation for the missing transitionals cannot now be sustained.** Meyer explores this theme in detail.[55]

The one other avenue to be explored, then, is the question of sampling. How likely is it that additional future excavations will uncover the "missing" fossils? By way of analogy Meyer asks us to imagine reaching into an enormous barrel full of marbles and randomly pulling out three marbles, one blue, one red and one yellow. We continue selecting marbles at random, sampling the whole barrel until we have picked out a thousand marbles. Yet no rainbow of colours has emerged. Still only the three primary colours are represented in our samples. We now have reasonable grounds for suspecting that there are no orange, green or purple marbles in the barrel.

Of the fossils known today fewer than 1% were known in Darwin's day. While it may have been reasonable for him to speculate that many more fossil discoveries would fill in the transitional gaps, now, more than 150 years on, statistical analyses by palaeontologists such as Michael Foote of the University of Chicago render this possibility highly improbable: "Foote's analysis suggests that since palae-ontologists have reached repeatedly into the proverbial barrel, sampled it from one end to the other, and found only representatives of various radically different phyla but no rainbow intermediates, we shouldn't hold our breath expecting such intermediates to emerge".[56] His view is that we can rely on the patterns already observed in the fossil record.

An orchard – not a tree

As Gould candidly affirms, "Instead of a narrow beginning and a constantly expanding upward range, multicellular life reaches its maximal scope at the start …"[57] and "… the basic pattern is a disproof of our standard and comfortable iconography – the cone of increasing diversity".[58] Fig. 6.6 then, amends the tree-of-life "iconography" to match the actual evidence of the fossil record. Instead of a tree with a universal trunk, an orchard of bushes better represents the actual data. The pattern of fossil evidence refutes the punctuated equilibria hypothesis too. Just like the tree, Punk Eek is also essentially gradualist: diversity *then* disparity.[59] As Meyer puts it, "The fossil record amply documents organisms corresponding to the terminal branches on the Darwinian tree of life (animals representing new phyla or classes, for example), but it fails to preserve those organisms representing the internal branches or nodes leading to these representatives of novel phyla and classes of Cambrian-era animals … Yet these intermediates are the very forms required …".[60]

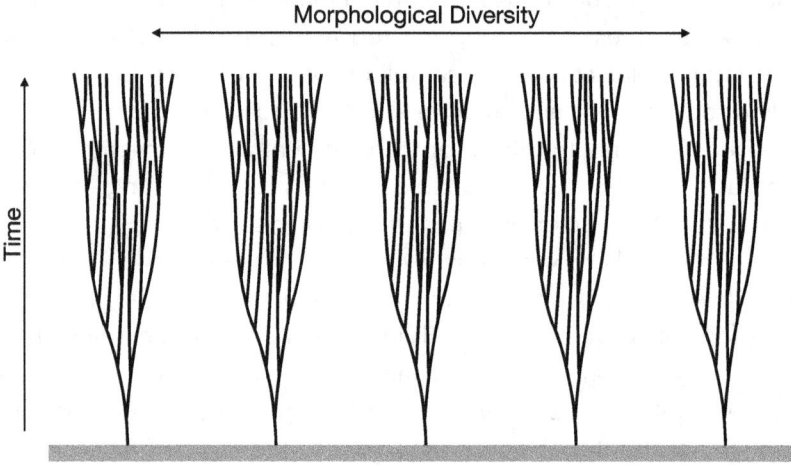

Figure 6.6 Rather than a single tree depicting universal common descent, an orchard of bushes better represents the actual fossil data.

The information 'hole' again

It's at this point in our journey below decks, having discovered the water welling up from the gaping hole in the 'watertight compartment' we're in the process of surveying, that we are met by the torrent overflowing from the first two compartments caused by the collision with the molecular biology 'iceberg'. The first surprise is the sudden appearance in the Cambrian of this large number of new animal forms: phyla, classes and orders. The second surprise is that most of these novel, and in some cases mysterious, animals are not "primitive" organisms as evolutionary theory would lead us to expect. Many already have sophisticated anatomies, including digestive and circulatory systems, exoskeletons, gills, notochords, compound-lensed eyes and relatively large brains. Clearly these animals are much more sophisticated than single-celled organisms. So where did the information to build these animals – clearly present in their respective genomes – come from? As Meyer points out, Whittington recognised that **the central unsolved problem** of the Cambrian explosion is **"the origin of biological form** [emphasis added]".[61]

One indicator of increased complexity, and therefore information requirement, is **the number of different cell types** that these life forms needed to perform the functions in their digestive, vision and other systems, though this probably underestimates the complexity hikes in evidence. As we know from earlier chapters, a bacterium (prokaryote) exists as a single cell. Protists, such as algae, also only have one cell type, albeit a much more complex one. They are eukaryotes and therefore have a nucleus together with other functional organelles within their cell wall. The **sponges** that appeared in the late Precambrian needed **five to ten distinct** (eukaryotic) **cell types**; arthropods, such as **trilobites about fifty**; and **chordates more than sixty**.[62]

Another measure of information content can be genome size. Prokaryotes are estimated to have 300,000 to 500,000 DNA base pairs, whereas eukaryotic single-celled organisms need over a million. We can't sequence the DNA of the extinct trilobite but a modern arthropod such as the fruit fly *Drosophila melanogaster*, has about 140 million base pairs.[63] Clearly these genomes would have included the instructions to build the large number of additional proteins that would have been required for these animals to survive: enzymes for digestion and to catalyse other chemical reactions; structural proteins to form tissues of various kinds, and so on. And we know from Chapters 4 and 5 that novel protein designs are extremely rare, meaning they exhibit high information content.

Other explosions

While it may be argued that fossil evidence for the gradual emergence of some classes exists, nevertheless, the explosion of novel life forms in the Cambrian period is not unique. About 485-460 mya, the *Ordovician explosion*, **when 300 new families of marine invertebrates appeared**, has been described as "every bit as momentous for animal evolution as the Cambrian one".[64]

The **abrupt appearance of all major groups of jawed fish** with teeth between 425 and 415 mya, has been labelled the *odontide explosion* in the Late Silurian/Early Devonian periods.[65] Also in this time interval, the sudden appearance and diversification of vascular land plants has been described as "the terrestrial equivalent of the much-debated Cambrian 'explosion' of marine faunas".[66]

In the Carboniferous, 318-300 mya, a large diversity of **winged insect groups appeared suddenly** without any known transitional forms in the Devonian, including mayflies, dragonflies, wasps and beetles – the *Carboniferous insect explosion*.[67] In the Triassic period, three explosions:[68]

- 251-240 mya, **modern tetrapods** (four-footed animals) **appeared abruptly**, including the first dinosaurs, turtles and lizards, the first crocodile-like and mammal-like creatures.
- 248-240 mya, **fifteen different families of marine reptiles**, including ichthyosaurs (swimming reptiles).
- 230-228 mya, **gliding and flying reptiles appear suddenly**, including pterosaurs.

The **sudden appearance of angiosperms** (flowering plants which produce seeds with a female reproductive organ, a carpel) from 130 to 115 mya in the Cretaceous period, was to Darwin, an "abominable mystery".[69] There are no transitional forms in the fossil record and, as Wilson has it, "Angiosperms ... provide **one of the most devastating challenges to Darwin** [emphasis added]".[70]

About **fifteen of today's mammalian orders appear without precursors** in the Paleocene epoch between 62 and 49 mya. They appear already in their distinctive forms: Carnivora, such as bears; Chiroptera, such as bats; Perissodactyla, such as horses. This is known

6 - FAILED PREDICTION #3: The tree-of-life is recorded in the fossils

as the *mammalian radiation*. The *avian explosion* or "Big bang for Tertiary birds" also occurred in the Paleocene epoch, between 65 and 55 mya. This was **the abrupt appearance of modern bird orders**.[71]
The sudden appearance of humans, *Homo sapiens*, will be the subject of Chapter 8.

HOW DO BIOLOGISTS ACCOMMODATE THIS FAILED PREDICTION?

Fig. 6.7 represents a typical example of how a palaeontologist in a recent book, which purports to tell us "What the fossils say",[72] copes with this failed prediction. Two features of this stereotypical diagram are significant.

First, the elongated bubbles represent the actual fossil evidence: the classes of synapsids/mammals, crocodilians, turtles, etc. **all appear abruptly**, each with their distinct biology: *disparity*. They may then exhibit slight changes in size, etc.: *diversity*, the bubbles becoming wider. Classes then continue to the present day or become extinct.

Second, the textbook author has drawn in connecting "tree" lines, **on the assumption that evolutionary common ancestry is true**, even

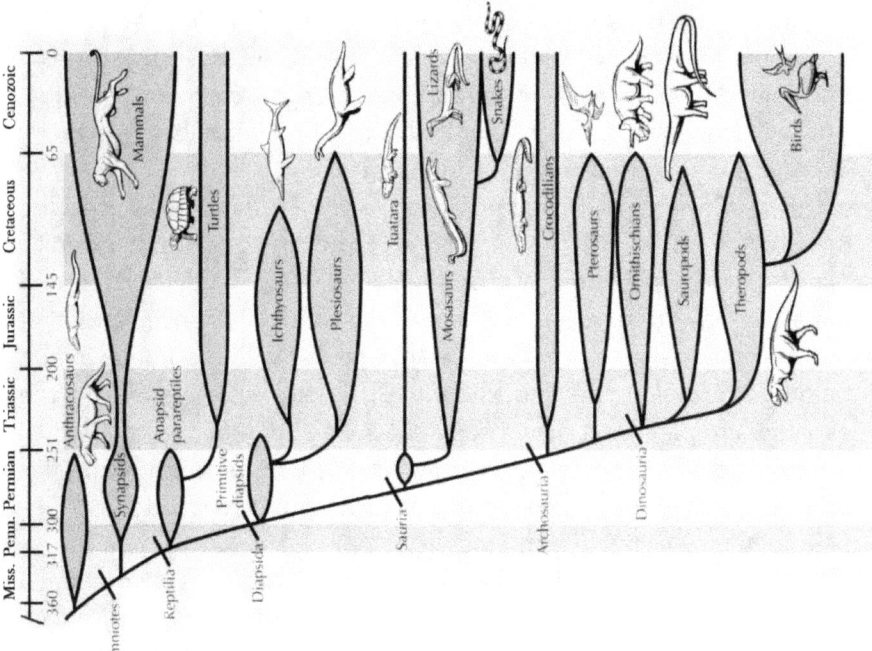

Figure 6.7 A typical contemporary textbook depiction of a tree-of-life, in this case Amniotes, which includes mammals, reptiles, dinosaurs and birds. It's presented on its side here so that the time axis, from around 360 mya to the present, is vertical similar to Figures 6.1, 6.2 and 6.6.

though there are no connecting "transitional" fossils at the branching points. A tree-like structure has been shoehorned in simply because common ancestry has been assumed.

Lost at sea: Extinctions

The fossil record exhibits evidence of extinction events such as the end-Permian, around 250 mya, when it has been estimated that 96 percent of marine species (including trilobites) and around 70 percent of terrestrial organisms were eliminated. Similarly the dinosaurs disappeared at the K-T event (a German abbreviation for the Cretaceous-Tertiary boundary) about 65 mya.[73] Much is often made of these extinctions in popular evolutionary literature as evidence for "evolution". But **what evolutionary theory needs to explain is** not extinctions, but rather **the sudden appearance of novel animal forms**: phyla, classes, orders and families **and the genetic information needed** to build these new classifications of animals.

Ice warnings... and stories of intermediates

Six "ice warnings" were received by RMS *Titanic*'s radio operators in the hours leading up to her nemesis. Not all of these messages – transmitted by other ships as they spotted 'bergs – reached the bridge, but we know that Captain Smith did respond to one of them by altering course to steer a more southerly route.

Both Coyne and palaeontologist Donald Prothero have used the phrase, "What the fossils say".[74] Now, obviously fossils don't literally "say" anything, but there are problems with this mindset even as a metaphor. Evidence does not speak for itself. Evidence, and that includes fossil evidence, has to be interpreted within a framework, a paradigm of belief and understanding (Chapter 1). Adherents to the evolutionary paradigm have proposed a small number of candidates as intermediates or so-called "missing links". But prior to surveying this particular section of the 'watertight compartment' we should first take heed of our own six 'ice warnings':

1. **There's a risk that we see what we want to see**. We've already come across this with Walcott. Recall from Part 1 that palaeontology is one of the historical, observational sciences. Neither palaeontologists nor anyone else was around to see animals prior to their fossilisation, so any conclusions we reach about their species identity should be tentative. There's a significant risk that

conclusions will be overstated, subject to bias, perhaps dependent upon unverifiable assumptions. Phillip Johnson put it this way, "Persons who come to the fossil record as convinced Darwinists will see a stunning confirmation, but skeptics will see only a lonely exception [e.g. *Archaeopteryx*] to a consistent pattern of fossil disconfirmation".[75]

2. **Different looking fossils could actually be from the same species.** Returning to the theme of domestic dogs, if we consider the huge differences in skull shapes amongst chihuahua, bulldog and Great Dane, even Coyne admits that "If somehow the recognized breeds existed only as fossils, paleontologists would consider them not one species but many ...".[76]

3. **Similar looking fossils may be interpreted erroneously as an ancestral sequence**. Where only skeletal detail has been fossilised,[77] potentially vital distinguishing evidence contained only in the soft biology is missing. The rhipidistian lobe-finned fishes had long been regarded as intermediate between fish and amphibians. This was due to similar bone patterns in their fins, vertebral column and skull. The coelacanth, a relative of the rhipidistia class, was thought to have become extinct around 100 mya. But then in 1938 a living coelacanth turned up in the nets of fisherman in the Indian Ocean. The soft biology of this living-fossil reality disappointed evolutionary biologists. Barbara Stahl writes, "the modern coelacanth shows no evidence of having internal organs preadapted for use in a terrestrial environment".[78] Similarly, a Tasmanian wolf skull is barely distinguishable from that of some dogs, yet the former has a marsupial rather than a mammalian reproductive system.

4. **Objects can be "sorted" into an "evolutionary" sequence where none actually exists**. Nails, tacks, screws, staples and so on, have been used to teach "tree-of-life" evolutionary principles,[79] see Fig. 6.8. Similarly, biologist Tim Berra's demonstration used various models of automobiles: "If you compare a 1953 and a 1954 Corvette, side by side, then a 1954 and a 1955 model, and so on, descent with modification is overwhelmingly obvious".[80] Yet the nails and cars were all *designed*; they were products of intelligent minds, not natural selection acting upon random mutations. Given that these examples have been used as illustrations of *unguided*

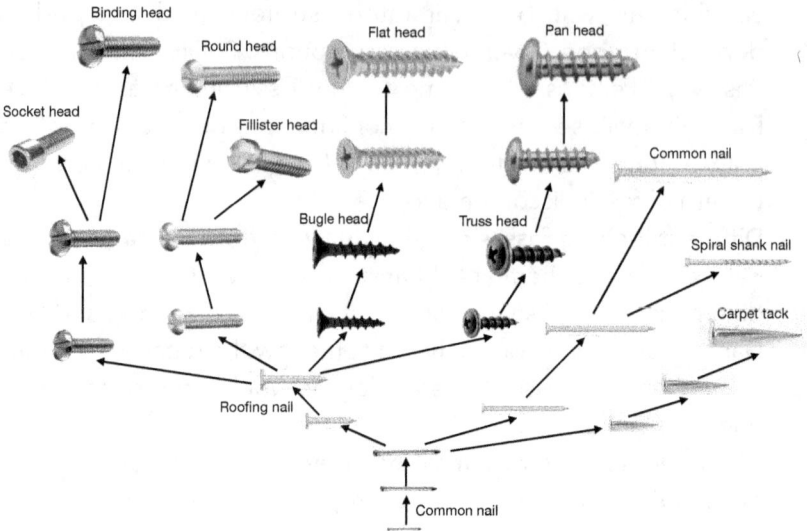

Figure 6.8 Nail "evolution". In this (fictitious) example, the "common ancestor" is a small nail with one branch exhibiting nails of increasing length and diameter; a second branch "evolves" pointed shafts (tacks); a third branch "evolves" a novel feature on the shaft – a thread – such that screws of increasing length and diameter "evolve".

evolution, we should therefore be circumspect when it comes to interpreting fossil evidence.

5. **Sequence by chance**. Millions of fossils have been found. Seemingly plausible evolutionary sequences could be arranged simply by chance.[81]
6. **Fossils sometimes don't appear in the predicted order**. Putative ancestors can sometimes appear later in the fossil record than the assumed descendent.

FISH TO TETRAPODS. Coyne begins the story, "Until about 390 million years ago, the only vertebrates were fish. But, thirty million years later, we find creatures that are clearly *tetrapods*: four-footed vertebrates that walked on land [emphasis in original]".[82] There seemed to be no intermediate between fossils that were clearly fish – *Eusthenopteron* and *Panderichthys* - and tetrapod representatives: *Acanthostega* and *Ichthyostega*, Fig. 6.9. Then in 2006 Neil Shubin and his team searching on Ellesmere Island in the Arctic Ocean north of Canada announced the discovery of a fossil that Coyne hailed as "a stunning vindication of evolutionary theory".[83] Found in riverbed strata dated at

6 – FAILED PREDICTION #3: The tree-of-life is recorded in the fossils

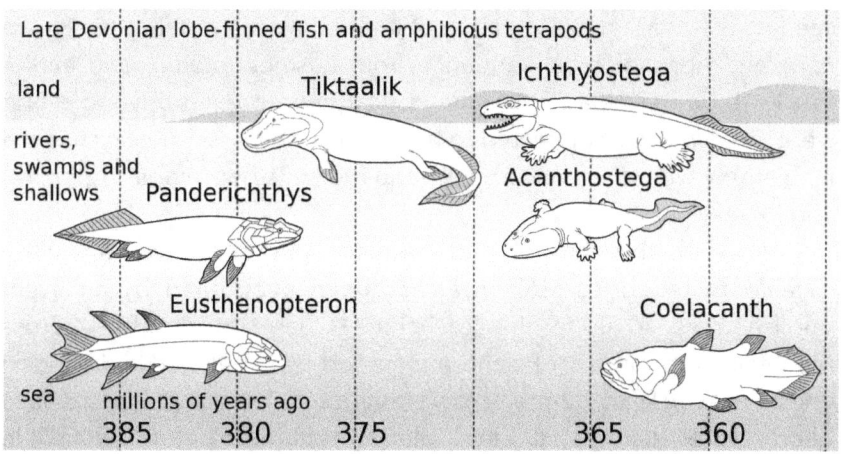

Figure 6.9 *Tiktaalik*, the much acclaimed transitional species between fish and tetrapods.

375 mya, Shubin named it *Tiktaalik roseae* in honour of the Inuit people ("Tiktaalik" means "large freshwater fish"). Like fish, it had gills, scales and fins, while its amphibian-like features were a flattened head with eyes and nostrils on top like a salamander. Its fins were more robust and, unlike fish, it had a neck. This combination was thought to allow it to "flex itself upward to help survey its surroundings."[84] But it still had gills and the "more robust fins" were not able to act as fully weight-bearing legs.[85] Critics are not convinced by the fin cladogram,

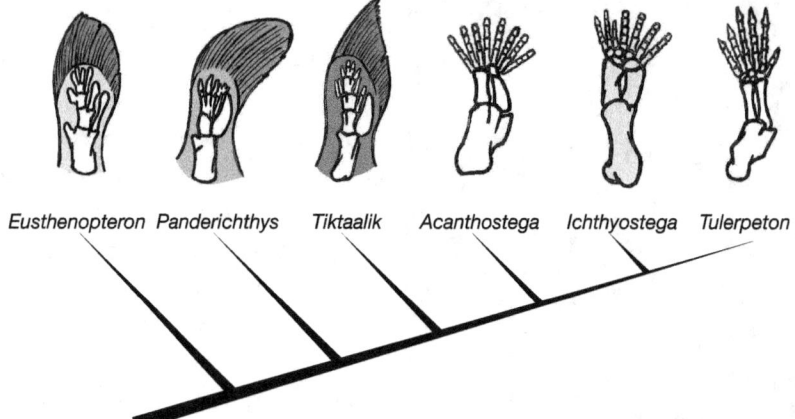

Figure 6.10 This cladogram (a branching diagram showing the relationship between a number of species putatively descended from a common ancestor) shows the claimed transformation of the pectoral fin of lobefins into the hand and forelimbs of primitive tetrapods.

see Fig. 6.10 for a representation of it: Shubin's team claims to show a coherent morphological sequence from *Eusthenopteron,* and earlier fossils, through *Tiktaalik,* to limbs in *Acanthostega* and beyond.[86] Nor were *Tiktaalik*'s fins connected to the main skeleton, so drastic changes in anatomy would still have been required.[87] 'Ice warnings' (1), (3), (4) and (5) may apply.

However, **the chronological sequence** from fish (385 mya) via *Tiktaalik* to tetrapods (365 mya) **has been overturned** by an event published in 2010. In the Zachelmie Quarry in the Holy Cross Mountains in south-east Poland a team led by Grzegorz Niedźwiedzki uncovered tracks of a 2-metre-long tetrapod.[88] These trace fossils have been securely dated at 395 mya, **placing tetrapods before *Tiktaalik* in the fossil record and even earlier than the *Panderichthys* fish**. The tracks are of a five- or perhaps six-toed creature, whereas even *Acanthostega*, thirty million years later, still has eight toes. 'Ice warning' (6) now applies.

DINOSAURS TO BIRDS. In 1861 Hermann von Meyer discovered a fossil specimen of *Archaeopteryx* in a limestone quarry near Solnhofen in Germany. It was a fully feathered bird with some reptilian features such as teeth, a long tail and claws on its wings, Fig. 6.11. It is believed to have lived some 150 mya. Two years after the publication of *The Origin*, the discovery of *Archaeopteryx* (literally "ancient wing") delighted Darwin. It was exactly the kind of fossil evidence he had hoped for.[89] Thomas Henry Huxley (Darwin's bulldog) saw similarities between *Archaeopteryx* and *Compsognathus*, a small bird-like dinosaur, and as a result of this favourable comparison Huxley gave birth to the belief that birds had evolved from dinosaurs. This is still the majority view today though not entirely without opposition among biologists.[90]

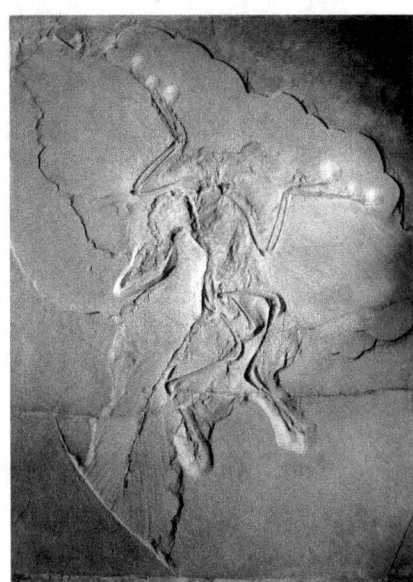

Figure 6.11 Archaeopteryx.

Palaeontologists agree, however, that **modern birds are not desc-**

ended from Archaeopteryx, nor is there consensus on its own ancestry. Cladistics (literally "branching") – the discipline that groups species according to their biological similarities and in what order their similarities were acquired or lost – considers *Archaeopteryx* to be descended from extinct bird-like dinosaurs that don't appear in the fossil record till about 20 million years *after Archaeopteryx* was itself thought to be extinct![91] 'Ice warnings' (1), (4), and (6) may apply here.

The big unanswered conundrum in relation to putative bird evolution from dinosaurs, however, is the origin of flight and its essential attendant biology. *Archaeopteryx's* fossilised feathers appear to be fully-formed flying feathers just like modern birds, including asymmetric vanes producing individual aerofoils[92] – not some hybrid reminiscent of reptilian scales. *Archaeopteryx*, it would seem, could fly like a modern bird. The avian lung is a second major biological discontinuity relative to the reptilian respiratory system,[93] Fig. 6.12. We see echoes here of the *irreducible complexity* challenge: **how could the avian system of parabronchi and interconnected air sacs with its unidirectional air flow have evolved step-by-step from the bi-directional bellows-style reptilian lung system?**

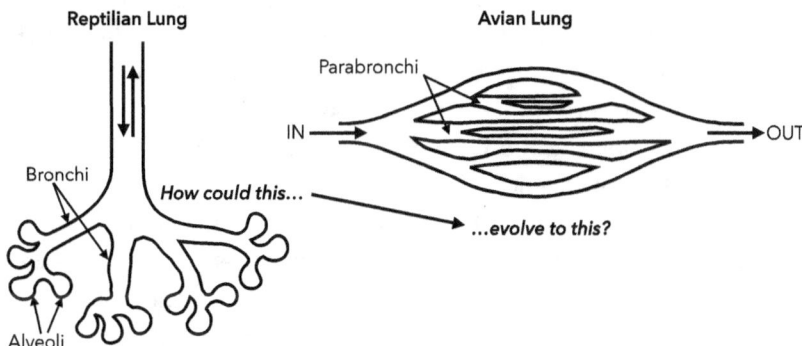

Figure 6.12 Step-by-step transition from a bidirectional airflow reptilian lung (left) into the unidirectional avian lung (right) is a challenge for gradual evolution by natural selection.

THE HORSE. Prothero documents the fact that Huxley was also involved in the promotion of horse evolution.[94] The early version of this sequence was a neat linear progression, beginning with genera known as *Eohippus* or *Hyracotherium*. It has now been updated to a more bushy, branching pattern which initiates with the genus *Protorohippus* in the Eocene epoch 55 mya. These were tiny beagle sized animals with four toes on their front feet and three on their hind. Size then increased through "*Orohippus* and *Epihippus,* culminating in the German-shepherd-sized horse *Mesohippus* and *Miohippus* in the late Eocene and [into the] Oligocene ... These horses had three robust toes on their hands and feet".[95] The sequence also involved changes in teeth and snout morphology. There were around a dozen extinctions along the way on side branches in the Eocene, Oligocene and Miocene, "leaving only the lineage leading to the modern [one-toed] genus of *Equus* to flourish in the Pliocene and Pleistocene".[96]

Most of the 'ice warnings' almost certainly apply here, but even if we take the constructed sequence at face value, this is no more than a demonstration of microevolution – increases in body size and adjustments to teeth and snout – species and genus level differences. There has been no change at family level or above and certainly no novel body plan. Yet this microevolutionary sequence apparently took 50 million years. For more detail on horse microevolution, see Swift.[97]

MAMMALS RETURN TO THE SEA.[98] Darwin thought that whales had evolved from bears.[99] More recently, primarily due to similarities found in their DNA sequences, the hippopotamus has become the mammal believed to be the whale's nearest terrestrial living relative. Their putative common ancestor is sometimes endearingly referred to as the "whippo". Following a number of fossil finds in the late 1990s, popularisers have become very excited about whales as the confirmatory "poster-child" of *Evolution*. According to Coyne, "**This is one of our best examples of an evolutionary transition**, since we have a chronologically ordered series of fossils, perhaps a lineage of ancestors and descendants, showing their movement from land to water [emphasis added]".[100] Dawkins uses Prothero's diagram to illustrate the whale's presumed evolution,[101] see Fig. 6.13.

There are two misleading elements in this diagram. First notice that it is depicted (correctly) as a cladogram rather than as a conventional evolutionary tree (unlike in some textbooks[102]). In other words it is not an ancestor-descendant sequence. So for example modern whales are not believed to be descended from *Pakicetus* (meaning "whale from Pakistan") or from *Ambulocetus* (walking whale) or even from *Basilosaurus* (king lizard). This is important because it means the animals shown in sequence are not "intermediate" in the sense of grandfather, father, son ..., but rather "intermediate" in the

6 – FAILED PREDICTION #3: The tree-of-life is recorded in the fossils

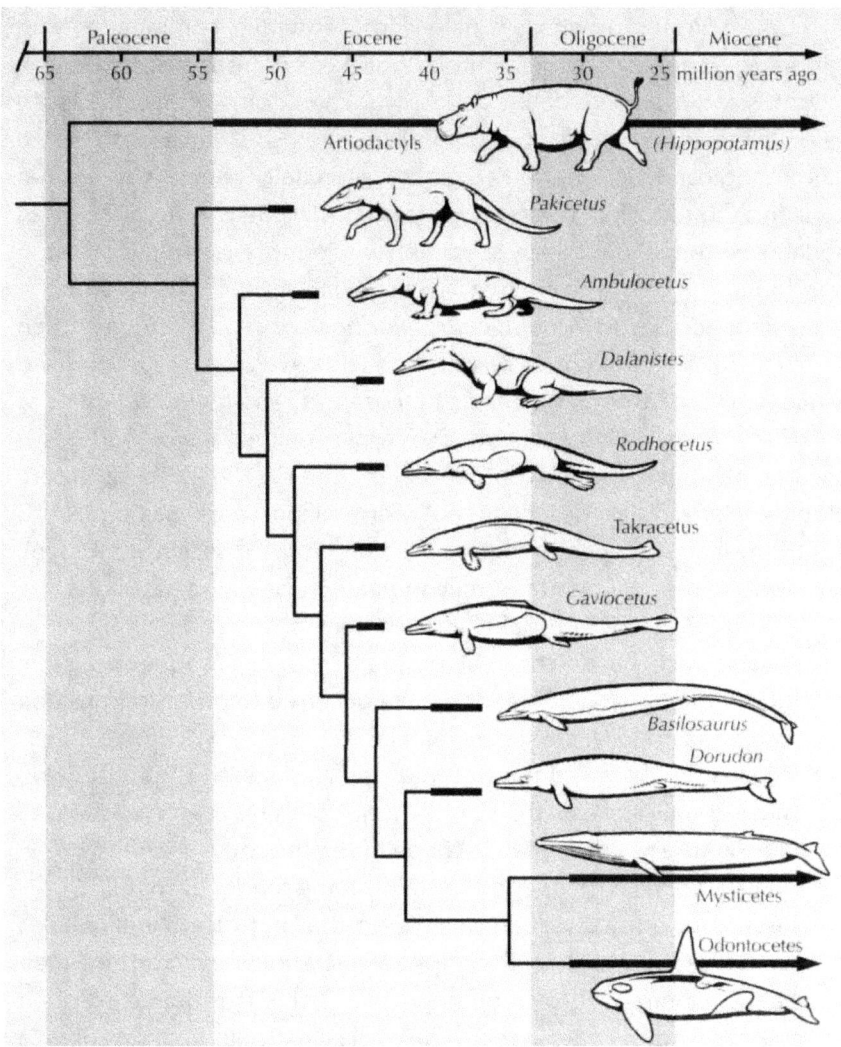

Figure 6.13 The standard whale evolution story.

sense of sharing some biological features in common. So what we have is a tree populated by unique animals at the tips of its branches – each with distinguishing features that would have to have been lost in order to be considered as direct ancestors one of the other – but no evidence of the actual ancestral line at the major branching points.

Second, for understandable reasons, the animals all appear to be about the same size. In fact the modern whale is, of course, massively larger than the wolf-sized *Pakicetus* by every physical measure (Coyne's diagram does attempt to address this problem).[103]

Unlike Prothero, whose whale-ward sequence commences with *Pakicetus*, Coyne begins his "chronologically ordered series" with the racoon sized *Indohyus* dated at 48 mya. Then comes *Pakicetus*, even though he dates it at 52 mya. We seem to have lost some "chronological order" here. *Pakicetus* was initially known only from a skull and the rest of its anatomy was *assumed* to be well adapted to an aquatic existence. But then a specimen with a more complete skeleton was found which revealed that it was in fact a wolf-like creature.[104] According to Coyne *Ambulocetus*, *Rodhocetus* and *Dorudon*, then follow at 50, 47 and 40 mya respectively. However, in 2016 a fossilised whale similar to the fully aquatic *Basilosaurus* was found in Antartica dated at 49 mya.[105] So, contra Coyne, we neither have "perhaps a lineage of ancestors and descendants", nor do we have "a chronologically ordered series of fossils". Ten million years was already a tight timescale for such a major transition, as we'll see in a moment, but now it's reduced to three million years at best. 'Ice warnings' (1), (3), (4) and (6), at least, probably apply here.

In any case here's the real problem with this sequence. What changes in biology would need to have occurred in order to transition from terrestrial to fully aquatic mammals?[106]

- Whales are powered through the water by massive up-and-down moving tail flukes which use huge muscles and tendons to contour their hydrodynamic shape independently of the tail.
- A large dorsal fin is needed to stabilise the tendency to roll.
- Instead of normally-open nostrils on the end of a snout, whales have normally-closed thick-lipped blowholes on top of their heads. Contraction of a number of muscles is required to open the blowhole against the highly elastic tissue that ensures a watertight seal.
- Deep diving to 2000 metres requires that the lungs can collapse safely under 200-times atmospheric pressure. In turn this needs "floating ribs", not attached to the sternum, together with a diaphragm that runs parallel to the spine rather than perpendicular to it. This ability allows these creatures to avoid narcosis (due to too much nitrogen in the bloodstream) and "the bends" (nitrogen bubbles in the blood) when returning to the surface.
- Also upon resurfacing, special fluids called "surfactants" in the lungs are essential to facilitate their re-inflation.

- In most terrestrial mammal males, sperm production requires that their testes are a few degrees below normal body temperature. Whales achieve this, even though the testicles are internal to their bodies: warm blood from the heart is cooled in a counter-flow heat exchanger around the testes by blood returning in special blood vessels from the (cold) tail flukes and dorsal fin.
- Young are born breach delivery. Head first would be fatal underwater.
- Whale's milk is three to four times more concentrated than cow's milk and, since the whale calf doesn't have proper lips, the mother needs to squirt her milk into its mouth.
- Some whales use echolocation to hunt their prey and some have the ability to communicate over very large distances.
- … and there are many more.[107]

Yet we are told that these very significant novel features evolved in 3 million years maximum. By comparison it took more than 50 million years, we're told, for the horse to lose a couple of toes and lengthen its snout. And meantime, "living fossils" such as scorpions, the coelacanth, the horseshoe crab, and jelly fish have hardly changed at all after, 360, 370, 445 and 500 million years, respectively.[108] It would seem then that evolution is very slow – except, of course, when we're assured that it's very fast.

If we now consider the implications at the molecular level, how many genetic mutations would be required to evolve these numerous and extensive changes in whale morphology? At present there is no definitive answer to that question. But we can still make an assessment of the plausibility of the whale evolutionary story. And this is where, once more, we meet the water pouring over the 'bulkheads' from the first two 'watertight compartments'. In Chapter 5, from the work of Behe, Gauger and Axe we know that just four specific simultaneous mutations could not be achieved even by bacteria, the most populous organism on Earth, even over its entire four billion year history. Geneticists Durrett and Schmidt find that the waiting-time for a specific pair of mutations in fruit flies would require a few million years, but that "for humans with a smaller effective population size, this type of change would take >100 million years".[109]

In terms of population size and generation times, whales are going to be nearer to, if not beyond, the human end of this waiting-time spectrum – and that's the waiting-time for only two specific mutations. Comparisons between the okapi and its stretched-neck cousin, the giraffe, revealed differences in as many as seventy genes.[110] If that's the case for the relatively similar giraffe and okapi, surely many more than 70 mutations would have been required to turn wolf-like creatures into fully aquatic whales. Yet, for Coyne, this is "one of the best examples of an evolutionary transition" that was "only a few mutations away".[111] Is Coyne's confidence justified?

Lower lifeboat 6!

Here's a summary of Chapter 6.

When asked what observation could conceivably *disprove* evolution, the curmudgeonly J.B.S. Haldane reportedly growled, "Fossil rabbits in the Precambrian!"[112] Now, given that everybody, including even the most ardent critic of *Evolution*, would be as surprised[113] as Haldane if such a find were to occur, this would seem to set the bar of disproof at an absurdly high level.

Our survey of the damage in the third watertight compartment has revealed:
- Darwin knew that the fossil record, in his time, did not provide evidence of the millions of intermediate species that his theory predicted simply ought to be there.
- His hope was that succeeding generations of palaeontologists would discover the "missing links" in unexplored strata.
- Darwin clung to the belief that the fossil record was "imperfect"; that only a tiny fraction of fossils had been preserved in the rocks.
- Unfortunately for Darwin, the last 150 years - in which more than 99% of all fossil discoveries have been made - have merely confirmed and accentuated the overwhelming pattern of the fossils.
- Palaeontologist Steven Stanley concluded, "The known fossil record is not, and never has been, in accord with gradualism".[114]
- Niles Eldredge also admits that "[Evolution] never seems to happen. Assiduous collecting up cliff faces yields zigzags, minor oscillations, and the very occasional slight accumulation of change over millions of years ... When we do see the introduction of evolutionary novelty, it usually shows up with a bang ... Evolution cannot forever be going on some place else. Yet that's how the fossil record has struck many a forlorn paleontologist looking to learn something about evolution".[115]

- Perhaps because fossil reality is so unsupportive, Dawkins has simply declared, "We don't *need* fossils … We are … lucky to have fossils at all [emphasis in original]".[116]
- Yet as Phillip Johnson testily remarked, "Just about anyone who took a college biology course during the last sixty years or so has been led to believe that the fossil record was a bulwark of support for the classic Darwinian thesis, not a liability that had to be explained away".[117]
- A small number of stories of fossil "intermediates" are popularly promoted, such as *Archaeopteryx*, *Tiktaalik* and whale evolution. But these are the exceptions, their chronologies are in disarray, and they simply beg the question, "Where did the additional biological information come from and how did it arise so quickly?"
- Crucially, the waiting-time for the essential specific mutations is far longer than the transition times available according to the putative fossil sequences.
- The overwhelming pattern of the astonishing Cambrian Explosion with its complex animals, and the many other explosive radiations of jawed fish, winged insects, angiosperms, mammals and more, is the *sudden* appearance of novel phyla (body plans) and classes, followed by orders, families, genera and species.
- This disparity-first (sudden appearance of novel phyla) followed by diversity (minor change within species and genera), is the very opposite of the diversity-first pattern predicted by evolutionary theory.
- Contrary to the Darwinian prediction, the fossil record fails with statistically "mathematical certainty" to record the tree-of-life.

Darwin's contemporary and opponent, Louis Agassiz with his encyclopaedic knowledge of fossils recognised that, straightforwardly interpreted, rather than imposing a theory upon the evidence, the fossil record contradicts Darwinian theory. He saw the Darwinian position as an abdication of responsibility, "Both with Darwin and his followers, a great part of the argument is purely negative, thus throwing off the responsibility for proof …".[118]

Agassiz turned out to be right. But at the time Darwin was the ideological victor. Agassiz became 'man overboard'. Perhaps we should 'rescue him in lifeboat six'.

Chapter 7

FAILED PREDICTION #4

Similar embryos imply common ancestry

If anyone should object to or deride the doctrine of the evolution ... of the animated forms which constitute that unbroken organic chain reaching from the beginning of life on the globe to the present times, let him reflect that he has himself passed through modifications the counterpart of those he disputes. For nine months his type of life was aquatic, and during that time he assumed, in succession, many distinct but correlated forms.[1]

John William Draper

Will our survey reveal any iceberg-seared gashes in the hull of this fourth 'watertight compartment'?

First we'll put the significance of embryology in context, including its relationship with homology:
- Was embryology important to Darwin?
- What is homology?
- Ice warnings… is the argument from homology sound?

Then dropping down through the decks, we'll ask these **three key related questions**:
- Does a developing embryo repeat the organism's evolutionary history?
- Does embryonic development provide evidence for universal common descent?
- Do genes provide evidence for universal common descent?

Was embryology important to Darwin?

Darwin came to regard observations in the development of embryos as fundamentally important evidence of evolutionary descent from a common ancestor: "… if [two groups of animals] pass through the same or similar embryonic stages, we may feel assured that they have both descended from the same or nearly similar parents ... Thus, community in embryonic structure reveals community of descent".[2] Having already asserted that he regarded the facts of embryology as "second in importance to none" he further enthuses, "Embryology rises greatly in interest, when we thus look at the embryo as a picture, more or less obscured, of the common parent-form of each great class of animals".[3]

This chapter's opening quote is by John Draper, the late-nineteenth-century Professor of Chemistry at the University of the City of New York, whom we came across in Chapter 2. At the 1860 Huxley-Wilberforce debate in Oxford, Draper had spoken in support of Huxley. His theme included the phrase "Progression of Organisms by Law."[4] Notice that he draws a parallel between (human) *embryonic* development and our assumed *evolutionary* history.

Making a similar connection, the story is told of J.B.S. Haldane's quick-witted response to an unfortunate questioner at one of his public lectures. One version of the anecdote renders the question to the celebrated population geneticist as, "Professor Haldane, even given the billions of years that you say are available for evolution, I simply cannot believe it is possible to go from a single cell to a complicated human body, with its trillions of cells organised into bones and muscles and nerves ... a heart that pumps ... and a brain capable of thinking and talking and feeling". According to the story, the professor's quipped rejoinder was, "But, madam, you did it yourself. And it only took you nine months".[5]

However, a human embryo contains all the information necessary to grow into a human, whereas a primitive single-cell organism doesn't. So, setting aside Haldane's diversionary smokescreen (echoing Draper) - which shrewdly distracted everyone's attention from the foundational question of whether the neo-Darwinian mechanism (Chapter 3) is *capable* of generating the information that specifies the very embryological development to which he alludes (the 'water' relentlessly gushing in from the first three 'watertight compartments' answers that question with a resounding "No") - here we see Haldane explicitly equating *embryological* development (ontogeny) with *evolutionary* development (phylogeny).

So, why were Darwin, Draper, Haldane - and of course today's evolutionists - so excited about embryology? But first we need to survey the topic of *homology* and its significance in relation to embryology.

What is homology?

Darwin asked his readers, "What can be more curious than that the hand of a man ... the leg of the horse, the paddle of the porpoise, and the wing of the bat, should all be constructed on the same pattern, and should include similar bones, in the same relative positions?"[6] Morphologically similar patterns such as these are defined in biology as homologous (from the Greek *homos* "same" and *logos* "ratio, proportion"). See Fig. 7.1.

For Darwin, the fact that the same bone structures are present in all these different animals – yet used for different purposes: walking, paddling and flying – was strong evidence that they have descended from a common ancestor. And the reason he was so excited about embryology was that he believed its evidence would underpin the testimony of homology and therefore his common ancestry claim. How? Well, if organisms were closely related on his tree-of-life, their unfolding embryonic development should follow similar patterns, at least in the early stages, and they should exhibit significant elements

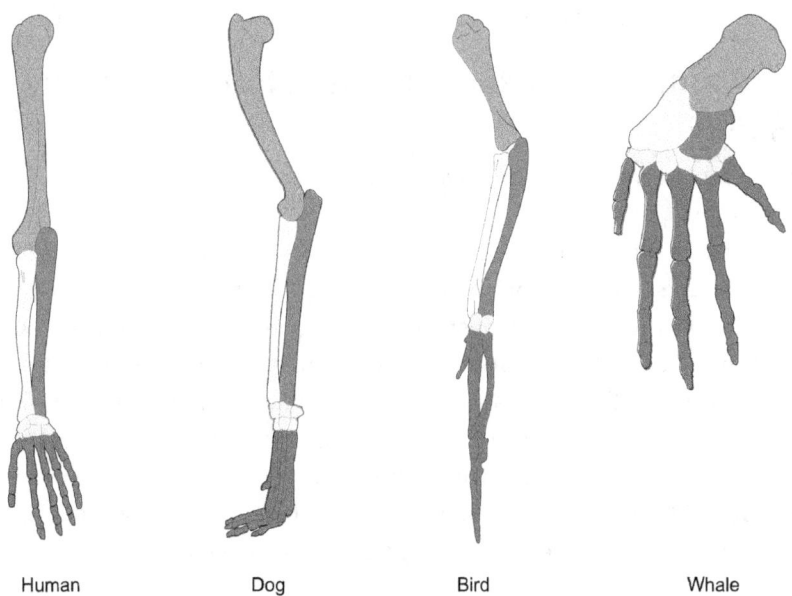

Human   Dog   Bird   Whale

Figure 7.1 Homologous vertebrate forelimbs.

or stages in common. If Darwin had been alive today, and, given the revolutionary advances made in molecular biology in recent times, he would surely also have predicted that homologous morphology would not only emerge from homologous *embryonic* development, but also from homologous *genetic* inheritance. Indeed, in the 1960s, effectively acting as Darwin's surrogates, chemist Linus Pauling and anatomist Emile Zuckerkandl made just such a prediction.[7]

Putting it another way, if we found that species believed to be descended from a common ancestor because of, for example, forelimb homology, also exhibited homologous embryonic development and homologous genes in their DNA, then these three lines of evidence, while not proving common descent, would offer very strong mutual support for such a conclusion. More significantly for our damage-surveying journey below decks in this fourth 'watertight compartment', if these predictions fail, then we will have good reason to doubt the theory of common ancestry. That's to say, if we discover instances of substantial differences in embryonic development and of non-homologous genes – even in the formation of apparently homologous organs – then these will count as evidence against the theory of universal common descent.

Before addressing our three key questions, there are a number of difficulties with the argument from homology that we should explore.

Ice warnings ... is the argument from homology sound?

Here are some problems with the logic of the argument from homology.[8]

First, a reminder is appropriate that we are in the realm of **low-confidence science** according to Stadler's criteria. We can't repeat by experiment the historical descent from a common ancestor – if such descent did indeed happen – and homology is therefore an *observational* rather than an *interventional* study. The evidence is what a detective investigating a crime would describe as "circumstantial".

Second, The argument from homology is in danger of invoking the **logical fallacy** known as *affirming the consequent*. It's of the form:
   a. If it had rained overnight, the grass would be wet.
   b. The grass is wet.
   c. Therefore it rained overnight.

But there are other potential causes of the grass being wet. For instance, the gardener may have watered it in the late evening or early morning. Similarly, the argument from homology *affirms the consequent*:
   a. If universal common descent (UCD) is true, we would expect homologous features in biology.
   b. We do observe homologous features.
   c. Therefore UCD is true.

However, as in the wet grass example, there could be other reasons why animals have features in common. Engineers reuse designs all the time. The classic example is, of course, the wheel. Wheels of various forms appear in bicycles, cars, lorries, aeroplanes, ship's propeller shafts and in toothed, and sometimes bevelled form, in gearboxes. Similarly, electronics engineers use standard components - capacitors, transistors, and microprocessors - in many different design applications: radios, computers, smartphones, washing machines, measurement instrumentation and so on.

Third, even if it were true that homologous patterns, such as forelimb bone structures, had been inherited from a common ancestor, **this would tell us nothing about how the information specifying that structural pattern arose in the first place.**

Fourth, there is the question of similar morphological structures, systems or behaviours that are not - according to evolutionary theory - the result of inheritance from a common ancestor. So for example, echolocation has, we are told, evolved separately in bats, dolphins and even some birds;[9] sight has apparently evolved independently at least forty times in the history of life on earth - the vertebrate camera eye is similar to that of the octopus, yet the putative common ancestor of chordates and molluscs had no vision system: so vertebrates and the octopus have similar features, yet no common ancestry.[10] There are numerous examples of this, including: the remarkable similarities of many placental and marsupial mammals such as the sabre-toothed cat and the thylacosmilus, Fig. 7.2; the Australian marsupial mole and its placental equivalent.[11] Birds, insects and mammals (bats) are all capable of flight, yet their putative common ancestor was earthbound. The evolutionary biologist, Simon Conway Morris, whom we came across in Chapter 6 in connection with his work on the Burgess Shale, is struck by how often adjectives like "'remarkable', 'striking', 'extraordinary', or even 'astonishing' and 'uncanny' are common-

Figure 7.2 Smilodon cat (left); the marsupial thylacosmilus (right). Their sabre-tooth features are strikingly similar, yet not derived from a common ancestor. This phenomenon is sometimes labelled as "convergent evolution".

place"[12] in descriptions of **the emergence of almost identical features not due to common ancestry.** So, rather than "homologous", this phenomenon has been tagged "analogous" or, more commonly, **"convergent evolution"**.

Dawkins, for example, expounds in fascinating detail the physics of sonar and radar to explicate how bats "see in the dark" by analysing echoes from the very high-pitched clicks they generate. He eloquently explains how they identify the position and speed of their insect prey using Doppler and "chirp" radar techniques. Following this impressive science-y sounding elucidation, we might reasonably expect at least a tentative account of *how* bat echolocation evolved by, in Darwin's words, "numerous, successive, slight modifications". But no. Appealing to vast amounts of time, Dawkins simply asserts, "the job was done in gradual evolutionary stages by natural selection."[13] Despite his supreme confidence based on an unshakeable belief in neo-Darwinism, we already know – from the damaged second 'watertight compartment' in Chapter 5 – that the power of the mutations plus natural selection mechanism is severely limited.

It would seem that similar anatomical features are sometimes evidence of UCD and sometimes not. This difficulty has supposedly been resolved by redefining "homology" as "similarity due to common ancestry". But defined in this way **homology can no longer be used as evidence for common descent without begging the very question at issue**. Wells quotes the philosopher of biology Ronald Brady, "By making our explanation [common ancestry] into the definition of the condition to be explained [homology], we express not scientific hypothesis but belief. **We are so convinced that our explanation is true that we no longer need to distinguish it from the situation we were trying to explain** ... [emphasis added]."[14] Notice the echoes here of the *scientific priesthood* mindset (Chapter 2).

Does a developing embryo repeat the organism's evolutionary history?

With this background in homology, we now ask our first key question. Coyne enthusiastically claims the fulfilment of Darwin's prediction: "... all vertebrates begin development in the same way, looking rather like embryonic fish ... Eventually, the dance of development culminates in the very different adult forms of fish, reptiles, birds, amphibians, and mammals. Nevertheless, when development begins they look very much alike".[15] This prompts the question ...

DO EARLY EMBRYOS ALL LOOK SIMILAR? The Prussian-Estonian biologist Karl Ernst von Baer (1792-1876) is notable for his important contributions to our understanding of how embryos develop. He published his four laws of embryology in 1828 in which he aimed to refute two, as he saw it, incorrect views.[16] The first was that of the *preformationists*, who held that the final form of the organism existed from the beginning and simply grew in size during its embryonic development. Think of a newborn human baby. Now shrink it down to a microscopic size of the same form. Preformationists believed embryos developed from the latter. Von Baer's first two laws debunked that belief, summarised here by Pallen, "at an early point in their development the embryos of different species are much harder to distinguish from each other than are the equivalent adult forms."[17] If von Baer was implying that early embryos look almost identical, he wasn't quite correct, as we'll see later, because he wasn't comparing the very earliest stages of development. But his key point that animal embryos do not look like miniature versions of their respective adult body forms is not controversial. Von Baer's third and fourth laws countered what had become known as the (erroneous) Meckel-Serres law – that embryos pass through successive stages representing the adult forms of less complex organisms. As we'll see, Darwinian evolution became entangled with this "recapitulation" theory. Von Baer, on the other hand, held (correctly) that instead of passing through other forms, embryos rapidly differentiate from one another.

In 1866, Ernst Haeckel, Darwin's first and perhaps greatest convert in Germany, promoted what became known as his "biogenetic law": *ontogeny recapitulates phylogeny*. As Prothero (whom we came across in Chapter 6) puts it, this rather opaque language, "is simply a fancy way of saying embryonic development ("ontogeny") repeats ("recapitulates") evolutionary history ("phylogeny")".[18] Haeckel's law – basically a resurrection of the Meckel-Serres law which von Baer had refuted – made the claim that as, for example, a human embryo develops in its mother's womb, it repeats its evolutionary history,

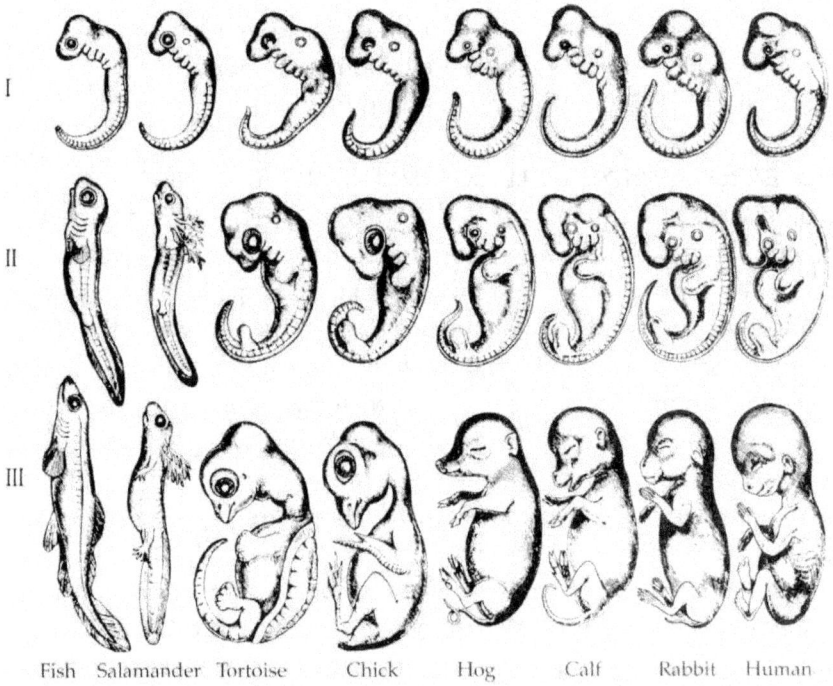

Figure 7.3 In a figure entitled, "The evidence from embryology", Prothero uses Haeckel's discredited 1874 drawings to claim that "all vertebrates start out with a fish-like body plan early in embryology, including the predecessors of gills and long tails". See main text.

7 – FAILED PREDICTION #4: Similar embryos imply common ancestry

transitioning through the adult forms of fish, amphibians and reptiles on its way to becoming a mammalian human. As part of Prothero's exposition of embryology, he includes a diagram which claims to compare the embryonic development of eight vertebrates including fish, tortoise, rabbit and human, Fig. 7.3. The legend in his diagram informs us that "… all vertebrates start out with a very fish-like body plan early in embryology, including the predecessors of gills and a long tail. As they develop, many lose their fish-like features on their way to becoming reptiles, birds and mammals".[19] Writing in 2007, Prothero attributes[20] the drawings in his diagram to G.J. Romanes, a publication by the latter in 1896. But Romanes (correctly) acknowledges[21] Haeckel, who produced and published the original drawings in 1874 in support of his biogenetic law. Now why is this important? It turns out that **no one, in more than 120 years, had published drawings that challenged Haeckel's.**

In 1997 Michael Richardson and his team realised this and set about collecting and photographing embryos representing – crucially – a significantly wider range of vertebrate animals than Haeckel had portrayed.[22] The team focused on what's known as the *tailbud* stage which corresponds to the first row in Fig. 7.3. Richardson first notes that some of Haeckel's contemporaries had challenged his drawings. In 1894, for example, a Cambridge University embryologist, Adam Sedgwick, contradicted Haeckel, "There is no stage of development in which the unaided naked eye would fail to distinguish between [vertebrate embryos] … a blind man could distinguish them".[23] What did Richardson's research reveal?

The ebullient Haeckel had promoted his drawings with missionary zeal and Richardson begins by recognising that these drawings represented the primary source of putative evidence that embryos pass through a common stage in which they look virtually identical, "Haeckel's drawings of the external morphology of various vertebrates remain the most comprehensive comparative data purporting to show a conserved [very similar] stage".[24] And their conclusion? "Our survey seriously undermines the credibility of Haeckel's drawings …"[25] **They discovered that there is no stage at which embryos of different species are identical** and that these embryonic variations often (unsurprisingly) foreshadow differences in the adult body plan. Fig. 7.4 illustrates what real embryos look like.

Figure 7.4

Real embryonic development documented photographically by Michael Richardson's team.

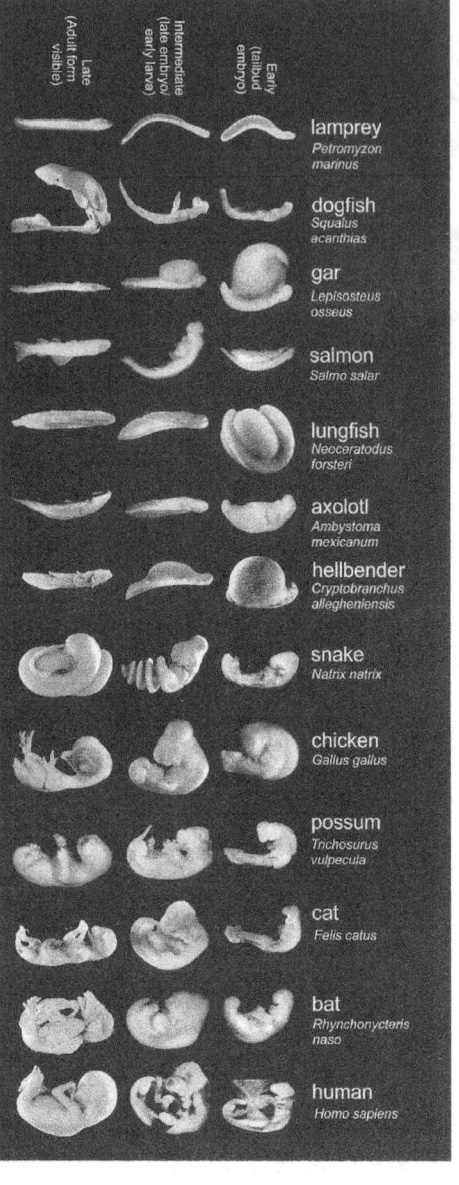

In addition to differences in body size and in the sequence and timing of organ development, the team found significant differences in:[26]

- Body plan – for example, the presence or absence of paired limb buds.
- The number of units in repeating series, such as the somites (transitory or temporary embryonic segments of the embryo) – varying from 11 to over 60 in the Puerto Rican tree frog and blind worm (a reptile) respectively.

Haeckel had depicted the branchial apparatus (the region of the embryo in which gills – in fish – develop) as being virtually identical in all species at his stage 1 (top row in Fig. 7.3). Richardson et al. point out that this is contrary to their own findings. They go further, **"Haeckel's drawings are inaccurate and we have provided persuasive evidence that this is the case** [emphasis added]".[27]

Their paper includes a revealing insight by Goldschmidt writing in 1956 about Haeckel's influence.

> *The present generation cannot imagine the role he played in his time, far beyond his actual scientific performance ... Haeckel's easy hand at drawing made him improve on nature and put more into the illustrations than he saw ... one had the impression that he first made a sketch from nature and then drew an ideal picture as he saw it in his mind.*[28]

In other words, **Haeckel**, so convinced that his biogenetic law must be true, **was able to legitimise** – at least in his own mind – **falsifying the evidence**. Here we see a classic instantiation of Stadler's latter three criteria of low-confidence science: overstated confidence, unsubstantiated assumptions and plenty of opportunity for bias. It's relatively easy to weave a seemingly plausible story around a *historical* event, one which cannot be repeated and consequently such a story is difficult to falsify. But in this case Haeckel has been caught out, because making drawings, or better still, taking photographs of developing embryos, is a series of experiments that *is repeatable*. Nevertheless, ever since Haeckel, most biologists have been unquestioning in their acceptance of his drawings, presumably owing to what's known as "confirmation bias" – they too were committed to *Evolution* and therefore to any evidence that *appeared* to support it. Richardson is surprised that biologists have adopted, without proof, Haeckel's claim of a common virtually identical stage for all embryos: "One puzzling feature of the debate in this field is that while many authors have written a conserved embryonic stage, no one has cited any comparative data in support of the idea. **It is almost as though the phylotypic [near identical] stage is regarded as a biological concept for which no proof is needed** [emphasis added]".[29] Von Baer, on the other hand, did not believe that fish, amphibians, reptiles, birds and mammals had descended from a common ancestor. His concern, as recorded by historian Timothy Lenoir, was that **Darwinists had "already accepted the Darwinian evolutionary hypothesis as true before they set to the task of observing embryos"**.[30]

HAECKEL'S DRAWINGS DIDN'T BEGIN AT THE BEGINNING.

Haeckel's drawings misrepresented reality in three ways:

1. He selected examples which best represented his theory.
2. He 'doctored' the drawings.
3. The earliest stages of development were missing because little was known about them at the time.

In the *Descent of Man*, Darwin includes a similarly misleading diagram purporting to represent a "very early period" of development.[31] Neither did von Baer take account of the earliest stages. In 1996, Rudolf Raff clarified this, "It should be noted that von Baer's laws provide an incomplete description of development in that von Baer considered the [tailbud] stage to represent early development. In fact he was dealing only with the later half of ontogeny".[32] The significance will become clear shortly when we explore our second key question.

SOMETHING FISHY? On one occasion when the author was discussing embryology with a biologist, the latter explained that the reason newborn human babies are able to 'swim' when submerged in water is because the embryo passed through a fish stage during its development in the womb. Where does this, clearly widely believed, idea come from? Here's Dawkins on the topic, "... **five-week human embryos can be regarded as little pink fishes, with gills** [emphasis added]".[33] Similarly, in his textbook *Evolutionary Biology*, Douglas Futuyma has this, "Early in development, human embryos are almost indistinguishable from those of fishes, and briefly display **gill slits** [emphasis added]".[34] Is this true? At the most similar tailbud stage, all vertebrate embryos possess a series of folds in the neck region or pharynx. Wells describes them: 'The convex parts of the folds are called pharyngeal "arches" or "ridges" and the concave parts are called pharyngeal "clefts" or "pouches"'.[35] But are these "pouches" gills? The British embryologist Lewis Wolpert offers a corrective: "A higher animal, like a mammal, passes through an embryonic stage when there are structures that resemble the gill clefts of fish. But this resemblance is illusory and the structures in the mammalian embryo only resemble the structures in the *embryonic* fish that will give rise to gills [emphasis in original]".[36] **The pharyngeal arches are not gills - even in fish embryos at this stage**. In fish they will *later* develop into gill structures. But in reptiles, mammals and birds they will develop into completely different structures, such as the inner ear and parathyroid gland.[37] **There is therefore no justification for references to "gills" or "gill slits" in human embryos.** Echoing von Baer, **it's simply a reading of an evolutionary prediction back into the evidence.**

In terms of a newborn baby's ability to 'swim' - which it loses within six months - it would seem that adherence to the evolutionary paradigm induces blindness to the obvious and more parsimonious explanation: that the baby has been comfortably floating around in amniotic fluid (not breathing) for almost nine months.

HAECKEL'S BIOGENETIC LAW IS FALSE BUT THE MYTH LIVES ON.
The fact that embryos are far from identical at any point, including from their earliest stages, as we'll soon discover, leaves in tatters Haeckel's claim that *ontology recapitulates phylogeny*. Richardson clarifies the

logic here, "The drawings were intended to demonstrate Haeckel's recapitulation theory or biogenetic law. A conserved stage was a necessary part of this theory because evolution was claimed to progress principally by the terminal addition of new adult stages to the end of ancestral developmental sequences".[38] We can therefore conclude from Richardson's findings that **there is no evidence that the embryological development of a species repeats its alleged evolutionary history.** In spite of this, Haeckel's drawings "are still widely reproduced in textbooks and review articles, and continue to exert a significant influence on the development of ideas in this field".[39] Prothero's *Evolution: What the Fossils Say* textbook[40] provides a perturbing example of Richardson's prophetic remark that biologists have adopted the nearly identical embryonic stage without proof. What is particularly shocking, written ten years after Richardson's work, is Prothero's assertion that Haeckel's "errors and over-simplifications" do "not change the overall fact that the sequence of all vertebrate embryos show the same patterns in the early stages, and all of them go through a "fish-like" stage with pharyngeal pouches ... and a long fish-like tail ...".[41] Even more disturbing perhaps, is that in his diagram, he continues to promote Haeckel's drawings – and not Richardson's – while citing Romanes as the source and mentioning only von Baer in the diagram caption. Could it be that he wished to disguise the fact that they were Haeckel's drawings, aware that they had been discredited? Or perhaps he was simply following Futuyma who, in his 1998 *Evolutionary Biology* textbook, presented Haeckel's incorrect drawings, claiming that they demonstrate von Baer's law and similarly attributing them to Romanes.[42] But Prothero certainly, and arguably also Futuyma, should have known that Haeckel's drawings had been called out.

Though Jerry Coyne concedes that there is no recapitulation of the *adult* forms of our alleged evolutionary ancestors, nevertheless he also assures us that each vertebrate undergoes development in a series that recapitulates ancestral *embryonic* stages, he claims "a lizard begins development resembling an embryonic fish, then somewhat later an embryonic amphibian, and finally an embryonic reptile. Mammals go through the same sequence, but add on the final stage of an embryonic mammal".[43] Yet we know from Richardson's work and that of others that this is false. Meantime, **Coyne, Dawkins, Prothero,**

Futuyma and other biologists continue to promote this myth which the evidence contradicts.

So then, despite the fact that Haeckel's biogenetic law has been refuted and discredited, its misleading influence lives on into recent times. This 'fake news', which fails to provide corroborative evidence for *Evolution* from embryology, has been recycled as 'science' for almost 150 years in textbooks and review articles, influencing with its falsehoods many generations and countless individuals.

The answer, then, to our first key question "Does a developing embryo repeat the organism's evolutionary history?" is "No".

Does embryonic development provide evidence for universal common descent?

We continue our survey of this fourth 'watertight compartment' with the second key question.

Sequence was crucial in the building of RMS *Titanic* in Harland & Wolff's shipyard. First the keel was laid and then the double bottom with its "tank top" was built out on either side of the keel. This was followed by fitting of the rib-like transverse framing to which steel plates were riveted to form the hull. Next the decks were added and the basic superstructure assembled. Boilers, engines and other out-fittings were added after the ship had been launched, and finally the three massive propellers were fitted in the Thompson Dry Dock. Modern shipbuilding follows a different pattern. Instead of laying down a keel and constructing the hull along its entire length, ships are assembled in modules, effectively vertical slices through the hull. The completed sections are then joined together end-to-end. Clearly hierarchical levels of planning, sequencing, timing, procurement and logistical support are crucial to the success of any such enterprise.

What about embryonic development? It begins with a single fertilised cell which then divides successively. As the organism's body plan emerges, cells develop into different tissue types and different organ types, finally becoming the fully formed animal. The human body has hundreds of different cell types. Leisola and Witt stress that position, sequence and timing are essential, "the right types of cells have to be made at the right times and brought to the right places … During the development of a human, for instance, embryonic red cells contain hemoglobin that is different from that in adult red cells. Brain cells produce enzymes involved in transmitting nerve impulses, while intestinal cells produce enzymes to degrade food in the alimentary tract. These proteins function in totally different environments and have completely different tasks".[44]

ARE THE EARLIEST STAGES OF DEVELOPMENT SIMILAR? Fig. 7.5(a), (b) and (c) illustrate four stages of development leading up to that "first" stage in Haeckel's drawings, the tailbud (and we already know from Richardson's work that the timing of most stages varies amongst species). The six main classes of vertebrate are represented. Only a very brief overview is given here and only of the first two stages. The interested reader will find much more detail on David Swift's website.[45] The central purpose here is to illustrate how *different* the very early development processes are in different classes of vertebrate.

During "cleavage" the initial embryonic cell divides into a population of cells, without noticeably growing in size, forming the "blastula". Even this initial stage of cleavage is carried out in different

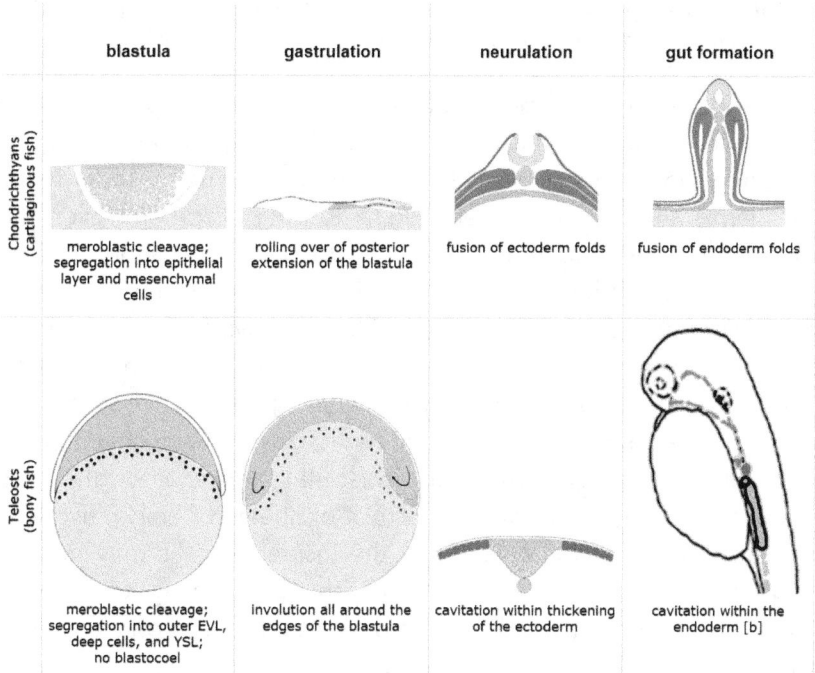

Figure 7.5(a) Four early stages of embryonic development (proceeding from left to right). These occur prior to Haeckel's "first" stage. Here we see the sequence for the embryos of cartilaginous and bony fish. See main text.

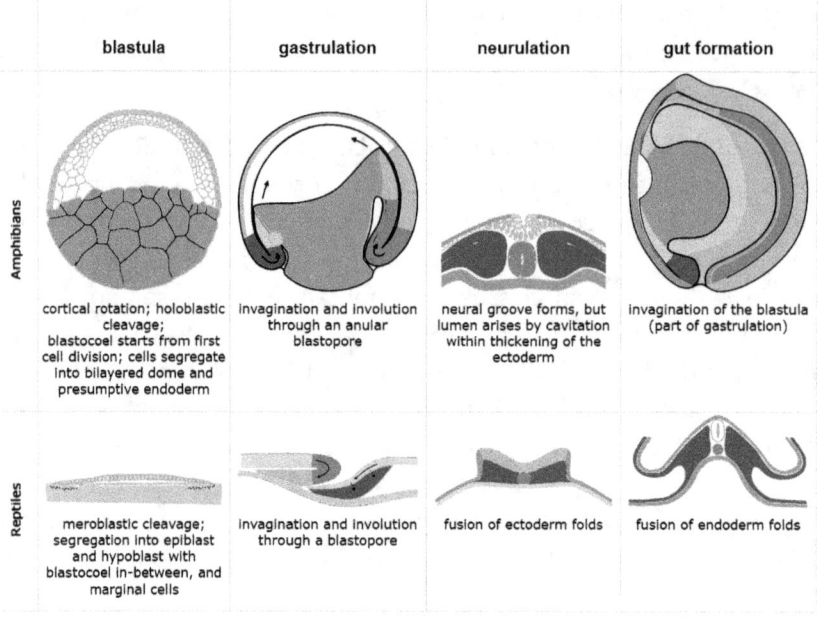

Figure 7.5(b) The same stages of embryonic development as in Fig. 7.5(a), but for amphibians and reptiles. See main text.

ways, and the resulting cells move and segregate in distinct ways to form the very different blastulas. The next phase, "gastrulation", is a key stage in which the three germ layers form (ectoderm, mesoderm and endoderm) and the body plan begins to take shape. Yet even this occurs in radically different ways. Even the subsequent formation of the neural tube (the beginning of the nervous system) and early alimentary canal form in substantially different ways. In *Evolution Under The Microscope*, David Swift enlarges on this, "there is considerable – and surprising – diversity in the ways in which gastrulation occurs, even between what are generally regarded as closely related groups of organisms. In many cases the [gastrula] arises through deep invagination of one side of the blastula, or sheets of cells may move over the surface of the blastula to the inside, or cells may migrate individually from the outside through the intervening cells to the inside, or a combination of these processes. Then not only are there different ways in which the gastrula forms, but there is also remarkable variety in which parts of the gastrula develop into apparently homologous tissues".[46] By way of example, Swift then quotes from Sir Gavin de Beer.

7 – FAILED PREDICTION #4: Similar embryos imply common ancestry

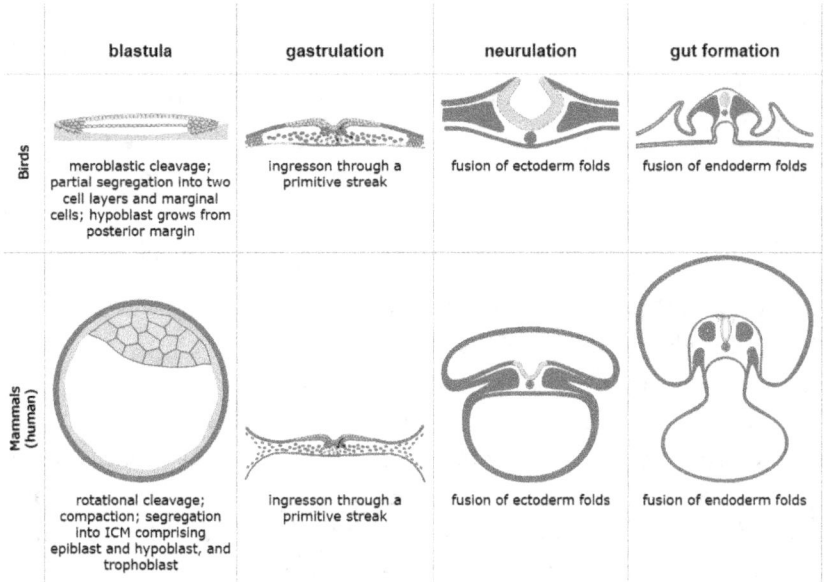

Figure 7.5(c) The same stages of embryonic development as in Fig. 7.5(a), but for birds and humans. See main text.

> Structures as obviously homologous as the alimentary canal in all vertebrates can be formed from the roof of the embryonic gut cavity (sharks), floor (lampreys, newts), roof and floor (frogs), or from the lower layer of the embryonic disc, the blastoderm, that floats on the top of heavily yolked eggs (reptiles and birds).[47]

If these vertebrate classes had all descended from a common ancestor, we would expect that they would be most similar in their earliest embryonic stages of development – that's what Darwin was excited about. Yet, it's clear from the diagrams that these **example species of cartilaginous fish, bony fish, amphibians, reptiles, birds and mammals are each unique. There is no common pattern**.

Sheena Tyler of the John Ray Research Field Station summarises the key question, "**How can different early cleavage patterns be traced to a common ancestor? The proposed existence of such ancestors appears to be imposed on the evidence rather than emerging from it** [emphasis added]".[48] She goes on, "… cleavage patterns, cell fates, and developmental mechanisms can be radically different between different forms of animals during these early [embryonic] stages".[49] She quotes from Eric Davidson's conclusion, "the differences among the taxa in their modes of development are anything but trivial and superficial".[50]

Günter Bechly and Stephen Meyer similarly affirm that 'It turns out ... that different classes of vertebrates do not progress through similar phases of embryological development. Yet, Darwin regarded alleged similarities in vertebrate development as "the strongest single class of facts in favour of common descent"'.[51]

But what about slightly later stages of embryonic development?

DO HOMOLOGOUS FEATURES ARISE FROM HOMOLOGOUS DEVELOPMENT PROCESSES IN THE EMBRYO?

Vertebrates, for example, are believed to exhibit homologous features due to descent from a common ancestor. The most obvious homologous feature of vertebrates is, of course, their eponymous skeletal vertebrae. According to *Evolution*, all vertebrates have descended from a common ancestor, so the theory would predict that the embryonic development of their backbones would follow a common pattern inherited from that ancestor. Not so, it turns out. Different classes develop by distinct routes. A rod-like structure called the notochord acts as the focus for development of the vertebrae in

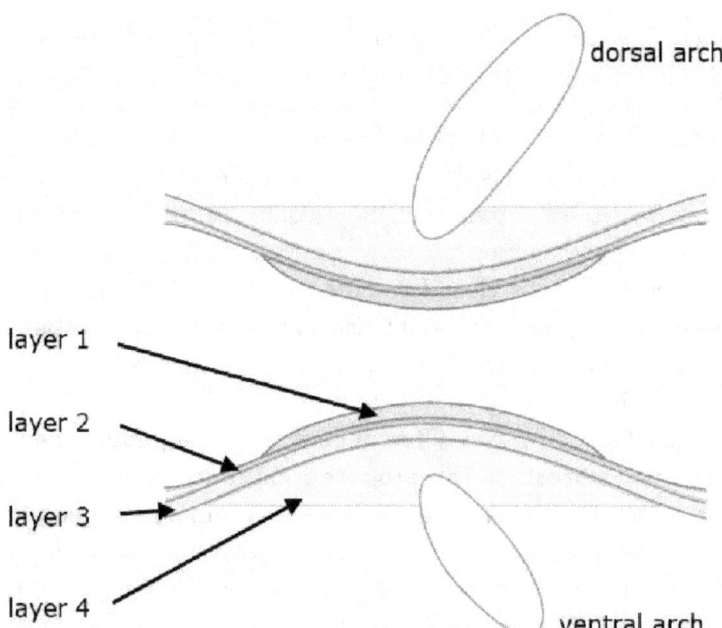

Figure 7.6 A longitudinal section through a teleost (bony fish) vertebra developing in the embryo. See the main text for identification of the layers.

7 - FAILED PREDICTION #4: Similar embryos imply common ancestry

each type of embryo, but its role differs greatly in different classes. David Swift describes examples of the major differences.[52]

In most fish (teleosts), the innermost part of the vertebrae arise directly from the notochord. Cartilaginous elements (layer 1 in Fig. 7.6.[53]) form to produce the inner layer of each vertebra. Next a layer of collagen fibres encases the notochord extending over its full length. A layer of dense bone is then deposited. Meanwhile above and below the notochord dorsal and ventral arches of cartilage form. Finally a fourth layer of bone is deposited connecting to the arches.

In reptile, bird and mammal (tetrapod) embryos the vertebrae develop quite differently, however, see Fig. 7.7. Here the neural tube which will develop into the spinal cord forms running parallel to the notochord. But this time, the vertebrae do not form from the notochord itself. Instead, they arise from pairs of somites (segments of the embryo), one on either side of the neural tube running along its length, Fig. 7.7(a). The somite cells differentiate into three layers: dermatome, myotome and sclerotome which develop respectively into connective tissue, muscle and the vertebrae themselves, Fig. 7.7(b). The sclerotome layer migrates towards and envelops the notochord to

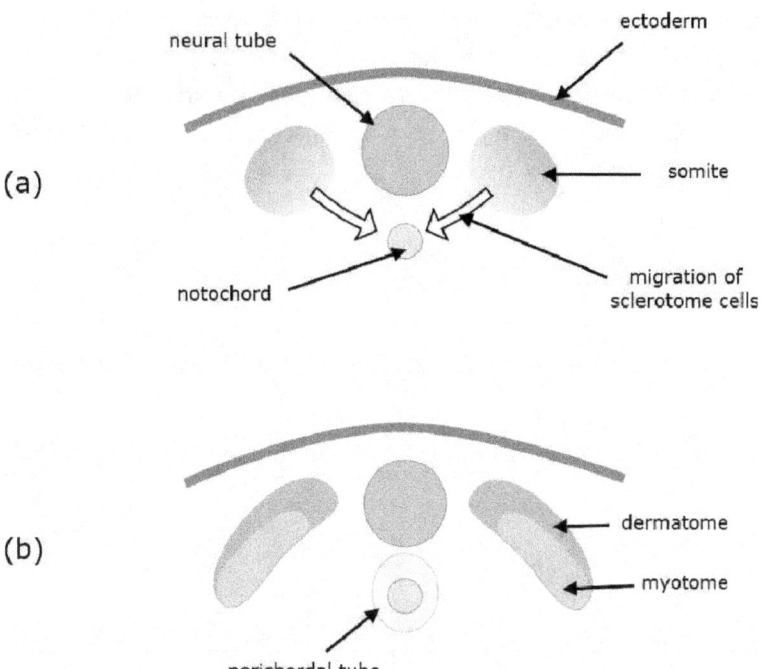

Figure 7.7 How reptile, bird and mammal vertebrae develop in the embryo (longitudinal section). See main text.

form the perichordal tube. One surprising feature of tetrapod embryology is known as re-segmentation. Each vertebra forms not simply from the two somites on either side of the notochord. Rather each somite spilts into two halves, one posterior (tail-ward) and one anterior (head-ward), Fig. 7.8 (b). Each half then combines with half of the somite adjacent to it, Fig. 7.8 (c). In this way, each vertebra has developed from four re-segmented somites. The notochord contributes slightly to intervertebral discs but otherwise disappears. The vertebrae form as cartilaginous tissue in the first instance which later ossifies.

Cartilaginous fish, such as the shark, are different again. Here each pair of somites produces four pairs of cartilaginous tissue called arcualia. Each pair of arcualia then becomes a specific part of a given vertebra as it emerges, see Fig. 7.9 (a) and (b).

Amphibians (such as frogs) are tetrapods, but they exhibit yet another variation. Fig. 7.10[54] compares more typical tetrapod embryology with that of the amphibian *Xenopus laevis*. In the former the somites are a composite of an outer dermatome layer and an inner myotome layer. The hollow in the middle is called a myocoel. In amphibians, however, the somites form exclusively from the myotome layer, the dermatome retains its characteristic as a distinct layer and there is no myocoel. One further variation in the amphibian is that, in the course of their formation, somite cells rotate through 90 degrees

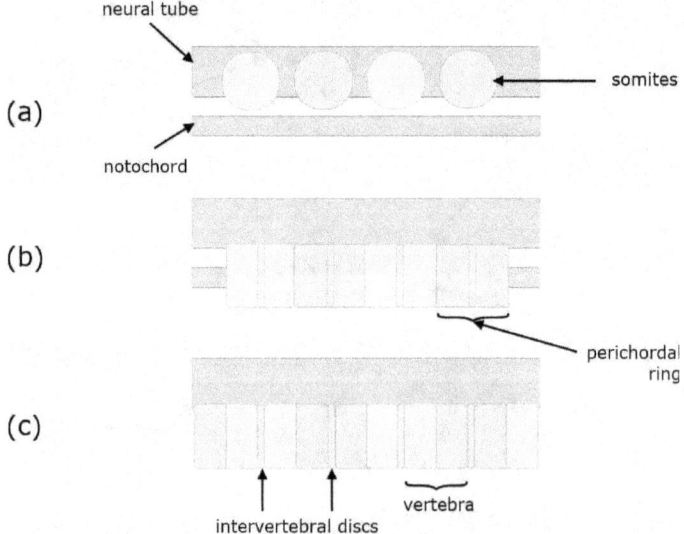

Figure 7.8 Re-segmentation of somites in tetrapod vertebra formation (side view). See main text.

7 – FAILED PREDICTION #4: Similar embryos imply common ancestry

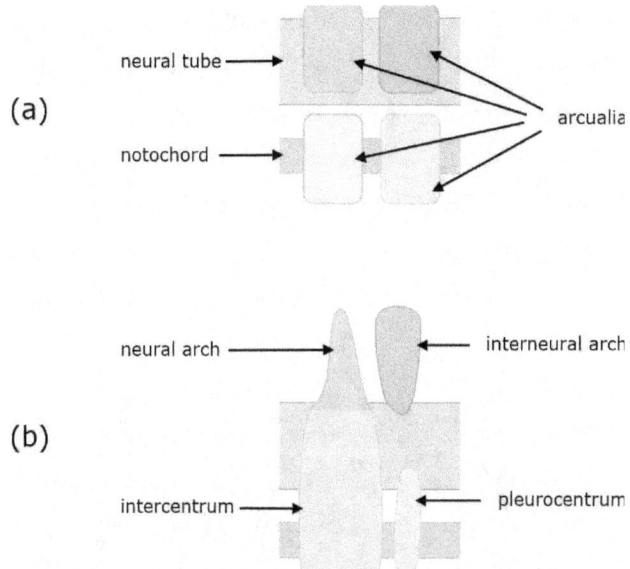

Figure 7.9 Side view of vertebra development in cartilaginous fish (e.g. shark). Each of the arcualia shown is paired with another on the far (hidden) side of the neural tube and notochord respectively.

to run parallel to the neural tube rather than perpendicular to it in the typical tetrapod case.

We have here a clear example of a failed prediction. According to the theory mammals evolved in turn from reptiles, amphibians and lobe-finned fish – part of the circumstantial evidence being homologous skeletal structures. Yet here we see **a key feature of these vertebrates – their backbone – that develops in different ways in their respective embryos. Their embryonic formation is clearly non-homologous.** This is evidence of a huge hole in RMS *Evolution*'s hull. Or to introduce another nautical metaphor, a single broken link in a chain is sufficient to set a ship adrift from its anchor.

As we discovered in Chapter 5 from the work of Ann Gauger *et al.*, *how* could the coordinated sets of mutations, needed to effect these startling embryonic developmental differences, have evolved by, "a series of numerous, successive, slight modifications"? And given that the adult morphologies are so similar, *why* would natural selection select for such different sets of mutations?

Another defining homologous feature of tetrapods is the pentadactyl limb with its five digits (fingers and toes), Fig. 7.1. Yet frogs and humans, for example, differ in how their digits develop in the

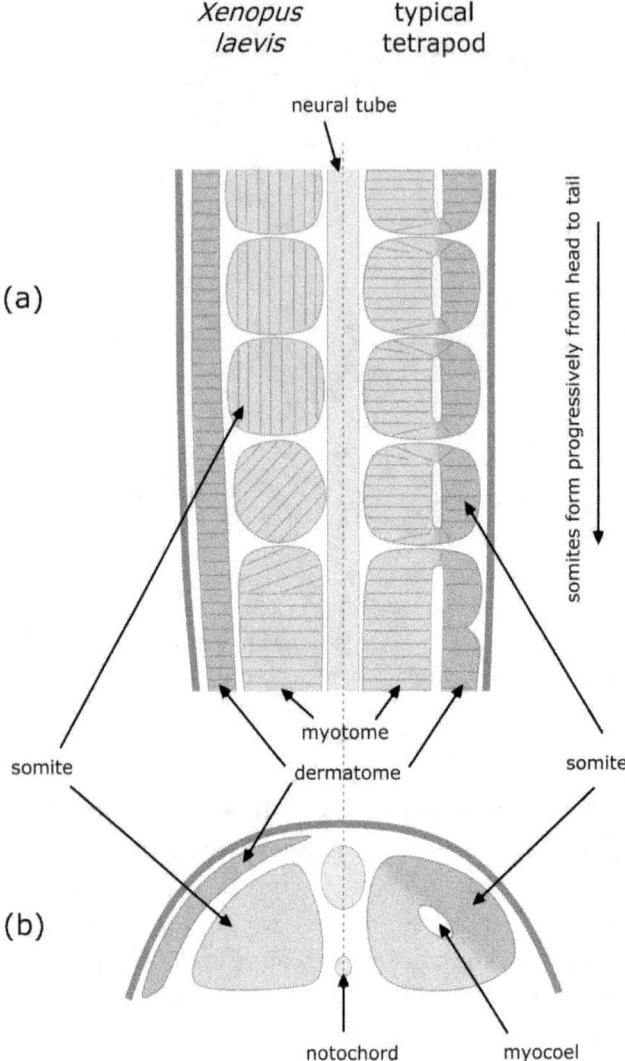

Figure 7.10 Comparison of vertebrae development in amphibians (*Xenopus laevis*) versus a more typical tetrapod. (a) Longitudinal section showing progressive formation of somites. (b) Cross-section through newly formed somites.

embryo. **Ironically its the frog that ends up with webbed hands and feet, yet in the embryo it's the human** whose hands and feet begin as plate-like shapes **with effectively webbing between the fingers and toes**. Apoptosis (cell death) then removes the 'webbing' tissue between the digits. Whereas in frogs, the fingers begin as buds which extend outwards from the palm of the 'hand', each individual digit growing by cell division.⁵⁵ The pentadactyl forelimb itself often develops from different body segments in different classes of vertebrate: from the trunk segments 2, 3, 4 and 5 in the newt (amphibian), segments 6, 7, 8 and 9 in the lizard (reptile) and from segments 13, 14, 15, 16, 17 and 18 in humans (mammal).⁵⁶

Continuing with the vertebrate skeleton theme, the majority of fish existing today are ray-finned as opposed to lobe-finned. Yet although both are assumed to be descended from a common ancestor, the skull of the ray-finned fish is quite distinct not only from that of lobe-finned fish, but also from all other vertebrates. Swift elaborates, "[Webster and Webster] pointed out that the actinopterygian (ray-finned) skull is markedly different from any other type of vertebrate, past or present, commenting that 'Although many of these bones are given the same names as bones of other vertebrate skulls, the homologies are dubious at best'".⁵⁷

Günter Wagner of Yale University admits that "**The disturbingly many and deep problems associated with any attempt to identify the biological basis of homology have been presented repeatedly** [emphasis added]".⁵⁸ The answer, then, to our second key question "Does embryonic development provide evidence for universal common descent?" is "No".

Do genes provide evidence for universal common descent?

This brings us to our final key question. We descend one more deck in our investigative quest. Speaking of "descent", in the *Ancestor's Tale*, Dawkins conducts us on a metaphorical pilgrimage, beginning with *Homo sapiens*, and tracing the putative evolutionary tree-of-life in the reverse direction back in time to the single-celled last universal common ancestor (LUCA). Along the way we are introduced to what he calls "concestors" – convergent ancestors – such as the assumed common ancestor of all vertebrates. He regards the fact that the same genetic code is common to most species as "near conclusive proof that all organisms are descended from a single common ancestor".⁵⁹

> We can be very sure there really is a single concestor of all surviving life forms on this planet. The evidence is that all that have ever been examined share ... the same genetic code; and the genetic code is too detailed, in arbitrary aspects of its complexity, to have been invented twice.⁶⁰

(Dawkins does however admit that the genetic code is, in fact, not quite universal; many variants in the genetic code are known to exist.)[61]

His logic here is another example of the fallacy, *affirming the consequent*. There could be another explanation. Via an email conversation, Phillip Johnson quizzed Dawkins, "On what basis are you so confident that the hypothetical common ancestor of lobsters and humans is not merely an artefact of evolutionary theory but actually lived on earth?". Responding, he asserted, "the reason we know for certain we are all related, including bacteria, is the universality of the genetic code …" Johnson, recognising the fallacy, as well as Dawkins' philosophical commitment to materialism and reductionism, commented, "biochemical similarities, like the musical similarities in Beethoven's symphonies, may be evidence of a common designer rather than a common physical ancestor".[62] In Johnson's analogy, Beethoven's symphonies all make use of crotchets, quavers and triplets, just as all genomes code for amino acids in an (almost) universal way. Musical similarities don't explain away the need for Beethoven. Equally, and with the eye of an engineer, a common designer could be the correct explanation for biochemical similarities.

Back in the *Ancestor's Tale*, a few lines later Dawkins lets slip, "If we now were to discover a life form sufficiently alien to have a completely different genetic code, it would be the most exciting discovery in my adult lifetime …".[63] This seems rather smug, given that neither Dawkins nor anyone else has offered a plausible explanation of how the genetic code came into existence in the first place by, "numerous, successive, slight modifications". Francis Crick's description of it as a "frozen accident"[64] (prophetic of RMS *Evolution*'s collision with the 'molecular biology iceberg' perhaps!) would seem to be an indicator of evolutionary desperation. Meantime Dawkins' slip suggests that he would be "certain" of *Evolution*, whether or not the genetic code was, in fact, universal. RMS *Evolution* just keeps sailing on. It's unsinkable after all.

But, do genes provide evidence that universal common descent is true? If a universal common ancestor did "actually live on earth", we ought to be able to construct a tree-of-life by comparing gene sequences that code for proteins common to many organisms and inferring what mutations would have been required to occur if there had been a common line of descent. The smaller the number of assumed mutational differences in a given common gene, the more closely related any two species could be inferred to be. Then we could compare our *genetic* tree-of-life with the orthodox *phylogenetic* tree – the conventional tree derived from anatomical and morphological similarities. **Coyne explains** that "Until about thirty years ago, biologists used visible features like anatomy and mode of reproduction to reconstruct the ancestry of living species ... But **now we have a powerful new and independent way to establish ancestry: we can look directly at the genes themselves** [emphasis added]". He goes on to claim that there is congruence between tree-of-life relationships found in the genes and those already derived from anatomy, "both the visible traits of organisms and their DNA sequences usually give the same information about evolutionary relationships".[65] Coyne here rehearses Zuckerkandl and Pauling's prediction. But was their prediction fulfilled? And is Coyne's claim confirmed by the evidence?

DIFFERENT GENES – DIFFERENT TREES.

Many papers published in *Nature*, *New Scientist* and other prominent scientific journals within the last couple of decades provide evidence that the congruence between molecular and phylogenetic trees-of-life may be less secure than Coyne has claimed. Here are some examples:

- In a paper entitled, "Understanding phylogenetic incongruence" Liliana Dávalos *et al.* have this to say: "Incongruence between phylogenies [trees-of-life] derived from morphological *versus* molecular analyses, and between trees based on different subsets of molecular sequences has become pervasive as datasets have expanded rapidly in both characters and species [emphasis in original]".[66] In other words **phylogenies derived from genes often disagree with phylogenies based on morphology**.

- Salichos and Rokas from the University of Vanderbilt examined 1,070 genes in 23 different species of yeast. It had been hoped that just one gene tree could be inferred, but they "identified 1,070 distinct gene trees".[67] Commenting on this finding, Yale evolutionary biologist, Michael Donoghue admitted, "**We** are trying to figure out the phylogenetic relationships of 1.8 million species and **can't even sort out 20 [types of] yeast** [emphasis added]".[68]

- Degnan and Rosenberg of the University of Michigan note that "[w]ith the increasing abundance of molecular data" there is a "recognition that evolutionary trees from different genes often have conflicting branching patterns ...". They also cite other studies that have found, "**considerable discordance across gene trees**: studies of hominids ... pines ... cichlids ... finches ... grasshoppers ... and fruit flies ... have all detected genealogical discordance so widespread that no single tree topology predominates [emphasis added]".[69]

- Trisha Gura reported in *Nature* magazine that "[b]**attles between molecules and morphology are being fought across the entire tree of life** [emphasis added]".[70]
- According to Teeling and Hedges of University College Dublin and Pennsylvania State University respectively, there is disagreement between palaeontologists and molecular evolutionists over which placental mammal tree is correct (if any): "Untangling the root of the tree of placental mammals has been nearly an impossible task. The good news is that only three possibilities are seriously considered. The bad news is that all three are seriously considered".[71] Palaeontologists "favour" sloths and anteaters giving rise to all the others, while molecular evolutionists "favour" elephants, hyraxes and tenrecs.
- Michael Syvanen compared 2000 genes that are common to humans, frogs, sea squirts, sea urchins, fruit flies and nematodes. His idea was to use the gene sequences to examine the relationships among the six animal groups and infer an evolutionary tree. He expected this to agree with the conventional morphological tree: "He failed". **Not only could he not identify a confirmatory tree, but also different genes implied different trees**, "The problem was that different genes told contradictory evolutionary stories".[72] With sea squirts, for example, 50% of its genes clustered with chordates, which was to be expected, but the other 50% correlated with sea urchins of the phylum echinodermata. Such a mosaic-like pattern was not predicted by evolution.
- A peculiar "chunk" of DNA was discovered in the genomes of the mouse, rat, bushbaby, little brown bat, tenrec, opossum, anole lizard and African clawed frog – "but not in 25 others, including humans, elephants, chickens and fish ... As ever more multicellular genomes are sequenced, **ever more incongruous bits of DNA are turning up** [emphasis added]".[73]

ORPHAN GENES. One of the discoveries that has been frustrating for geneticists on a mission to construct genetic trees – phylogenies – is that as more and more genomes are sequenced, **perhaps 10% of the protein-coding DNA of each species is turning out to be unique**. In 1999 Fischer and Eisenberg compared the genomes of a dozen bacteria and found that between 4% and 22% of their protein-coding regions were unique. Protein-coding regions are also known as "open reading frames" so they referred to these unique regions as "ORFs" or "ORFans". **This level of uniqueness is entirely unexpected** on the assumption of a gradually branching evolutionary tree pattern. Fischer and Eisenberg ask, "Why, if proteins in different organisms have descended from common ancestral proteins by duplication and adaptive variation, do so many today show no similarity to each other?"[74]

Further studies have confirmed the ORFan pattern. By 2014 evolutionary biologist Seirian Sumner explained, "We have sequence data for algae, pythons, green sea turtles, puffer fish, pied flycatchers, platypus, koala, bonobos, giant pandas, bottle-nosed dolphins ... and each new genome brings with it a suite of unique genes. Twenty percent of genes in nematodes are unique. Each lineage of ants contains about 4000 novel genes ...".[75]

Because these novel genes would frustrate the identification of phylogenetic trees, studies have labelled them as "uninformative" and ignored them, using only data that exhibits genetic commonality. Jonathan Wells points out that "counter-informative" might be a better description. He summarises the typical approach to constructing phylogenetic trees as, "(1) Assume that common ancestry is true. (2) Cherry-pick the data to construct a tree that includes various organisms. (3) Conclude that these organisms are related to a common ancestor".[76]

EVO-DEVO. The challenge of how to explain large-scale macro-evolution – change of body plan – came to a head in the early 1990s. One major focus, then, was upon the mechanisms involved in embryonic development. The biologist Brian Hall gave birth to a new discipline: evolutionary developmental biology, or *evo-devo* for short. The thought was that it's all very well to have protein structures specified in DNA, but how is their production and deployment orchestrated? Perhaps it's all in the relative timing of developmental events and of the growth of particular features relative to one another.

Eric Davidson, a developmental biologist, used the term "gene regulatory networks" (GRNs) to refer to interworking sequences of DNA, RNA and proteins to control which genes are transcribed and when, as embryos develop. The hypothesis was that simple mutations in GRNs *early on in development* could have a much more significant body-plan-changing effect than an equivalent mutation in later embryonic development.

It was intriguing, then, when "Hox" genes – the first subset of "homeobox" regulatory genes to be discovered in the mid 1980s – were found to be common to a wide range of animals both vertebrates and invertebrates (including insects). *Hox* genes determine the identity of embryonic regions along the anterior-posterior (head-to-tail) axis. The most famous *Hox* gene, *antennapedia*, can place a leg on the head of a fruit fly where there ought to be an antenna. The fact that *Hox* genes are similar across a wide range of animals has been seen as another pointer to universal common ancestry. But take the example of *distal-less* which is associated with jaw and limb development. It is expressed in the development of various types of legs, feet and other appendages: "vertebrate fins and limbs … arthropod legs, echinoderm tube feet, ascidian syphons and ampullae, and annelid parapods".[77]

Yet as Swift goes on to point out, "It is thought that divergence of animal phyla occurred so early that the last common ancestor did not have appendages". So if *distal-less* was present in the common ancestor and inherited from it, the gene's function in that ancestor could not have been the development of appendages. This argues against the theory that *distal-less* was inherited from a common ancestor.

Another subset of homeobox genes is the "Pax" family which is involved in eye and nervous system development. The *Pax-6* gene was originally called *eyeless*, because a mutated gene could result in reduced or missing eyes. Once again *Pax-6* is similar across disparate phyla. In fruit flies, experimenters used *Pax-6* to artificially induce the occurrence of eyes on wings, legs and antennae; these "ectopic" (out-of-place) eyes appeared to be fully formed, although evidently not transmitting images to the brain. Experiments also showed that inserting a mouse *Pax-6* gene into a fruit fly embryo could produce similarly ectopic eyes. They were not mouse eyes, however, but normal fruit fly-type eyes. In a form of complementary exchange, inserting a fruit fly *Pax-6* gene into a frog embryo also resulted in ectopic eyes;

but frog, not fruit fly, eyes. Biologists have claimed that *Pax-6* is a master control gene for eye development and provides evidence of evolutionary common descent. It certainly acts as a controlling switch, triggering the embryonic development of mouse eyes in mice and compound eyes in fruit flies. The echo of engineers reusing wheels, transistors and capacitors should not be missed here. As Wells concludes, a "very similar gene can switch on a developmental pathway in many different kinds of animals - though the resulting structures are determined by the species, not the gene".[78]

But here's the problem. As already discussed, eyes are claimed to have evolved independently at least 40 times in different phyletic lineages. *Pax-6* variants are common to them all. In addition, the key protein used in light absorption in each of the visual systems is rhodopsin. But the claimed common ancestor of all these animals could not have had eyes, so would have use for neither *Pax-6* nor rhodopsin.[79]

And there are other dilemmas for Evo-Devo. In insects for example, different, **unrelated genes are instrumental in the same embryonic development process** - differentiating head and tail ends. Researchers reported that "[u]nrelated genes establish head-to-tail polarity in embryos of different fly species, raising the question of how they evolve this function". Genes called *bicoid* in fruit flies and *panish* in common midges accumulate at the anterior (head) end of their respective eggs to distinguish head from tail. In moth flies, a third gene, *odd-paired* is the active differentiator. In one species of mosquito it's the gene *cucoid*. In another it's *pangolin*.[80]

FRUIT FLIES - *Drosophila* - are a favourite target for laboratory experimentation that seeks to explore the impact of genetic mutations induced during embryonic development. Probably the best known example of this is the four-winged mutant. A fruit fly normally has one pair of wings. In Fig. 7.11 the normal wings are the pair closer to the head (anterior). A series of three mutations over three generations induced the second (posterior) pair of apparently normal wings. However, there's a problem: the additional wings don't work - there are no muscles to operate them so instead of aiding flight, they have introduced debilitating drag. Additionally, the new wings have replaced the pair of small appendages called "halteres" which act like tiny gyroscopic pendulums giving the fly information about its

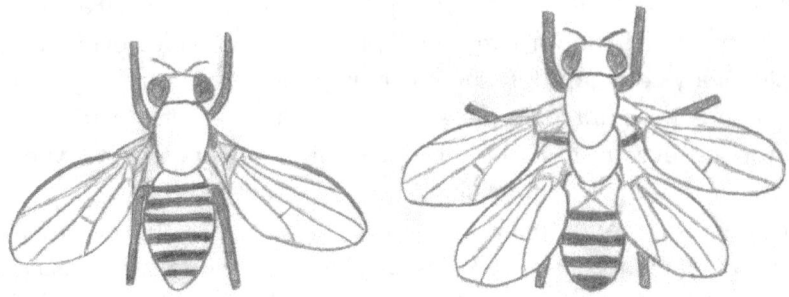

Figure 7.11 Normal and mutated four-winged fruit flies.

orientation in space and hence stabilising its flight. As a result the mutated insects are disabled fliers.

The mechanism appears to be that a gene called *Ultrabithorax* is normally turned on in the third thoracic segment of the fly resulting in the production of halteres. In this carefully controlled experiment, highly skilled geneticists induced three separate mutations all of which were necessary to completely turn *Ultrabithorax* off, leading to the production of a normal-looking extra pair of wings. There are echoes here of the irreducible complexity principle: not just one, but three specific mutations were required to induce this body plan change. We already know from Chapter 5 how unlikely this would be in nature. Yet the mutant fly is *less* fit than the original. And experiments inducing mutations in countless fruit fly embryos have produced only fruit flies, disabled or otherwise. **This is the dilemma: early-acting mutations are overwhelmingly likely to be lethal or severely debilitating – natural selection will eliminate them; later-acting mutations can produce viable organisms, but no new body plans.** Wells concludes, "… mutating the DNA of a fruit fly embryo leads to only three possible outcomes: a normal fruit fly, a defective fruit fly, or a dead fruit fly. Hardly the raw materials for evolution".[81]

Hox and *Pax* genes offer some insight into the astonishing hierarchical layers of control and regulation involved in embryonic development, yet no Darwinian theorist predicted their existence nor has yet explained their emergence. As discussed in Chapter 5 and as David Berlinski puts it, "How could the [Darwinian mechanism] have produced an instrument capable of *anticipating* the course of morphological development and controlling its expression in widely different organisms [emphasis in original]?"[82]

There will be a little more exploration of *Evo-Devo* in Chapter 10.

7 – FAILED PREDICTION #4: Similar embryos imply common ancestry

Lower lifeboat 7!
Here's a summary of Chapter 7.

- **Developing embryos do not repeat an organism's putative evolutionary history**:
  - Primarily due to drawings of embryonic stages of development published in 1874 by Ernst Haeckel, it became widely believed that, for example, a human embryo first resembles a fish, then an amphibian and finally a reptile on its way to becoming a recognisably human fetus.
  - It turns out that Haeckel falsified the evidence in his drawings and that his 'biogenetic law' – that embryos repeat their putative evolutionary history – has been demonstrated to be false.
  - Despite this, recent biology textbooks and other sources have continued to present his drawings and rehearse a version of his "law", confusing generations of young people into believing that they were once fish/amphibians/reptiles in the womb.
- **Embryonic development does not provide evidence for universal common descent**:
  - The earliest stages of embryonic development – the very ones *Evolution* would predict to be most similar – are surprisingly different in all of the main vertebrate classes: cartilaginous fish, bony fish, amphibians, reptiles, birds and mammals.
  - Even the embryonic development processes of vertebrates' key homologous feature – their vertebrae – differ strikingly.
- **Genes do not provide evidence for universal common descent**:
  - Contrary to the claims of popularisers of *Evolution*, trees-of-life derived from comparison of different genes most often disagree with one another as well as with conventional trees based on anatomy.
  - What's more, as the genomes of hundreds of species have been sequenced in the last twenty years, researchers have been surprised to discover that typically around 10% of the protein-coding DNA of each species is unique.

The implications are profound. Writing in the *New Scientist* in 2009, Graham Lawton affirmed the prominence of the theory of common ancestry, the tree-of-life, in Darwin's mind, **"The tree of life concept was absolutely central to Darwin's thinking, equal in importance to**

natural selection ... For much of the past 150 years, biology has largely concerned itself with filling in the details of the tree ... [emphasis added]".

Glimpsing only the tip of the iceberg, there was perhaps hope. But now a better understanding of what lies below the surface, makes fatal damage inevitable. Lawton continues, "A few years ago it looked as if the [holy] grail was within reach. But **today the project lies in tatters**, torn to pieces by an onslaught of negative evidence. Many biologists now argue that the tree concept is obsolete and needs to be discarded [emphasis added]".[83]

- **Darwinian theory makes the prior assumption that nature is fundamentally continuous**: that simple mutations in genes will induce smooth transitions in embryonic development and hence anatomy. In this way all species would be connected via a gently branching tree of universal common descent.
- The facts, however, are that anatomical homology is neither underpinned by homologous patterns in embryology nor in genetics.
- Meanwhile Conway Morris has documented another feature of nature, "the ubiquity of convergence"[84] (very similar morphology *not* believed to be due to common descent).
- Instead, as research director Sheena Tyler explains, **the evidence points to discontinuity**, and to "the existence of types [distinct forms] that are real in nature. Distinct forms are apparent at various hierarchical levels, ranging from the phylum level [body plan] down to the basic types, **most commonly identifiable with the family level**, and recognisably distinguishable from the nearest forms by clear gaps or discontinuities [emphasis added]".[85]

Much is made of the similarities amongst organisms, whether by putative common descent or by convergence and the much cited (almost) universal genetic code. But **what evolutionary theory needs to explain is** – not the similarities – but **the clear differences** between phyla, classes, orders and families. **This it has signally failed to do.** The problem for Darwinists is that universal common ancestry is assumed to be true, so the theory is imposed upon the evidence, no matter how many incompatible facts continue to flood in through gaping holes in the hull.

The bubbling sea is pouring into the fourth 'watertight compartment' and waves are beginning to break over the perilously dipping bow of RMS *Evolution*.

Chapter 8

FAILED PREDICTION #5

The human species evolved from apes

We ... learn that man is descended from a hairy, tailed quadruped, probably arboreal in its habits and an inhabitant of the Old World ... probably derived from an ancient marsupial animal, and this through a long line of diversified forms, from some amphibian-like creature, and this again from some fish-like animal.[1]

Charles Darwin

As we survey the lower decks in the fifth 'watertight compartment' of RMS *Evolution*, we begin with some deck-clearing:
- The March of Progress 'fact'.
- What's the popular story of human evolution?
- Survival of the first class: the western superiority culture that infused Darwin's time.
- The sociology of human fossil-hunting.
- Ice warnings... and palaeoanthropology: debatable scientific practices, assumptions and pitfalls.

Then we'll ask three important questions:
- Is the fossil evidence convincing?
- What about the differences – can evolution explain them?
- Similar genes – are they similar enough?

The March of Progress 'fact'

Neither in the first edition of *The Origin*, published in 1859, nor in subsequent editions, did Darwin make any direct reference to human evolution, perhaps apprehensive that explicit exploration of human origins might be too controversial for public disclosure at that time. Nevertheless, the implications of his thesis in *The Origin* would surely have led most of his 1859 readers to make that inference. Within

Figure 8.1 Iconic "March of Progress" images such as this promote the view that human evolution from an ape-like ancestor is a 'fact'.

twelve years it would seem that there had been sufficient acceptance of his ideas for him to publish *The Descent of Man* in which he made the bold claim that humans have evolved from an ape-like ancestor, summarised in the opening quote.[1]

Much more recently Jerry Coyne updated the assertion, "We are apes descended from other apes, and our closest cousin is the chimpanzee whose ancestors diverged from our own several million years ago in Africa. These are indisputable facts".[2] Steven Pinker chimes in to the conversation, "We know, but our ancestors did not, that humans belong to a single species of African primate that developed agriculture, government, and writing late in its history".[3] Dawkins is even more emphatic, "It is the plain truth that we are cousins of chimpanzees, somewhat more distant cousins of monkeys, more distant cousins of aardvarks and manatees, yet more distant cousins of bananas and turnips …".[4]

The familiar image in Fig. 8.1 has become an icon which ubiquitously appears in popular magazines, documentaries and educational materials purporting to demonstrate the "fact" of human evolution. It typically begins with a knuckle-walking ape-like primate and progresses video-frame-like through ever more human-looking stages en route to becoming a fully upright modern human being. The iconic image pops up even in popular novels. In his 2018 novel *Origin*, Dan Brown has his futurist character Edmond Kirsch speak these words, "Yes, humans evolved," and as the screen behind him shows what Brown describes as "a primitive ape slouching behind a line of increasingly erect hominids, until the final one was fully erect, having shed the last of his body hair" Kirsch continues, "This is an irrefutable scientific fact, and we've built a clear timeline based on the fossil

8 – FAILED PREDICTION #5: The human species evolved from apes

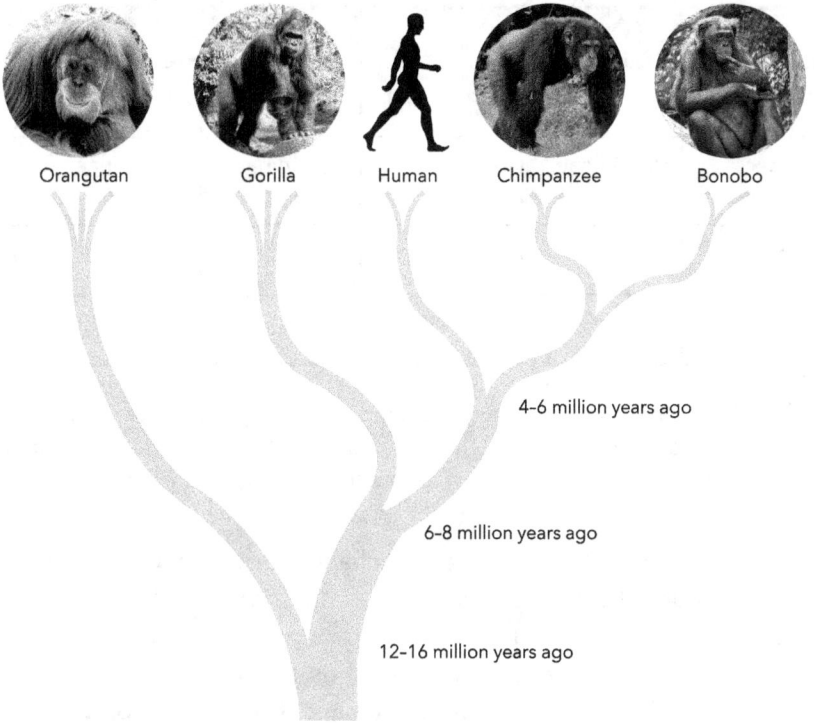

Figure 8.2 A typical representation of the Hominidae (human–ape) family tree, showing the claimed sequence of divergence of today's species from an unnamed common ancestor.

record".[5] The icon powerfully communicates the impression that science has demonstrably verified this version of human history. The "March of Progress" was first created by natural history painter Rudolph Zallinger in 1965 and reproduced as a fold-out in the Time-Life Nature Library book, *Early Man*.[6]

What's the popular story of human evolution?

Fig. 8.2 shows the *Hominidae* family tree, illustrating the major species groups that exist today and their hypothetical sequence of divergence from an unknown common ancestor.[7] As Coyne indicated, our closest relatives today are believed to be chimpanzees. We've even been described as "just a third species of chimpanzee, along with the common chimpanzee and the bonobo".[8] We, chimps and gorillas are all classed as Hominins (sub-family) of the family Hominidae (see Table 8.1), but each in a different genus: *Homo*, *Pan* and *Gorilla* respectively. Orangutans have been placed in a different sub-family, Ponginae. Such

	Human	Chimpanzee	Gorilla	"Lucy"
Family	Hominidae	Hominidae	Hominidae	Hominidae
Sub-Family	Homininae	Homininae	Homininae	Homininae
Genus	*Homo*	*Pan*	*Gorilla*	*Austrolopithecus*
Species	*sapiens*	*troglidytes*	*gorilla*	*afarensis*

Table 8.1 The Hominidae family belongs to the order *Primates* and in turn to the class *Mammalia*, phylum *Chordata*, kingdom *Animalia* and domain *Eukaryota*. The classification (taxonomy) of "Lucy" is included for later comparison.

taxonomic classification is subject to change, however. Only a couple of decades ago, *Homo sapiens* was the only species in the Hominidae family and chimps and gorillas were grouped in a separate family, Pongidae.[9] Family groupings are thus somewhat arbitrary or inconsistent. For example, **while humans cannot interbreed with chimps or other extant members of the *Hominidae* family**, within the Felidae (cat) family, lions, leopards, tigers and jaguars are known to interbreed.[10] Likewise, in Canidae (the dog family), wolves, jackals, dingoes, coyotes and domestic dogs can all interbreed.[11]

So what, then, is the popularly understood evolutionary story? Birmingham professor Mark Pallen tells us that the human line of descent diverged from that of chimpanzees and bonobos 4 to 6 million years ago (mya). According to the lavishly produced book, *Evolution: The Human Story* by Alice Roberts, professor of Archaeology and Anthropology at the University of Bristol, "The term 'hominin' is used to describe living humans and all other species comprising the lineage that diverged from that of chimpanzees around 7 million years ago".[12] As fossil discoveries were being made in the 1960s and 1970s the most commonly popularised "March of Progress" was a linear progression from an ape-like last common ancestor (LCA) which evolved into "Ardi" (*Ardipithecus ramidus*). The evolutionary sequence then continued with "Lucy" (*Australopithecus afarensis*), followed by "Handy Man" (*Homo habilis*) and "Upright Man" (*Homo erectus*), who then evolved to become modern *Homo sapiens* (Wise Man). The tree in Fig. 8.3 captures a typical late twentieth century representation of

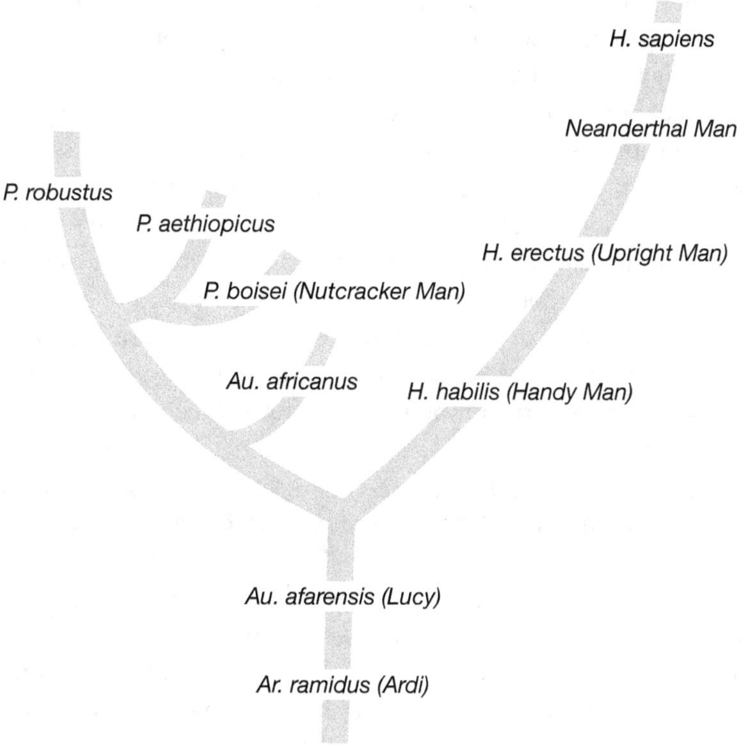

8 – FAILED PREDICTION #5: The human species evolved from apes

H. sapiens

Neanderthal Man

P. robustus

P. aethiopicus

H. erectus (Upright Man)

P. boisei (Nutcracker Man)

Au. africanus

H. habilis (Handy Man)

Au. afarensis (Lucy)

Ar. ramidus (Ardi)

Figure 8.3 This was a typical understanding of hominin evolution from the late 20th century [based on Futuyma (1998) figure 26.6]. Following the split from the assumed common ancestor of chimps and bonobos, *Lucy* evolved from *Ardi* (Ardipithecus ramidus) and thereafter via three *Homo* species: *habilis, erectus* and *neanderthalensis* to *Homo sapiens*. In addition to the genus *Homo, Australopithecus* (*Au.*) and the more robust *Paranthropus* (*P.*) genera are also shown. (Ardi's discovery was not published until 2009 but is included here for completeness.)

this evolutionary ascent. Today, however, as we will see, this tidy story has been discarded, at least by the experts if not in the public mind – which has been deeply influenced by the March of Progress icon.

Survival of the first class

Only 25% of the third class passengers survived *Titanic's* sinking compared with 62% of those in first class (97% of the women in first class).[13] It would seem that first class passengers were regarded as of more 'value' than those travelling third class.

With this in mind, we pause to survey the context in which Darwin's human evolutionary ideas became accepted. Darwin was a man of his time. In the mid-19th century, Europe was at the peak of its colonial exploration and, as many have argued, *exploitation* of the world. Europeans had come to view their civilisation as far superior to those in other geographies and cultures. For example, in 1795 German doctor Johann Friedrich Blumenbach described five "types" of humans: Caucasians, Mongolians, Ethiopians, Americans and Malays and he elevated Caucasians – those from Europe, India and North Africa – to the status of most beautiful of all.[14] Darwin was no exception in adhering to this view. For Darwin, Australian Aborigines for example, were seen as occupying one of the lowest rungs in the human evolutionary hierarchy.

> *... how little can the hard-worked wife of a degraded Australian savage, who uses very few abstract words, and cannot count to four, exert her self-consciousness, or reflect on the nature of her own existence.*[15]

He was shocked, too, by the nakedness and apparent savagery of Terra del Fuegans,[16] and most Africans were regarded as inferior, indeed sub-human.[17] In Germany, Haeckel considered black Africans to be a "missing link" between apes and white Europeans.[18] Darwin's theory appeared to provide a scientific explanation, and hence scientific justification for this conviction: that white Europeans were more highly evolved than other human populations. Indeed, the British anthropologist, Tim Ingold, contends that Darwin began to frame evolution as an "imperialist doctrine of progress".[19] Darwinism gave legitimacy to this (what today would be labelled) "racist" view.

The predominant view among Europeans at the time – that they were more highly evolved than other ethnicities – had two consequences. First, it led to the prediction that the "lower", "less evolved" races would die out within a few hundred years through natural selection[20] – even setting in motion the desire to 'help' evolution along the way. Appendix B briefly explores this latter theme, including the eugenics movement. Second, Darwin's science encouraged the already prevalent suspicion that some human races could be viewed as intermediate evolutionary stages between gorillas (and other apes) and white Europeans.

However shocking such views are to us in the 21st century, nevertheless, Darwin subscribed to both of these propositions.

8 - FAILED PREDICTION #5: The human species evolved from apes

> *At some future period, not very distant as measured by centuries, the civilised races of man will almost certainly exterminate, and replace, the savage races throughout the world ... The break between man and his nearest allies will then be wider, for it will intervene between man in a more civilised state, as we may hope, even than the Caucasian, and some ape as low as a gibbon, instead of as now between the negro or Australian and the gorilla.*[21]

Fig. 8.4 shows Haeckel's putative evolutionary gradation from apes to humans. Above all, Darwin's explanation for what could be understood as *biological progress* chimed with the conviction that Victorians had been instrumental in achieving ongoing *cultural and technological progress*.

Not all of Darwin's contemporaries shared his racist views: Alfred Russel Wallace, co-discoverer of natural selection, who had travelled and lived much more widely than Darwin, insisted that all peoples everywhere "possess human qualities of the same kind as our own"

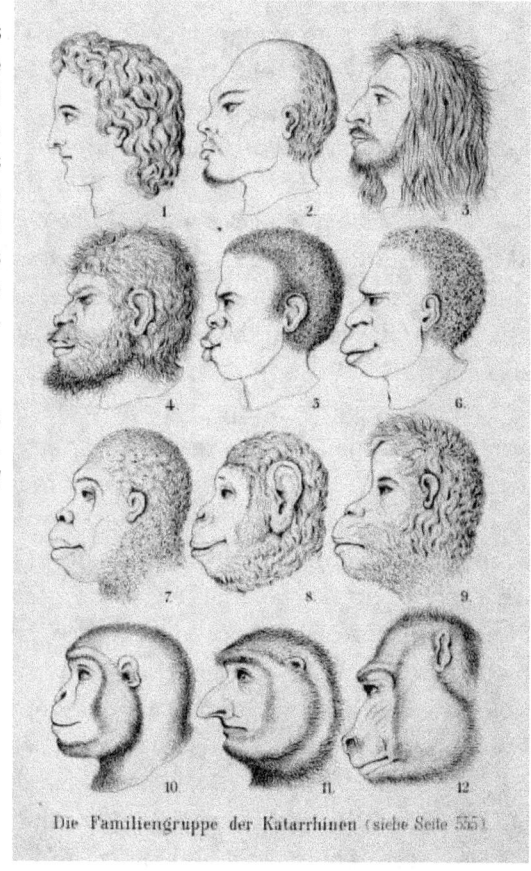

Figure 8.4 Ernst Haeckel's drawings compare the heads of various apes and human races. His intention was to show a continuous evolutionary gradation from apes, through presumed "less evolved" human races to what he believed to be the "most evolved" Caucasian.

This is the frontispiece in his *Natürliche Schöpfungsgeschichte* (1868) - *Natural History of Creation.*

and that there was "no marked superiority in any race or country" in terms of "intelligence and morality".[22]

Nevertheless, Darwin's theory of human evolution from lower ape-like animals offered a scientific justification for racism which was already endemic in 19th century Europe – some 'passengers' were apparently of more 'value' than others. Consequently, the idea that humans had evolved from lower animals became axiomatic; and while it was widely believed that no further proof was really needed, it was nevertheless assumed to be certain that confirmatory ape-man fossils *would* be found.

The sociology of human fossil-hunting

The White Star Line was determined to make headlines with RMS *Titanic* by crowning her maiden voyage with an ostentatious early arrival in New York. The pressure was on. It meant steaming full speed ahead and taking the most direct great-circle route. Captain EJ Smith and White Star Line management believed that *Titanic* was unsinkable, so it was tacitly assumed that to largely ignore ice warnings was an acceptable risk. The passengers and most of the crew – apart from those few in command on the bridge that fateful night – were quite unaware of the risks being taken. And even those few still did not doubt that *Titanic* would remain afloat even if the worst happened. RMS *Titanic* did, of course, make headlines, but instead of achieving celebrity status, the reports were of tragedy, scandal and humiliation.

As we descend further into this fifth 'watertight compartment', we should peek inside the locker of fossil hunting culture. Palaeo-anthropology is the study of fossils relating to human evolution. It's about the origin of our very own species, and therefore of great interest to the public. If there was pressure to secure good headlines in response to *Titanic's* maiden voyage, the publicity stakes are perhaps even higher amongst those searching for hominin fossils. From Chapter 1 we know that scientists suffer from the foibles and temptations of ordinary people. In this context historian of science Richard Delisle asks an important question, "Do those paleoanthropologists who discover and pronounce upon fossils follow good and sound scientific practices that are in the best interests of their field?"[23] There are good reasons to have doubts. Here are some of the factors Delisle lists[24] that influence the motivation and therefore potentially the practices of human fossil-hunters:

Achieving scientific fame. "Paleoanthropologists are in no way different from other people: they want to be popular, they are desirous of fame and they compete against each other."[25] They therefore seek recognition and prestige both within and beyond their discipline.

Gaining media attention. Any new discoveries relating to human evolution attract a high level of fascination from the media including magazines, journals, television documentaries, radio, and of course the internet. Once more this plays into the desire for recognition and prestige, what might be called the "prima donna" temptation.

The need for funding. Competition is severe and those who have a track record of discovering "missing links" are much more likely to secure future funding.

The dream of being lucky. As we'll see shortly, Donald Johanson dreamed of being one of those lucky ones who would make breakthrough hominin fossil discoveries. Nor is he the only example of a fossil-hunter with childhood dreams of being lucky and famous.[26]

Ice warnings... and palaeoanthropology

As a result of these motivating factors, Delisle warns that "... history reveals an alarming adherence to debatable scientific practice ...".[27] We will find some echoes of the Chapter 6 'ice warnings' here.

1. **The paradigm rules**. Because the "fact" of human evolution is unquestionable, there is a risk that we see what we want to see. In 1908 Charles Dawson and A. Smith Woodward discovered a fossil skull and jawbone. In recognition of the first finder's name it was assigned to a new species, *Eoanthropus dawsoni*, but became better known as "Piltdown Man". Forty years later it was realised that the fossil was in fact fake: it had been deliberately constructed from the cranial bones of a recent human and the mandible of a recent orangutan. Why was it accepted as genuine for so long? Delisle points out that new fossil finds are assessed in relation to the ruling paradigm, how well they fit with the orthodox story: "... discoverers present their discoveries to an opinionated scientific community that then evaluates them in the context of received wisdom".[28] Henry Gee, senior editor at *Nature*, recognises preconceptions at work, "The fact that it took 40 years to expose Piltdown as a fraud is a mark of how deeply rooted such prejudices are".[29] Science Magazine identifies Dawson as the culprit: "Dawson was able to fool the experts of the day by employing the

same trick used by successful con artists since time immemorial: he showed them what they wanted to see".[30]

2. **This is low confidence science.** As Stadler has already warned us, distinguished evolutionary biologist Ernst Mayr also cautions, "Evolutionary biology, in contrast with physics and chemistry, is a historical science – the evolutionist attempts to explain events and processes that have already taken place. Laws and experiments are inappropriate techniques for the explanations of such events and processes. Instead *one constructs a historical narrative*, consisting of a tentative reconstruction of the particular scenario that led to the events one is trying to explain [emphasis added]".[31] The "fact" of human evolution from an ape-like ancestor is assumed to be 'unsinkable'. As such there are clear opportunities for confirmation bias, and it's tempting to overstate the confidence in or scope of results.

3. **Skeletal reconstructions are speculative.** Fossil bones are often fragmentary and/or crushed, spread over a wide area (sometimes miles apart), and often found alongside the fossil remains of many other species. Most reconstructions are based on a small number of bones. It is rare to have even 50% of a skeleton.

4. **Face and body reconstructions are even more speculative.** Preservation of soft biology in hominin fossils is extremely rare.[32] So, while clever forensic science techniques may have been used, the size and shape of the nose/nostrils, mouth and ears, the colour of skin and eyes, the presence – or not – of body and facial hair, the texture of the skin, and whether clothes were worn, is largely speculative. Yet the images created by such remarkably life-like reconstructions are most effective at overstating confidence in the discoverer's (inevitably) biased assumptions. The case of "Kennewick Man" described[33] by science historian Angela Saini serves as an example. "Dated at around 8,500 years old, his middle-aged bones were discovered in 1996" in Washington State. Archaeologists concluded that he didn't look like a modern-day Native American and was described as "Caucasoid". His reconstructed face, which was given an off-white colour, "weirdly resembled the English actor Patrick Stewart" of *Star Trek* fame. Nearly twenty years later, in 2015, Kennewick Man was DNA tested and found to be closer to Native Americans than to any other group. He was therefore given a makeover. The new forensic

reconstruction was "starkly different" with long hair and dark skin – most unlike Patrick Stewart! Vindicated native Americans were finally able to put his bones to rest near his ancestral home by the Columbia River. A recent paper explains how displays in natural history museums can easily mislead the unwary visitor; it describes the "variability present in reconstructions of the same individual across separate museum displays". Meaning, for example, that a given reconstruction can be made to look more ape-like or more human-like to fit the desired narrative. The authors continue, "it is clear that very little effort has been made to produce reconstructions that are substantiated by strong empirical science. This is surprising given how museums boast about decades of success presenting scientific knowledge and education to the public".[34]

5. **Lump or Split?** Some researchers are "lumpers". They prefer to combine finds that exhibit strong similarities into a single genus, or even into a single species. "Splitters" argue over minor skeletal differences and prefer to assign most finds to different species or even different genera (plural of genus). The highly motivated fossil hunters themselves tend to be splitters. After all, much more prestige is likely to accrue from claiming to have discovered a previously unknown species. Splitters, not knowing about dogs, would likely identify different breeds found in a dog graveyard as different species. Geneticist John Sanford and biologist Christopher Rupe point out that according to splitters, "There are 5 different species of [living] baboon, possibly 7 depending on whom you ask ... yet they are ... all very similar in their general anatomy (and can probably interbreed) ... Other taxonomists ... would say that all the baboon species should be lumped together as a single variable species".[35] If this can happen with living species today, the scope for error and uncertainty must be significantly higher where there is no soft biology to study. The problem at the root of this ambiguity is the variable definition of the word "species". The "biological species concept" states that if members of the same or different populations are able to interbreed and produce fertile offspring, then they are considered the same species. The "morphological species concept" separates animals into different species based on distinctive anatomical features.[36] Lumpers tend to use the former. Hominin fossil-hunters,

as splitters, tend to use the latter. To be fair, they don't have the option of testing the interbreeding potential of skeletal remains!
6. **Objects can be "sorted" into an "evolutionary" sequence where none actually exists.** Palaeontologist Steven Stanley reminds us, "In fact, the fossil record does not convincingly document a single transition from one species to another".[37] Colin Patterson, former palaeontologist at London's Natural History Museum, candidly points out, "Fossils may tell us many things, but one thing they can never disclose is whether they were ancestors of anything else".[38]

Is the fossil evidence convincing?

So let's now check out some stories of fossils that have been claimed to be on the evolutionary ancestor-descendent route from apes to modern humans. We'll survey them in the order in which they were discovered over a period of nearly 150 years. Their claimed evolutionary sequence, as depicted in Fig. 8.3, is based on dates assigned to the rock layers in which the fossils were found. A discussion of dating techniques and their merits is beyond the scope of this book. Assigned dates are simply accepted here.

We may be surprised to discover that the human fossil evidence is relatively sparse, fragmentary and hotly disputed amongst experts in the field.

NEANDERTHAL MAN (*Homo neanderthalensis*). In 1856 hominin fossils were discovered in a cave in the Neander Valley in Germany which gave its name to the new species. In subsequent decades the remains of some 275 individuals from over 70 sites in Europe, the Middle East and western Asia were unearthed, variously dated between 350,000 and 28,000 ya, according to Roberts.[39] Neanderthal Man had a number of distinctive skeletal features: an elongated skull with a low forehead and a swelling or "bun" at the rear, strong brow ridges, a pushed-forward lower face with reduced chin. Their brain capacity averaged 1475 cm^3, larger than the modern human average. Although their arms and legs were relatively short and their bones more robust – suggesting heavy musculature – they walked upright just like modern humans. Where do Neanderthals fit in? Were they an ape-like "missing link" between apes and *H. sapiens*? Were they a now extinct separate sub-human species, or were they fully human?

The "Neanderthal" descriptive has long been a term of abuse, associated with "knuckle-dragging thugs".[40] Even to this day, a typical

8 – FAILED PREDICTION #5: The human species evolved from apes

Figure 8.5 The Czech artist František Kupka's 1909 rendering of Neanderthal Man. It was heavily influenced by palaeontologist Marcellin Boule's view of the skeleton and depicted as more ape-like than human.

dictionary definition includes adjectives such as "unintelligent", "uncivilised" and "uncouth". How did this come about? William King (1809-1886), an Irish professor of geology, began the de-humanisation process, "I feel myself constrained to believe the thoughts and desires which once dwelt within [Neanderthal Man] never soared beyond those of a brute".[41] Regarding them as sub-human, a new species name was required and it was King who proposed: *neanderthalensis*, perhaps an improvement upon Haeckel's suggested *Homo stupidus*.[42] Within five years of the discovery, Thomas ("bulldog") Huxley, and others, compared Neanderthal Man to Australian Aborigines, whom Victorians regarded as "savages" and a "primitive, fossilised stage in human evolution".[43] Some years later, the French palaeontologist Marcellin Boule was called in to examine a skeleton found in a cave at La Chapelle-aux-Saints. His 1911 reconstruction of the skeleton presented Neanderthal as a bent-knee, bent-hip figure with similarly ape-like opposable big toe. The first published artist's impression was of a hairy, semi-upright ape, Fig. 8.5.

Boule's faulty reconstruction convinced the scientific community at the time. His iconic caricature of Neanderthal Man has cast a long shadow to this day. It wasn't until 1957 that re-examination of this "Old Man of La Chapelle" skeleton, together with other discoveries, allowed Neanderthal to be seen in quite a different light. The Smithsonian National Museum of Natural History reports that "many of the features thought to be unique in Neanderthals fall within the range of modern human variation".[44] People with, for example, a sloping forehead and prominent brow ridges are alive today.[45] As anatomists Straus and

Figure 8.6 Neanderthal has had a makeover. A more recent reconstruction of a Neanderthal child.

Cave put it, "If he could be reincarnated and placed in a New York subway – provided that he were ... dressed in modern clothing – it is doubtful whether he would attract any more attention than some of its other denizens".[46] In 2010, DNA extracted from a well-preserved specimen registered at 99.7% identical to present-day humans. Geneticist Svante Pääbo concluded, "we had shown that Neanderthals and modern humans are the same species".[47] The result is that Neanderthal Man has now been credited with "sophisticated cultural behaviour" and described as "cognitively indistinguishable" from modern humans.[48]

Neanderthal reconstructions have had a makeover, Fig. 8.6. Science historian Saini describes the transformed situation, "For more than a century the word 'Neanderthal' had been synonymous with low intelligence. In the space of a decade [announced in January 2014], once the genetic link to modern Europeans was suspected and then confirmed, that all changed". She then poses a question, "If it had turned out that Aboriginal Australians were the ones to possess that tiny bit of Neanderthal ancestry instead of Europeans, would our Neanderthal cousins have found themselves quite so remarkably reformed?"[49] Quite so. Meanwhile, although the paleo-community has accepted that Neanderthal Man interbred with *Homo sapiens* and is therefore, by the "biological species concept" definition, the same species, the perception persists among the general public that Neanderthal is less evolved than modern humans. All of the 'ice warnings' apply.

UPRIGHT MAN (*Homo erectus*). Inspired by Darwin's prediction in *The Descent of Man* and by Haeckel's prediction[50] in his *History of Creation* published in 1876, Eugène Dubois, a Dutch anatomist, travelled to the Indonesian islands in the 1890s eagerly expecting to find a "missing link". And, of course, he did. He found a skullcap (only part of a skull) a femur and a molar. (This was after several years of discovering fossils of fish, reptiles, elephants, rhinoceros, hippopotamus, deer, cats and more, all on the same site.) On the basis of these three fossils he announced a new species: *Pithecanthropus erectus* (upright ape-man). But his "Java Man" fossils have been described by Delisle as of "questionable association". Why? Well it's unclear whether Dubois personally witnessed the uncovering of these key fossils by his team.[51] His patchy record keeping indicated that the human-like femur had been found some 10 to15 metres away from the other two fossils and almost a year later.[52] Prior to the discovery of the thigh bone he had believed the skullcap and tooth belonged to a chimpanzee.[53] As a consequence of these uncertainties, his discovery was immediately "subject to heated debate".[54] The femur was unquestionably human, but Dubois interpreted some of the skullcap features as ape-like. Those who doubted his conclusion suspected the three fossils did not all belong to the same individual. However, Dubois could not be dissuaded from his firm conviction that he had found a "missing link".

Since that time, around 300 finds have been unearthed in China (Peking Man), Indonesia, Europe and Africa and reassigned, along with Java Man, to *Homo erectus* – considered to be the immediate ancestor of *Homo sapiens*. Roberts reports that, in total, only one relatively complete cranium, several incomplete ones, some teeth and jaws, and a few limb bones have been catalogued as *H. erectus* fossils, believed to span a timeline from 1.8 mya to 30,000 ya.[55]

Because it was the first find, Java Man became the holotype – the species type specimen. This has become problematic when assigning other finds to *H. erectus* since we only really have a skullcap and a femur. While splitters such as Tattersall and Schwartz think several *different* species have been classified (wrongly) as *H. erectus*,[56] lumpers, on the other hand, such as Milford Wolpoff, Alan Thorne and others believe that the anatomical features of *H. erectus* cannot be clearly distinguished from those of *H. sapiens:* "today, it is more reasonable to include *Homo erectus* within the species *Homo sapiens* as these paleospecies are not separated by cladogenesis [formation of a new group], or even a distinct, definable boundary".[57]

Until the 1980s *H. erectus* fossil finds were mainly skulls and teeth. By 1986, Richard Leakey, of the legendary fossil-hunting Leakey family, along with Alan Walker had unearthed an almost complete skeleton, thought to have been a twelve-year-old. This find became known as "Turkana Boy", dated at 1.6 mya,[58] Fig. 8.7. Some authorities,[59] of the

Evolution's Iceberg

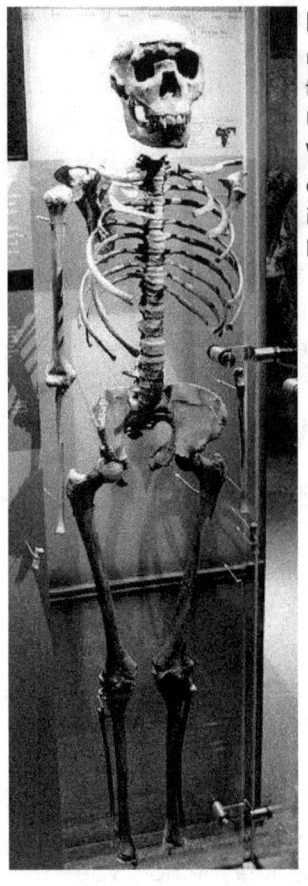

Figure 8.7 "Turkana Boy" dated at 1.6 mya. The most complete *Homo erectus* skeleton ever found, thought to be of a 12-year-old boy. Unearthed in 1986 by Richard Leakey and Alan Walker. Notably, the skeleton is almost indistinguishable from modern humans. The image is of a cast displayed in the American Natural History Museum.

splitter variety classify Turkana Boy as *Homo ergaster* (workman), but most include him within *erectus*.

What is remarkable about the most complete *H. erectus* skeleton ever found is how almost indistinguishable it is from modern humans. John Reader asks, "... is he a missing link? The answer must be no ... the skeleton is too human-like for that".[60] According to the Institute of Human Origins, founded by Donald Johanson, the postcranial (below the neck) skeleton of *H. erectus* exhibits "striking similarities" to *H. sapiens*.[61] Surgeon and anatomist Vij Sodera's assessment is that when adult, Turkana Boy would have had "the body proportions that we would expect of modern Kenyan bushmen".[62]

H. erectus skulls tend to have a low or sloping forehead, large brow ridges, prominent upper jaw (prognathism) and little in the way of a chin. Many experts believe these "primitive" features separate the *H. erectus* species from modern humans. But there are two factors whose consideration might cast doubt on that view. Reader recounts Owen Lovejoy's excavation of an American Indian burial site no more than 1000 years old. Some 1300 individual skeletons were examined.

> Some skeletons demonstrate **strange physical deformities**, others appear to exceed the 'normal' limits of the human form. In all, the collection presents a convincing example of the **extraordinary degree of variation** to which the human skeletal frame is susceptible; in particular it shows very clearly that human living bone is a plastic material which can be moulded to suit the demands of behaviour and anatomy ... disease or broken or distorted bones may force the skeletal frame to function quite differently

8 – FAILED PREDICTION #5: The human species evolved from apes

... morphological variations in the form of the bones are not necessarily ... indicative of taxonomic distinction [emphasis added].[63]

First, then, these Amerindian skeletons were all of the same species, *H. sapiens*, yet their skeletons exhibited an "extraordinary degree of variation". Recall Coyne admitting that if different varieties of domestic dog had only been known from fossil discoveries, they would almost certainly have been classified as different species, if not different genera. Some modern people groups span many of these erectus-like features; Rampassa pygmies from the island of Flores are prone to prognathism and a receding chin; Eskimos and Aleuts exhibit skull features similar to erectus finds in Asia. Anthropologist William Laughlin sums up, "When we find that significant differences have developed, over a short timespan, between closely related and contiguous peoples, as in Alaska and Greenland, and when we consider the vast differences that exist between remote groups such as Eskimos and Bushmen, who are known to belong within the same species of *Homo sapiens*, it seems justifiable to conclude that *Sinanthropus* (Peking Man) [later renamed *Homo erectus*] belongs within this same diverse species".[64] So these so-called "primitive" features are found within *H. sapiens* and are not unique to *H. erectus*.

Second, Lovejoy noted the surprising presence of "strange physical deformities" perhaps as the result of disease, meaning that if these 1300 skeletons had been found in different geographical locations rather than in a single recent burial site, they would most likely have been assigned to different species. Some of the skulls assigned to *H. erectus* display similar distortions. Such characteristics could be symptomatic of pathologies. For example, when the Zika virus, spread by the *Aedes* mosquito, infects a pregnant woman, the child may be born with severe microcephaly.[65] This results in reduced brain volumes similar to some of the *erectus* specimens. Rickets (vitamin D deficiency) and diseases we no longer experience today could perhaps have been factors. Developmental disorders can also be the result of inbreeding, often a characteristic of small isolated hunter-gatherer communities. Other possibilities could include various tribal practices which deliberately deformed the skull and other body parts, such as skull banding, extreme corsets and Chinese feet binding.

What about brain size? Smaller cranial capacity is often cited as evidence that *H. erectus* was sub-human and of lower intelligence. *H. erectus* brain volumes vary between 700 and 1400 cm^3, with an average of 940 cm^3. This compares with the modern human range of 800 to 2220 cm^3 with an average of 1345 cm^3. These are huge ranges – 2:1 and almost 3:1 in *erectus* and *sapiens* respectively and they overlap significantly. Given that *H. erectus* specimens were generally physically smaller individuals, their relative brain capacities actually compare well. Meantime, there are counter examples to the view that larger brain volume implies high intelligence. In 1921 the Nobel prize for literature was won by Anatole France whose cranial capacity was 933 cm^3, which is just below the *erectus* average. In the late 1800s, Daniel Lyon, with a brain capacity of 660 cm^3 was able to read and write and had no signs of mental deficiency.[66] An autopsy following the death of the famous Louis Pasteur (1822-95) revealed that for the last more than thirty years of his life he had continued with his demanding research with only half a brain. The other half had completely atrophied following a cerebral accident.[67] And it is now known that, in determining intelligence, the *organisation* of the brain is more important than brain *size*.

Given these insights, it seems highly likely that the lumpers are correct in conflating *erectus* and modern humans into our species, *H. sapiens*. All six 'ice warnings' apply.

HANDY MAN (*Homo habilis*). Richard Leakey's father Louis and colleagues, working in the Olduvai Gorge in the African Great Rift Valley, announced the discovery of a new species in 1964. World-renowned palaeoanthropologist Bernard Wood tells the story that this find "shifted the search for the first humans from Asia to Africa and began a controversy that endures to this day". He continues, "In 1960, the twig of the tree of life that contains hominins … looked remarkably straightforward. At its base was *Australopithecus*, the apeman that palaeoanthropologists had been recovering in southern Africa since the 1920s. This, the thinking went, was replaced by the taller, larger-brained *Homo erectus* from Asia, which spread to Europe and evolved into Neanderthals, which evolved into *Homo sapiens*. But what lay between the australopiths and *H. erectus*, the first known human?"[68] In 1959, Louis's wife Mary Leakey uncovered the cranium of a young adult which had a small brain, a large face and tiny canines. Its huge molars earned it the name "Nutcracker Man". Louis announced him as *Zinjanthropus bosei* (now renamed as *Paranthropus bosei*). Some primitive stone chopping tools had been found in the same layers as the cranium which led the Leakeys to initially believe Nutcracker Man was the toolmaker. In 1960 however, Jonathan Leakey, Louis and Mary's eldest son, found the lower jaw and top of the head of a juvenile hominin. Nicknamed "Johnny's Child" and believed to be the real toolmaker, it was recognised as a different species from *bosei* (now regarded as an extinct robust ape) and was included within the 1964 *Homo habilis* announcement.

Have many *Homo habilis* fossils been found? The Johnny's Child defining specimen consists of a broken and deformed lower jawbone with 13 teeth, an isolated molar, two small skull fragments and 21 finger, hand and wrist bones (Fig. 8.8). Six of the 21 finger bones were later found to be non-hominin, one turned out to be a vertebral fragment and two others belonged to an arboreal monkey.[69]

In the intervening years the total *habilis* fossil inventory has amounted to several skulls and crania, fragments of hand, arm, leg and foot bones.[70] Nothing approaching a complete skeleton has been found. None of the bones were found physically connected to other bones. They were mostly isolated bones and fragments, often described as distorted, poorly preserved, scrappy, crushed, flattened, broken into little pieces – and found in mixed beds containing many different animal species.[71] In 1966, Wood analysed an ankle bone excavated alongside Johnny's Child. He concluded, "Far from it being like that of modern humans, the bone is a much better match for an australopith. Other features of *H. habilis* have turned out to be less like those of modern humans than Louis and his team suggested ... my sense is that handy man should belong to its own genus, neither australopith nor human... In my view, the species is too unlike *H. erectus* to be its immediate ancestor, so a simple linear

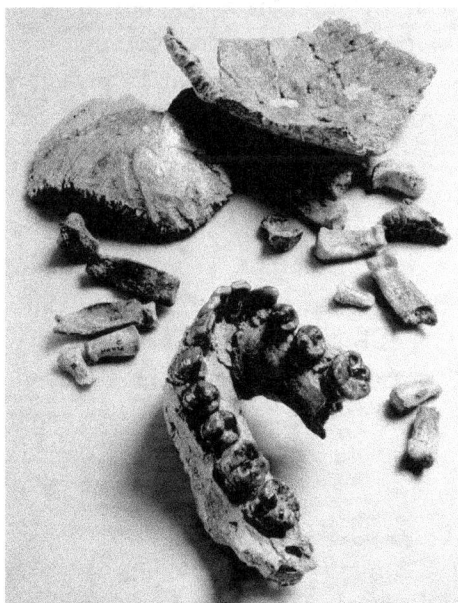

Figure 8.8 The type specimen of *Homo habilis* (handy man), nicknamed "Johnny's Child". It was announced in 1964 by Louis Leakey, dated at 1.7 mya.

model explaining this stage of human evolution is looking less and less likely".[72]

Experts Tattersall and Schwartz characterised *H. habilis* as an "all embracing 'wastebasket' species into which a whole heterogeneous variety of fossils could be conveniently swept".[73] They go on to use the word "mess" to describe the situation: "The mystery of *H. habilis* thus persists. The ancestry of later hominids is presumably represented somewhere within the large and miscellaneous aggregation of fossils that have at one time or another been called *H. habilis*. But for the time being there is no agreement on exactly how many species are included in this assemblage ... One thing is clear, however. Sorting out this mess (and we make no apologies for the term) to everyone's satisfaction is very unlikely to occur as long as linear notions of human evolution linger in paleoanthropology".[74] In *Missing Links*, John Reader concludes, "Nearly half a century of accumulating evidence and discussion has left *Homo habilis* more open to question, more insecure than it ever was ... *Homo habilis* remains more of an evolutionary idea than an example of anatomical fact linking one species to another".[75]

LUCY (*Australopithecus afarensis*) is the most famous hominin fossil ever discovered, see Table 8.1. In 1974, she was unearthed by Donald Johanson near the Hadar river in the Afar region of north-east Ethiopia, and enigmatically named "Lucy" because the *Beatles* song *Lucy in the Sky with Diamonds* was popular on the radio at the time of his team's celebration. As a teenager Johanson had dreamed of going to Africa and finding a "missing link".[76] Lucy was dated at 3.2 mya and in *Evolution: The Human Story* we read, "It is thought that [*Lucy*] could be the ancestor of the genus *Homo* to which modern humans - *Homo sapiens* - belong".[77] But there are significant disagreements as Pallen reveals, "experts still squabble as to how the early hominin, australopithecine and *Homo* lineages relate to one another".[78]

Lucy's skeleton is said to be 40% complete, but taking into account the absence of hand and foot bones, this drops to more like 20% (Fig. 8.9) and later another expert realised that one of Lucy's vertebrae segments actually belonged to a baboon.[79] To date some 400 specimens have been assigned to *Au. afarensis*. They are mostly isolated bones or bone fragments.

She was not "immediately recognised as a separate species".[80] Indeed, the year before, during the 1973 fossil-hunting season, Johanson had found jaw bones and a knee joint that he reported to be

Figure 8.9 Probably the most famous hominin fossil collection. A partial skeleton of Lucy (*Australopithecus afarensis*) discovered by Donald Johanson and team in 1974.

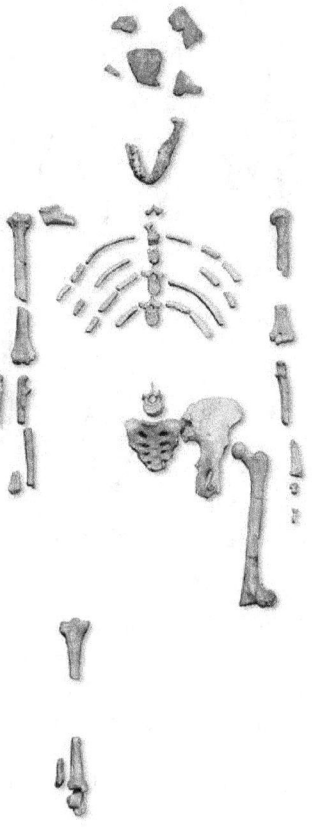

of the genus *Homo*, describing them as "true man" or "near man". And in the year after, he found the remains of at least 13 individuals[81] of different ages from infant to adult. They became known as the "First Family". Johanson reported several of these bones as being indistinguishable from those of *Homo sapiens*.

> Reaching across the millenniums, hand bones from [the First Family specimens] ... bear an uncanny resemblance to our own - in size, shape, and function. The backs of the meta-carpal heads have no ridges, so these individuals did not walk on their knuckles as African apes do. The thumb rotates making it possible to manipulate tools with finesse. Prehistoric foot bones also appear. A fossil fifth metatarsal ... corresponds closely to that of modern man ... One evening, for a lark, members of the research expedition made clay casts of their own teeth. One woman's jaw bore a startling resemblance to a three-million-year-old specimen.[82]

At this point in time Johanson believed that *Homo* had coexisted with *Australopithecus* in the Afar region, 3 to 4 mya.[83] This was consistent with the view of the dynastic palaeoanthropological Leakey family. The by now late Louis, Mary and their son Richard had championed the view that the origin of the *Homo* genus would be established at 4-6 mya or even earlier and that **the genus *Australopithecus* was not involved in the *Homo* line of descent**.[84] At the end of the 1975 field season, Johanson met with Mary and Richard in Nairobi to show them the Hadar collection of bones. Here are Mary's recollections: "To me and to Richard, it seems that they included a considerable range of variation such that there must be at least two hominid types present. Lucy herself was a very small creature ... In contrast, several of the other Hadar hominids were much larger and seemed to us far more

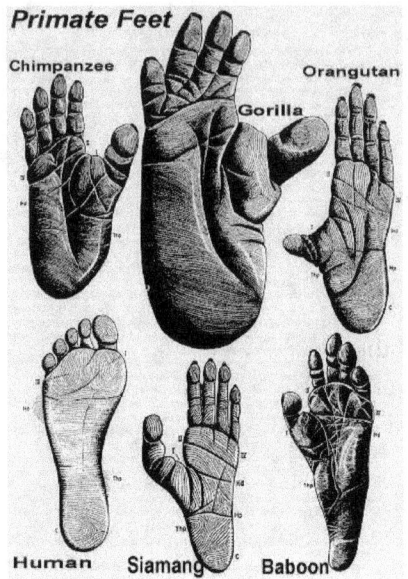 

Figure 8.10 (Left) the feet of various apes in comparison to a human foot. Notice that in apes the grasping big toe splays out to the side. (Right) a close-up sample of the "undoubted human footprints" discovered by Mary Leakey's team at Laetoli, Tanzania in 1978. A total of 77 prints were found, thought to have been left in volcanic ash by three individuals, dated to 3.7 mya. Note the lack of a splayed big toe. While initially in agreement with Mary, White and Johanson later assigned the footprints to Lucy's *A. afarensis* species even though her fossil skeleton had no feet! The justification for this change of mind was the **assumption of 'sexual dimorphism', that the male of Lucy's species must have been much larger and more human-like.**

Homo-like than australopithecine. There was nothing unusual in the idea that two different kinds of hominid should be contemporary in one region".[85]

Some of the Hadar specimens compared well with jaws recently found by Mary about 1000 miles away in Laetoli, Tanzania, dated to 3.6-3.7 mya, and assigned to *Homo*.[86] **So at this point, Johanson and the Leakeys agreed that *Australopithecus* could not be ancestral to modern man.** Instead they were co-existing lineages – and assumed to have an unknown common ancestor.[87]

It was during the 1978-79 season that Mary's team discovered what later became known as the Laetoli footprints, dated at 3.7 mya[88] (Fig. 8.10). She described them as "undoubted human footprints ... The essentially human nature and the modern appearance of the footprints were quite extraordinary."[89] There were 77 prints, left by three individuals of different stature, "It is tempting to see them as a man, a woman and a child. Whether or not this is so, the middle-sized individual was stepping deliberately in the prints left by the largest."[90] Tim White, by this time a young member of Johanson's team agreed, "Make no mistake about it, they are like modern human footprints. If one were left in the sand of a Californian beach today, and a four year old were asked what it was, he would instantly say that somebody had walked there".[91]

Fast forward to May 1978 and a Nobel Symposium at the Royal Swedish Academy of Sciences.[92] Johanson had been invited to speak. Mary was due to speak about her Laetoli finds immediately after him. As Johanson's presentation progressed, Mary was in shock. Why? First he claimed that all of the Hadar material belonged to a single species, which overturned their previously agreed assessment of two separate species. Second, without consulting her beforehand, he included her Laetoli finds within the same, single, newly announced *Australopithecus afarensis* species.

Moreover, it turned out that shortly before the symposium Johanson and White had prepared a paper for publication in the 1978 *Kirtlandia*, the house journal of the Cleveland Natural History Museum.[93] It documented the same shocking volte-face and, unknown to Mary, it included her as one of its authors.[94] She confronted Tim White and insisted that her name be removed from the paper.

What made Mary particularly furious was that they had adopted one of her Laetoli jawbones (a less well preserved one at that) as the *Au. afarensis* "holotype" (the specimen that is definitive of the species). This compounded hubris with scientific error, "It seemed to me unjustifiable, and also scientifically quite wrong, to choose for a species named *afarensis* a type specimen that came from a site … 1000 miles away … and one which was also supposed at the time to be half a million years older … Not only that, but surely no one should choose as type specimen a fragmentary mandible when there is a fossil as complete as Lucy to hand …".[95]

In a subsequent more detailed paper[96] Johanson and White claimed that *Lucy* was the ancestor of all later hominins, including *Homo sapiens*. They illustrated this belief in the family tree diagram subsequently widely used by others, including in the textbook by Douglas Futuyma (see Fig. 8.3).

To add insult to injury, this radical realignment meant assigning the Laetoli footprints to Lucy, even though her partial skeleton had no foot bones! What about the problem of some individuals being tall and others short? Johanson and White's solution was "sexual dimorphism", a phenomenon in which – like today's gorillas – the male of the species is much larger than the female. But critics argue that smaller *afarensis*-size primates alive today exhibit much less sexual size variance than the Hadar-Laetoli specimens.

And size isn't the only problem. **The reason the Leakeys and others regarded some fossils as *Homo* and others as *Australopithecus* was because their post-cranial bones (all of the skeleton apart from the skull) looked distinctly human in the former and distinctly ape-like in the latter**. So, did the males look and act like humans while the females looked and acted like apes?[97] The dispute over Johanson and White's sexual dimorphism hypothesis is unresolved to this day.[98] Indeed some experts[99] want to rename Lucy as "Lucifer" since certain features of the skeleton suggest 'she' was male, though others[100] dispute this. If true, this would wreck the sexual dimorphism defence.

The obvious interpretation of the disparity between the human-like and ape-like bones found in the same fossil beds at Hadar and Laetoli is that they are indeed separate species, and that similar-to-modern humans lived around the same time as ape-like creatures 3 mya, or more. Indeed, in the years that followed, **several authorities agreed with the Leakeys that the *Au. afarensis* collection was best interpreted as two (or more) different species.**[101] **But this view *had* to be rejected by Johanson and White at the time because they claimed that Lucy was a direct ancestor of *Homo sapiens* who must therefore have evolved much later**. In a high profile media interview the charismatic Johanson easily upstaged[102] the more staid and, in the moment, less well prepared Richard Leakey. In the public mind, then, Lucy's "missing link" status became firmly established. Johanson and White had achieved their respective teenage dreams.

A new paradigm had become the ruling one. It had defeated the more obvious interpretation – an example of 'ice warning' (1). Disturbingly, fossil-hunting sociology and most of the other 'ice warnings' also apply here. But the Lucy narrative is almost certainly a mistake as Sanford and Rupe summarise, "The invention of a 'new species' by combining bones from different species has occurred several times in the field of paleoanthropology. Paleo-experts

8 – FAILED PREDICTION #5: The human species evolved from apes

acknowledge that it is not uncommon for hominin-bearing sites to contain a commixture of *Homo* and *Australopithecus* bones. Making an "ape-man" out of human and ape bones is an easy mistake to make, especially when disconnected bones from multiple species are randomly jumbled together in the same bone bed" and this is what "appears to have occurred with Lucy's kind [*afarensis*]".[103] Although in this case, we are left wondering whether "deliberate deception" would be nearer the mark than "mistake".

ARDI (*Ardipithecus ramidus*) is, according to the popular press, man's oldest known ape-like ancestor, closest to the human divergence from the chimp lineage. Veteran of the *Lucy* saga along with Johanson, American anthropologist Tim White originally classified the fossils in the genus *Australopithecus* in 1993. His team had found pieces of 35 individuals in the Middle Awash River valley in Ethiopia, mostly represented by teeth. In 1995 the find was reclassified as *Ardipithecus*

and dated between 4.5 and 4.3 mya (DNA sequencing is no help here because of significant degradation in fossils of this age).[104] White's team recovered 45% of a single skeleton including fragments of the skull and jaw, broken limb bones, a few vertebra fragments and a full set of teeth (Fig. 8.11).[105] New discoveries such as this usually create a bit of a stir and, true to form, *Archaeology* magazine enhanced the drama with, "… we are going to have to re-write our textbooks …".[106]

It was 2009 before the results were published. Why so long? According to the announcement in *Science*, the recovered skeleton was in a terrible condition, "The bones literally crumbled when touched". White had described the remains as "road kill … And parts of the skeleton had been

Figure 8.11 Tim White's team recovered fossils attributed to *Ardipithecus ramidus* (*Ardi*). Around 45% of the skeleton was found including skull and jaw fragments.

trampled and scattered into more than 100 fragments; the skull was crushed to 4cm in height".[107] The bones were scattered over nearly four miles[108] and virtually none were connected together. Those parts of the skeleton that *were* well preserved were clearly ape-like. Sanford and Rupe catalogue Ardi's features: "overall ape-like body proportions with long upper limbs compared to lower limbs, long and curved fingers typical of tree-dwelling primates, and ape-like feet with a highly divergent opposable great toe indistinguishable from a chimp's".[109] The brain case at 300-350 cubic centimetres (cm^3) was also ape-like.

White's team claimed that three features indicate *Ardi* was a human ancestor: **one detail in the skull, the shape of the pelvis and the profile of her canine teeth**.

First the skull: the foramen magnum (the entry point of the spinal column into the skull) was believed to be positioned under the base of the skull, whereas in many apes it is positioned towards the rear. Recall that the skull was crushed. It had been digitally reconstructed from 65 separate pieces of the cranium. The base of the skull was missing.[110] It was the tenth attempt at reconstruction following 1000 hours of work before the researchers were satisfied. Now there's no doubt this was an amazing piece of highly-skilled work. However, since the first nine attempts were rejected, one is left wondering how much artistic interpretive allowance was involved. In any case, even assuming the foramen magnum *was* positioned at the base of the skull, this is not necessarily indicative of upright walking. Experts point out that gibbons and short-faced monkeys have a similar feature, yet don't stand erect and are not connected with human evolution.[111]

Second, the pelvis reconstruction by Owen Lovejoy of Kent State University similarly required 14 attempts before *Ardi's* far-from-complete pelvis was deemed to be presentable. On the basis of these two reconstructions White's team concluded that *Ardi* had habitually walked upright.

Third, *Ardi's* upper canine teeth lacked the dagger-like shape common to chimpanzees. Again, other experts have pointed out that "the same dental features have been found in other species of extinct apes that have nothing to do with human evolution".[112]

Fourth, the artist's portrayal of the skeleton (Fig. 8.12) was given a very human-like upright posture with a straight backbone incorporating its slight 'S' shape rather than a curved (ape-like) one. Given that

8 – FAILED PREDICTION #5: The human species evolved from apes

only one vertebra and one neck bone were recovered, this seems highly questionable conjecture.

It should come as no surprise, then, that some respected authorities disagree with White's upright walking analysis. Anthropologists Bernard Wood and Terry Harrison have this to say, "... the claim that *Ardipithecus ramidus* was a facultative terrestrial biped [living in trees and walking upright on the ground] is vitiated because it is based on highly speculative inferences about the presence of lumbar lordosis [inward curvature of the spine] and on relatively few features of the pelvis and foot, many of which also occur in the arboreally adapted *Oreopithecus* [an extinct ape]".[113] Anatomist William Jungers concludes, "This is a fascinating skeleton, but based on what [White's team] present, the evidence for bipedality is limited at best. Divergent big toes are associated with grasping, and this has one of the most divergent big toes you can imagine. Why would an animal fully adapted to support its weight on its forelimbs in the trees elect to walk bipedally [human-like] on the ground?"[114] David Begun, a palaeoanthropologist at the University of Toronto, has difficulty accepting the *Ardi* story, "It is hard for me to actually find a lot of characteristics that are not chimpanzee-like".[115] Jungers of Stony Brook University once more, "I see nothing in the foot that suggests bipedality". He describes Lovejoy and White's fossil reconstruction and conservation job as "heroic". And he's not convinced by Lovejoy's interpretations of the fossils, least of all the badly fragmented pelvis, "That's really kind of a 3-D Rorschach

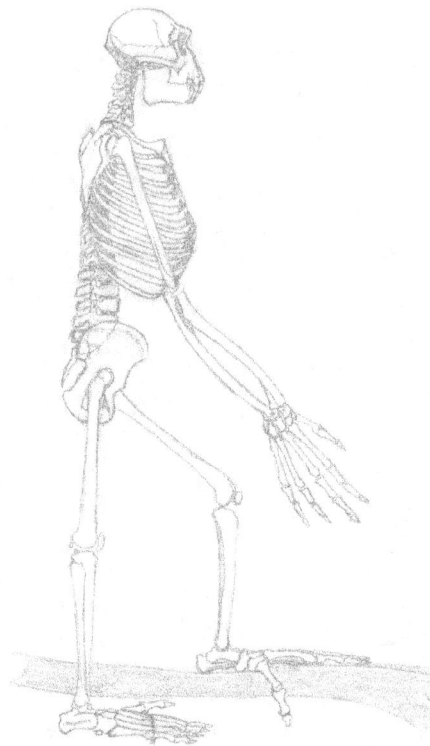

Figure 8.12 Artist's reconstruction of *Ardi's* skeleton suggesting the ability to stand and walk upright.

test[116] if you ask me ... I'm still not convinced that it's necessarily completely accurate".[117]

Taken together with fossil-hunting sociology and the 'ice warnings', why should we believe *Ardi* is anything more than an extinct chimpanzee-like ape?

THE THEORY OF EVOLUTION HAS BEEN IMPOSED UPON THE FOSSIL EVIDENCE.

So where does the fossil evidence leave us? Eminent evolutionist Mark Pallen admits that **"The evolution of humans and our relatives is no longer seen as a tidy ladder** but as a bushy branching tree ... Attempting to identify the earliest hominins ... is problematic [emphasis added]".[118] Most recent depictions of the human family tree do not even attempt to define ancestor-descendent relationships amongst up to 23 different hominins catalogued.[119] They don't make

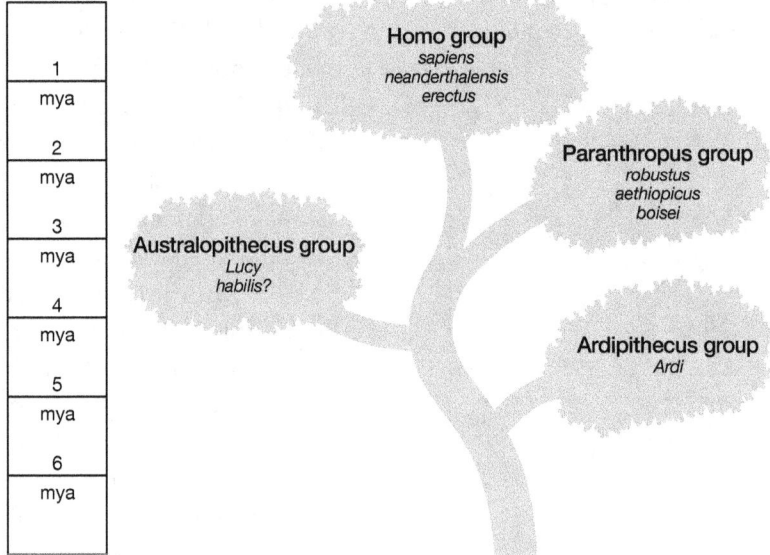

Figure 8.13 Typical of more recent depictions of the hominin family tree, this is adapted from the Smithsonian Natural History Museum version.[114] Note that the *Homo* group, which includes *Homo sapiens*, is not shown as descended from any of the other groups, not even from Lucy's *Australopithecus* group. We have evidence for species only at the outermost twigs of the tree, but no evidence of common ancestors where the branches join the trunk. Nor is there evidence of the putative common ancestor of them all. What makes the trunk and branch constructs any more than theory imposed upon the evidence?

8 – FAILED PREDICTION #5: The human species evolved from apes

any solid line connections. Any, such as Tattersall[120] and Klein,[121] who do embark on such a venture find themselves resorting to a diagram replete with dotted lines and question marks. Fig. 8.13 adapted from the Smithsonian National Museum of Natural History's "Human Family Tree",[122] is starkly honest. Fossil finds have simply been positioned within genus groupings and according to assigned age up to 6 mya (only the key species mentioned in this chapter have been shown). Side branches from the main trunk connect to the *Ardipithecus*, *Australopithecus* and *Paranthropus* genus groupings respectively. Yet **none is shown as descended from any of the others**. And crucially, even more revealing, **the *Homo* genus which includes *Homo sapiens*, is not shown to have descended from any of the other genera, even *Australopithecus***. Rather, **all four genera are claimed to have descended from an unknown ancestor for which there is no fossil evidence**. The claimed, presumably ape-like, common ancestor is absent from the diagram, anonymous. It looks like the "ladder" that Pallen criticised as untidy is in fact non-existent. So in more than 150 years of fossil hunting we are no further forward in establishing a factual basis for the hypothesis of human evolution.

Referring to the "March of Progress" icon, Fig. 8.1, the acclaimed palaeoanthropologist Bernard Wood summarises the current view, "Even with all the fossil evidence and analytical techniques from the past 50 years, a convincing hypothesis for the origin of *Homo* remains elusive[123] ... Our progress from ape to human looks so smooth, so tidy. It's such a beguiling image that even the experts are loath to let it go. But it is an illusion".[124]

In conclusion then, we can reasonably think of the various fossil finds in terms of two major groupings:
1. Various species of extinct apes including *Ardi*, *Lucy* and *Homo habilis*.
2. A modern human grouping that obviously includes *Homo sapiens*, but also *Homo erectus* and *Homo neanderthalensis*. The latter two, while currently classified as separate species, would nevertheless seem to fall within the range of modern humans.

What about the differences – can *Evolution* explain them?

> *The remarkable similarity in the genome of a great many organisms suggests that there is at bottom only one living system; but how then to account for the astonishing differences between human beings and their near relatives – differences that remain obvious to anyone who has visited a zoo?*[125]
>
> David Berlinski

The fossil-hunting art is all about identifying skeletal similarities and inferring evolutionary ancestry when such similarities are recognised. And there is no doubt that there are strong similarities between human and ape skeletal structures. But this assumption, that similarity must imply common descent, side-steps two important considerations.

First, what about the *differences*? It's the differences that really matter. Can evolution explain them? For instance, chimp and bonobo skeletons are almost identical. Now suppose they had both been extinct and we only had their fragmentary fossil record. Palaeo-anthropologists would probably have assigned all of the fossils to only one species. They almost certainly would not have predicted, from the fossil evidence, the dramatic behavioural differences between the two species that are recognised today.[126] David Premack of the university of Pennsylvania put it this way, "In examining claims of similarity between animals and humans, one must ask: **What are the dissimilarities?** This approach prevents confusing similarity and equivalence [emphasis added]".[127]

Second, as we'll see below, evolutionary mechanisms cannot explain these differences. *Design* is therefore a more likely explanation than common descent. Where similar behaviour in terms of function and performance is required, engineers re-use tried-and-tested designs time and again. Reciprocating steam engines were designed into trains and cotton mills as well as into ocean-going liners like *Titanic*. So for example, ape and human arms both use a three-joint configuration: shoulder, elbow and wrist. The ability to reach out at arm's length to grasp a branch, or to manipulate a tool, at different angles, while also being able to pick up food and bring it to the mouth, uniquely requires just such a structure.

So let's now explore some of these ape-human differences. We begin with the anatomical differences. In order to stand, walk upright,

8 – FAILED PREDICTION #5: The human species evolved from apes

and speak, **the human body has many *unique* physical features relative to apes**. Here are some of them:[128]

ARCHED FEET. TV celebrity and anthropologist Alice Roberts agrees that "Human feet look very different from those of other apes".[129] While apes' feet are prehensile, like a second pair of hands for grasping branches, human feet are more rigid and designed to make three points of contact with the ground (the heel, the ball of the foot near the big toe, and the ball of the foot near the little toe). Three arch structures connect each point of contact to the other two. Engineers know that three points of contact is the most precise way of supporting an object. It allows us to stand on one foot, for example.

LONG LEGS AND UPRIGHT KNEE JOINTS. Human legs are about half the length of the whole body versus about one third in apes. Ape knee joints do not fully extend and are always slightly bent, whereas human legs can be straight at the knee and the body fully upright. Indeed, the human knee can lock in the upright position, saving muscle energy and fatigue. Similarly the human hip joints allow legs to be straight, whereas the ape hip keeps the upper leg bent.

ANGLED FEMUR BONES. Apes hobble clumsily from side to side when walking, whereas human walking and running is much more stable. This is because human femurs angle inwards, resulting in each foot being more nearly under the centre of gravity of the body as each step is taken.

PELVIS AND SPINE DIFFERENCES. In chimpanzees and gorillas, the upper parts of the pelvic bones, the ilia, rise up much higher on each side of the spine trapping the lower lumbar vertebrae so that they can hardly move.[130] The ape spine is bent, similar to the letter 'C', which means the upper body projects out in front of the hips. This in turn necessitates relatively long arms for knuckle-walking to support their weight. In contrast, the human back is straight with a slight 'double-S' shape for cushioning. This positions the upper body directly above the pelvis. The position of the spinal column entry point – the foramen magnum – at the base of the skull, is essential for upright walking and looking forward (as already discussed).[131]

FINE HAND MOVEMENTS AND CONTROL. Apes have naturally curved fingers and a limited range of finger movement. Conversely, one estimate suggests human hands are capable of 58 distinct types of hand movement, each one involving up to 35 different muscles.[132] A larger section of the motor cortex in the human brain is dedicated to hand and finger control relative to that in apes. The human hand has the remarkable ability to range from strong and controlled power grips to much finer movements such as holding a pen in a tripod precision grip and the extraordinary feat of playing an average of 16 notes per second on a piano keyboard over sustained periods of time.[133]

FACIAL MUSCULATURE. The human face has around 50 separate muscles. This compares to fewer than 30 in the gorilla. As a result the range of human facial expressions greatly exceeds that of apes. Studies suggest humans are capable of 10,000 discernible expressions. This would have required not simply adapting pre-existing structures, but originating new ones.

SPEECH CAPABILITY. Distinctive features of the voice box, vocal tract and brain enable speech in humans; and the lack of these features probably renders apes and monkeys incapable of physically producing speech and language. In the human vocal tract, the low position of the voice box (larynx) atop the windpipe (trachea) and at the base of a deep throat (pharynx), together with uniquely agile lips and tongue allow the production of a wide range of vowel sounds.[134] It is estimated that about 100 muscles are involved in precisely shaping the vocal cords (in the larynx) and each element of the vocal tract. Conversely, apes have far fewer muscles and limited control over the shape of their vocal tract. David Berlinski quips, "the plain fact of the matter is that while other animals hoot, chatter, grimace, moan, whistle, chirp ... bark, meow, sing lustrously from the trees, screech in barns ... it is only human beings who talk ...".[135]

THE HUMAN BRAIN. When you plot brain weight against body weight for humans and animals on a graph, it is immediately obvious that humans are an outlier. The weight of the human brain is more than three times that of any comparable animal. As a proportion of body weight it is five times that of the gorilla.[136] In particular, the cerebral cortex - the grey matter and white matter - is much larger than that of apes. Distinctive size is one factor. Unique organisation is quite another. According to one brain expert, "Sitting on your shoulders is the most complicated object in the known universe".[137] The human brain is estimated to contain 100 billion nerve cells (neurons) and each neuron connects to around 10,000 others.[138] Premack reports that "Microscopic study of the human brain has revealed neural structures, enhanced wiring, and forms of connectivity among nerve cells not found in any animal, challenging the view that the human brain is simply an enlarged chimpanzee brain".[139]

OTHER PHYSICAL DIFFERENCES include differences in reproductive biology: among primates, the human female menopause is unique and only in the human female are breasts apparent when not nursing; male apes have a bone in the penis called the baculum, humans don't. Meanwhile, unlike apes, humans sweat and shed tears, are mostly right-handed and can hold their breath and swim.[140]

DISTINCTIVE CULTURE AND BEHAVIOURS. These are illustrative examples of *physical* dissimilarities between apes and humans. What about cultural and behavioural distinctions?

> *Horses, mammoths, reindeer, bison, mountain goats, lions and a host of other mammals cascade in image along the cave walls over a distance of almost a hundred yards, over three hundred depictions in all. Delicately executed and meticulously observed, these varied and overlapping images were made... perhaps thirteen thousand years ago.*[141]
>
> Ian Tattersall

Inspired by his exploration of the Combarelles cave in southwest France, celebrated palaeoanthropologist Ian Tattersall goes on to say, "this is not in any sense crude art ... Any preconceptions you may have had of the "primitiveness" of "cave men" are instantly dispelled ... we instinctively recognize [art] as something profoundly human. Not only is it humans, uniquely, who create [delicately executed and meticulously observed] art, but it is only we who indulge in behaviours as mysterious and unfathomable as this".[142]

It is uncontroversial that humans share some elements of anatomy, biology and behaviours with mammals and the animal kingdom generally, but it is similarly uncontentious that our cognitive abilities, including "mysterious and unfathomable" art, set us apart. We measure time and make plans, including sequential plans spanning years if not decades. We think about the past and the future. We wear clothes, domesticate animals and reconfigure landscapes in pursuit of agriculture. "Our consummate command of technology is unique ... it really does set us apart."[143] We design and build huge buildings, cities, roads, bridges, computers and space probes - as well as, of course, ocean going liners. We are capable of abstract thought in mathematics and philosophy. We seek to explain our origins, practise religion, bury the dead. We make music, write poetry and novels; we dance. As has been noted elsewhere, "We have empathy for others, and altruism on a scale unknown in the animal world. We care for the infirm and the elderly".[144]

While for the archaeologist, cave-art is perhaps the most distinctive feature of human activity – because it is preserved while speech isn't – experts generally argue that language is the fundamental type-defining factor that distinguishes humans from chimps. Tattersall again, "What modern human beings alone do (as far as we can tell) is to deconstruct their experience of the worlds both around and within them into a vocabulary of mental symbols."[145] Biochemist Michael Denton explains, "Some of our mental abilities and emotional traits are certainly shared to some degree by other species, but language, as [Noam] Chomsky comments, is 'without any homolog in any other species' ... it is not led up to by any empirically known sequence".[146]

From the age of two, language development in humans and chimps diverges dramatically. While the average high-school student acquires as many as 60,000 words with little difficulty, conversely **a Herculean effort is required to persuade even clever chimps to acquire a handful of words**.[147] The cognitive scientist and "father of linguistics",[148] Noam Chomsky, showed that all human languages share a deep invariant structure, what he called "universal grammar", as its organising principle. One significant grammatical feature of human language is recursion – the embedding of sentences within other sentences. Premack gives an, albeit slightly contrived, example: "Ida the red-haired woman who left her hat in the theatre, the old one that burned down, because arguing with Henry, her husband of forty years, who still has all his hair, wears a maroon smoking jacket in the evenings and is as broke as ever, had rattled her".[149]

Darwin believed that all species were interconnected by an entirely *continuous* "descent with modification" step-by-tiny-step evolutionary process, driven by natural selection. He claimed that the abilities of apes were simply different in degree only, "the differences in mind between man and the higher animals, great as it is, certainly is one of *degree* and not in *kind*".[150] Dawkins, too, believes that the evolutionary magic wand of natural selection produced the human

8 – FAILED PREDICTION #5: The human species evolved from apes

brain and that human "feats of intellect" are a by-product, "brains were naturally selected to increase in capacity and power for utilitarian reasons, until those higher faculties of intellect and spirit emerged as a by-product ...".[151]

Now it's at this point that we meet the upsurging waters that have already cascaded over *Titanic's* for'ard bulkheads. We already know from Chapter 5 that natural selection is no more than a tinkerer. It's not capable of inventing novelty, rather only of tweaking already existing functionality. But even if we didn't know that, is it credible, as Denton puts it, that "a brain capable of the intellectual feats of an Einstein, a Newton, or a Mozart"[152] – which far exceed the requirements of mere survival – simply emerged as a by-product of traits that enabled hunter-gathering activities? Is human cognitive capability – especially exemplified in language – not of a different "kind"? Does it not represent a huge *discontinuity* between chimps and humans?

Surprisingly, perhaps, Alfred Russel Wallace thought so. Recall that Wallace was Darwin's contemporary who had threatened to overtake Darwin in the race to publish his own thesis on natural selection. Even though Wallace, too, believed that natural selection was powerful, he was realistic that it could not select for features that *might* be useful in the future, "We are ... driven to the conclusion that in his large and well-developed brain he possesses an organ quite disproportionate to his actual requirements – an organ that seems prepared in advance, only to be fully utilised as he progresses in civilisation".[153] Chomsky agreed, "[Wallace] recognized that mathematical capacities could not have developed by natural selection; it's impossible because everybody's got them, and nobody's ever used them, except for some very tiny fringe of people in very recent times. Plainly, they developed in some other way".[154] Even the eminent evolutionist Ernst Mayr affirmed that human cognitive abilities are unique.[155]

In his paper, "Human and animal cognition: Continuity and discontinuity", Premack examines eight cognitive cases – teaching, short-term memory, causal reasoning, planning, deception, transitive inference, theory of mind, and language – and finds "in all cases, that similarities between animal and human abilities are small, dissimilarities large".[127] Another contemporary of Darwin, Richard Owen, the founder of the London Natural History Museum, disagreed with Darwin's continuity thesis. He believed that nature is fundamentally *discontinuous*, conforming to "primal patterns" and not led up to by a long series of functional transitional forms.[156]

In previous chapters, we've already come across discontinuities between non-living matter and a living cell, between different proteins, between different families in the fossil record, and between different embryonic development paths. Human cognitive and language abilities are surely another.

Similar genes – are they similar enough?

As we've ventured below deck within this fifth 'watertight compartment' we've discovered that the human fossil evidence is surprisingly sparse, fragmented, unconvincing and hotly disputed amongst experts in the field; and we've identified significant anatomical and behavioural discontinuities between apes and humans. It's time to descend one final stairwell to survey the *genetic* evidence – aware that the damage has already begun to flood this compartment.

The similarity between chimp and human genomes – their DNA – has been much trumpeted. Back in 1975 a paper published in *Science* announced that the genetic difference between humans and chimpanzees was only 1%.[157] Although this revelation was considered to be heretical at the time,[158] since then it has become axiomatic that humans and chimps are 99% similar, an iconic symbol of the apparent evidence for human evolution. In 1991 in *The Blind Watchmaker*, Dawkins propagated the ubiquitous claim, "Chimpanzees and we share more than 99 per cent of our genes".[159] Yet, within less than 10 years, the much acclaimed one percent difference had been exposed as a myth.[160] More recent estimates of the difference have ranged from 5% (2002) through 6.4% (2007), even to as much as 16% (2018).[161]

So how was the 1% figure derived? The initial work focused only on the protein coding regions of the DNA, which represent perhaps two percent of the whole genome. From the perspective of an engineer reusing designs, the commonality here is unsurprising. Indeed it should be anticipated. Why? We know from Chapters 4 and 5 that functional proteins are extremely rare in amino-acid sequence space. And we know that the 3-D shape of a protein is determined by that sequence (which is in turn coded in DNA) and critical to achieving specificity of function. And given that chimps and humans do share similar tissue structures and similar bodily functions – including digestion, cardiovascular respiration and reproduction – many proteins would be expected to be near identical. Close correlation between protein coding regions in human and chimp DNA is therefore to be expected.

Why the focus on this tiny fraction of the genome? In the 1970s it was not technically feasible to sequence entire genomes and since the purpose of the other ninety-eight percent was not understood it was thought to be not worth comparing. However, there is something else at work here, else why be so bold in making the 1% claim based on such a small fraction of the data? The focus on this tiny percentage of the genome was due to *Evolution*'s prediction that most of the DNA would be non-functional "junk DNA". The assumption was that this "junk" had been left over from millions of years of mutational trial-and-error. Now, to the engineering mind, a computer analogy could be appropriate here. Without an operating system, a computer might be an effective paperweight, but not much else. The operating system supports and regulates all the other applications such as word-processing, emailing and internet browsing. The prior assumption, therefore, that DNA would have only one "app" (protein coding) and no operating system (now known as "gene regulatory networks") is illustrative of the power of the evolutionary paradigm: most of the DNA is "junk" so we don't need to compare these huge stretches of nucleotide strings. As we know from Chapter 5, the ENCODE project has revealed the myth of "junk DNA".

Yet in 2011, Alice Roberts' glossy-picture-filled hardback, *Evolution: The Human Story*, clearly intended to inform the interested layperson, gives the headline figure as 1.2% in a diagram comparing orangutan and gorilla, as well as chimp and human.[162] Even in 2014 she mentions only the 99% similarity figure.[163] However, this figure only takes account of base substitutions; that's to say, point differences where human and chimp nucleotide base sequences *do* align. It ignores those that *can't* be aligned: huge stretches of DNA that appear in the human (but not the ape) genome; and similarly, other sequences present in the ape (but not the human) genome. The evolutionary jargon uses the label *indels* because such sequences are assumed to have been *in*serted or *del*eted respectively. The accompanying text concedes that, taking indels into account, the total genomic difference is about 5%.

THE WAITING TIME PROBLEM. Whether, 1%, 5% or 16%, here's the real problem. And it relates to the water flowing over the bulkhead from the second 'watertight compartment' discussed in Chapter 5 - natural selection's *lack* of creative power. It's at this point that we will discover why the fifth 'watertight compartment' will flood with "mathematical certainty".

The human genome extends to about three billion base-pairs. So even if we adopt the 1% difference number, then at least 30 million nucleotide bases differ between chimp and human DNA. Let's assume we can attribute 15 million mutations from the putative common ancestor to each of the chimp and human lines of descent respectively (giving the 30 million total). This difference is approximately equivalent to the information content in one volume of Encyclopaedia Britannica (~1.4 million words). Chimps are programmed by their DNA to look and behave like chimps; humans are programmed by their DNA to look and behave like humans.[164] And given all the anatomical, organisational and behavioural differences between the two species described earlier, this huge genetic information difference in programming is entirely credible.

If we were simply to consider restructuring the foot, even it would be a very complex genetic undertaking. As Sanford and Rupe point out, "Many bones, ligaments, muscles and neurons would have to be reprogrammed, requiring the creation and reworking of many genes".[165] And it's not as if changes in the foot could function in isolation. Coordinated leg, knee, hip, backbone, neck and skull programming changes would be required in a timely manner too. What about the new information to specify the twenty extra facial muscles; the extraordinary brain and vocal tract organisational changes to enable speech and language? The probability that all the required programming differences could be accumulated by nucleotide base mutation events one or more at a time is vanishingly small. No software engineer would consider producing a new app by taking an existing app and changing one or two characters or symbols at a time - nor would she expect the program would still function following each 'mutation' occurrence. She would know that the program would crash long before novel functionality emerged. As we discovered in Chapter 5, Dawkins' "METHINKS IT IS LIKE A WEASEL" illustration suffers from more than one fatal logical flaw. In particular it depends upon fore-knowledge of the target string such that any single

8 – FAILED PREDICTION #5: The human species evolved from apes

'correct' mutation would immediately be selected and retained. This fallacy alone renders the *Blind Watchmaker* explanation non-Darwinian. How can we better simulate how long it might take for needed mutations to occur?

Back in 1957, the celebrated geneticist J.B.S. Haldane was first to recognise one element of what is now labelled *the waiting time problem*. It became known as *Haldane's dilemma*. He realised that once a beneficial mutation arose within a population it would take a large number of generations and a huge death-cost for that mutation to become 'fixed', meaning driving the previous variant to extinction. He published a paper in which he estimated that only about 1000 beneficial mutations could become 'fixed' in a pre-human population over the claimed 6 million years of its evolution.[166] This falls well short of the 15 million mutations needed and we know it's more likely to be 5 or 10 times this number. If Haldane had assumed a *ready* supply of beneficial mutations, it is now known that the vast majority of mutations are neutral or detrimental, not beneficial. "Beneficial mutations are rare and high impact beneficial mutations are extremely rare."[167]

Sanford *et al.* have developed a software program, *Mendel's Accountant*, that realistically simulates the mutation/selection process.[168] The program allows more than 25 parameters to be adjusted, such as population size, generation time, mutation rate per generation, and fitness benefit. Using generally accepted assumptions about early human evolution – a population size of 10,000, a generation time of 20 years, and a mutation rate per generation of one in 100 million – they then set out to determine the "average time required to *fix a specific set of linked mutations in a given population in order to establish a specific alteration in the genome, such that a specific new function is created that meets a specific evolutionary challenge [emphasis in original]*".[169]

The idea is that, in a given simulation run, everything in the genome is assumed already to be in place to give the organism an evolutionary advantage (here called a *fitness benefit*), *except* for a *small* number of specific nucleotide base mutations, all of which must occur simultaneously to provide that functional advantage. In their simulation runs they varied that *small* number from just 1 up to combinations of 8 nucleotide substitutions.

A *fitness benefit* of 10% was used, meaning individuals with the specified mutations would have a relative reproductive advantage of 10%. This is highly conservative; 0.1% fitness benefit is more typical in population genetics studies. **The results are revealing: the average waiting time for a combination of only 2 co-dependent beneficial mutations was 84 million years.** Yet supposedly, within 6 or 7 million years, pre-humans accumulated many, many more co-dependent beneficial mutations in order to achieve all the physical and behavioural changes outlined above. In *Mendel's Accountant*, even just one specific substitution averaged more than 1.5 million years waiting time and a combination of 6 co-dependent substitutions averages 4.2 billion years – about the age of the earth. With a string length of 8, the average is 18 billion years, more than the age of the universe.[170] These latter two parameter sets, strings of 6 and 8, straddle the requirements to create just one new functional protein from an already existing very similar one, as we discovered in Chapter 5. And these results offer independent confirmation of Chapter 5's waiting time conclusions.

Using a more realistic fitness benefit of 0.1%, a string of just 2 mutations becoming fixed in a human population would have a waiting time of nearly a billion years.[171] **Clearly, accumulating the new information required to transform an ape into a human by a Darwinian process requires a prohibitively long timescale.**

GENETIC ENTROPY. We came across "entropy" in Chapter 4: the inexorable tendency for systems to move from a state of order to one of disorder. Cars and ocean-going liners inexorably accumulate rust, for example. The same proclivity to disorganisation is true in the world of genetics. This brief overview of the topic is covered more fully elsewhere.[172]

Even though the genomes of living organisms have assemblies of protein machines which are able to correct most errors occurring during reproduction (unlike most viruses), nevertheless, errors – mutations – do occasionally occur. The human mutation rate, mentioned above, is around one in a 100 million per person per generation, which means that each newborn human being acquires around 30 mostly neutral mutations (independent of population size). And here's the crippling snag for evolution: natural selection will eliminate only the fatal or significantly debilitating combinations of mutations. Most bad mutations are too subtle to be quickly eliminated by natural selection. This innate, inescapable process is degenerative. It entails a relentless net loss of information over time.[173]

It follows from the genetic entropy evidence that *Homo sapiens*, far from <u>ev</u>olving (gaining genetic information), **is instead <u>dev</u>olving** (losing genetic information).

Lower lifeboat 8!
Here's a summary of Chapter 8.

- Darwin's theory that humans evolved from apes quickly gained acceptance because it gave scientific legitimacy to the widely held view that Europeans were superior to other "sub-human" races. It was then self-evident that transitionary species *must* have existed and that fossils *would* be found.
- If ever there were a discipline whose science was inherently low-confidence, palaeoanthropology (with the willing collusion of the headline-hungry media) is surely it.
- Science historian Richard Delisle has recognised that the sociology of fossil-hunting encourages poor scientific practices, "... paleo-anthropology should reduce reliance on personal preferences and preconceptions, and move toward more rigorous operational and analytical practice and procedure, elaboration of common rules of engagement, and more open and accessible discourse".[174]
- A prominent field worker is even more forthright: "Paleo-anthropology's ecosystem of publishing, access, fundraising, career advancement, media promotion and celebrity seems squarely aligned against the field's ability to self regulate, a condition exacerbated by the limited fossil resources available".[175]
- New fossil discoveries touted as "missing links" in our human ancestry instantly attract high profile media attention and celebrity status for the palaeoanthropologist in question. As often as not, when the new find is examined in succeeding months by other experts it turns out to be much less of a breakthrough – if at all – than the original hype and headlines promised. But the impression of human evolution as "fact" has already been reinforced in the public consciousness.
- Experts admit that the story just doesn't hold up, "For anthropology students 30 years ago, learning human evolution was a breeze. It went from *Australopithecus* to *Homo habilis* to *Homo erectus* to various *Homo sapiens*. It was a straight shot that one could learn in a

few minutes late at night while cramming for an exam. But in the late 1970s, we entered a golden age of human fossil discoveries that has repeatedly punched holes in the naïve idea that our evolution would be that clear, clean, and straight ... The straight line has blossomed into a spreading, rather uncontrolled bush and we don't like it. We want our history to be nice and neat, but the fossils keep messing us up".[176] To preserve an evolutionary narrative a trunk and branches seem to have been drawn for the "bush" on such charts despite the complete absence of supporting fossil evidence.

- *Nature* agrees: "We have all seen the canonical parade of apes, each one becoming more human. We know that, as a depiction of evolution, this line-up is tosh. Yet we cling to it. Ideas of what human evolution ought to have been like still colour our debates".[177]
- Fossil curator David Pilbeam admits, "If you brought in a smart scientist from another discipline and showed him the meagre evidence we've got, he'd surely say, 'forget it; there isn't enough to go on'".[178]
- "Imagine if we lined up human skeletons – including a 7 foot-tall Watusi tribesman, a dwarf, a professional wrestler, a midget, and various modern humans with various growth disorders or pathologies. This would represent a wider range of skeletal morphologies than all the variations seen among the fossils that are described as different species of the genus *Homo*."[179]
- It follows that most of the fossils classified in the genus *Homo*, including *erectus* and *neanderthalensis* easily fall within the range of modern human morphology.
- Meanwhile those in the genera *Australopithecus*, *Paranthropus* and *Ardipithecus* together with the "mess" of the *Homo habilis* classification are almost certainly no more than various species of extinct apes.
- Evidence from sites in Kenya, Tanzania and Ethiopia suggests that modern humans appeared suddenly and coexisted with various ape species including australopithecines, such as Lucy.
- Today no fossils are claimed to be clearly ancestral to modern humans in the putative lineage from an ape-like ancestor (see Fig. 8.13).
- The evolutionary mechanism fails to account for the *differences* – the major physical and cognitive *discontinuities* – between chimp-like animals and humans.

8 – FAILED PREDICTION #5: The human species evolved from apes

- Human characteristics are distinctive: "It is not that difficult to tell a human from an ape, after all. The human is the one walking, talking, sweating, praying, building, reading, trading, crying, dancing, writing, cooking, joking, working, decorating, shaving, driving a car, or playing football. Quite literally, from the top of our head (where the hair is continually growing, unlike gorillas) to the tips of our toes (the stoutest of which is non-opposable), one can tell the human part from the ape part quite readily if one knows what to look for. Our eye-whites, small canine teeth, evaporative heat loss, short arms and long legs, breasts, knees, and of course, our cognitive communication abilities and the productive anatomies of our tongue and throat are all dead giveaways".[180]
- "Types are distinct and isolated and not led up to via a long series of functional transitional forms as Darwinism demands. On the contrary, the evidence ... points ... to discontinuity and to the ultimate Darwinian nightmare – that gaps were crossed ... in a series of jumps, a mode of sudden emergence which eliminates any possibility of attributing agency to natural selection ..."[181]
- The genetic evidence against human evolution is devastating. It's here in the already severely punctured fifth watertight compartment that we meet the water gushing over the insufficiently high bulkheads from forward compartments.
- The genetic difference between humans and chimps is much greater than the apocryphal and widely touted 1%, and may be as much as 16%.[182]
- The waiting time for just two co-dependent beneficial mutations to occur in a pre-human species is more than ten times the claimed timespan in which modern humans supposedly evolved.
- Each human acquires about 30 new mutations which are likely to be detrimental and passes them on to the next generation – genetic entropy. This adds to the evidence from Chapter 5 that random mutations plus natural selection, instead of *accumulating* information and complexity – <u>ev</u>olution – will rather lead to <u>de</u>volution: a net and continuous *loss* of information.

RMS *Evolution*'s bow is now well below the waves and the freezing sea is rolling and bubbling up over the foredeck as the huge stern simultaneously rises out of the water.

Part 3

SHE'S SINKING!

But few people know this, or that there's a better theory

Thomas Andrews - *Titanic's* Chief Designer

"She's made of iron, sir, I assure you she can [sink] and she will, with mathematical certainty."

Introduction to part 3

DARWIN WAS WRONG. That was the unlooked-for conclusion to which I was inexorably led ...[1]

A.N. Wilson

If Darwin described *The Origin of Species* as "one long argument"[2] in favour of his theory, Part 2 of this book could be described as one long counter-argument demonstrating that RMS *Evolution* has collided with the 'molecular biology iceberg'. Hoyle and Wickramasinghe pointed out that, before modern molecular biology, it was difficult to refute *Evolution*.[3] But we have now ventured below deck and discovered holes – **five failed predictions** – in RMS *Evolution*'s 'watertight compartments' as a result of crashing into that molecular biology iceberg (arguably RMS *Evolution* sinks if any one of these compartments fails, whereas all five needed to be holed to sink *Titanic*):

1. **Life emerged from chemistry.** It would appear that the likelihood of the first living cell, and especially its enormous *complex specified information* content, emerging from inanimate molecules is so indescribably low as to be, for all practical purposes, zero. Atoms and molecules bumping around for billions of years, even given the size and putative age of the observable universe, struggle to produce even a single *functional* protein.
2. **Natural selection has creative power.** All the evidence, from dog breeding to observations of bacteria over tens of thousands of generations, indicates that natural selection is severely limited in its power. Its modus operandi will inevitably lead to <u>de</u>volution, loss of information, sliding *down* rather than *up Mount Improbable*. Why? First, because each successive round of adaptation is likely to eliminate some genes from the gene pool, meaning that less variability will be available for future adaptation; second, because *many* slightly deleterious mutations will accumulate (ultimately resulting in catastrophic failure of function) long before the *staggeringly rare* combinations of mutations required to generate *novel* functionality can possibly emerge.
3. **The "tree-of-life" is recorded in the fossils.** Despite what we have all been led to believe, the pattern displayed by the fossil record is in direct opposition to that anticipated by *Evolution*. The statistic-

ally dominant characteristic of the fossil record is the sudden appearance of entirely novel phyla with no evidence that such novelty has been led up to by a gradual sequence of intermediate forms.

4. **Similar embryos imply common ancestry**. The idea that as embryos develop they recapitulate their putative evolutionary history - fish to amphibian to reptile to mammal - is a myth that still lives on in evolutionary textbooks to this day. Instead it turns out that each embryo's development is recognisably unique. Neo-Darwinism makes much of homology: the biological, especially anatomical, *continuity* amongst species. But it's how the *differences* arose that the evolutionary mechanism needs to - and fails to - explain. Nor is there comfort for the idea of universal common descent from genes. Trees-of-life derived from similar genes often differ according to which gene is used, and differ from the orthodox tree based on anatomy. Further, to the great surprise of evolutionists, each time the genome of a new species is sequenced, around 10% of its protein-coding DNA is found to be unique.

5. **The human species evolved from apes**. The ubiquitous *March of Progress* parade of apes, each one becoming more human-like, is acknowledged as "tosh",[4] even amongst palaeoanthropologists. The fragmentary fossil evidence doesn't support it. Instead the evidence is consistent with the view that all of the *Homo* species, including *erectus* and *neanderthalensis* are indistinguishable from the range of modern human morphologies alive today, and that *Homo* was coexistent with other genera, such as *Australopithecus*. The apocryphal 1% difference between chimp and human genomes, derived in the 1970s, is now known to be at least 10%. Realistic simulations of the "waiting time" required for just 2 co-dependent mutations to evolve, never mind the much greater numbers needed, vastly exceeds the timeframe in which *Homo sapiens* is claimed to have evolved from apes.

Few of *Evolution's* critics doubt that natural selection is a real phenomenon: that it can explain cases such as bacterial resistance to antibiotics, variation in the shape of finch beaks in response to changing climate and why polar bears are white. These examples illustrate microevolution, small-scale change at the species or perhaps the genus level of taxonomy. But it soon runs up against the buffers of its limitations: its inability to build novel biological function due to the complexity – the *specified* complexity – of biochemical machines.

If *Titanic* hadn't hit an iceberg, she would have crossed the Atlantic in about 5½ days, a distance of about 3,600 miles. Does that mean in 366 days – a leap year – she could have sailed to the Moon, a distance of approximately 240,000 miles? Clearly, sailing to the Moon would be an extrapolation much too far for *Titanic*. Similarly, the "long counter-argument" in Part 2 demonstrates that small-scale-change-over-time microevolution by random mutation and natural selection *is* a real phenomenon at work in nature, but that all the other uses of the word "evolution" extrapolate the power of mindless, unguided processes well beyond their capability. In other words the scientific evidence neither supports particles-to-people *Evolution*, nor bacteria-to-Beethoven universal common descent, nor even evolution-of-new-body-plans macroevolution (see Table 3.1).

The limit of the mutations plus natural selection mechanism would appear to be at the taxonomic level of family or below. To put this in perspective, recall that living organisms are identified within 8 levels of taxonomy, from domain through kingdom, phylum, class, order, family, genus and species. Biochemist Michael Behe illustrates the severity of this limitation by representing the levels as an 8 digit number of dollars, say $213,754.36. The neo-Darwinian mechanism can only stretch to change within the pennies and dimes (to, say, $213,754.83).[5]

And rather than Darwin's *tree* of universal common descent with a single root, the evidence is instead consistent with an *orchard* full of bushes, one for each individual family, such as Felidae – the cat family (see Fig. 6.7). So Darwin's claim for the power of natural selection was a speculative *extrapolation* much too far.

Titanic had hoped to make headlines. She did, but instead of being fêted with rapturous praise for her elegance, luxury and speed, the public's unanticipated new realisation was that the unsinkable *Titanic* was in fact very sinkable. Similarly, despite the ubiquitous lauding of Darwin and his 'discovery' of natural selection, the reality is that **what is true about *Evolution* is rather trivial: that natural selection is a tinkerer, not a designer or creator. And by implication the grand claims of *Evolution* are simply untrue.** However, as we know, failed theories are nothing new in science. As author and journalist Arthur Koestler put it, "The progress of science is strewn, like an ancient desert trail, with the bleached skeletons of discarded theories which once seemed to possess eternal life".[6]

Two important questions arise. If the science supporting *Evolution* fails, as we've seen in Part 2:

- Why is *Evolution* still so widely believed by the majority of people, certainly in the West?
- Is there another explanation that better fits the evidence?

These questions will be explored in Part 3.

Another category of question arises which is beyond the scope of this book: if we believe *Evolution* to be true and interpret it, not just as a scientific theory, but also as a purely naturalistic, unguided process - sometimes labelled *evolutionism* - what are the logical consequences of such a view? What are the repercussions for our beliefs about humanity; our relationship with animals; our relationship with various people groups including the disabled, the unborn, the newborn and the senile; our beliefs about free will, the human mind, morality, justice, and the existence of a Creator? Appendix B offers an outline response to this line of questioning.

Chapter 9

Why is RMS *Evolution* still afloat?

I call it theory-induced blindness: once you have accepted a theory and used it as a tool in your thinking, it is extraordinarily difficult to notice its flaws. If you come upon an observation that does not seem to fit the model, you assume that there must be a perfectly good explanation that you are somehow missing. You give the theory the benefit of the doubt, trusting the community of experts who have accepted it.[1]

Daniel Kahneman

In this chapter we will explore the major reasons why RMS *Evolution* is (still) the dominant explanation for the origin of everything alive, despite the clear scientific evidence against it.
- The marketing hype says "She's unsinkable".
- Most people don't know there's been a collision (with the scientific evidence).
- Dissent (or even descent) below decks is not tolerated.
- Why so intolerant – is this a new religion?

The marketing hype is "She's unsinkable"

The zeitgeist of today's Western culture is, on the whole, one of almost universal scepticism. It is axiomatic that there is no such thing as "absolute truth". Everything and anything is questioned, doubted and often rejected. Fake news is everywhere. Institutional authority, whether political, religious or secular is held in disrepute and distrusted.

But there's one exception to this ubiquitous ethos. For many, belief in the evolutionary narrative is entirely intact. It's the one 'sacred' truth. Darwinian doctrine is so central to our upbringing and education, and so comprehensively promoted within the media, that few even think to question it. Science writer Angela Saini describes how such an all-pervasive narrative becomes foundational to our thinking, "... the stories we're raised on, the tales, myths, legends, beliefs, even the old scientific orthodoxies, are how we frame everything we learn. The stories are our culture. They are the minds we inhabit".[2] Nowhere is this influence more disturbingly true than in works of popular fiction. Think of Dan Brown's 2018 Robert Langdon novel, *Origin*. Having stated on an introductory page that the science he presents is real "Fact",[3] as the story then unfolds, he makes the false claim that a rerun of the Miller-Urey experiment in 2008 produced DNA![4] (See Chapters 4 and 5).

As an example of popular non-fiction, in his 2015 book, *Sapiens: A Brief History of Humankind*,[5] Yuval Harari weaves a historical account that unquestioningly assumes the truth of *Evolution*. He sees no need to justify it. He simply takes it for granted that he and everyone else believes it to be scientifically demonstrated "fact".

Then there's the constant drumbeat of documentaries promoted by the broadcast media in which we are informed that "nature has produced the neck of the giraffe, the farming techniques of leafcutter ants, the dance of bees, the compound eyes of flies, the sense of smell in dogs, the beauty of roses, and the big brains, upright posture, and moral and creative capacities of human beings. We are told that nature has made everything by itself, without intelligence or plan."[6] Views of this ilk are simply asserted over and over. Apparently there is no need to substantiate them. The *Evolution* hegemony has complete control of the media. Saini's analysis, albeit in a different context, is nevertheless apt here, "... knowledge is not just an honest account of what we know, but has to be seen as something manipulated by those who happen to hold power when it is written [or broadcast]".[7] As physician and science writer Ben Goldacre points out, journalists are short of time, yet are under pressure to fill pages and churn out documentaries. Such an atmosphere severely reduces the likelihood that thorough research will be undertaken. And this results in what has been described as "*Churnalism*, the uncritical rehashing of press releases into content".[8] Echoing many of our 'Ice warnings', Goldacre, too, has signalled how bias often results in unsound beliefs:

- In relation to a given hypothesis, we (and journalists) seek out and then overvalue *confirmatory* information.
- Our assessment of the quality of new evidence is biased by our previous beliefs.[9]

Perhaps, then, if journalists were to interrogate origin-of-life scientists as vigorously as they typically grill politicians, the public would have an opportunity to be better informed. As Goldacre states, "Journalists are used to listening with a critical ear to briefings from press officers, politicians [and others], and they generally display a healthy natural scepticism; but in the case of science, they don't have the skills to critically appraise a piece of scientific evidence on its merits".[10] (There will, of course, almost certainly be occasional exceptions to Goldacre's claim.)

As a consequence, there is a huge gulf between what is generally believed about *Evolution*, and the truth. In a recent survey of people, mostly of college degree education level, more than 72 percent of respondents thought (erroneously) that origin of life researchers had created "simple life forms from scratch" in the laboratory, such as bacteria (although we saw in Chapter 4 that bacteria are in fact very complex). More than 40% even thought scientists had created complex life forms, such as frogs, from scratch.[11]

When doubts are expressed about *Evolution* it is not uncommon to hear in response, "I am no expert, but lots of people, including scientists that I trust, have no doubts". Nobel prize-winning psychologist, Daniel Kahneman confirms how dependent we are upon others for some of our foundational beliefs.

> *For some of our most important beliefs we have no evidence at all, except that people we love and trust hold these beliefs. Considering how little we know, the confidence we have in our beliefs is preposterous ...*[12]

Picture this moment: *Titanic's* engines have come to a stop following the collision; EJ Smith's and Thomas Andrews' inspection party has discovered the extent of the damage, and passengers have been instructed to don lifejackets and muster at their lifeboat stations. A scene in Cameron's 1997 film then ensues in which passengers in the saloon are plied with drinks by stewards as they continue to enjoy animated and unhurried conversations, oblivious to the seriousness of the crisis. Why worry? After all, even if *Titanic* has bumped into an iceberg: the ship is unsinkable, is it not?

Here is a dramatic example of "groupthink" at work. Geneticist John Sanford was a committed evolutionist for most of his adult life. He believed *Evolution*, including ape-to-human evolution to be an "obvious fact of science". He goes on, "But I did not hold that view based upon careful examination of the evidence. Since I only had a superficial understanding of the topic, where did my certainty come from? Like any other scientist who is outside of their field of expertise, I was primarily persuaded by "groupthink", which is especially strong amongst the academic community ... this over-arching groupthink about evolution was powerfully reinforced by lay-level science articles and powerful visuals promoted through the mass media ... But I never took time to actually study the scientific literature (I was already certain) ... This would explain why so many academics are extremely certain of human evolution, yet have never actually studied it, and have almost no grasp of the subject".[13] Goldacre corroborates this phenomenon, "Communal reinforcement [and] testimonials within communities ... can supplant and become more powerful than scientific evidence".[14] Kahneman, too, confirms this curiosity:

> We know that people can maintain an unshakeable faith in any proposition, however absurd, when they are sustained by a community of like-minded believers.[15]

When steaming at full speed, *Titanic's* momentum was such that even with the engines throbbing full astern, she could not come to a stop in less than 800 yards. In a similar way, the momentum of groupthink and unquestioning loyalty to the ruling paradigm within the community of evolutionary biologists sustains belief – even in the face of counter-evidence. Recall Stephen Jay Gould's admission (Chapter 1) that "The greatest impediment to scientific innovation is usually a conceptual lock, not a factual lack".[16]

RMS *Evolution*'s momentum sanctions the use of iconic stories, such as the Miller-Urey experiment (Chapter 4), non-Darwinian computer simulations such as METHINKS IT IS LIKE A WEASEL (Chapter 5), the tree-of-life (Chapter 6), Haeckel's embryos (Chapter 7) and the March of Progress (Chapter 8). All of these stories are, at best misleading, and at worst, fraudulent. This momentum permits the dissemination of these and other myths in evolutionary biology, including the belief that proteins could have evolved from simple forms starting with small numbers of amino acids. This belief is propagated by evolutionary textbooks, but never actually substantiated, nor even scrutinised.

Because RMS *Evolution* is so widely believed to be unsinkable, any evidence that *appears* to support that conclusion is readily accepted. Here's Kahneman again.

> ... when people believe a conclusion is true, they are also very likely to believe arguments that appear to support it, even when these arguments are unsound ... [often] the conclusion comes first and the arguments follow.[17]

Other psychologists, such as Jonathan Haidt,[18] agree with Kahneman. They claim studies have shown that we believe less by reason than by intuition. That, contrary to the Enlightenment belief in the power of rationalism, we instead tend to reach a conclusion quickly and intuitively. Then we justify that conclusion, after the fact, by formulating supportive reasoning.

Science is not immune to this phenomenon, as we discovered in Chapter 1. So for example, Priestley never relinquished his belief in phlogiston; it took decades to vindicate Bretz's Lake Missoula flood theory; they laughed at Wegener's plate tectonics ideas and at Marshall and Warren's peptic ulcer theory; and Chernobyl operators' firm belief was that nuclear reactors *do not explode* so they failed to 'see' lumps of burning radioactive graphite before their very eyes.

Once a scientific paradigm has become mainstream and a conclusion reached, it's remarkably easy to:

1. Ignore counter-evidence. Kahneman lists two important facts about our minds, "... we can be blind to the obvious and we are also blind to our blindness".[19]
2. Accommodate counter-evidence within the current paradigm. There *must* be a good explanation. And surely someone *must* have found that explanation already.

Most don't know there's been a collision

At 11:40 pm on Sunday 14th April 1912, when *Titanic's* lookout, Frederick Fleet, realised that an iceberg was dead ahead, none of the passengers, nor even most of the officers and crew, had any idea that a catastrophic collision was both inevitable and imminent. The ship's chief designer Thomas Andrews was preoccupied, poring over ship's plans in his first class cabin, oblivious to the impending disaster. Even when the fateful collision occurred, he perhaps felt only a series of slight judders. Yet down below the waterline, as the iceberg ripped intermittently morse-code-like through steel, freezing north Atlantic ocean was gushing into the Forepeak, into Hold numbers 1, 2, and 3, and into Boiler Room number 6.

RMS *Evolution* has already collided with the molecular biology 'iceberg', as we've discovered in Part 2. Yet the vast majority of scientists, even most biologists, and certainly the general public, have no idea that evolutionary theory is in trouble, never mind sinking.

Bioengineer Matti Leisola recalls a conversation with biochemistry professor Michael Gold who died in 2015. When asked for his views on *Evolution*, Gold said that he had never really thought about it, but that it was probably true. Leisola was surprised that "an internationally known biochemist accepted evolution without ever having given it serious thought".[20] In Leisola's experience, however, this was not unusual. Michael Sherman of Boston University is also puzzled, "As a professional biologist, I have always wondered why the Darwinian idea of evolution is so accepted among my colleagues. If one were to poll biologists, I would bet that almost all of them would say that there has been evolution and that it has taken place in accord with Darwin's theory. Probably 95% of them, however, have never thought seriously about evolution …".[21]

Environmental scientist David Swift concluded that even those who should have properly scrutinised the evidence have not in fact done so: "I have also come to realise that most biologists haven't even looked at the evidence behind what they believe, and all too many are reluctant to do so … It seems evolutionists cannot risk questioning whether [their] basic belief … is actually well-founded, because if it is seen to fail then it undermines the whole (macro)evolutionary edifice".[22]

However, when someone does venture 'below decks' and examines the evidence, they are often shocked by what they find. A growing number of scientists and others are asking questions and seeking answers. Here are a few examples.

PERTTI MARKKANEN. Leisola, when he was acting professor of biochemistry at Helsinki's University of Technology, describes an occasion when he had a debate about *Evolution* in the student union with his former teacher, assistant professor of microbiology. It turned out that Markkanen had never critically examined the Darwinian claims and, to the surprise of everyone present, when Leisola presented his arguments against *Evolution*, Markkanen found himself agreeing with almost every point.[23] He later became a Darwin sceptic. Such admirable open-mindedness among biologists is as remarkable as it is rare. Leisola himself had begun his career as an 'insider', with no doubts about naturalistic neo-Darwinism. Later when his assumptions were challenged by a persistently recalcitrant student, among others, he set out in a new direction of research and discovery.

MICHAEL BEHE, too, was an 'insider' to begin with. As professor of biochemistry at Lehigh University, he had accepted *Evolution* as the received wisdom for much of his career. The idea that the science might be incorrect had not even occurred to him. One of the problems for 'insiders' is their focus on a single specialism. Geoscientist Lynn Margulis lists more than a dozen disciplines involved in studying *Evolution* (it's not exhaustive):

> Biochemistry, cell biology, geology, invertebrate zoology, metabolism, molecular evolution, microbial ecology, nutrition, paleontology, protistology [the study of single-celled organisms], sedimentary geology, and virology are all relevant to deciphering the origins of species.[24]

So even if a scientist were to have doubts about evolutionary theory as a result of observations within her or his own field of expertise, such thoughts are likely to be suppressed due to a lack of evidence that practitioners in *other* relevant disciplines are expressing similar doubts. Michael Polanyi explains that

> ... nobody knows more than a tiny fragment of science well enough to judge its validity and value at first hand. For the rest he has to rely on views accepted at second hand on the authority of a community of people accredited as scientists.[25]

But then Behe read Denton's *Evolution: A Theory in Crisis*,[26] a book which presents evidence across a range of branches of origins science. This opened Behe's eyes. He began to do his own research culminating in the publication of his own *Darwin's Black Box*.[27] He concluded that the result of

> ... cumulative efforts to investigate the cell - to investigate life at the molecular level - is a loud, clear, piercing cry of "design!"[28]

He goes on, "The result is so unambiguous and so significant that it must be ranked as one of the greatest achievements in the history of science. The discovery rivals those of Newton and Einstein ... The magnitude of the victory ... would be expected to send champagne corks flying in labs around the world ... But no bottles have been uncorked, no hands slapped. Instead, a curious, embarrassed silence surrounds the stark complexity of the cell. When the subject comes up in public, feet start to shuffle, and breathing gets a bit labored. In private people are a bit more relaxed; many explicitly admit the obvious but then stare at the ground, shake their heads, and let it go at that".[29]

A.N. WILSON. A surprise was in store for this author. Prior to commencing research for his biography of Darwin, *Charles Darwin: Victorian Mythmaker*, he had no idea he would later conclude that "Darwin was wrong".[30] He, like most people, doubted neither the veracity of Darwinian science nor project *Evolution*. Nor had he any intention at the outset of departing from mainstream scientific opinion. The thought hadn't even occurred to him, "There were a number of reasons why it did not even cross my mind that I would come to disbelieve in Darwin's theories".[31] First among these[32] was the plain fact that Wilson was not a scientist and was therefore dependent upon scientists for his knowledge of *Evolution*. Second, he recognised that the second half of the twentieth century had been a "neo-Darwinian Golden Age". Julian Huxley had published *Evolution in Action* in 1963, John Maynard Smith had updated *The Theory of Evolution* as late as 1993. Meantime, of course, Richard Dawkins had been busy with *The Selfish Gene*, *The Blind Watchmaker* and many more publications. Nevertheless, following much investigative research, he reached the "unlooked-for conclusion" that Darwin was wrong.

ANTONY FLEW. On 9th December 2004, an *Associated Press* headline read, "One of World's Leading Atheists Now Believes in God, More or Less, Based on Scientific Evidence".[33] Antony Flew (1923-2010), a British professor of philosophy who held academic positions at the Universities of Keele, Oxford, Aberdeen and Reading, a man who had spent much of his life in public debates in opposition to Christian apologists, 'came out'. He had announced at the beginning of his final public debate in May 2004 that he now accepted the existence of God. Why? In his book, *There Is ~~No~~ A God: How the world's most notorious atheist changed his mind,*[34] he explains that, following the evidence where it leads, he had reached the conclusion that intelligence must have been involved in establishing the "almost unbelievable complexity of the arrangements which are needed to

Figure 9.1 Antony Flew

produce life".[35] (Chapter 4 develops the argument which so influenced Flew.)

THOMAS NAGEL, Professor of Philosophy at New York University, in his book *Mind & Cosmos: Why the Materialist Neo-Darwinian Conception of Nature Is Almost Certainly False*,[36] candidly admits that

> [p]hysico-chemical reductionism in biology is the orthodox view, and any resistance to it is regarded as not only scientifically but politically incorrect. But for a long time I have found the materialist account of how we and our fellow organisms came to exist hard to believe, including the standard version of how the evolutionary process works.[37]

Much to the chagrin of establishment figures, Nagel lends credibility to the work of *Intelligent Design* proponents Michael Behe and Stephen Meyer among others.[38] Nagel did not change his atheistic worldview, however, which he describes as his "ungrounded intellectual preference".[39] The words "ungrounded" and "preference" are intriguing. Effectively he is admitting that he simply *dislikes* the idea that divine intervention might actually be the ultimate explanation of reality.

GÜNTER BECHLY, a palaeontologist, formerly curator at the State Museum of Natural History in Stuttgart, specialises in the fossil history and systematics of insects. Until his early 40s he had been a staunch supporter of neo-Darwinism. In 2009, as curator of the State Museum, he designed an exhibition to celebrate 150 years since the publication of *The Origin* (also 200 years since Darwin's birth). One of the exhibits he designed for the showcase event, which attracted over 100,000 visitors, was a large set of scales with a copy of *The Origin* in one pan while the other was loaded with a *stack* of books promoting Intelligent Design. The balance was of course rigged for the exhibit such that *The Origin* appeared to far outweigh the Intelligent Design stack – a striking visual image of a metaphorical message. But then Bechly, as he puts it, "made the mistake" of reading some of the books in the Intelligent Design pile, "**[W]hat I recognized to my surprise is that the arguments I found in those books were totally different from what I heard either**

Figure 9.2
Günter Bechly

from colleagues, or when you watch YouTube videos where the discussion is around intelligent design versus neo-Darwinian evolution. And I had the impression that on one side those people are mistreated, their position is mis-represented, and on the other hand that these arguments are not really receiving an appropriate response and they have merit [emphasis added]".[40] The result was a volte-face. His eyes were opened to the flaws of *Evolution* and he is now a senior scientist at the *Biologic Institute* and a senior fellow with *Discovery Institute's Center for Science and Culture*, which promotes the Intelligent Design movement.

DAVID GELERNTER, professor of computer science at Yale University, who is known for predicting the *World Wide Web* and for developing many complex computing tools, wrote an article in the highly respected *Claremont Review of Books* in the spring of 2019, entitled "Giving Up Darwin". In it he explained his defection from Darwinism:

Figure 9.3
David Gelernter

> ... there are many reasons to doubt whether [Darwin] can answer the hard questions and explain the big picture – not the fine-tuning of existing species but the emergence of new ones. The origin of species is exactly what Darwin cannot explain.[41]

Gelernter is an example of an academic who gives credit – for his change of mind about Darwin – to Stephen Meyer's *Darwin's Doubt* (2013) as well as to books by David Berlinski and David Klinghoffer[42] – all three of whom are senior fellows of the *Discovery Institute*.

JORDAN PETERSON. In 2018 this Canadian clinical psychologist and professor of psychology reached almost rock-star fame amidst the flurry of TV interviews following publication of his *12 Rules for Life: An Antidote to Chaos*.[43] As someone wedded to scientific materialism, he was surprised as he read Meyer's (and Axe's) discussion of the extreme improbability of a single protein fold arising within the universe over its entire existence[44] (as discussed in Chapter 4). Peterson's tweet exposes another example of a high profile academic who didn't know there had been a collision with the scientific evidence, "Is this an accurate claim? [Meyer] makes the case very carefully. It's not often I come across a book that contains so much that I did not know ...".[45]

Dissent (or even descent) below decks is not tolerated

If theory conflicts with the facts, so much the worse for the facts.[46]

Gottlieb Fichte

Once EJ and Thomas Andrews' party had completed their inspection of *Titanic's* no-longer-watertight compartments, a scene in the movie[47] ensues in which they report their findings to the officers on duty in the chart room next to the bridge. Bruce Ismay, chairman of the *White Star Line*, was also present. When Andrews announced that with five compartments flooding, it was inevitable that *Titanic* would sink, Ismay immediately rehearsed his unshakeable belief in no uncertain terms, "But this ship can't sink!" and "When can we get underway again, dammit?!" He foresaw no obstacle to *Titanic* completing her Atlantic crossing in record time. Delay (dissent) could not be tolerated. The character Rose, however, played by Kate Winslet, was not afraid to ask 'awkward' questions, such as why insufficient lifeboat capacity was an acceptable policy. So what has happened to those who 'dared' to venture 'below decks' (descent) on RMS *Evolution*?

Priests promote and defend an established orthodoxy. Prophets, however, challenge and 'call out' that establishment when its doctrine is in error. We already know that prophets are not welcome below deck. Recall that according to the 'priestly' Dawkins, "It is absolutely safe to say that if you meet somebody who claims not to believe in evolution, that person is ignorant, stupid or insane (or wicked, but I'd rather not consider that)".[48] Similarly he mocks those who disagree that natural selection has the power that evolutionists attribute to it, describing this stance as the "Argument from Personal Incredulity". He counters with a statement of his own faith position, "That is exactly what I firmly believe".[49]

It has become standard establishment practice to regard criticism of *Evolution* as forbidden. As one commentator has put it, "... the theory has taken on nearly dogmatic status with many in the profession, and ... anyone who dares to criticize it faces ostracism - or worse".[50] Commenting upon the Orwellian nature of a deteriorating atmosphere over the last several years, neurosurgeon Michael Egnor explained that, "... there has been a progressive loss of ordinary civility and ordinary conventions of scientific conduct. Challenging Darwinian groupthink in the biology community – merely asking questions about the adequacy of Darwinian theory to explain all of life – is professional suicide. Diversity of scientific opinion is not tolerated, and dissenters from the Darwinian mob have been hounded out of their jobs. Simply to speak up to question Darwinian orthodoxy is to invite professional and personal ruin – subjecting Darwinian orthodoxy to an objective discussion of the evidence is unthinkable in most public schools ...". Professional scientists who ought to "be devoted to academic freedom and open discussion"[51] are resorting to the law to silence dissent. "What inclines me now to think you might be right in regarding [*Evolution*] as *the* central and radical lie in the whole web of falsehood that now governs our lives", wrote C.S. Lewis in a letter to a friend, "is not so much your arguments against it as the fanatical and twisted attitudes of its defenders".[52]

Here are a few indicative examples of professionals whose experiences testify to such a toxic culture. But this is only the tip of the iceberg![53]

Following publication of the 1981 book, *Evolution from Space*,[54] which took a critical look at *Evolution*, someone threatened to burn down the house of one of the authors, Chandra Wickramasinghe, while he was in it. Police took the threat so seriously that Wickramasinghe fled from the UK with his family to his native Sri Lanka.[55]

In the year 2000, Chinese palaeontologist J.Y. Chen made a presentation in Seattle to faculty members of the University of Washington. While describing the exquisite fossils of the Chengjiang explosion (Chapter 6), his scientific credentials were cast in doubt when he highlighted the "apparent contradiction between the Chinese fossil evidence and Darwinian orthodoxy. As a result one professor in the audience asked ... if he wasn't nervous about expressing his doubts about Darwinism so freely - especially given China's reputation for suppressing dissenting opinion. With a wry smile, Chen responded, "**In China, we can criticise Darwin, but not the government. In America, you can criticise the government, but not Darwin** [emphasis added]".[56]

Thomas Nagel's claim, expressed in the subtitle of his book, that "the materialist neo-Darwinian conception of nature is almost certainly false" has attracted ridicule, anger and despair from loyal adherents of evolutionary orthodoxy. Andrew Ferguson's article, "The Heretic",[57] which headlines a cartoon image of Nagel being burned at the stake, includes a *Twitter/X* outburst from Steven Pinker, "What has gotten into Thomas Nagel?" Ferguson continues, "Tom, oh Tom ... how did we lose Tom? ...". It is simply taken for granted that by attacking materialism Thomas Nagel has rendered himself an embarrassment to his colleagues and a traitor to his class.

Leisola tells his story in his book *Heretic: One Scientist's Journey from Darwin to Design,*[58] published in 2018. The title of the book gives a sense of how he has been viewed by his colleagues and by the scientific community at large.

Director of the *Biologic Institute*, Douglas Axe, a chemical engineer and later a postdoctoral research scientist at the University of Cambridge, echoes these sentiments. He discovered early on that questioning the received wisdom is punished severely; during his final exams at Caltech, in answer to a question about the origin of life he gave the 'correct' answer in full and then followed on with an explanation of why he found the answer to be unconvincing. His exam paper was returned with points deducted for these remarks. They were clearly judged to be gratuitously heretical. He had learned his lesson: "We were there as much to be acculturated as educated. The stream of scientific consensus flows with an almost irresistible current".[59]

For Günter Bechly, who had co-authored around 150 scientific publications, had discovered and named over 160 new species, and had 10 biological groups named in his honour, the working atmosphere he experienced at the Stuttgart State Museum of Natural History now turned hostile. Following an exemplary seventeen-year career, the museum told him that "as a big threat to the credibility and reputation of the museum", he was "no longer welcome, and that it would be appreciated if [he] would decide to quit". He was forced to resign. In 2017, Wikipedia added to his 'punishment' by deleting its long-standing English-language page about Bechly.

When referring to his colleagues at Yale, David Gelernter had this to say, "Darwinism has indeed passed beyond a scientific argument as far as they are concerned. You take your life in your hands to challenge it intellectually. They will destroy you if you challenge it". He goes on, "Now, I haven't been destroyed, I am not a biologist, and I don't claim to be an authority on this topic ... but what I have seen in their behavior intellectually and at colleges across the West is nothing approaching free speech on this topic. It's a bitter, fundamental, angry, outraged rejection [of Intelligent Design], which comes nowhere near scientific or intellectual discussion. I've seen that happen again and again".[60]

Richard Sternberg who holds two PhDs in biology was a Research Associate at *Smithsonian's National Museum of Natural History*. On August 4th 2004, in his role as editor of *The Proceedings of the Biological Society of Washington* he published an article by Stephen Meyer entitled, "Intelligent Design: The Origin of Biological Information and the Higher Taxonomic Categories". The article had been through the normal peer review process. Although not a proponent of Intelligent Design at the time, Sternberg published it, "Because evolutionary biologists [had been] thinking about this. So I thought that by putting this on the table, there could be some reasoned discourse. That's what I thought, and I was dead wrong". The article was retracted. Around the Museum, it was rumoured that Sternberg wasn't even a scientist. His Research Associateship was not renewed. He lost his office. He was transferred to a hostile supervisor and demoted to research collaborator.

An independent investigation into the incident later concluded in a letter to Sternberg, "It is … clear that a hostile work environment was created with the ultimate goal of forcing you out of the [Smithsonian Institute]". In December 2006 a report by Staff of the House of Representatives Committee on Government Reform stated that, "… Dr. Sternberg's civil and constitutional rights were violated by Smithsonian officials … The failure of [two named officials] to take any action against such discrimination raises serious questions about the Smithsonian's willingness to protect the free speech and civil rights of scientists who may hold dissenting views on topics such as biological evolution".[61] In 2007, Sternberg, now a supporter of Intelligent Design, joined the *Center for Science and Culture* and he continues his research as a scientist with *Biologic Institute*.

There are many similar stories of scientists whose free speech has been censored, quashed or cancelled if they dared to dissent from materialistic evolutionary orthodoxy.[62] Many have been forced out of academic tenure. Similarly there are many examples of school biology teachers who have been demoted or forced out of their jobs for daring to make their pupils aware of counter-evidence to the ruling paradigm.[63]

The abusive language used by some is extraordinary. For example this by evolutionist professor P.Z. Myers, "The only appropriate response should involve some form of righteous fury, much butt-kicking, and the public firing of some teachers, many school board members, and vast numbers of sleazy far-right politicians ... It's time for scientists to break out the steel-toed boots and brass knuckles, and get out there and hammer on the lunatics and idiots".[64] Similarly, geologist Donald Prothero, having described the fossil record's evidence in favour of *Evolution* in effusively glowing terms,[65] later suggests that anyone who disagrees is a "creationist" who has "much in common with the Neo-Nazi Jew-hating Holocaust deniers".[66]

Sometimes the intolerance takes the form of a deliberate policy of not engaging with critics so as not to risk giving them credibility. Eugenie Scott, the Executive Director of the National Center for Science and Education at the time, advised her colleagues to "Avoid debates". Apparently reasoned discussion might promote "the mistaken idea that evolution is scientifically weak".[67]

A rather different tactic was invoked by the skeptic James Randi. In May 2005, he heard that the Smithsonian National Museum of Natural History had agreed to screen a new film entitled, *The Privileged Planet: The Search for Purpose in the Universe*,[68] in exchange for a donation of $16,000 from the Discovery Institute co-sponsors. Incensed, Randi offered the Smithsonian $20,000 to cancel the event!

Why so intolerant – is this a new religion?

This kind of rhetoric coupled with the language of "heretic" and the associated ostracising actions raises the question, "Are we dealing with a form of religion here, rather than simply with science?" What other scientific discipline evokes such vilifying invective in the face of disagreement over theory? Such tactics and touchy outbursts would tend to suggest that the ship is foundering. As Leisola puts it, "**This is not how the defenders of a theory react when they have the evidential goods. That is the behaviour of someone defending a theory in crisis** [emphasis added]".[69] And as sociologist Don McDonald asks, "How can it be that you have to believe a certain idea in order to be a member of the scientific community? If you have to believe a certain idea in order to be a member, doesn't that sound more like a religion that's pretending to be science? If you have a theory that cannot stand up against debate, then there's something wrong with the theory. If you do not allow scientists to debate a theory, then there's something wrong with the system. And no student should have to lie to get a degree he's earned".[70]

But what is the definition of "religious belief"? Must it include belief in the supernatural? *Sapiens* author Harari thinks not, since that would exclude Buddhism, Confucianism, Zoroastrianism, Jainism and many others. Here's Harari's definition: "a system of human laws that is founded on a belief in superhuman laws".[71] Using this approach Harari is able to include ideologies such as Communism and Nazism in addition to those generally classified as world religions.[72]

Table 9.1 lists criteria normally associated with religious belief and suggests that *Evolution* also exhibits many of the same characteristics. *Evolution*, too, has its 'prophet' - Charles Darwin, who revealed the 'one source of truth' in his 'holy text' - *The Origin of Species*. 'Priest', Alice Roberts, is currently *Professor of Public Engagement in Science* at the University of Birmingham.[73] Richard Dawkins was first to hold the chair of the *Professorship for the Public Understanding of Science* at Oxford University.[74] Brian Cox is the Royal Society's *Professor for Public*

	Islam	Christianity	Buddhism	Communism	*Evolution*
Prophet	Mohammed	Jesus	Siddhartha Gautama	Karl Marx	Charles Darwin
'Holy Text'	Qur'an	Bible	Tipitaka	Das Kapital	The Origin of Species
Priests	Imam/ Caliph	Priest/ Chaplain	Bhikkhu (Buddhist Monks)	Commissar	Professor of Public Engagement in Science
'Holy Wars'	Jihad	Crusades	Rohingya persecution	October Revolution	Huxley/ Wilberforce, Dover Trial
Heresies	Ismailis, Hurufiya, Alawis	Gnosticism, Arianism	The Six Heretics	Trotskyism, Theism	Creationism, Intelligent Design
'Holy days'	Ramadan	Easter	Nirvana Day	May Day	Darwin Day
Utopia	Paradise	Heaven	Nirvana	A Communist State	Autonomy (there is no god)

Table 9.1 *Evolution* displays similar characteristics to other religious ideologies. For Huxley/Wilberforce debate, see Chapter 3. For Professor of Public Engagement in Science see text. For Dover Trial, see Chapter 10.

Engagement in Science at the University of Manchester.[75] All three promote philosophical naturalism in the guise of *Evolution* via both broadcast and print media. (Now, of course, not all holders of such professorships *necessarily* promote naturalism.) *Evolution*, too, has its special day in the calendar: *Darwin Day* celebrates Darwin's birthday on 12th February each year.

Although *Evolution* neither requires adherence to ritualistic behaviours nor invokes the supernatural, nevertheless it claims to answer our most fundamental questions - normally the domain of religions - such as, "Who are we?", "Where have we come from?", "Why are we here?", "What is our destiny?" Influential philosopher and ardent evolutionist Michael Ruse received much opprobrium from many fellow evolutionists when he admitted that "Evolution is promoted by its practitioners as more than mere science. Evolution is promulgated as an ideology, a secular religion – a full-fledged alternative to Christianity, with meaning and morality".[76] Writer Richard Halvorson confesses that "…questioning the universal explanatory power of evolution is met with intellectual excommunication … expressing hesitation about Darwin is considered irretrievable intellectual suicide, the unthinkable doubt, the unpardonable sin of academia".[77] That's why *Evolution* is unchallengeable. Dissent is taboo.

Lower lifeboat 9!

Here's a summary of Chapter 9.

Given the counter-evidence presented in Part 2, why is RMS *Evolution* not lying at the bottom of the ocean?

- While most ideas, authorities and institutions are questioned, critiqued and often distrusted within Western culture today, *Evolution* - if thought about at all - is widely assumed to be "unsinkable." The academic establishment, with the willing collusion of the media, constantly reinforces this view.
- We believe it because others we trust tell us it's true. It's known as *groupthink*. Even amongst scientists, their evolutionary creed is sustained by their community of like-minded believers.
- The result is that most people don't even know there is a debate about the evidence.

- There's a general blindness to counter-evidence and any that is noticed is assumed to have been explained by someone, somewhere.
- Even most scientists' knowledge of *Evolution* is second hand. They haven't thought about it, far less checked out the evidence for themselves.
- When scientists and others do survey 'below decks' they are often surprised just how weak the evidence in favour of the theory is, and how strong the counter-evidence.
- Dissent is not tolerated. Those who dare to voice their criticisms, whether academics, teachers or scientists generally, risk losing their current job, the prospect of future work, and ostracism from the scientific community.
- Why so intolerant? *Evolution* is defended with such religious fervour and dogmatism because evolutionary theory underpins the atheistic worldview of scientific materialism. Materialism offers explanations of who we are, why we are here, and what is our destiny. This effectively makes it a religion in competition with other religions and ideologies. These "have become the new dogmatists".[78]
- It's a religion that is being taught via the theory of *Evolution* in schools and universities in the name of *science*.[79]

Jerry Coyne made this claim: "For those who oppose Darwinism purely as a matter of faith, no amount of evidence will do – theirs is a belief not based on reason".[80] However, given the materialistic 'religion' that we now know underpins Darwinism, perhaps an inversion of this logic would be more appropriate: "For those who unquestioningly *accept* Darwinism purely as a matter of faith, no amount of *counter*-evidence will do – theirs is a belief not based on reason".

Is it time for group-sink?

Chapter 10

A better theory: Intelligent Design

... even leading evolutionary biologists now doubt the creative power of the mutation and natural selection mechanism, and for many good scientific reasons. As evidence from across the biological subdisciplines shows, the mechanism can produce modest small scale modifications (or adaptations) to existing organisms, but it clearly lacks the ability to produce major innovations in biological form such as have arisen during the history of life.[1]

Stephen Meyer

The theory of intelligent design holds that certain features of the universe and of living things are best explained by an intelligent cause, not an undirected process such as natural selection.[2]

Discovery Institute website

In this chapter we'll discover that, in recent years, remarkably, we've begun to witness a number of mainstream evolutionary biologists confessing that there is a serious problem with *Evolution*. They're even looking for alternative (albeit naturalistic) theories to patch things up. We'll also explore the theory of Intelligent Design, what it says and what its critics have to say.

- Even 'insiders' critique the theory.
- The Extended Evolutionary Synthesis - can it save *Evolution*?
- Intelligent Design - what is it?
- Intelligent Design - attacked as a heresy.
- She will sink - with mathematical certainty.

Even 'insiders' critique the theory

Given the ire directed at dissenters who challenge the authority of the evolutionary establishment, as we've seen in Chapter 9, it is surprising that any scientist, or indeed any other academic, would dare to 'come out' as a Darwin doubter. Yet in the last couple of decades there have been a few high profile awakenings.

Suzan Mazur, a journalist who specialises in reporting on what she refers to as *The Evolution Industry*, interviewed attendees following a symposium held at the *Konrad Lorenz Institute* in Altenberg, Germany, in July 2008. Journalists had been specifically excluded from the meeting. She describes this private meeting of a select group as

> ... a gathering of 16 biologists and philosophers of rock star stature – let's call them "the Altenberg 16" – who recognise that the theory of evolution which most practicing biologists accept and which is taught in classrooms today, is inadequate in explaining our existence.[3]

The sixteen have two things in common. First, they are all mainstream academics within the biological family of sciences who believe the grand narrative of *Evolution* to be generally true. Second, unlike most other mainstream academics, **these insiders have all come to the view that the mutations plus natural selection mechanism**, by itself, **falls far short of explaining how life has evolved**: "... they recognize the need to challenge the prevailing Modern Synthesis [another name for neo-Darwinism] because there's too much it doesn't explain".[4]

Toward an Extended Evolutionary Synthesis – as the symposium was entitled – was, therefore, a working meeting of experts in the various relevant fields with the intention of, not necessarily replacing, but certainly supplementing, the 1930s and '40s neo-Darwinian Synthesis with other ideas and theories. Attendees included cell biologist Stuart Newman; biologist and anthropologist David Sloan Wilson; geophysical scientist David Jablonski; geneticist Eva Jablonka; theoretical biologist Gerd Müller; and geneticist and philosopher of science Massimo Pigliucci. These biologists are still regarded as 'insiders' because, as has been pointed out, "It's ok to dig up the road as long as you patch it up again afterwards [with purely *naturalistic* processes]".[5]

A few years after Altenberg, in November 2016, a conference was held at the prestigious *Royal Society of London* with the disarming headline title, *New Trends in Evolutionary Biology*.[6] The first speaker was Gerd Müller who had hosted the Altenberg 16 symposium in 2008. In his remarkably candid opening talk at the *Royal Society*, **Müller set out the problems with the orthodox mechanism of mutations plus natural selection.**

He said that what the current synthesis "**does not explain**, are all these complex levels of evolution ... such as **the origin of**:

- **Complex [biological] features** ...

- **Body plans** ...
- **Complex behaviours** ...
- **Non-gradual forms of transition** ... [emphasis added]".

This is an extraordinary 'insider' admission. These bulleted items are precisely what Darwin claimed to have explained. Müller goes on to point out that, "**The standard theory focused on characters that exist already** and their variation and maintenance across populations, but **not on how they originate** [emphasis added]".[7]

Of some twenty or so international speakers at the conference, around half supported the thrust of Gerd Müller's view, including Eva Jablonka and James Shapiro, while the other half broadly defended evolutionary orthodoxy. What's fascinating here is that, as philosopher of biology Paul Nelson put it, "They're still not looking outside the walls of the 'City of Naturalism'", but nevertheless, "No one looks for a better theory if they're happy with the one they have".[8]

Yet this devastating news did not make a single headline. RMS *Evolution* simply sails majestically onwards.

What is this *Extended Evolutionary Synthesis*? What are the other concepts that the Altenberg 16 have proposed?

The Extended Evolutionary Synthesis – can it save *Evolution*?

What follows is not an exhaustive list of theories within the *Extended Evolutionary Synthesis*, nor are the explanations detailed; some of them have been explored to some extent in Part 2.

- **Self-organization** is championed by Stuart Newman and Stuart Kauffman, among others. It's based on ideas like these: a snowflake *self-assembles*; a vortex, such as water swirling as it empties out of a bath, *self-organises*. However, as we've seen in Chapter 4, self-organization can produce simple *order*, but not the *specified complexity* required to produce biological function.
- **Evolutionary Developmental Biology (Evo-Devo)** promoted by Gerd Müller, Sean Carroll and others proposes that mutations in master regulatory (*Hox*) genes must have played a huge part in the early embryonic development of species, in particular evolving novel body plans. The problem here is that mutations occurring in the early embryo, while introducing changes at the body plan level, are likely to be fatal, or at best debilitating (fruit flies with an extra pair of wings for example, see Chapter 7).

Meantime mutations occurring late in the embryonic process will not produce novel body plans. For the engineer, there is an analogy here with complex interconnected systems, whether for example, in electrical distribution networks, in electronic circuitry, in software applications or in combinations of such systems: if you introduce a significant change into one element of a system, catastrophic failure of function is likely to ensue unless other system modules are also modified in an appropriately co-ordinated way. And that's the problem for the molecular biology of Evo-Devo.

- **Natural Genetic Engineering**, developed by James Shapiro, advocates that organisms respond to environmental stresses by inducing mutations in a self-directed way rather than 'waiting' for mutations to occur at random. However, this simply assumes the prior existence of functional genetic information. It offers no explanation for the origin of that information.
- **Symbiogenesis**. Lynn Margulis has put forward the idea – now widely accepted within evolutionary biology – that two previously distinct species may merge with one another, combining their respective functionalities to produce a new species. She argues, for example, that the DNA of lichens combines the DNA of a fungus with that of blue-green algae (cyanobacteria).[9] Once more, this tells us nothing about the origin of the key component: the genetic information in the prior putatively separate species.
- **Genetic Drift**. This is the fact that gene frequencies change in a population due to chance, including advantageous/disadvantageous mutations. Genetic drift will be particularly prominent in small populations. In 1968, Motoo Kimura argued that genetic drift is *the* major source of genetic change in a population. Professor Jonathan Pettitt[10] of the University of Aberdeen is a contemporary proponent of the theory. However, as we discovered in Chapters 4, 5 and 8, such a random search mechanism at the level of molecular biology will fail to find novel functionality.

So it would appear that **these theories are no more effective** – perhaps even less effective – **at originating biological information than natural selection.**

Meantime, a growing *international* body of insiders is beginning to express its scepticism. And they've gone public. What started out as a list of around one hundred (courageous) scientists, by May 2021, had reached over 1,200. They signed up to *A Scientific Dissent From Darwinism*, and by doing so endorsed the following statement:

> We are skeptical of claims for the ability of random mutation and natural selection to account for the complexity of life. Careful examination of the evidence for Darwinian theory should be encouraged.[11]

Perhaps this list is only the 'tip of an iceberg'. Many are reluctant to sign because they are afraid of the, as we've seen, very real consequences for their career and reputation.[12]

Intelligent Design – what is it?

The evidence in Part 2 points to a "loud, clear, piercing cry of 'design!'" as Michael Behe exclaimed. And the conclusion of this book is that Intelligent Design (ID) is the main challenger to unguided *Evolution*. Unlike undirected processes, ID has the necessary explanatory power. (Other perspectives are explored and summarised in Appendix A.)

So what is ID? Repeating one of the opening quotes to this chapter, according to the *Discovery Institute* (which represents the main proponents of ID):

> The theory of intelligent design holds that certain features of the universe and of living things are best explained by an intelligent cause, not an undirected process such as natural selection.[13]

In the context of this book, then, ID is the view that design – the signature of an intelligent mind – can be detected in the molecular biology of a living cell. The detection process, working as does a detective or forensic scientist investigating a murder, identifies clues, gathers data and then, having posited and evaluated a number of possible explanations, reaches a conclusion as to which is the "best explanation": the cause which, in our uniform experience, is most capable of explaining all the observed data. This method is called *inference to the best explanation* or *abduction*. The historical sciences often have recourse to this method. Charles Lyell, the father of modern geology, and even Darwin himself made use of *abduction*.

Part 2 makes the case that purely unguided naturalistic processes such as natural selection, self-organization, and so on – all ultimately reducible to the laws of physics and chemistry – cannot explain the origin of the extraordinary information content evident in molecular biology. We can therefore eliminate such causes since they are incapable of explaining the observed data. Conversely, it is our uniform experience that only an intelligent mind can account for the presence of complex specified information, whether in a morse code message, a text book or a piece of software code (the information content is independent of the medium). By the same logic, only a designing intelligence can explain the complex specified information in DNA and in molecular biology generally.

However, opponents of the intelligent design view claim that this is a religious conclusion, not a scientific one. Is it?

Intelligent Design – attacked as a heresy

Adherents of a religion or an ideology tend to show contempt for those who promote what the former believe to be heresies. So, for example, evolutionists direct particular ire towards what they regard as the heresy of ID. The attacks come in two varieties: ID is disparaged as being 1. "not science" (or "pseudoscience"), or 2. "anti-science", or both. Let's examine these in turn.

CLAIM (1): INTELLIGENT DESIGN IS NOT SCIENCE. As acclaimed chemist and philosopher Michael Polanyi put it, any theory competing with current orthodoxy is not science by definition, "Every great scientific controversy tends ... to turn into a dispute between the established authorities and a pretender ... who is as yet denied the status of scientist, at least with respect to the work under discussion".[14] We now turn to a court case in Pennsylvania which became a focus for those wishing to attack ID.

In early 2005 the Dover Area School District issued a policy requiring teachers to read a statement to senior high school biology pupils indicating that *Of Pandas and People*,[15] a book which gives "an understanding of what Intelligent Design actually involves", had been made available. The statement went on to encourage "those who might be interested"[16] to access it. Whatever the wisdom or otherwise of the School District's policy,[17] on the face of it, this would seem to be fairly consistent with encouraging senior school pupils to investigate alternatives and to think for themselves. Not so, apparently. On this topic, pupils have to be taught *what* to think not *how* to think.

The Dover School District's act was interpreted by evolutionists as an incitement, in effect, to 'holy war'. In late 2005 a six-week court case ensued: Kitzmiller versus Dover Area School District, with District

Judge John E. Jones III presiding. The suit filed by the plaintiffs contended that "the ID policy constitutes an establishment of religion prohibited by the First Amendment to the United States Constitution ...".[18] The legal challenge was led by the American Civil Liberties Union (ACLU) and supported by Eugenie Scott of the National Center for Science Education (NCSE).[19]

The Judge's ruling was much lauded in evolutionist quarters, for example as a "masterpiece of wit, scholarship and clear thinking", despite the subsequently-revealed fact that 5,458 of his 6,004 word section about ID had been copied and pasted, virtually verbatim, from a document submitted by the ACLU attorneys.[20] What, then, was 'his' opinion of ID? Judge Jones concluded that "ID is not science". Now from Chapter 2 we know that philosophers of science have been unable to agree upon a universal definition of science. Untroubled by this fact however, the judge fearlessly, as he put it,[21] "traipse[d] into this controversial area":

> ... we find that while ID arguments may be true, a proposition on which the Court takes no position, ID is not science. We find that ID fails on three different levels, any one of which is sufficient to preclude a determination that ID is science. They are: (1) ID violates the centuries-old ground rules of science by invoking and permitting supernatural causation; (2) the argument of irreducible complexity, central to ID, employs the same flawed and illogical contrived dualism that doomed creation science in the 1980's; and (3) ID's negative attacks on evolution have been refuted by the scientific community.[22]

Judge Jones' conclusion (1) is that ID invokes supernatural causation. ID, he argues in effect, is guilty of the 'unforgivable sin' of invoking the Deity.[23] Is the judge correct? Not according to the *Discovery Institute* website statement above. There is no mention of the supernatural. **ID theory argues that the cause of certain features of, for example, living organisms is *design***, having examined other possible causes and found them to be incapable of explaining how such features came into existence. As we saw in Chapter 4, if we limit our range of possible causes to those of chance and mindless law-like behaviours, we will never find an explanation for Mount Rushmore.

Some argue that we cannot invoke "design" unless we know that the prior cause of that design exists. But there's a logical flaw here. Take the example of the *Search for Extra-Terrestrial Intelligence (SETI)*. Intelligent extra-terrestrials may exist, or they may not. We don't know

the answer to that question. The logic of SETI exhibits the following pattern:
- If we detect a signal that we are confident did not originate on Earth,
- and if we are confident that the content of the signal cannot be explained by existing unguided law-like processes in nature (such as electromagnetic radiation emitted by quasars or pulsars),[24]
- and if the signal contains complex specified information, such as a series of prime numbers, or some other complex sequence of symbols that conforms to a specification external to itself,

then it can be concluded that the signal was *designed*. It was generated by a *mind*. Now some believe there are no other intelligent civilisations in the universe, or at least not in our galaxy, but there is little dispute that if such a signal were received, then *SETI* would rightly go on to infer that at least one extra-terrestrial mind does exist.

ID theory follows exactly the same pattern. This time the "signal" is the complex specified information in DNA, proteins and other cellular apparatus and systems. The conclusion that this information exhibits design, and was therefore derived from a mind, has explanatory power, unlike unguided law-like processes.[25] The theory has nothing to say about the nature of that mind.

In finding (2), when Judge Jones dismisses the irreducible complexity argument (see Chapter 5) with the phrase "flawed and illogical contrived dualism" he is probably referring to the *god-of-the-gaps* rebuttal often rehearsed by evolutionists. The accusation here is that when we don't yet understand how unguided nature has achieved a particular outcome (our ignorance, a *gap*), there can be a tendency to conclude that "God must have done it". But irreducible complexity is an argument from *knowledge*, not *ignorance*, of the scientific evidence. We now know that cells are full of molecular machines which fail to function upon removal of almost any *one* of their many finely tuned and purposefully arranged components. And we know that natural selection has no foresight: it cannot initiate and progress the construction sequence of a complex multi-component molecular machine that offers no functional advantage until *all* the components are in place. The irreducible complexity argument is neither "illogical" nor does it invoke god-of-the-gaps "dualism".

The judge's statement (3) is defeated by its own logic: if ID "is not science", then what locus does "the scientific community" have in refuting it? But on the other hand, if, as he claims, "the scientific community" has "refuted" it, then ID must make scientific arguments after all.

In any case, if you have been persuaded by evidence presented in Part 2 then it follows that Judge Jones was incorrect in his second and third findings.

So much for the judge's three levels of argument that "ID is not science." Here, now, are some positive reasons to regard ID as a scientific argument:

First, we've already seen that **ID theory *is* science because it uses the scientific method known as "abduction", or "inference to the best explanation"**.

Second, **ID theory is science because**, contrary to the claims of its detractors, **it does make testable predictions**. Meyer lists twelve predictions inspired by ID theory.[26] Here are five adapted from his list:

- The functional sequences of amino acids within amino-acid sequence space should be extremely rare, rather than common.
- Most of the DNA in the genomes of species should turn out to be functional (i.e. so-called "Junk DNA" should be a small percentage of the genome).
- If an intelligent (and benevolent) agent designed life, then studies of putatively bad designs in life – such as the vertebrate retina and virulent bacteria and viruses – should reveal either (a) reasons for the designs that show hidden functional logic or (b) evidence of decay of originally good designs.
- The fossil record should show evidence of discrete infusions of information into the biosphere at episodic intervals as well as a disparity-before-diversity (see Chapter 6) pattern of appearance of new fossil forms.
- Palaeontology and possibly other subdisciplines of biology should show evidence of polyphyly (an 'orchard' rather than a 'tree' pattern, see Fig. 6.7).

It should be noted that while Part 2 constituted evidence that five predictions of neo-Darwinism fail, it also offered evidence that the above five predictions of ID succeed. Did you notice that, perhaps surprisingly, Judge Jones acknowledged that "ID arguments may be true". Even Jerry Coyne has admitted that "… scientific truth is decided by scientists, not by judges".[27] Quite so.

Third, despite ill-founded claims to the contrary, **well over a hundred pro-ID papers have been published in prominent peer-reviewed scientific journals.**[28]

CLAIM (2): INTELLIGENT DESIGN IS ANTI-SCIENCE. Continuing with Coyne, he claims - nor is he alone in this - that ID not only disputes evolutionary theory, but that it also strikes at the very heart of the whole scientific enterprise.

> The battle for evolution seems never-ending. And the battle is part of a wider war, a war between rationality and superstition. What is at stake here is nothing less than science itself and all the benefits it offers to society.[29]

More than one logical error is in play here. First, the fallacy of bifurcation, or the false dilemma. Coyne makes the unsubstantiated assertion that attacking *Evolution* will kill off the entire scientific enterprise and that we must choose between both or neither. We're being tempted to think that if we reject *Evolution*, all scientific research will come to a halt and we will no longer have access to mobile phones, the internet, aeroplanes, medical treatment, agricultural technology, electric vehicles, satellites, wind turbines, and so on. Clearly, this is untrue. Falsifying *Evolution* would not even be detrimental to research in most subdisciplines of biology never mind other fields of science. Anatomy and physiology, for instance, have no need of evolutionary theory. Yet the false taunt that disagreement with evolutionary theory necessarily entails rejection of all scientific research has been widely circulated. It has become a modern myth, commonly believed by many in the intelligentsia.

Second, the question-begging epithet fallacy. Couched in emotional language, Coyne claims that adherence to *Evolution* equals "rationality" and that rejection of it equals "superstition". The intent is to equate criticism of *Evolution* with belief in witchcraft or astrology. Sometimes criticism of *Evolution* is even branded as "anti-intellectual".[30] Hopefully, Part 2 of this book demonstrated that the use of rational, intellectual argument is not exclusive to evolutionists.

On the contrary, as we discovered in Chapter 9, the prominent promoters of ID theory love science and what it has achieved. Many of them are highly qualified career scientists working, researching and publishing across a range of scientific disciplines. The claim that those who support ID, this author included, intend to subvert the whole scientific enterprise is ill-judged and unhelpful to healthy discussion and debate. Science and technology - rightly to be celebrated - will continue to provide insights into the workings of this amazing universe along with benefits to society and the world.

She will sink – with mathematical certainty

In the 1997 movie, chief designer Thomas Andrews is unequivocal about *Titanic's* fate, "She's made of iron, sir, I assure you she can [sink], and she will, with mathematical certainty".[31]

In Part 2, as we surveyed below the waterline inside RMS *Evolution*'s first five 'watertight compartments', we discovered that five predictions of neo-Darwinian theory fail. Specifically, it's the mathematics of molecular biology that sinks *Evolution*. As we saw in Chapter 1, however, all science is provisional and may need to be revisited in the light of new evidence.

The thesis of this book is that 19th century Darwinian science, developing as it did in an age that also gave rise to supreme confidence in *Titanic's* unsinkability, has collided with an 'iceberg': the 'iceberg' of new evidence from 21st century molecular biology. In the light of the evidence, RMS *Evolution* will sink. The adoption of Intelligent Design theory is a rational conclusion from the evidence and, far from undermining the scientific enterprise, will offer new avenues for future below-the-waterline 'iceberg' research.[32]

Lower lifeboat 10!

Here's a summary of Chapter 10.

- A growing number of mainstream biologists have concluded that neo-Darwinism can't explain the origin of novel biology – the very thing it is supposed to explain.
- These 'insider' critics of neo-Darwinism have proposed the addition of a number of theories with the intention of rescuing unguided, naturalistic evolutionary theory. This so-called *Extended Evolutionary Synthesis* (EES) includes ideas such as self-organization and symbiogenesis.
- However, the various theories within the EES still assume the prior existence of, and are unable to explain the origin of, complex specified information which is so evident in molecular biology. Such unguided processes cannot explain the evidence.
- Intelligent Design (ID) – design derived from a mind – is the best explanation for the origin of the information that is essential to the

existence of life in all its variety of body plans. Only ID has the necessary explanatory power.
- ID is variously attacked as unscientific and/or anti-scientific, operating under the subterfuge that "critics of evolution must be motivated by religion, whereas defenders of evolution are supposedly the disinterested pursuers of truth".[33]
- However, ID *is* science because (1) it uses the scientific method known as abduction: inference to the best explanation; (2) it makes testable predictions; and (3) it has published peer-reviewed papers in prestigious scientific journals.
- RMS *Evolution* will sink – with mathematical certainty. Why so? Because of the evidence: it's the mathematics of molecular biology that sinks RMS *Evolution*.

Epilogue

The real tree-of-life

*There are, probably, ultimately only two possible answers to the question of origins ... : [either] that **the universe is the result of free personal agency, or that in some way or other it creates itself. The two answers are not finally compatible, and require a choice**, either between them or an attitude of agnostic refusal to decide [emphasis added].*[1]

Colin Gunton

British theologian Colin Gunton articulates the two possible answers to Dan Brown's fundamental question, "Where do we come from?"[2] He describes two opposing worldviews, two explanations for the existence of the universe and of life. There is nothing new about either of these views. Both have been debated by philosophers and theologians since at least ancient Greek times. The first worldview has been described as *Oneism*: the belief that the world is self-creating and self-explanatory (the universe is all there is). The (only) alternative is *Twoism*: the belief that the universe is the free work of a personal, transcendent (separately existing) God who created it from nothing. In so creating, God was not constrained by any preexisting conditions.[3]

As beliefs, both of these views are effectively 'religions'. *Twoism* leads to worship of the Creator. *Oneism* leads to worshipping (holding in highest reverence) nature itself (as it's own creator).

Darwin's publication of *The Origin* in 1859 seemed to give the imprimatur of science to the *Oneism* self-creation view. Suddenly it seemed that evidence-based rationalistic science had demonstrated that life was self-created. This understanding then stimulated, infused and underpinned philosophical materialism and consequently atheism. In 1810, most of the Western elite were theists; by 1890, most were atheistic naturalists.[4]

Science, too, was overtaken by naturalism. David Williams reveals the trick that has been played upon all of us, including – perhaps surprisingly – most scientists. In *Taken Without Consent*,[5] he explains that by conflating *science* and *philosophical materialism*, atheists have hijacked science for their own purposes. Philosophical materialism dogmatically insists that the universe is closed (*Oneism*).

And so it has become widely believed in academia, the media and within the general public that life has "created itself" by mindless, unguided natural processes and that *design* in biology is only *apparent*.[6] This philosophy, sometimes described as *scientific materialism*, is taught in schools, colleges and universities – for the most part implicitly rather than explicitly. It would therefore appear that the "establishment of religion" boot, prohibited by the First Amendment of the U.S. Constitution, is actually on the other foot. Contrary to the Constitution, the religion, or ideology if you prefer, of scientific materialism *is* being taught in biology classrooms – and its implications in other classrooms – and not only in the U.S.

The First Amendment *also* protects freedom of speech.[82] But as we saw in Chapter 9 freedom to critique *Evolution* is simply not tolerated by the hegemony of the evolutionary 'priesthood'. Having provided an anchor for atheism, materialistic philosophy now acts to protect failing Darwinian science.

Recall Dick Lewontin's candid admission that materialism is the evolutionist's adopted 'religion' by default, "**We take the side of science** [notice how he conflates science and materialism here] **in spite of the patent absurdity of some of its constructs ... in spite of the tolerance of the scientific community for unsubstantiated just-so stories, because we have a prior commitment ... to materialism. It is not that the methods and institutions of science somehow compel us to accept a material explanation of the phenomenal world but, on the contrary, that we are forced by our a priori adherence to material causes to ... produce material explanations, no matter how counter-intuitive, no matter how mystifying to the uninitiated. Moreover, that materialism is absolute, for we cannot allow a Divine Foot in the door** [emphasis added]".[7]

All ideas have consequences. The late biologist and atheist William Provine spelled it out: "Let me summarize my views on what modern evolutionary biology tells us loud and clear – and **these are basically Darwin's views. There are no gods, no purposes, and no goal-directed forces of any kind. There is no life after death. When I die, I am absolutely certain that I am going to be dead. That's the end of me. There is no ultimate foundation for ethics, no ultimate meaning in life, and no free will for humans, either** [emphasis added]".[8]

Similarly Francis Crick understands that, if *Evolution* is true, our sense of identity and self-worth is threatened, "**your joys and your sorrows, your memories and your ambitions, your sense of personal identity and free will, are in fact no more than the behavior of a vast assemblage of nerve cells and their associated molecules** [emphasis added]".[9]

Fig. E.1,[10] a Tree-of-Death, tries to capture the worldview of Provine and Crick visually. It begins with the belief that *Evolution* - a mindless, unguided process - is true. The logic then implies that life was not designed. While it does not follow from this that scientific materialism *must* be true, nevertheless, for Provine *et al.*, it counts as strong evidence that a designing deity *does not exist*. Appendix B outlines these and other implications of unguided neo-Darwinian evolutionary theory upon the way we think about ourselves: who we are.

However, if you have been persuaded by Part 2 then you will now realise that neo-Darwinism is a theory built upon sand. The science is sinking. The grand claims of evolutionary science are no longer credible. And as you will have seen throughout Part 2 and explicitly in Part 3, Intelligent Design offers a more cogent explanation for the astonishing evidence uncovered in molecular biology.

As a Christian, it seems to the author that such evidence is consistent with the designing mind being that of the Judaeo-Christian God of the Bible.[11] Almost two thousand years ago the apostle Paul would appear to have got it right.

> *For since the creation of the world God's invisible qualities – his eternal power and divine nature – have been clearly seen, being understood from what has been made, so that people are without excuse.*   Romans 1 v 20

In contrast to following the logic of *Evolution* and reaping the consequences articulated by Provine and Crick, a harvest of 'good fruit' is now on offer with the potential to ground our sense of identity and wellbeing. See Fig. E.2, The Real Tree-of-Life.

> *The tongue that brings healing is a tree of life, but a deceitful tongue crushes the spirit.*   Proverbs 15 v 4

Here's the apostle Paul once more.

> *Do not conform any longer to the pattern of this world, but be transformed by the renewing of your mind.*   Romans 12 v 2

Are you ready to think the unthinkable, sink the unsinkable?

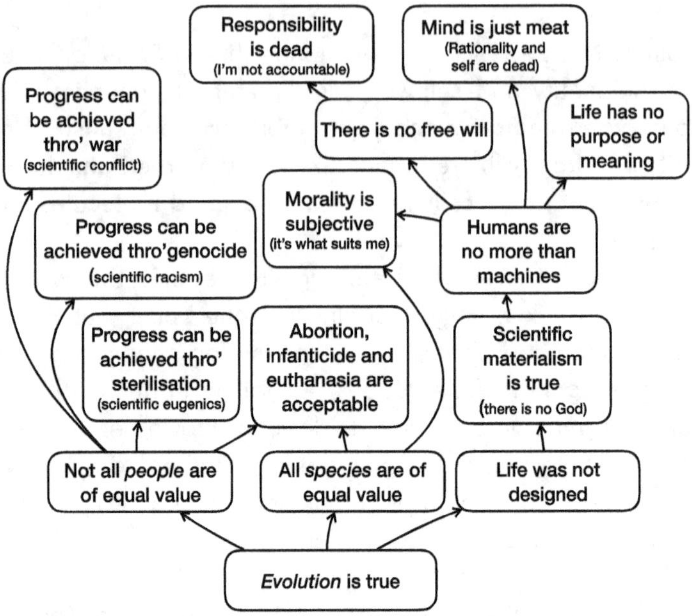

Evolution's Iceberg

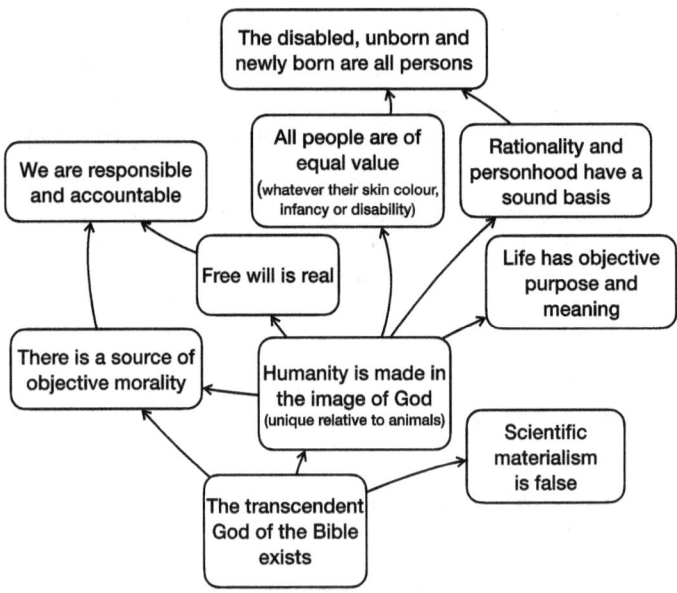

Figure E.1 A Tree-of-Death. Read the diagram from the root upwards: "**If** *Evolution* is true **then** Not all *people* are of equal value"… "**If** *Evolution* is true **then** Life was not designed", etc. See Appendix B for more detail.

Figure E.2 The Real Tree-of-Life that offers good 'fruit'. The existence of a transcendent designer is consistent with the God of the Bible. If such a God exists then lots of good 'fruit' is available to support human wellbeing. Once more, read the diagram from the root: "**If** the transcendent God of the Bible exists **then** Scientific materialism is false", etc.

Further Reading

These are only initial suggestions for further reading. In what follows each surname and following date(s), e.g. Youngson (1998), refer to a book listed in the *References* section.

Relating to Part 1
- Errors in science: Offit (2017), Youngson (1998).
- High/low confidence science: Stadler (2016).
- Is there a conflict between science and Christianity: Lennox (2007).
- The scientific priesthood: Sheldrake (2013).
- The Galileo, Dark Ages and other myths: Stark (2014), Keas (2019).

Relating to Part 2
- Evidence against the grand claims of *Evolution*: Axe (2016), Behe (1996, 2007 and 2019), Denton (1985 and 2016), Johnson (1993), Meyer (2009 and 2013), Swift (2002), Tan and Stadler (2020), and Williams (2020).
- *Long Story Short* cartoons, videos of typically only ten minutes, are entertaining as well as informative: https://www.youtube.com/playlist?list=PLR8eQzfCOiS0AfFPsMAUYr_VVkpU13uv9

Relating to Part 3 and the Epilogue
- The evolutionary science cover-up: Hedin (2021), Leisola & Witt (2018), Williams (2020).
- The social and philosophical implications of materialistic Darwinism: West (2015, 2012), Weikart (2016, 2022), Bergman (2014).
- Evidence for design: Meyer (2021), Galloway (2021), Burgess (2013).
- The problem of suffering and evil: Lewis (1986), Keller (2008) - especially Chapter 2, Lennox (2011), Orr-Ewing (2021).
- Human identity: Fretwell (2019).
- The scientific, philosophical and theological problems with evolutionary creationism (or theistic evolution): Moreland *et al.* (2017).
- The case for Christ: Strobel (1998).

Appendix A

Evolution's protagonists and their religious views

Probably today's best known critics of neo-Darwinism as an explanation for all of life's complexity are Biblical Creationists (BC), sometimes referred to as "Young Earth Creationists", together with members of the Intelligent Design (ID) movement. Confusion is often caused when these two positions, BC and ID, are conflated or misrepresented. Both groups are 'outsiders' in the sense that they reject the putative "fact" that purely unguided, purposeless, naturalistic processes can account for all of life's complexity. They are therefore viewed by the scientific establishment, the 'priesthood' if you will, effectively as 'heretics'. To help clarify who the most significant protagonists are, Fig. A.1 maps out the principal groupings involved in the debate over *Evolution* and their relationship to theism. In the diagram a number of writers and speakers, many of whom have been mentioned in this book, are arranged in groups along a spectrum from atheism to theism. Space necessarily limits the number of representatives of each group who can be shown in the chart.

ATHEISTIC EVOLUTIONISTS (AE). Beginning on the right of Fig. A.1 we find this grouping. Its members are high profile promoters of *Evolution* and its concepts. These particular individuals are also openly atheistic. Indeed some have been described as anti-theistic: not only disbelieving in God themselves, but also actively campaigning to dissuade others from belief in a Creator. They interpret all scientific evidence on the assumption that *Evolution* (particles-to-people) is true. Coyne and Dawkins have featured in most chapters. We've also encountered Brian Cox (Chapter 4) and Alice Roberts (Chapter 8), who are both writers and TV personalities, well-known for their document-

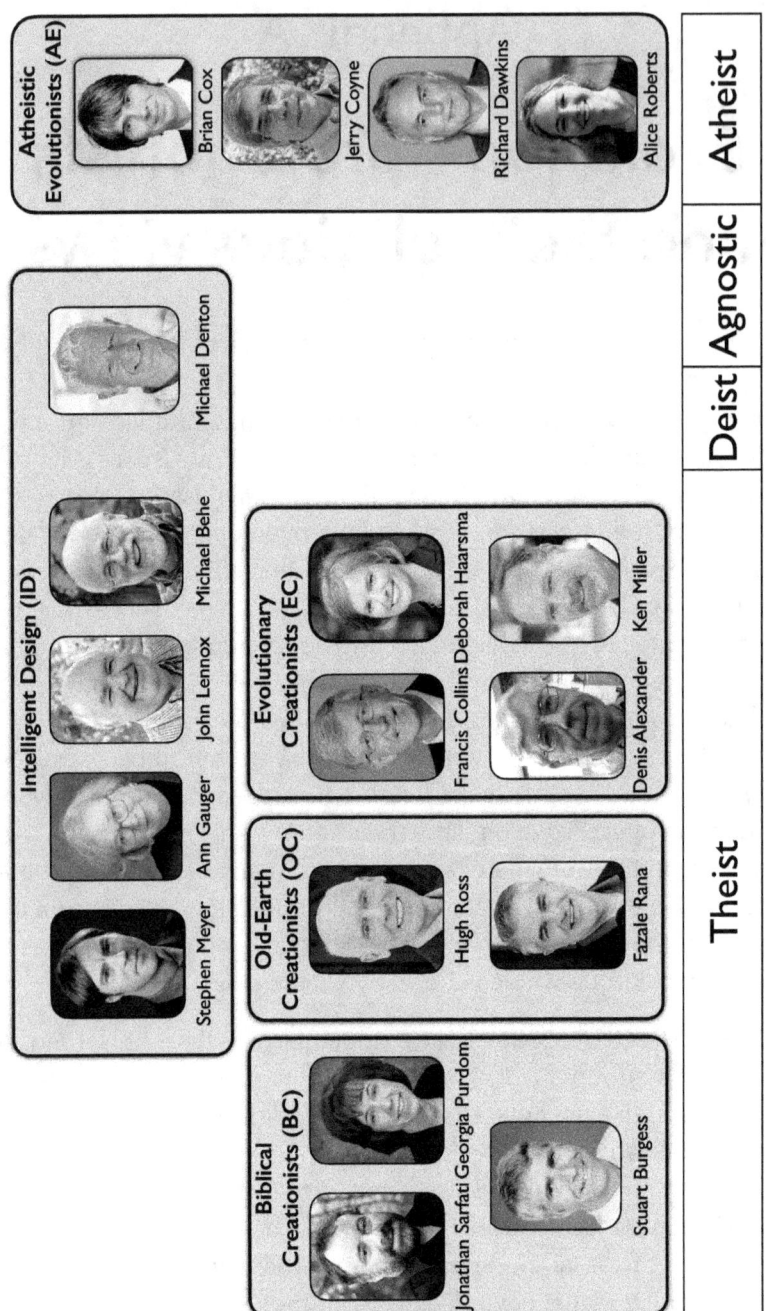

Figure A.1 A theological 'map' of some of the protagonists in the debate about *Evolution*. Positioning of the proponents of ID is not intended to be precise.

aries featuring aspects of science relating to the origin of the universe and of life.

EVOLUTIONARY CREATIONISTS (EC). Francis Collins (Chapter 5), who led the *Human Genome Project* which completed in 2003, was one of the founders of the *BioLogos* organisation which promotes the EC view. What proposition do ECs hold to? According to the *BioLogos* website

> [w]e believe that the diversity and interrelation of all life on earth are best explained by the God-ordained process of evolution with common descent. Thus, evolution is not in opposition to God, but a means by which God providentially achieves his purposes. Therefore, we reject ideologies that claim that evolution is a purposeless process or that evolution replaces God ... We believe that God created humans in biological continuity with all life on earth, but also as spiritual beings. God established a unique relationship with humanity by endowing us with his image and calling us to an elevated position within the created order.[1]

So ECs, or as they are sometimes designated, "Theistic Evolutionists", believe that *Evolution* was the process God used to create life; that *apparently* random mutations in species may actually have been guided by God – but in an undetectable way. So generally speaking, ECs don't quibble with the scientific basis of *Evolution*. The current President of *BioLogos* is astrophysicist Deborah Haarsma. Denis Alexander is a molecular biologist and author. Ken Miller (Chapter 5) is professor of biology at Brown University and co-author of several school and college biology textbooks.

Before tracking further to the left to critical 'outsider' groups, let's review the other two divisions on the atheism-theism spectrum. An "agnostic" is someone who believes nothing can be known about the existence or nature of God. The distinction between a "deist" and a "theist" is that the former believes the universe had its ultimate source in a Creator of some kind but this supreme being no longer intervenes in creation; whereas a theist believes that God is present within as well as beyond his creation, and free to work out his purpose. Specifically a Christian theist believes that God stepped into history as a human being in the form of Jesus of Nazareth and is a God who hears prayer.

OLD EARTH CREATIONISTS (OC). This is the first critical 'outsider' group. Astrophysicist Hugh Ross established *Reasons To Believe* in 1986. According to the RTB website

> [w]e open people to the gospel by revealing God in science ... We engage skeptics and cultivate communities where scholars and others learn to integrate science, theology, and philosophy so they can open the world of science to the gospel.[2]

Ross says that he has "been working to develop a biblical creation model that is testable and predictive". While accepting current scientific orthodoxy on the age of the universe and of the Earth, OCs believe that science nevertheless points to the Bible and to "Jesus Christ as Creator, Lord and Savior". President and CEO of RTB Fazale Rana offers this summary, "As a graduate student studying biochemistry, I was captivated by the cell's complexity, elegance, and sophistication. The inadequacy of evolutionary scenarios to account for life's origin compelled me to conclude that life must come from a Creator".

BIBLICAL CREATIONISTS (BC) regard the Bible as the revealed word of God and where the biblical narrative impinges on the historical, BCs take that content to be true history. They believe that the Earth and universe were created in six calendar days less than ten thousand years ago, that the Earth was repopulated following a global flood around four thousand years ago and that all the air-breathing species alive today throughout the world are descended from representatives on Noah's ark. So for example they believe that all members of the cat family – lions, tigers, leopards, panthers, and so on, including domestic cats – descended from an original cat family pair onboard the ark and have since migrated throughout the world, the diversity of cat species emerging in the process.

The BC view is that all scientific evidence either already does support their biblical assumptions about history, or if not yet, eventually will do so. Australian born Jonathan Sarfati's doctorate is in physical chemistry and he has written a number of books critiquing *Evolution* and supporting the BC view. Stuart Burgess is professor of mechanical engineering at Bristol University. He designed, for example, the gearbox mechanism which deployed the solar panel array on the European Space Agency's *Envisat* satellite. He now specialises in Biomimetics – the study and imitation of complex systems found in nature to help solve problems important to humanity. Georgia Purdom's doctorate is in molecular genetics. She has written and contributed to a number of publications.

Appendix A

INTELLIGENT DESIGN (ID). According to the *Discovery Institute* website

> [t]he theory of intelligent design holds that certain features of the universe and of living things are best explained by an intelligent cause, not an undirected process such as natural selection.[3]

For this grouping of critical 'outsiders', you'll notice that proponents of ID span across from deism, if not agnosticism, towards strong theism (positioning of individuals along the spectrum is not intended to be precise). Biochemist Michael Denton (Chapters 4, 6 and 8), for example, has been described as regarding the universe and life as "pre-planned" and a "providential dispensation", but is no more explicit than that.[4] In some ways Denton was a pioneer of the contemporary ID movement when he published *Evolution: A Theory in Crisis*[5] in 1985. Michael Behe (Chapters 5 and 6), biochemist, inspired by Denton and others then published *Darwin's Black Box: The Biochemical Challenge to Evolution*[6] in 1996. We've come across John Lennox in Chapters 1, 2, 3 and 9, emeritus Professor of Mathematics at the University of Oxford. Matti Leisola (Chapters 4, 7 and 9), is a bioengineer and former Dean of Chemistry and Material Sciences at Helsinki University of Technology. Ann Gauger (Chapters 5 and 6), senior research scientist at *Biologic Institute* in Seattle, researches protein evolution and human origins. She co-authored *Science and Human Origins*[7] with Douglas Axe (Chapters 4, 5, 6 and 9). Stephen Meyer (Chapters 1, 4, 6 and 7), is the Director of the *Discovery Institute's Center for Science and Culture* in Seattle. A former geophysicist, he holds a Ph.D. in the philosophy of science from the University of Cambridge and has published some important works promoting ID. The first, in 2009, was *Signature in the Cell: DNA and the Evidence for Intelligent Design*.[8] In his second book, *Darwin's Doubt*, Meyer summarises his view of *Evolution*.

> ... popular defences of the theory continue apace, rarely if ever acknowledging the growing body of critical scientific opinion about the standing of the theory. Rarely has there been such a great disparity between the popular perception of a theory and its actual standing in the relevant peer-reviewed scientific literature.[9]

The views of these groupings are summarised in Table A.1 in relation to two assertions.[10]

Assertions	BC/OC	ID	EC	AE
1. An evolutionary process is incompatible with the existence of a Creator.	Agree	No View	Disagree	Agree
2. An evolutionary process accounts for the existence of all of life's complexity	Disagree	Disagree	Agree	Agree

Table A.1. The different groupings in Fig. A.1 take different positions in relation to Assertions 1 and 2 above.
BC=Biblical Creationists; OC=Old Earth Creationists; ID=Intelligent Design; EC=Evolutionary Creationists; AE=Atheistic Evolutionists.

The BC, OC and ID groupings are 'outsiders' in the sense that they all disagree with Assertion 2. That is, they believe the scientific evidence does not support *Evolution*. Meantime, while BCs and OCs agree with AEs on Assertion 1, ECs, on the other hand, say it *is* possible to believe in both God *and Evolution*. To be clear, notice that the ID movement takes no view on Assertion 1 (individual members of this group may take a particular view, but the focus of the ID movement is entirely on the science as it relates to Assertion 2). The evidence of five failed predictions presented in Part 2 strongly suggests the verdict that Assertion 2 is false.

What do the groupings tend to think about one another? It's clear that Dawkins holds in contempt anyone who "claims not to believe in evolution" (by which, of course, he means particles-to-people *Evolution*). As Matti Leisola puts it, "The temptation is to consider a contrary paradigm to be, not just in error, but heretical".[11] Using satire Dawkins paints the ID "style of argument" as "lazy".[12] Dawkins and others find it convenient, as hinted earlier, to conflate and misrepresent the BC and ID positions. So for example, Jerry Coyne broadcasts a misleading story.[13]

> *The most commonly suggested alternative ... is creationism, known in its latest incarnation as "Intelligent Design" (ID). Advocates of ID suggest that a **supernatural designer** has intervened at various times ... either instantly calling into being the complex adaptations that natural selection supposedly can't make, or producing **"miracle mutations"** that can't occur by chance. (Some **IDers** go further: they are the extreme "young Earth"*

creationists who believe that Earth is about 6,000 years old and that life has no evolutionary history at all) [emphasis added].[14]

Coyne offers no reference for these assertions, so we may be left wondering if he simply made them up.

First then, the ID movement makes no claims about the existence or identity of a designer, "supernatural" or otherwise; nor does it invoke "miracle mutations". The ID argument is that the scientific evidence - relating to life and the universe - that has accumulated over the last two generations, defies the capabilities of unguided materialistic processes to explain. They then invoke the scientific approach of "making an inference to the best explanation" which, in this case, is design.[15]

Second, Coyne conflates "IDers" and "young Earth creationists". This is misleading in relation to both groups. As we have seen BCs begin with the assumption that Biblical history from the beginning of Genesis is true and then interpret the scientific evidence accordingly.[16] The ID movement, however, does not dispute current beliefs about the age of the earth. As discussed, their sole argument is that design *is* detectable within the scientific evidence. Similarly to Dawkins and Coyne, Steven Pinker misleads by conflating BC and ID groupings:

... policies set in motion during George W. Bush's administration, including his encouragement of the teaching of creationism (in the guise of "intelligent design") ...[17]

Obfuscation of this kind creates an atmosphere in which genuine questions about the scientific evidence (for or against *Evolution*) cannot be discussed with transparency.

One of the features of this debate is that labels, often inaccurate ones at that, are used as a substitute for genuine discussion and rational argument. We have been conditioned by the scientific establishment and by the media to link the word "creationist" with descriptors such as "uneducated", "ignorant", "unintelligent", "bigoted", "anti-science" and, of course, "fundamentalist" (and we 'know' that fundamentalists are irrational).

Contra Dawkins' "It is absolutely safe to say that if you meet somebody who claims not to believe in evolution ..." the leading scientists who align with ID, OC and BC are neither "ignorant" nor "stupid", never mind "insane". There may well be critics of evolution who would merit these descriptives, but these are the easy targets. Experience of the key people in each of these groups confirms that they are highly educated and intelligent. Their penetrating questions and cogent arguments, if not taken seriously, will not go away.

What about Evolutionary Creationists? AEs regard ECs with a kind of patronising tolerance. On one hand they are viewed positively as supporters of *Evolution*, but negatively on the other, in the sense that they seem to have missed the point: that, for AEs, neo-Darwinism's naturalistic process makes God redundant.

How do ECs regard promoters of Intelligent Design and Biblical Creation? Because they believe the scientific evidence for *Evolution* to be unassailable, ECs are embarrassed equally by BC and ID groupings, generally conflate and misrepresent them just as AEs do, and consequently treat them with a kind of patronising *intolerance*.

Meantime many of those who support Intelligent Design, including this author, take the view that Evolutionary Creationists occupy a worst-of-both-worlds position. ECs have hitched their wagon to a (now failing) science, a science which also undermines key tenets of Christian theology. Stephen Meyer articulated it well in an interview with John Zmirak of *The Stream*. When asked about EC he said that

> ... many Christians are attracted to [evolutionary creation] because it purports to offer a way to reconcile the findings of science with their belief in God. Nevertheless, [evolutionary creationists] have been famously diffident about saying what, if anything, they think God is doing to create life beyond upholding the laws of nature. Instead, they affirm, as do secular evolutionary biologists, the creative power of the main evolutionary mechanisms such as natural selection and random mutation. These mechanisms were formulated as alternatives to the idea that God designed or directed the process of creation. After all, it's "nature", not God, that does the "selecting" in the natural selection and random mutation mechanism. Thus, I do think this view is theologically and logically problematic. How, for example, can God direct an undirected process? And if He's not actively directing the process – as [evolutionary creationists] typically think – then in what way is He actually sovereign over the process of creation? In any case, my main objection to [evolutionary creation] is not theological. It's scientific. As I detail in my last book Darwin's Doubt, even leading evolutionary biologists now doubt the creative power of the mutation and natural selection mechanism, and for many good scientific reasons. As evidence from across the biological subdisciplines shows, the mechanism can produce modest small scale modifications (or adaptations) to existing organisms, but it clearly lacks the ability to produce major innovations in biological form such as have arisen during the history of life. Thus, it is highly ironic for Christians and other traditional theists to be insisting that natural selection and random mutation are "God's way of creating" at just the time when evidential

challenges to the creative power of mutation and natural selection are mounting and when even many secular evolutionary biologists are acknowledging these evidential problems.[18]

The book *Theistic Evolution* edited by J.P. Moreland *et al.* critiques the Evolutionary Creation position in terms of its science, its philosophy and its theology.[19]

Appendix B

The ideology of evolutionism

Within a few decades of Darwin's publication of the *Origin of Species* in 1859, Western civilisation had boarded RMS *Evolution* and set a course that has taken it over the horizon towards a new destination. The new landscape is entirely different: a land in which *design* in biology is simply an *illusion*; where matter, energy and natural law can explain the existence of everything; where mind is nothing more than chemical reactions occurring in the brain; where the human species is of no exceptional value. In this land there is no objective meaning or purpose; no personhood; we are simply another species of animal. In this new world we are nothing but biological machines.

The prominent evolutionist, Ernst Mayr, described the Darwinian influence in this way, "A 21st century person looks at the world quite differently than a citizen of the Victorian era did … But what is not at all appreciated is the great extent to which this shift in thinking indeed resulted from Darwin's ideas".[1] All ideas have consequences. If a thoroughly naturalistic worldview, underpinned by Darwinism, is taken on board, it can be - and has been - used to justify a range of unpalatable and destructive propositions for humanity.

Three key ideas emerge from naturalistic Darwinism, or evolutionism:
- Biology was not designed (nor was there a designing agent).
- All species are equal (no one species is privileged over another).
- Humans are unequal (some are more "fit" than others).

In many cases Darwin's own words have been used to justify:
- **Conflict and war**: "… when of two adjoining tribes one becomes less numerous and less powerful than the other, the contest is soon settled by war, slaughter, cannibalism, slavery, and absorption".[2]

- **Racism**: "At some future period, not very distant as measured by centuries, the civilised races of man will almost certainly exterminate, and replace, the savage races throughout the world …",[3] "We have now seen that a naturalist might feel himself fully justified in ranking races of man as distinct species".[4] More recent confirmation of the influence of Darwin's work comes from none other than Stephen Jay Gould, "Biological arguments for racism may have been common before 1859, but they increased by orders of magnitude following the acceptance of evolutionary theory".[5] In these first two we see the seeds of, for example, Nazi genocides.
- **Social Darwinism and eugenics**: "We civilised men … do our utmost to check the process of elimination; we build asylums for the imbecile, the maimed, and the sick; we institute poor-laws; and our medical men exert their utmost skill to save the life of every one to the last moment. There is reason to believe vaccination has preserved thousands, who from a weak constitution would formerly have succumbed to smallpox. Thus the weak members of civilised societies propagate their kind. No one who has attended to the breeding of domestic animals will doubt that this must be highly injurious to the race of man … excepting in the case of man himself, hardly anyone is so ignorant as to allow his worst animals to breed".[6]

And Darwinian science has been used by others to justify:
- **Abortion, infanticide and euthanasia**: Australian bioethicist Peter Singer has been one of the most robust and clinical expositors of the logic of evolutionism, "All we are doing is catching up with Darwin. He showed in the 19th century that we are simply animals. Humans had imagined that we were a separate part of Creation … Darwin's theory undermined the foundations of that entire Western way of thinking about the place of our species in the universe".[7] Singer continues, "… on any fair comparison of morally relevant characteristics, like rationality, self-consciousness, awareness, autonomy, pleasure, pain, and so on, the calf, the pig, and the much-derided chicken come out well ahead of the fetus at any stage of pregnancy – while if we make the comparison with a fetus of less than three months, a fish would show more signs of consciousness".[8] Infants too: "Now it must be admitted that these arguments apply to the newborn baby as much as to the fetus …

and the life of a newborn baby is of less value to it than the life of a pig, a dog, or a chimpanzee is to the nonhuman animal".[9] He concludes, "Killing a snail or a day-old infant does not thwart any desires" for its future life, "because snails and newborn infants are incapable of having such desires".[10]

- **Philosophical materialism (or naturalism) is true**: It is clear from Darwin's notebooks that he had become a "Materialist" though he was coy about sharing this view widely, seeing it as not "safe" to do so.[11] In *Darwin Day in America*, John West summarises Darwin's influence upon the zeitgeist of the late 1800s, "By describing in detail natural mechanisms that could produce the complexity of life as we know it, Darwin helped transform materialism from a fantastic tale told by a few thinkers on the fringe of society to a hallowed scientific principle enshrined at the heart of modern science".[12]

- **Meaning, purpose, objective morality, self and free will are illusions**: Francis Crick, co-discoverer of the structure of DNA claims that "you", "your joys and your sorrows, your memories and your ambitions, your sense of personal identity and free will, are in fact no more than the behavior of a vast assemblage of nerve cells and their associated molecules".[13] Biologist William Provine said this, "Let me summarize my views on what modern evolutionary biology tells us loud and clear – and these are basically Darwin's views. There are no gods, no purposes, and no goal-directed forces of any kind. There is no life after death. When I die, I am absolutely certain that I am going to be dead. That's the end of me. There is no ultimate foundation for ethics, no ultimate meaning in life, and no free will for humans, either".[14]

- **God is dead**: Historian Yuval Harari insists that "Just as people were never created, neither, according to the science of biology, is there a 'Creator' who 'endows' them with anything. There is only a blind evolutionary process, … when modern humans discovered that they actually evolved from reptiles, they rebelled against God and stopped listening to Him – or even believing in His existence … God is dead – it's just taking a while to get rid of the body".[15] Similarly, philosopher Michael Ruse claims that "[Darwin] cracked the final cause problem … He was the Newton of biology … God is out of the picture". He's a "retired engineer, and from this to His complete elimination was only a step".[16] And this is the message delivered to students in universities and even via popular fiction to the public at large.[17] Meanwhile for Dawkins, belief in God is "a kind of mental illness"[18] and until Darwin it was impossible to be "an intellectually fulfilled atheist".[19] Author Gene Veith also recognises the link between Darwinism and atheism. He's worth quoting at length.

> ... in the nineteenth century, science did strike a blow against Christianity and against religion in general, one that continues to reverberate today. Charles Darwin's theory of evolution has indeed undermined Christianity ... in purporting to account for the origins of human life in purely naturalistic terms, Darwin seemed to have rendered God unnecessary. When Darwin's Origin of Species was published in 1859, it was seized upon by many in the educated public who were interested not so much in its technical scientific claims as in its potential for freeing them from the "shackles" of religion. To this day, modernists and postmodernists and secularists in all of their variety invoke the theory of evolution as the definitive refutation of biblical faith.[20]

The connection between *Evolution* and disbelief is borne out by opinion polls: in a 2019 survey of fifteen thousand 18- to 35-year-olds in 25 different countries, nearly half (46%) of those who had no religious affiliation listed "science" as their biggest barrier to belief.[21] Homing in on questions specifically about *Evolution*, in a 2016 survey of American adults, 66% of atheists and 44% of agnostics said that for them personally, the idea that "life began from non-life through an unguided process of chemical evolution" has made the existence of God "less likely". And almost identical percentages said the idea that "all life forms on Earth (including humans) were produced by an unguided process of mutation and natural selection" has made the existence of God "less likely".[22] A 2003 survey found that 87% of leading evolutionists denied the existence of God.[23]

Acknowledgements

While I have had an aspiration to write this book for many years, several lockdowns during the COVID-19 pandemic demolished any excuses I may have been harbouring and provided the perfect opportunity to begin in earnest.

While I alone am responsible for the content of the book, I am most grateful to a number of others who have been a great help and encouragement to me during the project.

Mike Ross was first to be actively involved as he kindly read and insightfully critiqued each chapter draft as it was written. Through his dedicated efforts and encouragement the initial rough edges were excised from the text.

Helpful discussions with David Swift have been invaluable throughout the project. Each chapter has profited from his critical review and efforts and I am especially grateful for his input to Chapter 7 which has benefited greatly from his knowledge of embryology. I'm also much indebted to David for permission to use a number of diagrams from his website https://evolutionunderthemicroscope.com

I express my thanks to John Henry, Professor emeritus of History of Science at Edinburgh University for his feedback and for his critique of the text – and indeed my thanks go to John Magnus Sandberg for connecting me to this reviewer.

I'm much indebted to Mark Dykes, Roddy Evans and Jock Stein, each of whom devoted many hours to detailed review of the manuscript. As a result, the structure and readability of the text is much improved. Their inputs included suggestions to improve the book subtitle and its part and chapter titles. The phrase "think the unthinkable, sink the unsinkable" arose out of these discussions, for example. My thanks also go to Malcolm Macdonald and Moray Rumney for their enthusiasm, support and helpful input.

Insights, suggestions and encouragement from Doug Axe, Alistair Donald, David Galloway, Alastair Noble, John Richardson and David Williams have been very important to the project. Discussions around their own publishing experiences have also been very helpful.

James Gentles made the mistake of asking, "How is your book project going?" As a result, James has been my project manager and encourager from early on. His knowledge of book design and printing and his attention to detail have been invaluable throughout. The cover design is his. My grateful thanks also go to him for enabling and supporting the review and publishing processes and for his photographic skills in connection with capturing images from the James Clerk Maxwell Foundation collection.

Last but not least I thank my wife, Janet, for her permission to embark upon this project and for her unfailing patience throughout.

Notes

The bibliographic information is given in the References section which follows this one.

About the Author

1. For example, Alice Roberts speculates on the "why": why natural selection might select for loss of colour vision in some species (because it might be an unnecessary luxury in nocturnal mammals) and then later why natural selection might select for a regaining of colour vision in other species (perhaps to help find the right kinds of food). Roberts (2015), pp. 107-108.

Prologue

1. When *Gigantic* was eventually launched in 1915, her name had been changed to *Britannic*.
2. A video animation of how *Titanic* is thought to have sunk can be found here: https://video.nationalgeographic.com/tv/00000144-2f3a-df5d-abd4-ff7f31f90000
3. The major reference for the Prologue was Green (2005).

Introduction

1. Green (2005), p.140.
2. There is a view that the "unsinkable" myth developed after the *Titanic* disaster, but there is evidence, apart from Smith's quote, that she was *believed* to be unsinkable before the event. For instance, when reports reached the White Star Line New York office that *Titanic* was in trouble, the Vice President, P.A.S. Franklin announced "We place absolute confidence in the *Titanic*. We believe the boat is unsinkable". A White Star Line 1910 publicity brochure stated that *Titanic* and her sister ships were "designed to be unsinkable". In 1911, analyses in the *Irish News*, *Belfast News* and *Shipbuilder* magazine concluded that *Titanic* was "practically unsinkable". See "Why Did People Consider the *Titanic* Unsinkable?", *History on the Net*, Salem Media, https://www.historyonthenet.com/the-titanic-why-did-people-believe-titanic-was-unsinkable. Accessed 7 June 2022.
3. *Titanic*, film produced by James Cameron, distributed by Paramount Pictures (North America), 20th Century Fox (international), (1997), widescreen, 195 minutes.
4. This quotation, made famous by Cameron's film, is reputed to have been the answer given by a deck hand when asked if *Titanic* was really unsinkable. See "Why Did People Consider the *Titanic* Unsinkable?", op. cit.
5. On 1 January 2017, the United Kingdom's Channel 4 premiered a documentary titled "Titanic: The New Evidence" which claimed that *Titanic* would not have sunk if it had not been for a fire that had raged for days in coal bunker 10 which seriously damaged one of the bulkheads. For comment (suggesting *Titanic* might not have sunk so quickly if there had not been a fire, but would have sunk nevertheless due to the extent of the iceberg caused damage) see here: https://www.snopes.com/news/2017/01/06/coal-fire-sink-the-titanic/
6. Biles, J.H., "The loss of the *Titanic*", *Engineer*, April 19, 1912, pp. 409-410.

7. Ibid., p. 409.
8. For example, Richard Dawkins' statement, "Today the theory of evolution is about as much open to doubt as the theory that the earth goes round the sun ...", Dawkins (1989), p. 1.
9. Wagner, Günter P., "The Changing Face of Evolutionary Thinking", *Genome Biology and Evolution 5* (2013): 2006-7, quoted within Behe (2019), p. 226.
10. I'm grateful to Aitken (2018), p.10 for this analogy.

Chapter 1 – Science: its limitations

1. Gould (2000), p. 276.
2. Breast feeding and cuddling infants hardly seems a scientific achievement. However, a couple of generations ago it was fashionable, supposedly supported by the science, to encourage breast milk substitutes. And some multinationals made a mint from this fashion! Ditto, it was scientifically fashionable to treat babies as machines, including not cuddling them. Unsurprisingly, research has now confirmed that nature is best. In that sense, Pinker is correct.
3. Pinker (2019), p. 67.
4. Baden Aniline and Soda Factory
5. Offit (2017), p. 71.
6. Pinker (2019), p. 75.
7. Ibid., p. 94.
8. Youngson (1998), p. 261.
9. Plokhy (2018), p. 85.
10. Ibid., pp. 339-340.
11. Ibid., p. 343. Steven Pinker (2019), underplays the impact of Chernobyl relative to Plokhy, saying only, "... thirty-one deaths in the 1986 Chernobyl, the result of extraordinary Soviet-era bungling, together with a few thousand early deaths from cancer above the 100,000 natural cancer deaths in the exposed population", p.146.
12. Reaktor Bolshoy Moshchnosty Kanalny, high-power channel reactor.
13. Plokhy (2018), p. 66.
14. Ibid., pp. 319-320.
15. Ibid., pp. 268-269.
16. Ibid., p. 125.
17. Youngson (1998), pp. 155-159.
18. Ibid., pp. 13-19.
19. Ibid., p. 14.
20. Oard (2004).
21. Lyell (1830-33), pp. xvi-xvii.
22. Some sources spell "Harland" as "Harlan" or "Harlen"
23. Oard (2004), p. 9.
24. Ibid., pp. 34-35.
25. Offit (2017), p. 131 ff.
26. Ahmed, N., "23 years of the discovery of *Helicobacter pylori*: Is the debate over?", *Annals of Clinical Microbiology and Antimicrobials*, 31 October 2005. doi: 10.1186/1476-0711-4-17

27. Barrow (2003), p. 148.
28. Youngson (1998), pp. 135-141.
29. Ibid., pp. 82-88.
30. This analogy has been used by Stephen Hawking among others, see Hawking & Mlodinow (2011), pp. 168-169.
31. Polanyi (1974), p. 164. In the 1970's it was acceptable to use 'he', 'him' etc., as gender neutral pronouns.
32. Kuhn (1970), p. 24.
33. Ibid., p. 140.
34. Ibid., p. 144.
35. Ibid., p. 151, quoted from Max Planck, *Scientific Autobiography and Other Papers*, trans. F. Gaynor (New York, 1949), pp. 33-34.
36. Sheldrake (2013), p. 19.
37. The Wikipedia entry for "science", https://en.wikipedia.org/wiki/Science. Accessed 1 May 2023.
38. Lennox (2007), p. 31.
39. Gould (1986), p. 60-69.
40. Meyer (2009), p. 400-401.
41. Orwell, George, *Animal Farm*, New York, The New American Library, 1946.
42. Kuhn (1970), p.49.
43. Stadler (2016).
44. Adapted from Stadler (2016), p. 8.
45. Stadler (2016), p.9.
46. Ibid., p. 15.
47. Stark (2014), p. 319.
48. Stadler (2016), p. 10
49. Ibid., p. 35 ff.
50. Ibid., adapted from table on p. 38.
51. Ibid., p. 37.
52. Ibid., p. 39.
53. Thaxton, *et al.* (1984).
54. Ibid., p. 203.
55. For example, Walley, Stephen M., "Aristotle, Projectiles and Guns", *SMF Fracture and Shock Physics Group, The Cavendish Laboratory*, pp. 9-12, https://arxiv.org/pdf/1804.00716.pdf. Accessed 17 April 2023.
56. Thaxton *et al.* (1984), p. 204.
57. Sheldrake (2013), pp. 308-309.
58. See for example, Vogel, G., "Macchiarini guilty of misconduct, but whistleblowers share blame, new Karolinska Institute verdict finds", *Science*, 26 June 2018, https://www.science.org/content/article/macchiarini-guilty-misconduct-whistleblowers-share-blame-new-karolinska-institute. See also, "*Lancet* MMR autism fraud", https://en.wikipedia.org/wiki/Lancet_MMR_autism_fraud. Accessed 18 April 2023. See also, "The Replication Crisis", https://en.wikipedia.org/wiki/Replication_crisis. Accessed 11 October 2021. A core element of the scientific method is that experimental results are valid only if they can be independently replicated. One study suggested that only 39% of psychological studies could be replicated: Baker,

Monya, "Over Half of Psychology Studies Fail Reproducibility Test", Nature, 27 August 2015: doi:10.1038/nature.2015.18248. More than 70% of researchers in a wide range of disciplines, including physics, chemistry and medicine, have tried and failed to reproduce another scientist's experiments, and more than half have failed to reproduce their own experiments: Baker, Monya, "1500 Scientists Lift the Lid on Reproducibility", *Nature*, Vol 533, 26 May 2016. Others cite similar problems: Ioannidis, John P. A., "Why Most Published Research Findings Are False", *PLOS Medicine*, 30 August 2005: https://doi.org/10.1371/journal.pmed.0020124. See also Couronne, Ivan, "Beware Those Scientific Studies - Most Are Wrong, Researcher Warns", *Yahoo! News*, 5 July 2018, https://news.yahoo.com/beware-those-scientific-studies-most-wrong-researcher-warns-164336076.html. Accessed 11 November 2021. See also Ridley, M., "Science fiction: the crisis in research", *The Spectator*, 12 August 2023, https://www.spectator.co.uk/article/science-fiction-the-crisis-in-research/?utm_medium=email&utm_source=CampaignMonitor_Editorial&utm_campaign=WEEK%20%20230810%20%20AL+CID_833d18d0c0793efbf27885be419ad723
59. Sheldrake (2013)., p. 312.
60. Gould (2000)., pp. 277-284.

Chapter 2 - Scientists: the new priesthood

1. Writing in 1955, it was still generally regarded as acceptable for George Sarton to reference men only.
2. Sarton, G., 1955, Introductory Essay, in J. Needham, (ed.), *Science, Religion and Reality*, New York, Braziller, p. 12. This historian of science is cited by Sheldrake (2013), p. 16.
3. Marx, Karl, *A Contribution to the Critique of Hegel's Philosophy of Right*, Introduction, 1843. https://www.marxists.org/archive/marx/works/1843/critique-hpr/intro.htm
4. Polanyi (1974), p. 141.
5. Sheldrake (2013), p. 13.
6. Ibid., p. 14.
7. Ibid., p. 14.
8. For example, Pope Innocent III was the highest ranking person in Europe in the 13th century.
9. Eldredge (1982), pp. 26-27.
10. Russell, B., 1970, *Religion and Science*, Oxford, Oxford University Press, p. 243.
11. Medawar, P., 1979, *Advice to a Young Scientist*, London, Harper and Row, p. 31. Also, 1984, *The Limits of Science*, Oxford, Oxford University Press, p. 66.
12. Faith and Science Lecture Forum debate between William Lane Craig and Peter Atkins, 1998, https://www.youtube.com/watch?v=jnqiiNEOqP0. Accessed 10 November 2021.
13. Gervais, 2010.
14. Sheldrake (2013), p. 27.
15. Dawkins (2006).
16. Dawkins (2006), p. 5.

Notes

17. Carrier (2011), p. 56 ff.
18. Draper (1873).
19. White (1895).
20. Draper (1873), p. 174. Draper's specific target is the Roman Catholic Church.
21. Loftus (2011), David Eller's Chapter 11, p. 258.
22. Cited in Stark (2014), p. 70: Voltaire, *Works*, Vol. 12.
23. Stark (2014), p. 71
24. O'Neill, T., ""The Dark Ages" – Popery, Periodisation and Pejoratives", *History for Atheists*, 19 November 2016: https://historyforatheists.com/2016/11/the-dark-ages-popery-periodisation-and-pejoratives/. See also Keas (2019), Chapter 2.
25. Stark (2014), pp. 169-170.
26. Ibid., p. 171.
27. William of Ockham is best known for his eponymous principle Ockham's razor which states that explanations should, "not be multiplied beyond necessity." Cited in Ibid., p. 175.
28. Stark (2014), pp. 170-178.
29. Ibid., p. 303.
30. Ibid., p. 309.
31. Ibid.
32. Ibid., pp. 309-310.
33. Cited in Lennox (2007), p. 20.
34. The term, 'scientist' was first coined in 1830 by William Whewell, Professor of Mineralogy, later Master of Trinity College, Cambridge. See Wilson (2017), p. 66. Wilson also notes that Thomas Huxley, often described as Darwin's bulldog, ignorant of Whewell's innovation, wrote in 1894 "…with absurd pomposity… to the Science-Gossip magazine to protest against its use of a vulgar Americanism - the word 'scientist'. The English term he insisted was 'man of science'".
35. Spencer (2016), p. 85.
36. Psalm 111 verse 2, cited in Lennox (2007), p. 50. The words were inscribed over the archway in Latin.
37. Stark (2014), pp. 38, 315-316; also Lennox (2007), p. 20; also Spencer (2016), pp. 96-98; also Polanyi (1974), p. 181; also Kuhn, (1970), p. 168. Meantime Harari seems to indicate that "We don't know" why science thrived in a sustained way in Europe rather than China or India - Harari (2015), pp. 271-272. Historian Tom Holland offers an excellent insight into how European Jesuit astronomers had been appointed by the Chinese Emperor to sort out the Chinese calendar, especially in relation to its prediction of eclipses, where local astronomers were failing. Holland (2019), pp. 331-336.
38. Spencer, (2016), p. 104. Harrison's quote cited from his book, *The Fall of Man and the Foundations of Science*. A similar point is made by Francis Schaeffer, "In [Thomas] Aquinas's view the will of man was fallen, but the intellect was not. From this incomplete view of the biblical Fall flowed subsequent difficulties… man's intellect was seen as autonomous". Schaeffer (1990), p. 211.
39. Lennox (2007), p. 23.
40. Spencer (2016), pp. 104-105.

41. Schaeffer (1990), p. 226. Also, "And [Galileo, Kepler, Newton, etc.] believed… that because God was a reasonable God one could discover the truth of the universe by reason. So modern science was born. Greeks had almost all the facts that the early scientists had, but it never turned into a science like modern science", p. 326.
42. Lewis (1974), p. 110.
43. This is the argument from contingency: that the Judaeo-Christian God had freely chosen various laws with which to order His creation. These early scientists believed there was contingency here, in that He might have chosen different laws.
44. Lennox (2007), p. 16.
45. Lennox (2019), pp. 16-17.
46. For example: Stark (2014), pp. 318-320; Lennox (2007), pp. 22-25. Holland gives an excellent account, Holland (2019), pp. 335-341. Also Keas (2019), Chapter 5.
47. Based on a specific interpretation of Psalm 93, verse 1: "The world is firmly established; it cannot be moved". In fact, the final piece of evidence to confirm the Copernican model did not come for another 200 years when better and more accurate telescopes could measure parallax error between mid-summer and mid-winter observations of distant stars.
48. In 16th century Europe the Protestant Reformation resulted in Protestant churches splitting off from the Roman Catholic Church arising from a rejection of papal authority in favour of Biblical authority. See: https://en.wikipedia.org/wiki/Reformation
49. Stark (2014), p. 320.
50. Ibid.
51. Wells (2017), p. 18.
52. Plantinga (2011), p. 83
53. Ibid., p. 84. As Plantinga points out, in practice an analytical solution for the equations of motion for three bodies has not so far been solved, let alone the classical n-body problem for large n.
54. Ibid., p. 85.
55. Lennox (2019), p. 34.
56. Lewontin, Richard C., "Billions and Billions of Demons" (a review of Carl Sagan's book, *The Demon Haunted World: Science as a Candle in the Dark*), New York Review of Books, 9 January 1997.
57. Plantinga (2011), p. 307 ff. He argues that the real conflict, the deep conflict, instead of being between science and theism, is actually between science and naturalism (or materialism).
58. Cited in Lennox (2007), p. 39.
59. Cited in Ibid., p. 14.
60. Ibid., p. 20.

Chapter 3 – Evolution: thinking the unthinkable

1. Dawkins, Richard. Quoted from, https://en.wikiquote.org/wiki/Richard_Dawkins
2. Dawkins (1996), p. 81.
3. Dawkins (2010), p. 8. One of the most prominent biologists of the 20th century, Ernst Mayr has this to say, "No educated person any longer questions the validity

of the so-called theory of evolution, which we now know to be a simple fact". Mayr E., "Darwin's Influence on Modern Thought", *Scientific American*, 24 November, 2009.
4. Coyne (2010), p. xviii.
5. Dawkins (1989), p. 1. Alice Roberts tries a similar tack, "There are some theories, some facts that are so unlikely to be disproved that we can depend on them. So, for instance, that the Earth really is spherical, not flat, and that evolution has definitely happened". Roberts (2015), p. 302. In this case, critics of evolution are being likened to flat earthers.
6. Some processes within microevolution are directly observable, such as mutation and speciation, but the grand claims of *Evolution* are not (see Table 3.1).
7. Dawkins (2004), p. 18. The sentence about aeronautical engineers getting their sums right, Dawkins has quoted from p. 36 of his own *River Out of Eden* (1996).
8. Popkin (1998), p. 28.
9. Jason, Jean and Yixi, Lu, "Evolution as a fact? A discourse analysis", *Social Studies of Science*, Vol. 48(4) 615-632 (2018).
10. Wilson (2017), p. 358.
11. "scientific" meaning "naturalistic" as discussed in Chapter 2. Recall the Richard Lewontin quote.
12. "Science Heritage", *Engineering & Technology Magazine*, December 2019/January 2020, p. 71.
13. Hoyle, Sir Fred & Wickramasinghe, Chandra, (1984), p. 151.
14. Wilson (2017), p. 54.
15. Ibid., pp. 50-54. Schelling, 1812; Robinet, 1786 and Immanuel Kant (1724-1804) promoted evolutionary ideas, Veith (2020), p. 51. Patrick Matthew's 1831 *On Naval Timber and Arboriculture* completely pre-empted Darwin's theory, Sutton (2022).
16. Ibid., pp. 191-195.
17. Ibid., p. 149. Darwin also plagiarised Patrick Matthew's work, Sutton (2022).
18. Hoyle & Wickramasinghe, (1984), p. 152.
19. Ibid., pp. 153-4. See also Wilson (2017), p. 149.
20. Wilson (2017), p. 139.
21. Ibid., pp. 145-150.
22. Ibid., pp. 51-53 ff. Also Hoyle and Wickramasinghe, pp. 152-4.
23. Ibid., p. 279. See also Dawkins (2010), p. 29.
24. Mackean (2004), p. 206.
25. The Momentum of an object = its mass (in kilograms) times its velocity (in metres per second). The Kinetic Energy of an object = one half of its mass (in kilograms) times the square of its velocity (in metres per second). The definitions are unambiguous.
26. Coyne (2010), p. xvii.
27. Ibid., p. 3.
28. Christopher Hitchens was one of the self-styled "Four Horseman" of the New Atheist movement. Wikipedia defines New Atheism as: "…a term coined in 2006 by the journalist Gary Wolf to describe the positions promoted by some atheists of the twenty-first century. This modern-day atheism is advanced by a group of thinkers and writers who advocate the view that superstition, religion and

irrationalism should not simply be tolerated but should be countered, criticized, and exposed by rational argument wherever their influence arises in government, education, and politics". The article also lists the other "Horsemen" as Richard Dawkins, Daniel Dennett and Sam Harris. https://en.wikipedia.org/wiki/New_Atheism, viewed February, 2020.
29. Quoted in Wilson (2017), p. 266.
30. Ibid., p. 263.
31. Ibid., Chapter 13; also Youngson (1998), pp. 43-48; Lennox (2007), pp. 25-26.
32. A British literary magazine published 1828-1921.
33. Lennox (2007), p. 26.
34. Wilson (2017), p. 258.
35. Quoted in Lennox (2007), p. 25.
36. Wilson (2017), pp. 279-80.
37. Quoted in ibid., p. 289.
38. Ibid., pp. 264-5.
39. Coyne (2010), p. 13.
40. Ibid., p. 57.
41. Ibid., p. 62.
42. Ibid., p. 73.
43. Ibid., p. 132.
44. Dawkins (1996), p. 123.
45. It is premature to counter the specifics of Coyne's and Dawkins' arguments here. The content of Parts 2 and 3 will tackle such themes. The key point here is that popularisers of evolution use theological arguments - their understanding of what a Creator would or would not do - when we would perhaps be justified in expecting purely scientific ones. Cornelius Hunter goes even further. He argues that for Darwin in the first instance, and for his subsequent disciples, theological concerns actually have primacy over the science. See "Evolution as a Theological research Program", *Religions* 2021, *12*, 694. https://doi.org/10.3390/rel12090694
46. Coyne (2010), p. 149.
47. Wilson (2017), p. 287.
48. Dawkins (2006), p. 264.

Introduction to part 2

1. Kuhn (1970), p. 185.
2. None of the critics of evolutionary theory, including promoters of Intelligent Design and Biblical Creationists (sometimes known as Young Earth Creationists), doubt this kind of small-scale adaptation.
3. Mayr (1963), p. 586.
4. Pinker (2019), p. 366.
5. Ibid., p. 29.
6. Ibid., p. 27.
7. Coyne (2010), pp. 16-17.

Chapter 4 – FP #1: Life emerged from chemistry

Notes

1. Cox & Cohen (2014), p. 104.
2. Darwin (1860), p. 396.
3. From a letter Charles Darwin wrote to Joseph Hooker on 1 February 1871. See Darwin Correspondence Project: https://www.darwinproject.ac.uk/letter/DCP-LETT-7471.xml
4. Cox & Cohen (2014), p. 192.
5. See for example, "How many stars are there in the Universe?", European Space Agency website, https://www.esa.int/Science_Exploration/Space_Science/Herschel/How_many_stars_are_there_in_the_Universe. Accessed 19 April 2023.
6. Crane, L., "How old is the universe?", *NewScientist*, https://www.newscientist.com/question/how-old-is-the-universe/. Accessed 19 April 2023.
7. Cox & Cohen (2014), p. 66 ff.
8. Adapted from Ibid., p. 71.
9. The apparent contradiction between the high probability of extraterrestrial civilisations' existence and humanity's lack of contact with, or evidence for, such civilisations is known as the Fermi Paradox, named after Enrico Fermi the great 20th century physicist. By early 2020, over 4,000 planets outside our solar system had been discovered and confirmed with another ~3,000 candidates awaiting confirmation (or otherwise). So far no 'exoplanet' has been found with Earth-like characteristics likely to be able to support life (see NASA Exoplanet Exploration website: https://exoplanets.nasa.gov)
10. Cox & Cohen (2014), p. 103.
11. *Planets*. Directed by Stephen Cooter, BBC Studios with NOVA and WGBH Boston, 2019, Episode 2.
12. Ibid. Arguably, the widely held view that the emergence of life is 'inevitable' and maybe even 'easy', is a significant factor driving NASA's exploration of the Solar System.
13. Leisola (2018), p. 116.
14. Cox & Cohen (2014), p. 58.
15. Ibid., pp. 104-5.
16. See, for example, https://www.esa.int/Science_Exploration/Space_Science/Is_the_Universe_finite_or_infinite_An_interview_with_Joseph_Silk
17. I'm grateful to John Lennox for this analogy.
18. Rothery (2003), p. 213.
19. Lane (2010), p. 10. See also p. 20.
20. Brockman (2005), p. xi.
21. Ibid., p. 11. Other similar views were stated by, for example, Carolyn Porco, a NASA planetary scientist, p. 15; physicist Kenneth W. Ford, p. 19; genomic researcher J. Craig Venter, p. 23.
22. Dawkins (2006), p 137.
23. Ibid., pp. 137-8.
24. Another respected researcher has estimated the odds of life arising: "If the probability of life in the universe is one in a million billion, then in a million billion planets there is a chance approaching 1 that life should emerge somewhere… However exceedingly rare life might be, in an infinite universe there is always a probability of life emerging on one planet…". Nick Lane (2018), p. 9.

25. Dawkins (1997), p. 260.
26. Haeckel, Ernst, *The History of Creation*, vol. 1, Project Gutenberg. www.gutenberg.org/files/40472.
27. Steele, E. J., *et al.*, "Cause of Cambrian Explosion - Terrestrial or Cosmic?", *Progress in Biophysics and Molecular Biology*, 136 (2018), p. 5.
28. It has been argued elsewhere that Haeckel actually had no excuse for asserting that the internal working of a living cell entailed only simple processes. For example: Axe, Douglas (2016), p. 191.
29. Denton (1985), p. 328.
30. Ibid., p. 329.
31. Plantinga (2011), p. 232.
32. Alberts, B., "The Cell is a Collection of Protein Machines: Preparing the Next Generation of Molecular Biologists", *Review* 92(3), pp. 291-294, 06 February 1998. DOI:https://doi.org/10.1016/S0092-8674(00)80922-8
33. Eberlin (2019), p. 21.
34. This is an adaptation of an analogy used by Matti Leisola. Leisola (2018), p. 179. Leisola's analogy compares a microorganism to a sports car and, in turn to a garden spade.
35. Meyer, Stephen C., "Where does the information come from?" animation: https://www.youtube.com/watch?v=TVkdQhNdzHU
36. Dawkins (1991), p. 147.
37. Brockman (2005), p. 17.
38. A habitable world fine-tuned to support life is itself not trivial, but the requirements for that are beyond the scope of this book. See for example Gonzalez and Richards (2004).
39. Lane (2010), p. 31.
40. See for example, Pallen (2009), pp. 151-2.
41. Lane (2010), p. 11.
42. Leisola (2018), pp. 27-8.
43. Thaxton *et al.* (1984), p. 24.
44. Lane (2010), p. 11.
45. Thaxton *et al.* (2019), pp. 410-11.
46. Pallen (2009), pp. 152-3.
47. Lane (2010), p. 18.
48. Ibid., p. 20.
49. The movement of protons over a membrane has the formal name of 'chemiosmosis', a process elucidated by the British biochemist, Peter Mitchell which gained him a Nobel Prize in 1978. See Lane (2010), p. 31.
50. Lane (2010), p. 33.
51. Ibid.
52. Thaxton *et al.* (1984), pp. 93-4.
53. Brooks, J and Shaw, G, 1973, *Origin and Development of Living Systems*, New York, Academic Press, p. 212, quoted in Thaxton *et al.* (1984), p. 110.
54. See for example a conversation between synthetic organic chemist James Tour and physicist Brian Miller in "Thermodynamics & the Origin of Life", https://

www.youtube.com/watch?v=RJeUH7IhQHo&t=350s, especially from 5:50 to 10:00 minutes.
55. Matti Leisola tells the story of an interchange he had with astronomy professor, Esko Valtaoja, who claimed that "…the basic law of nature, the second law of thermodynamics, clearly says that order increases in nature". See Leisola & Witt (2018), p. 71. Valtaoja's understanding is the very opposite of the truth!
56. Pinker (2019), p. 19.
57. Quoted in Thaxton *et al.* (1984), p. 127.
58. Pinker (2019), p. 61.
59. Thaxton *et al.* (1984), Chapters 7 & 8.
60. Ibid., p. 125.
61. Ibid., p. 127.
62. Ibid., p. 125.
63. Berlinski (2009), p. 126.
64. Thaxton *et al.* (2020).
65. Human beings use ~2 mW/gram, or ~130 Watts for an average person weighing 65 kg. See Denton (2020), p. 76.
66. Thaxton *et al.* (2020), p. 363.
67. Thaxton *et al.* (2020), p. 382.
68. Moreland *et al.* (2017), pp. 169-70.
69. Thaxton *et al.* (2020), pp. 330-334. Also talk by James Tour: https://www.youtube.com/watch?v=zU7Lww-sBPg
70. Tour, James, 2020, talk on "The Mystery of the Origin of Life", https://www.youtube.com/watch?v=zU7Lww-sBPg. See also Thaxton *et al.* (2020), pp. 326-7, 334-5.
71. Regis (2008), p. 103.
72. Thaxton *et al.*, (2020), p. 341.
73. Steele *et al.*, op. cit.
74. Hoyle & Wickramasinghe (1984).
75. Ibid., p. 24.
76. Ibid., p. 103.
77. Ibid., pp. 36-7.
78. Lane, op. cit., pp. 9-10.
79. Hoyle & Wickramasinghe (1984), p. 31.
80. Quoted in Thaxton *et al.* (2020), p. 260.
81. Leisola & Witt (2018), p. 70.
82. Quoted in Coyne (2010), p. 114.
83. Hoyle & Wickramasinghe (1984), p. 3.
84. Hoyle & Wickramasinghe (1984), p. 4.
85. Sabatini, Riccardo (2016), "How to read the genome and build a human being", TED talk, https://www.ted.com/talks/riccardo_sabatini_how_to_read_the_genome_and_build_a_human_being?language=en#t-117229
86. For example, Dawkins (2004), p. 119.
87. String 3 could be *compressible*. For example, "five" could be replaced by "5". Alternatively, the whole string could be rendered in Pitman shorthand or some

other coded format. Similarly, the string has some elements of *redundancy*. Through knowledge of the language and the sender, the recipient (or a predictive text computer program) may be able to guess all or parts of words. Experience of predictive text suggests, however, that there are dangers in this!

88. Denton (2020), p. 116. Many human cells contain several billion protein molecules, p. 117.
89. Leisola & Witt (2018), p. 194.
90. Eberlin (2019), p. 67.
91. Leisola & Witt (2018), p. 181. The average is 267 for bacterial prokaryotic proteins and 361 for eukaryotic proteins.
92. Meyer (2009), p. 93.
93. Ibid., p. 94.
94. Meyer (2009), p. 211.
95. Axe, Douglas D., "The Case against a Darwinian Origin of Protein Folds", *BIO-Complexity* 2010, no.1 (2010), p. 2. doi:10.5048/BIO-C.2010.1. The mean and median lengths are both greater than 300 residues.
96. Carrier (2011), pp. 56-7.
97. The number of possible outcomes is 6^6. But 5^6 outcomes cannot produce a 6. So the probability of a 6 is $(6^6-5^6)/6^6 \sim 0.66$
98. Dembski (2005), pp. 209-210.
99. Barrow (2003), p. 85. See also Leisola (2018), p.181 and Thaxton *et al.* (2020), p. 342.
100. The smallest proteins are 70 amino acid residues in length (recall that the overwhelming majority are >150 residues. The number of trials needed for this is >20^{70}, or >10^{91} So while the universe may be able to 'find' *one* of these smallest proteins, given the very generous assumptions, finding a second one (10^{182}) would be short by 10^{41} trials.
101. One such story in Dawkins (1991), p. 46. The sonnet refutation in Flew & Varghese (2007), pp. 75-77.
102. Flew (2007), pp. 74-78.
103. Axe, Douglas, "Extreme Functional Sensitivity to Conservative Amino Acid Changes on Enzyme exteriors." *Journal of Molecular Biology* 301 (2000): 585-95. See also: Axe DD (2010), "The Case Against a Darwinian Origin of Protein Folds". BIO-Complexity 2010(1):1-12. doi:10.5048/BIO-C,2010.1
104. The radius of the observable universe is 46.5 billion light years. Multiply this by the speed of light (3×10^8 metres/second) and by the number of seconds in a year ($3.15 * 10^7$) to find the radius = $4.4*10^{26}$ metres. The surface area of the sphere is then $4\pi r^2 = 2.4 * 10^{54}$. The diameter of a hydrogen (H) atom is $1.2 * 10^{-10}$ metres. So number of H atoms per square metre = $0.7 * 10^{20}$. Hence number of atoms on the surface of a sphere the size of the observable universe is $\sim 1.7 * 10^{74}$.
105. Denton (1985), p. 323.
106. Meyer (2009), pp. 206-7.
107. Ibid.
108. Ibid., p. 212.
109. Hoyle & Wickramasinghe (1984), p. 148.

110. Eberlin (2019), p. 76. Meyer (2009), p. 201 cites the simplest extant cell, *Mycoplasma genitalium* as requiring 482 different proteins.
111. For example, Meyer (2009), p. 94.
112. The shortest proteins are ~70 amino acid residues in length.
113. Steele *et al.*, op. cit., p. 7. Having, at least implicitly, recognised the limitations of Earth's probabilistic resources, the thrust of this paper - perhaps in desperation - is to seek recourse to the vastness of space and time available to the universe. Just as Crick and Hoyle & Wickramasinghe did before them. But as we've seen, even the observable universe falls far short of the required probabilistic resources.
114. Berlinski (2009), p. 128.
115. Hoyle & Wickramasinghe (1984), p. 7.
116. See for example, Moreland *et al.* (2017), pp. 150-163.
117. Dawkins (1997), p. 260.
118. As an indication of how precarious the situation has become, a business consultant has offered a US$10 million prize to anyone who can answer the question, "Where did life and the genetic code come from?" Perry Marshall *et al.* see the pivotal question clearly, "Where did the *information* come from?", see the "Evolution 2.0 Prize" website: https://www.herox.com/evolution2.0
119. Tan, C. L. & Stadler, R. (2020), p. 190. *The Stairway to Life* explores 12 "steps" of a "stairway" in which each step would require to have been achieved before the next could commence and all 12 would have been required to complete the journey from chemistry to biology, that's to say abiogenesis, the first life. A number of the steps are discussed in Chapter 4 of this book, such as, Formation and concentration of building blocks, Homochirality of building blocks, Consistent linkage of building blocks. Others include Biopolymer reproduction, Sequences forming a useful code, Gene regulation, Selectively permeable membranes, and a Coordinated cellular purpose. Tan and Stadler's message is that the probability of achieving any one of these twelve steps is vanishingly small. This means that the probability of success with all twelve is, for all practical purposes, zero.

Chapter 5 – FP #2: Natural selection has creative power

1. Coyne (2010), pp. 138-9. Other processes such as genetic drift, self-organization, evo-devo, and so on, are also invoked by more recent evolutionists - more on this in Chapter 10 - but mutation plus natural selection is the primary mechanism cited by neo-Darwinian orthodoxy.
2. Dawkins (1991), p. xiii.
3. Coyne (2010), p. 11.
4. Dawkins (2010), p. 31.
5. Pallen (2009), p. 50.
6. Miller, Kenneth R., "Life's Grand Design", *Technology Review 97* (February-March 1994), pp. 24-32, available free (2019) at http://www.millerandlevine.com/km/evol/lgd/index.html
7. Dawkins (2010), p. 405.
8. Pinker (2019), p. 20.
9. Darwin (1860), p. 70.

10. Ibid., p. 167.
11. Dawkins (2010), p. 416. Earlier he has explained, "Evolution not only is a gradual process as a matter of fact; it *has* to be gradual if it is to do any explanatory work [emphasis in original]". p. 155. And "you have to think 'smooth gradient of improvement'". p. 241.
12. Dawkins (2010), p. 22.
13. Luskin, C., "Problem 10: Neo-Darwinism's Long History of Inaccurate Predictions about Junk Organs and Junk DNA", *Evolution News*, 15 February 2015. https://evolutionnews.org/2015/02/problem_10_neo/#backfn157. Also, Wells (2017), pp. 115-124; Eberlin (2019), pp. 119-121. Also Wells, J., "The Myth of Vestigial Organs and Bad Design: Why Darwinism is False", *Evolution News*, 4 May 2009. https://evolutionnews.org/2009/05/the_myth_of_vestigial_organs_a/
14. Quoted in, "BioEssays Editor: "'Junk' DNA... Full of Information!" Including Genome-Sized "Genomic Code"", *Evolution News*, November 18, 2019. Accessible (2020) here: https://evolutionnews.org/2019/11/bioessays-editor-junk-dna-full-of-information-including-genome-sized-genomic-code/
15. Dawkins (2004), p. 116. See also Dawkins (2005), p. 20.
16. Miller, Kenneth R., op. cit.
17. **ENC**yclopedia **Of D**NA **El**ements. "The ENCODE Project", National Human Genome Research Institute, Bethesda, MD (December 28, 2009). Accessible (2020) here: https://www.genome.gov/Funded-Programs-Projects/ENCODE-Project-ENCyclopedia-Of-DNA-Elements/pilot
18. Functional **AN**o**T**ation **O**f the **M**ammalian Genome. FANTOM Consortium, Yokohama, Japan. Accessible (2020) here: https://fantom.gsc.riken.jp/4/
19. "The ENCODE Project", op. cit.
20. See also Leisola (2018), p. 218.
21. Collins, Francis S., 2010, *The Language of Life: DNA and the Revolution in Personalized Medicine*, New York, HarperCollins, pp. 5-6, 9-10.
22. Dawkins (2010), p. 332.
23. Wells (2011), p. 104.
24. Moore, Andrew, "That "junk" DNA ... is full of information!", *Advanced Science News*, November 12, 2019, accessible (2020) here: https://www.advancedsciencenews.com/that-junk-dna-is-full-of-information/
25. Gates, Bill, 1996, *The Road Ahead*, Rev. ed. New York, Viking, Penguin Group, p. 188.
26. Dawkins (1991), pp. 46-49.
27. In the 1991 Faraday Christmas Lectures, Episode 3, Dawkins says 50 offspring were used. Software engineer Winston Ewart thinks it was 100 "Digital Evolution: Predictions of Design" in Moreland, *et al.* (2017), p. 203. Ewart wondered how sensitive this scheme might be to the number of offspring in each generation. He simulated Dawkins' program using ten offspring in each cycle. This scenario required 723,232 and 461,300 generations in successive runs, p. 205.
28. Dawkins (2010), p. 35.
29. Dawkins (2006), p. 122.
30. Ewart, Winston, "Digital Evolution: Predictions of Design", in Meyer, Nelson *et al.* (2009), pp. 193-216.

Notes

31. Ibid., p. 214.
32. Pallen (2009), p. 79. Also, Meyer, Nelson et al. (2009), p. 88-9. Confirmed in later experiments by Majerus, M., De Roode, J., "The moths of war", *New Scientist*, 8 December 2007, pp. 46-49. Described in Alexander (2008), p. 82.
33. Pallen (2009), p. 91. Also Meyer, Nelson et al. (2009), p. 88; Sutton (2022), p. 176.
34. Pallen (2009), p. 80. Also Dawkins (2010), pp. 133-9.
35. Wells (2000), pp. 148-9.
36. Dawkins (2010), p. 33.
37. For example, Dawkins (2010), pp. 266-7.
38. Behe (2019), p. 164.
39. Quoted in, Behe (2019), p. 162.
40. Behe (2019), pp. 165-6.
41. Behe (2019), p. 169.
42. Ibid.
43. Spencer (2016), p. 38.
44. Dawkins (2010), p. 66.
45. Coyne (2010), p.137.
46. Dawkins (2010), p. 37.
47. Lane (2010), p. 185. In this passage Lane contrasts the rapid "evolution" of domestic dogs with the estimated 500,000 years or less for eyes to have evolved, p. 183.
48. Behe (2019), pp. 193-4.
49. vonHoldt, B. M. et al., "Structural variation in genes associated with human Williams-Beuren Syndrome underlie stereotypical hypersociability in domestic dogs", *Science Advances* 3, 2017, e1700398
50. Behe (2019), p. 195.
51. Taylor, C., "Is a Healthier English Bulldog Possible?" *Science Friday*, 8 May 2016, https://www.sciencefriday.com/segments/is-a-healthier-english-bulldog-possible/. Tonkin, S. "Now BULLDOGS could be banned", *MailOnline*, 25 July 2022.
52. Behe (2019), pp. 16-17.
53. Meyer, Nelson et al. (2009), pp. 99-105. See also Sarfati (2010), pp. 68-9.
54. Coyne (2010), p. 142.
55. Dawkins (2010), p. 132.
56. Meyer et al. (2009), pp. 102-103.
57. Quoted in Meyer, Nelson et al. (2009), pp. 104-5: Linton, Alan, "Scant search for the maker", *Times Higher Education Supplement*, (April 20, 2001):29.
58. Dawkins (2010), p. 351.
59. Dawkins (2010), p. 345.
60. See for example, New York University. "Progeny Of Blind Cavefish Can 'Regain' Their Sight", *ScienceDaily*, 8 January 2008, www.sciencedaily.com/releases/2008/01/080107120911.htm
61. Hen's teeth: Stephen Jay Gould (1983), pp. 183-185 describes Kollar and Fisher's 1980 experiment which combined some mouse embryonic tissue - from the region where first molar teeth form - with the appropriate tissue in an embryonic chick and observed the production of dentin in the chick embryo. Gould asks, "But is it possible that we are seeing, in part, the actual form of a latent bird's tooth -

potential structure that chick epithelium has encoded for sixty million years, but has not expressed in the absence of dentin to induce it?" Harris, M. P., et al. ("The Development of Archosaurian First-Generation Teeth in a Chicken Mutant", *Current Biology* 16, 21 February 2006, pp. 371-377) describe the appearance of teeth similar to alligators' first-generation teeth in a mutant chicken embryo. This autosomal recessive mutation affects the development of several organ systems, which is probably why, as Harris points out (p. 372), the *"talpid^2"* mutated chick rarely survives beyond 12 days. Harris quotes the standard evolutionary view that "avian teeth were lost at least 70-80 million years ago" when the claimed separation from their reptilian ancestors occurred. They conclude (p. 376), "Our work demonstrates [an evolutionary] framework in which to interpret the latent ability of avian embryos to form teeth".

62. However, there are problems with this view as other evolutionists have pointed out. There's the "use-it-or-lose-it" problem. Casey Luskin: https://evolutionnews.org/2011/07/of_hens_teeth_and_neutral_muta/ quotes three sources that effectively confirm Dollo's Law which says that evolution is not substantively reversible. Crucially, even for traits that are determined by a single gene which is no longer subject to selection pressure (not being "used"), the mutation rate is such that the maximum estimated time a silenced gene, and its corresponding trait, could be reactivated is 10 million years. Imagine, for example, that a mutation occurs that duplicates a functional gene. The duplicate will no longer be 'conserved' (protected) by natural selection. Typical mutation rates predict that in less than 10 million years every nucleotide base location within the gene will have mutated. The original information will be long lost. As Luskin puts it, "Something is going on with hen's teeth, but it isn't the 'resurrection' of vestigial genes".

63. Human tails: Darwin regarded the human coccyx as vestigial (meaning no longer having a use) and therefore evidence of our descent from apes. However, we now know that the coccyx does have a function. It is not useless. It acts as the attachment point for various muscles, tendons and ligaments. Wells (2017, pp. 122-124) admits that, "Nevertheless, it is true that in very rare cases a human baby is born with an external projection in its lower back". Real cases, in summary, turn out to be birth defects, perhaps of the spinal cord - fatty projections containing no vertebrae and often occurring at locations other than the embryonic tail.

64. Meyer, Nelson, et al., (2009), p. 99. Also Sarfati (2010), pp. 52-3.
65. Behe (2007), p. 36.
66. Dawkins (2010), p. 37.
67. Ibid., pp. 109, 116 ff.
68. Behe (2007), p. 143.
69. Behe (2019), p. 177.
70. Behe (2019), p. 178.
71. Ibid., p. 179.
72. Ibid., pp. 188-9.
73. Hofwegen et al. affirm that "No new genetic information (novel gene function) evolved" in "Rapid Evolution of Citrate Utilization by *Escherichia coli* by Direct Selection Requires *citT* and *dctA*", *Journal of Bacteriology*, Vol. 198, No 7, 17 March

Notes

2016. See also (viewed 27 August 2021): https://evolutionnews.org/2021/06/viral-video-overstates-the-evidence-about-bacterial-evolution/
74. Behe (2019), p. 189.
75. Ibid.
76. Behe (2007), p. 57.
77. Ibid., p. 59.
78. Ibid., p. 137.
79. Ibid., p. 139.
80. Gerlt, J. A.; Babbitt, P. C., "Enzyme (re)design: lessons from natural evolution and computation", *Curr Opin Chem Biol 13(1)*, 2009, pp. 10-18: doi:10.1016/j.cbpa.2009.01.014
81. Gauger, A. K.; Axe, D. D. (2011), "The Evolutionary Accessibility of New Enzyme Functions: A Case Study from the Biotin Pathway". *BIO-Complexity* 2011(1):1-17: doi:10.5048/BIO-C.2011.1
82. For example, Alice Roberts speculates on gene duplication possibilities, "Millions of years ago, a few enthusiastic, duplicated genes, taking on a range of new roles in the developing embryo, led to the evolution of vertebrates, complete with neural crest and skulls". Roberts (2015), p. 82. Note the reification fallacy in attributing anthropomorphic agency to duplicated genes.
83. Gauger and Axe, op. cit., p. 13.
84. Behe (2007), p. 63.
85. Behe (1996), p. 193.
86. Behe (1996).
87. Darwin (1860), p.154.
88. Shapiro, James A., "In the Details... What?", *National Review*, September 16, 1996, p. 64.
89. Behe (1996), p. 72.
90. Coyne (2010), p. 154.
91. Dawkins (1997), pp. 148-154.
92. Lane (2010), pp. 182-3.
93. Nilsson, D. E.; Pelger, S., "A pessimistic estimate of the time required for an eye to evolve", *Proceedings of the Royal Society of London B* 256, 1994, pp. 53-8: https://doi.org/10.1098/rspb.1994.0048
94. Dawkins (1997), pp. 148-9.
95. This was confirmed in an email exchange between Dan-Erik Nilsson and David Berlinski in 2001, see Berlinski (2009), p. 379. In what Berlinski describes as a scientific scandal he also asks the question as to why Nilsson and Pelger have never dissociated themselves from unfounded claims about their work, p. 383.
96. The paper uses the term "acuity", meaning, sharpness of image.
97. Swift, D., "Evolution Under the Microscope - Eyes", https://evolutionunderthemicroscope.com/eyes02.html. Viewed 22 February 2023.
98. Berlinski (2009), p. 293.
99. Axe (2016), p. 177.
100. Behe (1996), pp. 18-21.
101. Ibid., p. 22. See also, Buranyi, Stephen, "Do we need a new theory of Evolution?", *The Guardian*, 28 June 2022, pp. 1-2.

102. Dawkins (2010), p. 354-5. Alice Roberts similarly believes the vertebrate eye to be wired backwards and sees this as an argument against design, Roberts (2015), p. 114.
103. Just because something is badly designed it doesn't mean it wasn't designed, e.g. William Paley pointed out that a watch that kept bad time had nevertheless been designed.
104. Strauss, O., "The Retinal Pigment Epithelium in Visual Function", *Physiological Reviews 85*, 2005, pp. 845-881: https://journals.physiology.org/doi/full/10.1152/physrev.00021.2004
105. Bergman, J., "Inverted Human Eye a Poor Design?", *Perspectives on Science and Christian Faith* 52, March 2000. https://www.asa3.org/ASA/PSCF/2000/PSCF3-00Bergman.html. Also Lumsden, R. D., "Not so Blind a Watchmaker", *Creation Research Society Quarterly* 31, June 1994. http://citeseerx.ist.psu.edu/viewdoc/download?doi=10.1.1.456.4779&rep=rep1&type=pdf
106. Bryson (2010), p. 206.
107. Behe (2019), p. 197.

Chapter 6 – FP #3: The tree-of-life is recorded in the fossils

1. Coyne (2010), pp. 18-19.
2. Darwin (1860), p. 380.
3. Ibid., pp. 140.
4. Darwin used the word "mutation" here, by which he simply meant "change". He was not using "mutation" in the neo-Darwinian sense of a "genetic mutation", since genetic mechanisms were unknown in Darwin's time.
5. Darwin (1860), pp. 373-374.
6. Lyell (1830-33), pp. xvi-xvii.
7. Palaeontologists Douglas Erwin and James Valentine in their 2013 book, *The Cambrian Explosion*, have this to say, "Few of Lyell's contemporaries agreed with him". They go on, "Today, geologists recognise that the rates of geological processes have varied considerably through the history of Earth and that many processes have operated in the past that may not be readily studied today". Quoted in Klinghoffer (2015), p. 199.
8. Biblical Creationists today, for example, believe that most of the fossil record accumulated rapidly during Noah's worldwide flood, and that the sequence reflects different habitats. Hence, marine creatures would have been catastrophically buried first, and so on.
9. Gould (1987), p. 134.
10. Mrs Lyell (1881), Vol 1, Lyell's letter to Scrope, 14 June 1830, p. 268. See also, Wilson (2017), p. 97. Also Lyell (1830-33), p. xxiv.
11. Darwin (1860), p. 375.
12. Denton (1985), p. 160.
13. Gould (1980), p. 181.
14. Ibid., p. 182. In 2009 this was still the case. Palaeobiologist Michael Benton affirms "it seems clear then that stasis is common, and that had not been predicted from modern genetic studies". The quote is from Benton M., and Harper D., (2009),

Notes

Introduction to Paleobiology and the Fossil Record, New York, John Wiley & Sons, pp123-124. Quoted in Wikipedia: https://en.wikipedia.org/wiki/Punctuated_equilibrium#Evidence_from_the_fossil_record
15. Eldredge (1985), p. 145.
16. Ibid., p. 75.
17. Stanley (1979), p. 39.
18. Eldredge (1985), p. 144.
19. Gould (1980), pp. 181-2.
20. Eldredge (1985), p. 146.
21. Ibid., p. 119.
22. Ibid., p. 75.
23. "Natura non facit saltum", Nature doesn't make jumps (saltations), e.g. in Darwin (1860), p. 158.
24. Eldredge, Niles and Gould, Stephen Jay, 1972, "Punctuated Equilibria: An Alternative to Phyletic Gradualism", in Schopf, Thomas J. M, ed., *Models of Paleobiology*, San Francisco, Freeman, Cooper and Company, pp. 82-115.
25. For example, Horgan, J., "Score One for Punk Eek: The fitful evolution of bacteria supports a controversial theory", *Scientific American*, 21 July 1996. https://www.scientificamerican.com/article/score-onefor-punk-eek/
26. Eldredge (1985), p. 120.
27. The arch-gradualist Dawkins and the punctuationist Gould, for example, conducted a correspondence war across the Atlantic for many years.
28. Eldredge (1985), pp. 72-3.
29. Denton (1985), p. 162.
30. Meyer (2013), p. 28.
31. Ibid., p. 10.
32. Ibid., pp. 36 and 53.
33. Gould (2000), p. 111.
34. Ibid., pp. 113, 273.
35. Ibid., p. 118.
36. Ibid., p. 127.
37. Ibid., p. 109.
38. Ibid., pp. 201-2, 206.
39. Meyer (2013), p 53.
40. Ibid., pp. 71-2.
41. Some argue the numbers of phyla are 25 of 33, e.g Erwin, see Ibid., p. 417, note 5.
42. Ibid., p. 31.
43. Dawkins (1998), p. 201.
44. Gould (2000), p. 49.
45. Meyer (2013), p. 41.
46. Ibid., pp. 74-5.
47. Dawkins (2005), p. 459.
48. Meyer (2013), pp. 56-7.
49. Ibid., pp. 46-7.
50. Gould (2000), p. 275.
51. The *Nature* article is quoted in Meyer (2013), pp. 84-5.

52. Meyer (2013), pp. 63-4.
53. Ibid., p. 62.
54. Ibid., pp. 64-7.
55. Meyer (2013).
56. Ibid., pp. 70-71. The reference is to Foote, Michael, "Sampling, Taxonomic Description, and Our Evolving Knowledge of Morphological Diversity", Paleobiology 23 (1997), p. 181.
57. Gould (2000), p. 233.
58. Ibid., p. 304.
59. Meyer (2013), pp 142-3.
60. Ibid., p. 69.
61. Ibid., p. 54.
62. Ibid., p. 163.
63. Ibid. However, genome size does not always correspond to what we would generally consider to be organisms of increased complexity.
64. Moreland et al (2017), p. 345.
65. Ibid.
66. Richard Bateman et al., quoted in Ibid., p. 346.
67. Moreland et al. (2017), p. 346.
68. Ibid., pp. 346-7.
69. Ibid., pp. 348-9.
70. Wilson (2017), p. 269.
71. Moreland et al. (2017), pp. 349-50.
72. Prothero (2007).
73. Pallen (2009), pp. 169, 174. Also now known as the K-Pg boundary (for Paleogene).
74. Coyne (2010), p. 55; Prothero (2007), the title of the book includes the phrase "What the Fossils Say".
75. Johnson (1993), p. 81.
76. Coyne (2010), p. 137.
77. Interestingly, examples of dinosaur fossils have been unearthed in recent years with some soft tissue present, such as blood vessels. For example this article describes some of the work of molecular palaeontologist, Mary Schweitzer: Fields, H., "Dinosaur Shocker", Smithsonian Magazine, May 2006: https://www.smithsonianmag.com/science-nature/dinosaur-shocker-115306469/
78. Quoted in Denton (1985), p. 179.
79. This example connected with King's College, London: Barker, John A. 2011, "Simulating Evolution", bioscience explained (viewed May 2020): https://bioenv.gu.se/digitalAssets/1580/1580960_simevoleng.pdf
80. Berra, Tim, 1990, Evolution and the Myth of Creationism, Stanford, California, Stanford University Press, pp. 117-19.
81. Meyer, Nelson et al. (2009), p. 27.
82. Coyne (2010), p. 38.
83. Ibid. The source paper is Shubin, N. H. et al., "The pectoral fin of Tiktaalik roseae and the origin of the tetrapod limb", Nature 440, 764–771 (2006). https://doi.org/10.1038/nature04637.
84. Ibid., p. 40.

85. Ibid., p. 41.
86. Meyer, Nelson et al. (2009), p. 28. Shubin's cladogram includes *Glyptoleps* and *Sauripterus* prior to *Eusthenopteron*, but doesn't include *Icthyostega*.
87. Sarfati (2010), pp. 132-133. According to Alice Roberts we are to believe that, "The evolution of limbs from fins involved reorganisation of the way these appendages attached to the rest of the skeleton. As pectoral fins became forelimbs, they detached themselves from the back of the skull, where they'd been attached in fish. Conversely, as pelvic fins became hindlimbs, they attached themselves very firmly to the spine." Roberts (2015), p. 278. Note the attribution of agency to the appendages.
88. Niedźwiedzki, G.; Szrek, P.; Narkiewicz, K. et al. (2010), "Tetrapod trackways from the early Middle Devonian period of Poland." *Nature* 463, 43-48. https://doi.org/10.1038/nature08623
89. Meyer, Nelson et al. (2009), p. 20.
90. Wells (2000), pp. 130-133.
91. Ibid., pp. 112, 118-121.
92. Feduccia, A., "Evidence from Claw Geometry Indicating Arboreal Habits of Archaeopteryx", *Science*, Vol 259, No. 5096 (Feb. 5, 1993), pp. 790-793. The vane of a feather is the usually curved surface formed from barbs (with their barbules) extending from the central shaft (rachis).
93. Denton (1985), pp. 210-211.
94. Prothero (2007), pp. 300-305.
95. Ibid., p. 302.
96. Ibid.
97. Swift (2002), especially pp. 282-284, 290-293, 377-378.
98. There's a great little cartoon, "Whale Evolution: Good Evidence for Evolution?", *Long Story Short Ep.2*, https://www.youtube.com/watch?v=wq_oYftA2ow
99. Darwin deleted this idea from his second edition onwards - owing to the incredulity of some critics - such that the vestigial text in Darwin (1860) reads, "In North America the black bear was seen by Hearne swimming for hours with widely open mouth, thus catching, almost like a whale, insects in the water." The original first edition followed up with these words, "I can see no difficulty in a race of bears being rendered by natural selection, more and more aquatic in their structure and habits, with larger and larger mouths, till a creature was produced as monstrous as a whale."
100. Coyne (2010), p. 52.
101. Dawkins (2010), p. 171.
102. See for example Wells (2017), pp. 101-102.
103. Coyne's diagram - Coyne (2010), p. 54 - does illustrate the enormous size differences with the aid of light-grey shading. Despite this, however, the eye is drawn to the bold outlines of the similarly sized skeletal forms.
104. The whale-like feature that justified the inclusion of *Pakicetus* is an involucrum (whale-like ears). Initially the rest of its body was imagined to be more aquatic and whale-like and appeared in drawings as such. But then a specimen was found with more skeletal parts in evidence, and it turned out to be a wolf-like, wolf-sized animal. *Indohyus* also had an involucrum, yet it has not been classified in the

cetacean (whale) infraorder, but rather with *artiodactyls*, even-toed hoofed animals such as pigs, giraffes, antelopes, sheep, cattle and hippopotamuses. So, it looks like the involucrum is diagnostic of cetaceans - except when it isn't. See Wells (2017), p. 103.
105. Mónica R. Buono, Marta S. Fernández, Marcelo A. Reguero, Sergio A. Marenssi, Sergio N. Santillana, Thomas Mörs, "Eocene Basilosaurid Whales from the La Meseta Formation, Marambio (Seymour) Island, Antarctica", Ameghiniana 53(3) (2016): 296-315 doi:10.5710/AMGH.02.02.2016.2922
106. See for example, Wells (2017), pp. 104-109.
107. See for example around 7 minutes into this video: https://www.youtube.com/watch?v=wq_oYftA2ow&feature=youtu.be
108. Carter (2014), pp. 140-142.
109. Durrett, Rick and Schmidt, Deena, "Waiting for Two Mutations: With Applications to Regulatory Sequence Evolution and the Limits of Darwinian Evolution", *Genetics*, 2008 Nov, 180(3):1501-1509 doi: 10.1534/genetics.107.082610
110. Agaba, M.; Ishengoma, E.; Miller, W. *et al.*, "Giraffe genome sequence reveals clues to its unique morphology and physiology", *Nature Communications* 7, 11519 (2016) doi: 10.1038/ncomms11519
111. Coyne (2010), pp. 52, 55.
112. Ibid., p. 57. Also Dawkins (2010), p. 147.
113. See note 8.
114. Stanley (1981), p. 71. On p. 95 he also claims that "...the fossil record does not convincingly document a single transition from one species to another".
115. Eldredge, N., *Reinventing Darwin*, London, Orion Publishing, 1996, p.95. Quoted in Carter (2014), p. 135.
116. Dawkins (2010), p. 146.
117. Johnson (1993), p. 58.
118. Quoted in Meyer (2013), p. 17.

Chapter 7 - FP #4: Similar embryos imply common ancestry

1. Draper (1873), p. 123. It was written in 1873 when the exclusive masculine pronoun could be applied without embarrassment.
2. Darwin (1860), p. 363.
3. Ibid., p. 364.
4. Wilson, A. N. (2017), pp. 261-2.
5. Dawkins (2010), p. 211. Elsewhere, when addressing what he calls the argument from incredulity, Dawkins recounts Haldane's "lateral thinking" as "Something like the transition from Amoeba to man... goes on in every mother's womb in a mere nine months. Development is admittedly a very different process from evolution but, nevertheless, anyone sceptical of the very possibility of a transition from single cell to man has only to contemplate his own fetal beginnings to have his doubts allayed". Dawkins (1991), p. 249-50. Alice Roberts also sees embryonic development as analogous to *Evolution*: Roberts (2015).
6. Darwin (1860), p. 351.

Notes

7. Zuckerkandl, Emil & Pauling, Linus, "Molecules as Documents of Evolutionary History", *J. Theoret. Biol.* (1965) 8, 357-366.
8. There's a great little video, "Is Homology Evidence for Evolution, *Long Story Short Ep. 1*, https://www.youtube.com/watch?v=lk1gDk1wGhQ&t=448s
9. Conway Morris (2003), p.181.
10. Swift, David, "Evolution Under the Microscope" website viewed 8 February 2021: https://evolutionunderthemicroscope.com/homology00.html
11. Conway Morris (2003), p. 139.
12. Ibid., pp. 127-8.
13. Dawkins (1991), Chapter 2 for the bat echolocation exposition. This quote on page 37.
14. Wells (2017), pp. 43-44.
15. Coyne (2009), p. 78.
16. Barnes, M. Elizabeth, "Karl Ernst von Baer's Laws of Embryology", *Embryo Project Encyclopedia* (2014-04-15). ISSN: 1940-5030 http://embryo.asu.edu/handle/10776/7821.
17. Pallen (2009), p. 97.
18. Prothero (2007), p. 109.
19. Ibid., p. 110, Figure 4.10.
20. Ibid., the legend of the diagram.
21. Romanes, G. J., 1896, *Darwin and After Darwin: An Exposition of the Darwinian Theory and a Discussion of Post-Darwinian Questions, I Darwinian Theory* (Second Edition), Chicago, The Open Court Publishing Company, pp. 152-3, FIG. 57 and FIG. 58.
22. Richardson, Michael K. *et al.*, 1997, "There is no highly conserved embryonic stage in the vertebrates: implications for current theories of evolution and development", *Anatomy and Embryology*, 196:91-106. DOI: 10.1007/s004290050082
23. Ibid., p. 91.
24. Ibid.
25. Ibid.
26. Ibid., pp. 103-105.
27. Ibid., p. 104.
28. Quoted in Ibid., p. 104. Goldschmidt R. B., 1956, *The golden age of zoology; portraits from memory*, Seattle London, University of Washington Press, pp. 31-33.
29. Ibid., p. 92.
30. Quoted in Wells (2000), p. 85. From Lenoir, Timothy, 1982, *The Strategy of Life*, Chicago, The University of Chicago Press, p. 258.
31. Darwin (1879), p. 25-7.
32. Raff, Rudolf A., 1996, *The Shape of Life: Genes, Development and the Evolution of Animal Form*, Chicago, University of Chicago Press.
33. Dawkins (2010), p. 357.
34. Futuyma (1998), p. 122. Another example of this occurs in Roberts (2015), e.g. p. 33.
35. Wells (2000), p. 105.
36. Wolpert, Lewis, 1991, *The Triumph of the Embryo*, Oxford, Oxford University Press, p. 185.

37. Wells (2000), pp. 105-6.
38. Richardson 1997 op. cit., p. 92.
39. Ibid., p. 104.
40. Prothero (2007).
41. Ibid., p. 110.
42. Futuyma (1998), p. 653.
43. Coyne, op. cit., p. 82.
44. Leisola & Witt (2018), p. 117.
45. Swift, D., "Evolution under the microscope" website, viewed 28 October 2022: https://evolutionunderthemicroscope.com/homology10.html
46. Swift (2002), pp. 324-5.
47. Ibid., p. 325. The quote is from: De Beer, G., 1971, *Homology: An Unsolved Problem*, London, Oxford University Press, p. 13.
48. Moreland *et al.* (2017), p. 317.
49. Ibid., pp. 317-8.
50. Ibid., p. 318. Quoted from Davidson, Eric H., "How Embryos Work: A Comparative View of Diverse Modes of Cell Fate Specification", *Development* 108, no. 3 (1990), p. 366.
51. Ibid., pp. 360-1.
52. Swift (2002), pp. 323-4. Also Swift's website viewed 27 October 2022: https://evolutionunderthemicroscope.com/homology02.html
53. Swift website, op. cit. Viewed 27 October 2022: https://evolutionunderthemicroscope.com/homology02.html
54. Ibid.
55. Futuyma (1986), p. 436.
56. Denton (1985), p. 146. Quoted from De Beer, G., 1971, *Homology: An Unsolved Problem*, London, Oxford University Press, p. 8.
57. Swift (2002), p. 321. His quote is from Webster, D. and Webster, M., 1974, *Comparative vertebrate morphology*, Academic Press.
58. Wagner, G., 1989, "The Origin of Morphological Characters and the Biological Basis of Homology" *Evolution* 43(6), p. 1163.
59. Dawkins (1991), p. 270.
60. Dawkins (2005), p. 7.
61. Moreland *et al.* (2017), p. 376.
62. Johnson (2002), pp. 82-3.
63. Dawkins (2005), p. 7.
64. Dawkins (2010), p. 409.
65. Coyne (2010), p. 10.
66. Dávalos, Liliana (2012), "Understanding phylogenetic incongruence: lessons from phylostomid bats", *Biological Reviews*, 87, pp. 991-1024. doi: 10.1111/j.1469-185X.2012.00240.x. Even trees based on morphology alone often fail to be tree-like 60% of the time. Using what's known as the tree's "consistency index". See Moreland *et al.* (2017), pp. 388-90.
67. Salichos, Leonidas & Rokas, Antonis, "Inferring ancient divergences requires genes with strong phylogenetic signals", *Nature*, 497, May 16, 2013, pp. 327-333. doi:10.1038/nature12130

68. Singer, Emily, "A New Approach to Building the Tree of Life", *Quanta*, June 4, 2013, accessed July 25, 2020, https://www.quantamagazine.org/a-new-approach-to-building-the-tree-of-life-20130604/#
69. Degnan, James & Rosenberg, Noah, "Gene Tree Discordance, Phylogenetic Inference and the Multispecies Coalescent", *Trends in Ecology and Evolution* 24, 2009, pp. 332-340.
70. Gura, Trisha, "Bones, Molecules... or Both?", *Nature* 406, July 20, 2000, pp. 230-233.
71. Teeling, Emma & Hedges, Blair, "Making the Impossible Possible: Rooting the Tree of Placental Mammals", *Molecular Biology and Evolution* 30(9), June 29, 2013, pp. 1999-2000.
72. Lawton, Graham, "Uprooting Darwin's Tree", *New Scientist*, January 24, 2009, p. 39.
73. Ibid., p. 38.
74. Fischer, Daniel and Eisenberg, David, "Finding Families for Genomic ORFans", Bioinformatics 15(9), 1999, pp. 759-762. doi: 10.1093/bioinformatics//15.9.759.
75. Sumner, S., "2014: What Scientific Idea is Ready for Retirement? Response: "Life Evolves Via A Shared Genetic Toolkit"", *Edge*, Annual Question. https://www.edge.org/response-detail/25533. Accessed 13 March 2023. "Each lineage of ants contains about 4000 novel genes..." (relative to other closely related non-ant species presumably).
76. Wells (2017), p. 39.
77. Swift (2002), p. 327.
78. Wells (2017), pp. 134-135.
79. Swift (2002), pp. 328-330.
80. Yoon, Yoseop *et al.*, "Embryo Polarity in Moth Flies and Mosquitos Rely on Distinct Old Genes with Localized Transcript Isoforms", *eLife*, October 8, 2019. eLife 2019;8:e46711. doi: 10.7554/eLife.46711. Back in 1971 British embryologist Gavin de Beer predicted this result, "Characters controlled by identical genes are not necessarily homologous" and "homologous structures need not be controlled by identical genes". Quoted in Wells (2017), p. 41.
81. Moreland *et al.* (2017), p. 256. See also Wells (2000), Chapter 9; Meyer, Nelson *et al.* (2009), p. 101 and p. 105; Leisola & Witt (2018), pp. 119-120.
82. Berlinski (2009), p. 117.
83. Lawton, op. cit., p. 34.
84. Conway Morris (2003), pp. 282-3.
85. Moreland *et al.* (2017), p. 324.

Chapter 8 – FP #5: The human species evolved from apes

1. Darwin (1879), pp. 678-9.
2. Coyne (2010), p. 209.
3. Pinker (2019), p. 394.
4. Dawkins (2010), p. 8. We also get here Dawkins' view that "The evidence for evolution is at least as strong as the evidence for the Holocaust."
5. Brown (2018), pp. 451-452.

6. Howell (1965), pp 41-45. This image had fourteen ape-like creatures in the "parade" leading up to "modern man".
7. For example, Pallen (2009) p. 181.
8. Pallen (2009), p. 180. Pallen quotes the evolutionary biologist Jared Diamond.
9. Futuyma (1998), p. 729. The recent recalibration is a very significant change, not only adding chimpanzees to the same family as humans, but even into the same sub-family. The grounds for this change seem to have been claimed molecular similarity. Schwartz explains, "Historically, the reason that humans were removed from their own family Hominidae and, with *Pan*, relegated to tribe Hominini is primarily due to Goodman's (Goldberg *et al.* 2003, Goodman *et al.* 1983, Goodman *et al.* 1998) insisting that molecular similarity between humans and African apes, and chimpanzees specifically, should be reflected in classification. At one point in time, he and his colleagues even suggested putting chimpanzees and all hominids in the same genus, *Homo* (Goodman *et al.* 1998)", Schwartz, Jeffrey H., "What's Real about Human Evolution? Received Wisdom, Assumptions and Scenarios." p. 82 in Schwartz (2017).
10. https://en.wikipedia.org/wiki/Panthera_hybrid
11. https://en.wikipedia.org/wiki/Canid_hybrid
12. Roberts (2011), p. 57. The "Hominins" chapter was authored by Dr Kate Robson-Brown with contributions by Dr Fiona Coward.
13. "Demographics of the *Titanic* Passengers: Deaths, Survivors, Nationality and Lifeboat Occupancy". Website viewed 15th October 2020: http://www.icyousee.org/titanic.html
14. Saini (2020), p. 3. Saini also describes how, in 1853, French aristocrat Count Arthur de Gobineau, published *An Essay on the Inequality of the Human Races*. In it he identified three races: "The negroid variety is the lowest, and stands at the foot of the ladder". Next in the hierarchy was the yellow race, "The yellow man has little physical energy, and is inclined to apathy… He tends to mediocrity in everything". For Gobineau, the white race is, of course, at the peak of the hierarchy, "… the white peoples… are gifted with reflective energy, or rather with an energetic intelligence… more courageous and ideal than the yellow races". pp. 53-54.
15. Darwin (1879), p. 105.
16. Saini (2020)., p. 19.
17. Saini (2020), p. 56 quotes from British anthropologist Tim Ingold saying that Darwin saw gradations between the 'highest men of the highest races and the lowest savages' and he thought that the 'children of savages' have a stronger tendency (than European children) to protrude their lips when they sulk due to being closer to the 'primordial condition', as in chimps.
18. Saini (2020), pp. 57-58.
19. Quoted in Saini (2020), p. 57.
20. Saini (2020), p. 19. Also pp. 56-57.
21. Darwin (1879), pp. 183-184.
22. Quoted in Flannery, Michael, "Charles Darwin: Racist Spokesman for Anglo-Male Superiority", *Evolution News*, 13 May 2021, https://evolutionnews.org/2021/05/charles-darwin-racist-spokesman-for-anglo-male-superiority/. Accessed 4 February 2022.

23. Delisle, Richard G., "The Deceptive Search for "Missing Links" in Human Evolution, 1860-2010: Do Paleoanthropologists Always Work in the Best Interests of Their Discipline?", in Schwartz (2017), p. 1.
24. Ibid., pp. 5-7.
25. Ibid., p. 5.
26. Another classic example not mentioned in the main text is Lee Berger. Inspired by Donald Johanson, he dreamed as a child of finding "missing links". In 2008 he discovered two partial skeletons at Malapa in South Africa. The skeletons manifested a mix of *Australopithecus* and *Homo* features. In 2010 he announced a new species, *Australopithecus sediba* as an intermediate between more "primitive" apes and *Homo* erectus and dated at ~2 mya. It would have replaced Lucy as our ancestor. Johanson was not impressed by this prospect. However, most experts concluded that the new species was not a transitional form, but rather a chimeric skeleton - simply a mix of human and non-human bones. Similarly, in 2015 via *National Geographic*, Berger announced another new species *Homo naledi*, found in a South African cave, claiming it as a "missing link". He anticipated that the find would be dated somewhere between 2 and 3 mya. However, two years later, the official dating placed *naledi* at 236,000 to 335,000 ya. This game-changer meant the "new species" could no longer be a transitional form. Despite all the media hype, *H. naledi*, may not even have been *Homo*. See Sanford and Rupe (2019), pp. 314-411.
27. Delisle, op. cit., p. 1.
28. Ibid., p. 1.
29. Gee, H., "Palaeoanthropology: Craniums with Clout", *Nature* 478, 6 October 2011, p. 34. https://doi.org/10.1038/478034a
30. Price, M., "Study reveals culprit behind Piltdown Man, one of science's most famous hoaxes", *Science Magazine*, 9 August 2016. https://www.sciencemag.org/news/2016/08/study-reveals-culprit-behind-piltdown-man-one-science-s-most-famous-hoaxes
31. Mayr, E., "Darwin's Influence on Modern Thought", *Scientific American*, 24 November, 2009.
32. Campbell, R. M.; Vinas, G.; Henneberg, M.; Diogo, R., "Visual Depictions of our Evolutionary Past: A Broad Case Study Concerning the Need for Quantitative Methods of Soft Tissue Reconstruction and Art-Science Collaborations", *Frontiers in Ecology and Evolution*, 26 Feb 2021, p. 7. doi: 10.3389/fevo.2021.639048
33. Saini (2020), pp. 196-199.
34. Campbell, R. M. *et al.*, op. cit., p. 11. Here's a portion of the paper's abstract, "Flip through scientific textbooks illustrating ideas about human evolution or visit any number of museums of natural history and you will notice an abundance of reconstructions attempting to depict the appearance of ancient hominins. Spend some time comparing reconstructions of the same specimen and notice an obvious fact: hominin reconstructions vary in appearance considerably. In this review, we summarize existing methods of reconstruction to analyze this variability. It is argued that variability between hominin reconstructions is likely the result of unreliable reconstruction methods and misinterpretation of available evidence. We also discuss the risk of disseminating erroneous ideas about human evolution

through the use of unscientific reconstructions in museums and publications. The role an artist plays is also analyzed and criticized given how the aforementioned reconstructions have become readily accepted to line the halls of even the most trusted institutions".

35. Sanford & Rupe (2019), p. 19.
36. Ibid., p. 60.
37. Stanley (1981), p. 95.
38. Patterson (1999), p. 109.
39. Roberts (2011), pp. 152-153.
40. Saini (2020), pp. 14-15.
41. Zimmer, C., "Are Neanderthals Human?", *NOVA*, 20 September, 2012. https://www.pbs.org/wgbh/nova/article/are-neanderthals-human/. Viewed 28 December 2020.
42. Saini (2020), p. 35.
43. Saini (2020), pp. 16-17. Also p. 37.
44. A description of the La Chapelle-aux-Saints exhibit item from the Smithsonian National Museum of Natural History. Last updated 30 March 2016. https://humanorigins.si.edu/evidence/human-fossils/fossils/la-chapelle-aux-saints. Viewed 28 December 2020.
45. For example, Sanford & Rupe (2019), pp. 61-62 cite Nikolai Valuev, a former boxing champion who was elected to the Russian Parliament in 2011.
46. Straus W. L. and Cave A. J. E., "Pathology and the Posture of Neanderthal Man", *Quarterly Review of Biology*, 32(4), December 1957, pp. 348-363. Quoted in Sanford & Rupe (2019), pp. 56-57.
47. Quoted in Sanford & Rupe (2019), pp. 70-71. See also, Saini (2020), p. 30.
48. Saini (2020), p. 36.
49. Ibid., pp. 37-38.
50. Reader (2011), p. 126.
51. Ibid., p. 129.
52. Ibid., p. 130.
53. Ibid., p. 130.
54. Delisle, op.cit., p. 2.
55. Roberts (2011), pp. 124-125.
56. Tattersall & Schwartz (2000), pp. 140-141.
57. Wolpoff, M. H., *et al.*, "Multiregional Evolution: A World-Wide Source for Modern Human Populations", in Nitecki M. H. & Nitecki D. V. (editors), *Origins of Anatomically Modern Humans*, 1994, New York, Plenum Press, p. 176.
58. Reader (2011), pp. 143-146.
59. Roberts (2011), pp. 116-117.
60. Reader (2011), p. 146.
61. Institute of Human Origins, *Homo erectus*. http://www.becominghuman.org/node/homo-erectus-0. Viewed 23rd December 2020.
62. Sodera (2003), p. 342.
63. Reader (1981), p. 232.
64. Quoted in Sanford & Rupe (2019), p. 111.
65. Sanford & Rupe (2019), pp. 110-111.

66. Ibid., p. 117.
67. Dembski & Wells (2008), p. 13.
68. Wood, B., "Fifty years after *Homo habilis*", *Nature* (508), 3 April 2014, pp. 31-33.
69. Sanford & Rupe (2019), pp. 293-294.
70. Roberts (2011), p. 100-101.
71. Sanford & Rupe (2019, p. 296.
72. Wood, B., op. cit.
73. Tattersall & Schwartz (2000), p. 111.
74. Ibid., p. 123.
75. Reader (2011), p. 332.
76. Johanson (2009), p. 3.
77. Roberts (2011), p. 76.
78. Pallen (2009), p. 192.
79. Meyer, M. R. *et al.*, 2015, "Lucy's Back: Reassessment of Fossils Associated with A.L. 288-1 Vertebral Column", *J Hum Evol* 85, pp. 174-180. DOI: 10.1016/j.jhevol.2015.05.007
80. Roberts (2011), p. 78.
81. Ibid. Also Reader (2011), p. 380 writes that 4 more were discovered later making a total of 17.
82. Johanson, Donald C., 1976, "Ethiopia yields first "family" of early man", *National Geographic Magazine* 150(6), pp. 790-811; quoted in Sanford and Rupe (2019), pp. 231-233.
83. Ottaway, David B., 1974, "3-Million-Year-Old Human Fossils Found", *International Herald Tribune*, Paris, October 28: https://archive.org/details/InternationalHeraldTribune1974FranceEnglish/Oct%2028%201974%2C%20International%20Herald%20Tribune%2C%20%2328548%2C%20France%20%28en%29/page/n3/mode/2up. The text includes this, "At the press conference Mr Johanson pulled out of a cigar box the three specimens plus another jawbone believed to belong to a creature called australopithecus [sic], contemporary in time to the genus *homo* [sic] from which modern man descended".
84. Reader (2011), p. 374.
85. Leakey, Mary (1984), p. 181.
86. Johanson & Shreeve (1989), p. 85.
87. Sanford & Rupe (2019), p. 234; also Reader (2011), p. 390.
88. Ibid., p. 244-245. The entry into the scene of another palaeoanthropologist now becomes pivotal to future events. The young Tim White had been working with the Leakeys. By this time, however, he had fallen out with Richard over the dating of a skull in Kenya and then moved to Laetoli to work with Mary's team. By 1978 relations had soured there too and on the rebound he formed a partnership with Johanson in Hadar.
89. Leakey, Mary (1984), pp. 176, 177.
90. Ibid., p. 178.
91. Johanson & Edey (1990), p. 250. In 1975 Johanson had agreed with the Leakeys that the bones found at the Hadar site attested to the coexistence of at least two genera, including *Homo* and *Australopithecus*.

92. The Symposium on the "Current Argument on Early Man" was being held in honour of the 200th anniversary of the death of Carolus Linnaeus, the father of the binomial classification system. As the American son of Swedish immigrants it seemed most appropriate that Johanson should speak. Reader (2011), p. 385.
93. Johanson, D. C, White T. D. and Coppens, Y., "A New Species of the Genus Australopithecus (Primates: Hominidae) from the Pliocene of Eastern Africa", *Kirtlandia* 28, pp. 1-14.
94. Mary would later conclude that "Tim White appear[ed] to have converted [Johanson] to the view that was eventually published." Leakey, Mary (1984)., p. 182.
95. Ibid.
96. Johanson, D. C. and White, T. D., 1979, "A systematic assessment of early African hominids", *Science* 203(4378), pp 321-330.
97. An angry interchange between White and critics Richard Leakey, anatomist Alan Walker and palaeontologist Andrew Hill ensued during an informal seminar in Nairobi. Walker opened the tetchy exchange, "If the degree of sexual dimorphism is outside the modern range, then you must justify your reasoning". White responded, "It's simplest to have only one species in the family collection, so …". Walker's retort exposed White's logical error, "Numerical simplicity is not necessarily the truth". Leakey's contributions to this short extract from the inquisition included, "It's my feeling that you are imposing what you think is right upon the fossils". When White countered with, "… we're trying to understand the evolution and biology - not just catalogue the fossils", Leakey's brusque conclusion was, "Well, we think the chances are that you've got it wrong". Reader (2011), pp. 383-384.
98. Sanford & Rupe (2019) document the opposing arguments of "terrestrialists" vs "arborealists" pp. 256- 265. The former group, led by Owen Lovejoy claims that *A. afarensis* was primarily a ground-walking biped, whereas the latter, championed by Jack Stern of Stony Brook University, sees *A. afarensis* as essentially a tree-climber.
99. Häusler, M., and Schmidt, P., 1995, "Comparison of the pelves of Sts14 and AL 288-1: implications for birth and and sexual dimorphism in australopithecines", *Journal of Human Evolution* 29(4), pp. 363-383. doi.org/10.1006/jhev.1995.1063
100. Wood, B. A. & Quinney, P. S., 1996, "Assessing the Pelvis of AL 288-1", *Journal of Human Evolution* 31, pp. 563-568. doi.org/10.1006/jhev.1996.0080
101. The following references, quoted in Sanford & Rupe (2019), pp. 267-8, conclude that the Hadar and Laetoli fossils are better interpreted as two separate species: Cartmill, M. and Smith, F. H., 2009, *The Human Lineage*, Hoboken, NJ, Wiley-Blackwell, p. 176; Day, M. H., 1985, *Guide to Fossil Man*, 4th Edition, Chicago, University of Chicago Press, p. 256; Ferguson, W. W., 1983, "An Alternative Interpretation of Australopithecus afarensis Fossil Material", *Primates* 24(3), pp. 397-409.
102. Reader (2011), p. 374.
103. Sanford & Rupe (2019), p. 305-306.
104. See for example Ridgeway, A., "Beyond DNA: How proteins let us get up close and personal to our ancient relatives", *BBC Science Focus*, 15th February 2021, https://www.sciencefocus.com/the-human-body/beyond-dna-how-proteins-let-us-get-up-close-and-personal-to-our-ancient-relatives/

105. Roberts (2011), pp. 70-71; Sanford & Rupe (2019), p. 171.
106. Zorich, Z., "Ardipithecus: Ape or Ancestor", *Archaeology* 63(1), January/February 2010.
107. Gibbons, A., "A New Kind of Ancestor: Ardipithecus Unveiled", *Science* 326, 2 October 2009, p. 38.
108. Ibid.
109. Sanford & Rupe (2019), p. 180.
110. Roberts, (2011), p. 71. The reconstructed skull does not include the base. See also Sanford & Rupe, p. 184.
111. Wood, B. and Harrison, T., "The Evolutionary Context of the First Hominins", *Nature* 470, 2011, p. 348.
112. Sanford & Rupe, op. cit., p. 191, including quote from Sarmiento, E. E, "Comment on the Paleobiology and Classification of *Ardipithecus ramidus*", *Science* 328:1105-1110, 2010.
113. Wood B. and Harrison T., op. cit.
114. William Jungers of Stony Brook University NY, quoted in Shreeve, J., "Oldest Skeleton of Human Ancestor Found", *National Geographic News*, 1 October 2009. Website viewed 17th October 2020: https://www.nationalgeographic.com/science/2009/10/oldest-skeleton-human-ancestor-found-ardipithecus/
115. Quoted in Zorich, Z., op. cit.
116. The Swiss psychiatrist, Hermann Rorschach (1884-1922) developed a tool for use in psychoanalysis in which the subject is presented with a standard pattern of ink blots of different shapes, sizes and colours and then asked to describe what they see.
117. William Jungers, op. cit.
118. Pallen (2009), pp. 181-182.
119. For example: Pallen (2009), p. 185; Roberts (2011), p. 65. Roberts catalogues 23 different hominins, but confesses that, "only some of them are our ancestors, and many became extinct without giving rise to new species", p. 57. And it is acknowledged that, "Their genetic relationships probably form a complex web, and until relatively recently several hominid species existed at any one time", p. 60.
120. Tattersall, I., "Brain size and the Emergence of Modern Human Cognition", in Schwartz (2017), p. 320.
121. Klein, R. G., "Darwin and the recent African origin of modern humans", *PNAS* 106(38), 22 September 2009. p. 16008. DOI: 10.1073/pnas.0908719106.
122. https://humanorigins.si.edu/evidence/human-family-tree. Viewed 26th February 2021.
123. Wood, B., "Fifty Years after *Homo Habilis*", *Nature* 508, 3 April 2014, p. 31.
124. Wood, B., "Who Are We?", *NewScientist*, 2366:44, 26 October 2002.
125. Berlinski (2009), p. 446.
126. Moreland *et al.* (2017), p. 440.
127. Premack, D., "Human and Animal Cognition: Continuity and Discontinuity", *PNAS* 104(35), 28 August 2007, pp. 13861-13867. https://doi.org/10.1073/pnas.0706147104
128. See Burgess (2013), Part 2.
129. Roberts (2015), p. 292.

130. Ibid., pp. 175-176.
131. Ibid., pp. 177-178.
132. Several muscles in our hands and thumbs are unique to humans. Roberts (2015), pp. 333-334.
133. Burgess (2013), p. 45.
134. See also Roberts (2014), pp. 124, 127.
135. Berlinski (2009), p. 456. It is sometimes claimed that this is an example of bad design since it leaves us vulnerable to a life-threatening choking hazard. However this view has been debunked: Roberts (2015), pp. 129-130. In summary, "The traditional story… that selection pressure for a descended larynx for speech must have been enough to override the risk of choking to death doesn't stand up to scrutiny".
136. Burgess (2013), p. 95. Roberts reports similarly, "Humans have an EQ [encephalisation quotient] of more than 5 - that's five times bigger than you'd expect for our size… Chimpanzees have an EQ of about 2…", Roberts (2015), p. 68.
137. Dr Michio Kaku, quoted in Ebbage, A., "Thinking Outside the Box: How does the brain work?", *Engineering & Technology*, March 2020. www.EandTmagazine.com
138. Ibid.
139. Premack, op. cit.
140. Dembski & Wells (2008), p. 8.
141. Tattersall, I., (1998), pp. 1-3. Chimps have been taught to paint, producing what has been described as "abstract impressionism", basically paint strokes on paper (https://en.wikipedia.org/wiki/Animal-made_art), but the gulf between this and "delicately executed and meticulously observed" human cave art is profound.
142. Ibid.
143. Roberts (2015), p. 335.
144. Gauger, A.; Hössjer, O.; Reeves, C., "Evidence for Human Uniqueness" in Moreland *et al.* (2017), p. 492.
145. Tattersall, I., op. cit., p. 323.
146. Denton (2016), p. 198.
147. Berlinski (2009), p. 459.
148. See Wikipedia article viewed 7th January 2021: https://en.wikipedia.org/wiki/Noam_Chomsky
149. Premack, op. cit., p. 13865.
150. Darwin (1879), p. 151.
151. Dawkins (2010), p. 402.
152. Denton (2016), p. 196.
153. Wallace, A. R., "The Limits of Natural Selection as Applied to Man", in *Contributions to the Theory of Natural Selection*, second edition, New York, MacMillan, 1871. Quoted in Denton (2016), pp. 196-197.
154. Quoted in Denton (2016), p. 197.
155. Even Ernst Mayr agreed that humans are unique, "The study of man showed that, in spite of his descent, he is indeed unique among all organisms. Human intelligence is unmatched by that of any other creature. Humans are the only animals with true language, including grammar and syntax. Only humanity, as Darwin emphasised, has developed genuine ethical systems. In addition, through high intelligence,

language and long parental care, humans are the only creatures to have created a rich culture". Mayr, Ernst, "Darwin's Influence on Modern Thought", *Biology*, 24 November, 2009.
156. Denton (2016), pp. 13-16. See also Roberts (2015), pp. 271-275.
157. King, Mary-Claire and Wilson, A. C., "Evolution at Two Levels in Humans and Chimpanzees", *Science* 188, 11 April 1975, pp. 107-116.
158. Cohen, J., "Relative Differences: The Myth of 1%", *Science* 316, 29 June 2007.
159. Dawkins (1991), p. 263.
160. For example, Cohen, J., op. cit., Batten, D., "The myth of 1%: Human and chimp DNA are very different": https://creation.com/1-percent-myth?utm_campaign=infobytes_uk&utm_content=Where+does+Stonehenge+fit+in+biblical+history%3F&utm_medium=email&utm_source=mailing.creation.com&utm_term=Fortnightly+Digest+-+2020.02.21
161. 5% – Britten, R. J., "Divergence between samples of chimpanzee and human DNA sequences is 5%, counting indels", *PNAS* 99(21), 15 October 2002, pp. 13633-13635. 6.4% – Cohen, J., op. cit. 16% – Buggs, Richard 2018, "How Similar are Human and Chimpanzee Genomes?" Website article accessed 7th October 2020: http://richardbuggs.com/2018/07/14/how-similar-are-human-and-chimpanzee-genomes/ Also Tomkins, J. P., "Comparison of 18,000 De Novo Assembled Chimpanzee Contigs to the Human Genome Yields Average BLASTN Alignment Identities of 84%", *Answers Research Journal* 11(2018), pp. 205-209.
162. Roberts (2011), p. 55.
163. Roberts (2015), p. 300.
164. It is now known that there are non-genetic (epigenetic) factors that also influence the growth and development of an organism from its embryonic state.
165. Sanford & Rupe (2019), p. 559.
166. Haldane, J.B.S., "The Cost of Natural Selection", *Journal of Genetics* 55, 1957, pp. 511-524.
167. Sanford, J.; Brewer, W.; Smith, F.; Baumgardner, J, "The waiting time problem in a model hominin population", *Theoretical Biology and Medical Modelling* 12(18), 2015, p. 3. Six references are cited.
168. The simulation is available online at: https://sourceforge.net/projects/mendelsaccount/. Accessed 15 January 2021.
169. Sanford *et al.* (2015), op cit., p. 25.
170. Ibid., p. 12. These results are consistent with independent work by Behe, M. J. and Snoke, D. W., "Simulating evolution by gene duplication of protein features that require multiple amino acid residues", *Protein Science*, Vol 13, Issue 10, October 2004.
171. Ibid., p. 14.
172. Sanford & Rupe (2019), pp. 567- 571. Also Sanford (2005).
173. Here's how the numbers might pan out: for *Homo sapiens* as a species in the 84 million years needed to accrue only 2 specifically co-dependent beneficial mutations, more than 4 million generations would have come and gone. This in turn would imply the accumulation of around 120 million random single-nucleotide mutations (4% of the entire genome) in each human being, the overwhelming majority of which would have been slightly detrimental. Clearly this

sequence of events is not sustainable and will surely lead to the extinction of humanity. Indeed, Russian biologist Alexey Kondrashov asks the question, "Why have we not died 100 times over?" Kondrashov A., "Contamination of the genome by very slightly deleterious mutations: why have we not died 100 times over?", *Journal of Theoretical Biology* 175(4), 21 August 1995, pp, 583-594.
174. Delisle, op. cit., p. 21.
175. White, T., "Paleoanthropology: Five's a Crowd in Our Family Tree", *Current Biology* 23(3), 04 February 2013, R112-R115. http://dx.doi.org/10.1016/j.cub.2012.12.001
176. Small, M. F., "Human Family Tree Now a Tangle, Messy Bush", *LiveScience*, 31 August 2007. https://www.livescience.com/7376-human-family-tree-tangled-messy-bush.html
177. Gee, H., op. cit.
178. Quoted in Leakey (1981), p. 43.
179. Sanford & Rupe (2019), pp. 396-397.
180. Marks, J., "What is the Viewpoint of Hemoglobin, and Does It Matter?" *Hist. Phil. Life Sci.*, 31, 2009, p. 246.
181. Denton (2016), pp. 222-223.
182. See note 161.

Introduction to part 3

1. Wilson (2017), p. 1.
2. Darwin (1860), the first sentence of Chapter 14, p. 371.
3. Hoyle and Wickramasinghe (1984), p. 133.
4. Gee, H., "Palaeoanthropology: Craniums with Clout", *Nature* 478, 6 October 2011, p. 34. https://doi.org/10.1038/478034a
5. Behe (2019), p. 154.
6. https://quotefancy.com/quote/1278326/Arthur-Koestler-The-progress-of-science-is-strewn-like-an-ancient-desert-trail-with-the. Viewed 11th March 2021.

Chapter 9 – Why is RMS *Evolution* still afloat?

1. Kahneman (2011), p. 277.
2. Saini (2020), p. 43.
3. Brown (2018), the unnumbered page prior to page 1.
4. Ibid., pp. 448, 449, 453, 454. His reference is to a genuine paper: Johnson, Adam P., et al., "The Miller Volcanic Spark Discharge Experiment", *Science* 322, 17 October 2008, p. 404. But Jeremy England, the real scientist, debunks Brown's science and disowns Brown's attribution of his world view: England, Jeremy, "Dan Brown Can't Cite Me to Disprove God", *Wall Street Journal*, 13 October 2017.
5. Harari (2015).
6. Leisola & Witt (2018), p. 111.
7. Saini (2020), p. 6.
8. Goldacre (2009), p. 228.
9. Ibid., pp. 247-250.
10. Ibid., p. 308.

Notes

11. https://evolutionnews.org/2021/02/great-expectations-origins-in-science-education/. See also Hedin (2021), p. 149.
12. Kahneman (2011), p. 209.
13. Sanford & Rupe (2019), p. 6.
14. Goldacre (2009), p. 253.
15. Kahneman (2011), p. 217.
16. Gould (2000), p. 276.
17. Kahneman (2011), p. 45.
18. For example, Haidt, J., *The Happiness Hypothesis*, London, Arrow Books, 2006.
19. Kahneman (2011), p. 24.
20. Leisola & Witt (2018), p. 157.
21. From a letter published in *Commentary* magazine in December 2002. Quoted in Berlinski (2009), p. 335.
22. Swift, D., *Evolution under the microscope*: https://evolutionunderthemicroscope.com/aboutme.html. Viewed 24th March 2021.
23. Leisola & Witt (2018), pp. 57-58.
24. Margulis & Sagan, (2003), p. 96.
25. Polanyi (1974), p. 163.
26. Denton (1985).
27. Behe (1996).
28. Ibid., p. 232.
29. Ibid., p. 233.
30. Wilson (2017), p. 1.
31. Ibid.
32. Ibid., pp. 1-3.
33. Flew & Varghese (2007), p. vii.
34. Flew & Varghese (2007).
35. Ibid., p. 75.
36. Nagel (2012).
37. Ibid., p. 5.
38. Ibid., p. 10.
39. Ibid., p. 26.
40. *Free Science* website viewed 30th March 2021. https://freescience.today/story/gunter-bechly/
41. Gelernter, David (2019), "Giving Up Darwin", *Claremont Review of Books*: https://claremontreviewofbooks.com/giving-up-darwin/
42. Berlinski (2009); Klinghoffer (2015).
43. Peterson (2018).
44. He read the argument in Meyer (2021), p. 211.
45. Peterson's twitter feed viewed 24 August 2021: https://twitter.com/jordanbpeterson/status/1426597853565276163?s=20
46. Quoted in Tinker (2020), p. 68.
47. *Titanic*, film produced by James Cameron, (distributed by Paramount Pictures (North America), 20th Century Fox (international), 1997), widescreen, 195 minutes.
48. Dawkins, Richard. Quoted from, https://en.wikiquote.org/wiki/Richard_Dawkins
49. Dawkins (1991), pp. 38-39.

50. West (2015), p. 241.
51. Egnor, M., "A Note from the Canaries", *Evolution News,* 18 June 2020: https://evolutionnews.org/2020/06/a-note-from-the-canaries/
52. Letter to Bernard Acworth, 13 September 1951 in Hooper, Walter (Ed.), *The Collected Letters of C.S. Lewis: Narnia, Cambridge and Joy 1950-1963,* vol III, HarperCollins e-books, pp. 179-180.
53. A couple more examples of censorship and career cancelling: https://evolutionnews.org/2021/01/happy-new-year-1-story-of-2020-biology-journal-demands-government-censorship-of-id/. See also the movie, *Expelled: No Intelligence Allowed,* by Ben Stein: https://www.youtube.com/watch?v=V5EPymcWp-g
54. Hoyle & Wickramasinghe (1984).
55. Leisola (2018), p. 110.
56. Meyer (2013), p. 52.
57. Ferguson, Andrew, "The Heretic", *Washington Examiner,* 25 March 2013: https://www.washingtonexaminer.com/weekly-standard/the-heretic
58. Leisola & Witt (2018).
59. Axe (2016), pp. 2-3.
60. Kabbany, Jennifer, "Famed Yale Professor Quits Believing Darwin's Theories", *The College Fix,* July 30th 2019: https://www.thecollegefix.com/famed-yale-computer-science-professor-quits-believing-darwins-theories/
61. *Free Science* website viewed 30th March 2021: https://freescience.today/story/richard-sternberg/
62. William Dembski's story is told for example in Wells (2006), pp. 89-91; Microbiologist Scott Minnich: https://freescience.today/story/scott-minnich/; Professor of Physics, Eric Hedin: https://freescience.today/story/eric-hedin/. Michael Behe is one of the fortunate ones, in the sense that he has not, as yet, lost his tenure within Lehigh University. But, clearly, he is only just tolerated within the Biological Sciences faculty, "The department faculty, then, are [sic] unequivocal in their support of evolutionary theory... The sole dissenter from this position, Prof. Michael Behe, is a well-known proponent of "intelligent design". While we respect Prof. Behe's right to express his views, they are his alone and are in no way endorsed by the department. It is our collective position that intelligent design has no basis in science, has not been tested experimentally, and should not be regarded as scientific." Viewed 31 March 2021, https://www.lehigh.edu/~inbios/News/evolution.html
63. West (2015), pp. 231-241.
64. Quoted in Wells (2006), p. 186.
65. Prothero (2007), p. xx.
66. Ibid., p. 44.
67. Quoted in Berlinski (2009), p. 445.
68. The hour long film was based on the book by Guillermo Gonzalez and Jay W. Richards, *The Privileged Planet: How Our Place in the Cosmos is Designed for Discovery,* 2004, Washington, Regnery Publishing: https://www.imdb.com/title/tt0495399/. Astronomer Gonzalez is another scientist who was denied tenure at Iowa State University in 2007 for his pro-ID views - see West (2015), p. 240.

69. Leisola (2018), p. 190.
70. *Free Science* website: https://freescience.today/story/don-mcdonald/
71. Harari (2015), p. 234.
72. Ibid., pp. 254-256.
73. https://www.birmingham.ac.uk/university/heroes/alice-roberts.aspx
74. https://www.simonyi.ox.ac.uk/about-marcus/the-oxford-simonyi-professor-for-the-public-understanding-of-science/
75. https://royalsociety.org/news/2015/01/professor-for-public-engagement-brian-cox/
76. Ruse, M., "Is Darwinism a Religion?", *Huffington Post*, July 21, 2011: https://www.huffpost.com/entry/is-darwinism-a-religion_b_904828. The original article was, Ruse, M., "How evolution became a religion: creationists correct?", *National Post*, May 13, 2000, pp. B1, B3, B7.
77. Halvorson, Richard T., "Confessions of a Skeptic", *The Harvard Crimson*, 7 April 2003. Accessed 13 April 2021: https://www.thecrimson.com/article/2003/4/7/confessions-of-a-skeptic-does-our/
78. West (2015), p. 267.
79. See for example, West (2015), pp. 231-268, 391.
80. Coyne (2009), p. xiv.

Chapter 10 – A better theory: Intelligent Design

1. Zmirak, J., "Philosopher of Science Stephen Meyer Answers the Tough Questions Darwinists Don't Even Ask", *The Stream*, 24 May 2021, https://stream.org/scientist-stephen-meyer-answers-the-tough-questions-darwinists-dont-even-ask/. Viewed 24 June 2021.
2. https://www.discovery.org/id/faqs/ [The Wikipedia definition of Intelligent Design, viewed 31 March 2021: "Intelligent design (ID) is a pseudoscientific argument for the existence of God, presented by its proponents as 'an evidence-based scientific theory about life's origins'. Proponents claim that 'certain features of the universe and of living things are best explained by an intelligent cause, not an undirected process such as natural selection'. ID is a form of creationism that lacks empirical support and offers no testable or tenable hypotheses, and is therefore not science". https://en.wikipedia.org/wiki/Intelligent_design. Attempts to edit this description are erased and Wikipedia's 'politically correct' version is quickly restored].
3. Mazur (2009), p. 19.
4. Ibid., p. vii. See also, Buranyi, Stephen, "Do we need a new theory of evolution?", *The Guardian*, 28 June 2022, p. 2 ff.
5. This has been attributed to Douglas Axe.
6. https://royalsociety.org/science-events-and-lectures/2016/11/evolutionary-biology/
7. http://downloads.royalsociety.org/events/2016/11/evolutionary-biology/muller.mp3
8. Paul Nelson attended the conference and he made these comments during an interview with *ID the Future* here: https://www.discovery.org/multimedia/audio/

9. 2019/05/first-the-royal-society-meeting-now-cambridges-evolution-evolves-paul-nelson-reports/
9. Margulis & Sagan (2003), pp. 13-14.
10. Pettitt, J., "What Darwin won't tell you about evolution", Lecture given at the Royal Institution, https://www.youtube.com/watch?v=7dzoGb-jcW4
11. The list can be found here: https://www.discovery.org/m/securepdfs/2021/07/Scientific-Dissent-from-Darwinism-List-07152021.pdf. Accessed 2 December 2023.
12. Leisola & Witt (2018), p. 144.
13. https://www.discovery.org/id/faqs/
14. Polanyi (1974), p. 174.
15. Davis, P.; Kenyon, D. H. and Thaxton, C. B. (academic editor), 2004, *Of Pandas and People: The Central Question of Biological Origins*, Dallas, Haughton Publishing Company.
16. Jones, *Kitzmiller, et al. v. Dover Area School District, et al.*; Jones, *Kitzmiller v. Dover Memorandum Opinion*, 2005, p. 2. https://aclupa.org/sites/default/files/legacy/8813/1404/6697/Dec20opinion.pdf
17. The Discovery Institute (that hosts the ID movement) strongly opposed the Dover board's policy. This fact was not reported in the media. The Institute lobbied the board against teaching of, or reference to ID, recommending instead its long-standing policy that "students shall be able to explain the scientific strengths and weaknesses of evolutionary theory". The school district in Grantsburg, Wisconsin, for example, followed this policy - and there was no court case. See West (2015), p. 259.
18. Jones, *Kitzmiller, et al. v. Dover Area School District, et al.*, op. cit., p. 2. The First Amendment states, "Congress shall make no law respecting an establishment of religion or prohibiting the free exercise thereof; or abridging the freedom of speech, or of the press; or the right of the people peaceably to assemble, and to petition the Government for a redress of grievances". https://www.whitehouse.gov/about-the-white-house/our-government/the-constitution/
19. Both the ACLU and the NCSE effectively operate as 'priestly' evolutionist organisations.
20. West (2015), pp. 260-261.
21. Jones, *Kitzmiller, et al. v. Dover Area School District, et al.*, op. cit., p. 63.
22. Ibid., p. 64. It would seem that (2) and (3) are pretty shaky grounds for declaring something not to be science. See Plantinga (2011), p. 171.
23. Wikipedia, too, contends that ID "is a pseudoscientific argument for the existence of God." Viewed 1 April 2021. https://en.wikipedia.org/wiki/Intelligent_design. Even Larry Sanger the co-founder of Wikipedia confesses its ideological bias. See "On ID, Myth Persists that *Wikipedia* Is Reliable, though Co-Founder Has Called It "Appallingly Biased"", Evolution News 26 July 2023, https://evolutionnews.org/2023/07/on-id-myth-persists-that-wikipedia-is-reliable-though-co-founder-has-called-it-appallingly-biased/
24. See for example, https://en.wikipedia.org/wiki/Quasar, and https://en.wikipedia.org/wiki/Pulsar Viewed 4 April 2023.
25. Meyer (2009), pp. 394-395.
26. Ibid., pp. 496-497.

27. Coyne (2010), p. xiii.
28. Assertions have been made that ID is "not science" because it hasn't had papers published in reputable scientific journals. This is actually not the case now, but the reason it once was true was because the 'wisdom' of peer review groupthink defined ID as "not science". We're then in a Catch 22 - ID is "not science" because no scientific papers have been published, yet no papers can be published because it's "not science". However, for some years now it could have been said that "… papers have appeared in scientific journals such as *Protein Science, Journal of Molecular Biology, Theoretical Biology and Medical Modelling, Journal of Advanced Computational Intelligence and Intelligent Informatics, Complexity, Quarterly Review of Biology, Cell Biology International, Physics Essays, Rivista di Biologia / Biology Forum, Physics of Life Reviews, Quarterly Review of Biology, Journal of Bacteriology, Annual Review of Genetics*, and many others. At the same time, pro-ID scientists have presented their research at conferences worldwide in fields such as genetics, biochemistry, engineering, and computer science." See: https://www.discovery.org/m/2018/12/ID-Peer-Review-July-2017.pdf
29. Coyne (2010), p. xiii.
30. Berlinski (2009), p. 82.
31. Darwin admits that "I attempted mathematics … but I got on very slowly. The work was repugnant to me, chiefly from my not being able to see any meaning in the early steps in algebra … in after years I have deeply regretted that I did not proceed far enough to at least understand something of the great leading principles of mathematics, for men thus endowed seem to have an extra sense". Darwin F. (ed.), *The Life and Letters of Charles Darwin*, Vol. I, London, John Murray, 1887, p. 46.
32. See for example Meyer (2009), pp. 477-480.
33. Ibid., p. 244.

Epilogue: The real tree of life

1. Quoted in Jones (2015), pp. 7-8.
2. Brown (2018), p. 98.
3. Jones (2015), pp. 12-13.
4. Christian philosopher and author Francis Schaeffer demonstrates that the nineteenth century spread of atheism occurred gradually, first of all geographically, "The ideas began in Germany and spread outward. They affected the Continent first, then spread across the Channel to England, and then the Atlantic to America. Second, it spread through society, from the real intellectual to the more educated, down to the workers, reaching the middle class last of all". Third, he traces the spread by discipline, from philosophy (Kant, Hegel, Kierkegaard) through art (Van Gogh, Gaugin, Cezanne), music and general culture (Debussy, Henry Miller, Dylan Thomas, The Beatles) and finally to theology (Karl Barth, Paul Tillich), Schaeffer (1990), pp. 7-9, 13-15, 27-29, 35-42, 51-55.
5. Williams (2010).
6. In Dawkins words, "Biology is the study of complicated things that give the *appearance* of having been designed for a purpose." Dawkins (1991), p. 1.

7. Lewontin's review of Carl Sagan's book, "The Demon Haunted World: Science as a Candle in the Dark", *New York Review of Books*, January 9, 1997. The full quote is given in Chapter 2.
8. Provine, William B., "Darwinism: Science or Naturalistic Philosophy", A debate at Stanford University with Phillip E. Johnson, 30 April 1994, *Origins Research*, Volume 16, Number 1: http://www.arn.org/docs/orpages/or161/161main.htm. Accessed 19 October 2021.
9. Crick, Francis, *The Astonishing Hypothesis: The Scientific Search for the Soul*, New York, Charles Scribner's Sons, 1994, p. 3.
10. Fig. E.1 is based on the idea of a "Current Reality Tree". It traces the undesirable effects that accrue from one or more current assumptions. See Goldratt, Eliyahu M., *It's Not Luck*, Aldershott, UK, Gower Publishing, 1994. Fig. E.2 adopts Goldratt's "Future Reality Tree" approach which is rooted in one or more different starting assumptions and traces its effects.
11. Meyer (2021). Stephen Meyer argues that evidence from the origin of the universe, and from the fine-tuning of the laws of physics, in addition to evidence from biology as presented here, is persuasive (having considered other "agency" options) that the most likely "free personal agency" candidate is the God of the Bible.

Appendix A – *Evolution*: its protagonists and their theistic views

1. BioLogos website:https://biologos.org/about-us/what-we-believe/ articles 9 and 10 of "What We Believe". Viewed 26 January 2023.
2. "Reasons To Believe" website, https://reasons.org/about. Accessed 1 May 2023.
3. https://www.discovery.org/id/faqs/ "What is the theory of Intelligent Design", viewed 26 January 2023.
4. Thomas, N., "In His New Book, Denton Shows How Science Leads the Charge to Theism", *Evolution News*, 20 May 2022, https://evolutionnews.org/2022/05/denton-shows-how-science-leads-the-charge-to-theism/
5. Denton (1985).
6. Behe (1996).
7. Gauger *et al.* (2012).
8. Meyer (2009).
9. Meyer, 2013, p. x.
10. Adapted from Lennox, (2007), p. 86.
11. Leisola & Witt (2018), p. 45.
12. For example, Dawkins (2005), p. 565.
13. There are lots of misrepresentation examples to choose from in Coyne (2010), including p. 36, pp. 95-97, p.115, p. 199, p. 201, p. 241.
14. Coyne, op. cit., p. 148.
15. More on 'inference to the best explanation' in Part 2.
16. Discussion about the age of the earth is not within the scope of this book. It should simply be noted in passing that none of us was present 6,000 never mind 4.6 billion years ago, so this would accord with Stadler's six *low* confidence science criteria in Table 1.1. For example, if someone were to say - and many media

presenters do indeed say - "We now know that the earth is 4.6 billion years old" this would be an example of overstating the case (criterion 6). Why? Because the words "now" and "know" suggest a certainty that is not justified in principle; it would have been more appropriate to say, "We *believe* that the earth *may* be 4.6 billion…"
17. Pinker (2019), p. 387.
18. Zmirak, J., "Philosopher of Science Stephen Meyer Answers the Tough Questions Darwinists Don't Even Ask", *The Stream*, 24 May 2021, https://stream.org/scientist-stephen-meyer-answers-the-tough-questions-darwinists-dont-even-ask/. Viewed 24 June 2021.
19. Moreland *et al.* (2017).

Appendix B – The ideology of evolutionism

1. Mayr, Ernst, "Darwin's Influence on Modern Thought", *Scientific American*, 24 November, 2009.
2. Darwin (1879), p. 212.
3. Darwin (1879), p. 183.
4. Darwin (1879), p. 202. However, Darwin seems to settle for different races being sub-species, p. 204.
5. Gould, Stephen Jay, 1977, *Ontogeny and Phylogeny*, Cambridge MA, Harvard University Press, p. 127.
6. Darwin (1879), p. 159.
7. "Peter Singer - an interview", originally in *The Independent*, 7 January, 2004, quoted in Johann Hari, https://web.archive.org/web/20060317041348/http://www.johannhari.com/archive/article.php?id=410. See also, Singer (2000), p. 210. And on page 320, he says that in the book of Genesis, "you see there the idea that humans are special, that God created humans in his own image and gave them dominion over the other animals. Since Darwin, at least, we've known that that's actually false…". And on page 324, the sanctity of life is "actually founded on fictions or outmoded views of the world". Part of the evidence Singer cites is, "We now know that we share 98.4 percent of our DNA with chimpanzees". Singer (2000), p. 80. However, we *now* know that this comparison is erroneous and in any case population genetics modelling shows even that gap to be unbridgeable in the evolutionary time available - see Chapter 8.
8. Singer (2000), p. 156.
9. Singer (2000), p. 160-161.
10. Singer (2000), p. 130. Elsewhere he adds, "If we compare a severely defective human infant with a nonhuman animal, a dog or a pig, for example, we will often find the nonhuman to have superior capacities, both actual and potential, for rationality, self-consciousness, communication, and anything else that can plausibly be considered as morally significant", p. 220. Or again, "Since neither a newborn infant nor a fish is a person, the wrongness of killing such beings is not as great as the wrongness of killing a person", p. 233. Also, "we cannot justifiably give more protection to the life of a human being than we give to a non-human animal, if the human being clearly ranks lower on any possible scale of relevant characteristics

than the animal. An anencephalic baby clearly ranks lower... than a chimpanzee", p. 222.

11. West (2015), pp. 39-40. Also according to Ruse, "He was as hardline a methodological naturalist as it is possible to imagine." Ruse, M., op. cit., in Harrison & Roberts (2019), p. 140.
12. Ibid., p. 41.
13. Crick, Francis, *The Astonishing Hypothesis: The Scientific Search for the Soul*, New York, Charles Scribner's Sons, 1994, p. 3.
14. Provine, William B., "Darwinism: Science or Naturalistic Philosophy", A debate at Stanford University with Phillip E. Johnson, 30 April 1994, *Origins Research*, Volume 16, Number 1: http://www.arn.org/docs/orpages/or161/161main.htm. Accessed 19 October 2021.
15. Harari (2015), pp. 123, 91, 313.
16. Ruse, M., "Removing God from Biology", in Harrison & Roberts (2019), pp. 139, 131.
17. For example, in his introductory talk to students each year, David Barash, an evolutionary psychologist at the University of Washington, effectively tells students there is no God, "The more we know of evolution, the more unavoidable is the conclusion that living things, including human beings, are produced by a natural, totally amoral process, with no indication of a benevolent, controlling creator". Barash, D., "God, Darwin, and My Biology Class", New York Times, 28 September 2014: www.nytimes.com/2014/09/28/opinion/sunday/god-darwin-and-my-college-biology-class.html. Quoted in West (2015), p. 391. Contemporary popular fiction picks up the idea. Dan Brown's hero, Robert Langdon, deciphers a piece of Kirsch's pictogram art in which an ancient Assyrian hieroglyph of a fish is depicted as *eating* a symbol that represents God. Langdon quips, "It's a playful version of the Darwin fish - evolution consuming religion". Brown (2018), p. 42.
18. Dawkins (1989), p. 330.
19. Dawkins (1991), p. 6. He goes even further, "if an individual doesn't succeed in shaking [religion] off, his mind is stuck in a permanent state of infancy, and there is a real danger he will infect the next generation [with its virus]". From *The Root of All Evil*, a television documentary on Channel 4 in January 2006. Quoted in Fretwell (2019), p. 78. Berlinski has a more tongue-in-cheek take, "It is atheism that makes it possible for a man to be an intellectually fulfilled Darwinist". Berlinski (2009), p. 507.
20. Veith (2020), p. 48.
21. "The Connected Generation: How Christian Leaders Around the World Can Strengthen Faith & Well-Being Among 18–35-Year-Olds", *Barna Group*, 2019, p. 59: www.barna.com
22. West, J. G., "Darwin's Corrosive Idea", *Discovery Institute*, Seattle, November 2016, https://www.discovery.org/m/2019/01/Darwins-Corrosive-Idea.pdf. Accessed 8 November 2021.
23. Graffin, G. W. and Provine, W. B., "Evolution Religion and Free Will", *American Scientist* 95(4), July-August 2007. Results of Cornell Evolution Project Survey http://www.polypterus.com/results.pdf, p. 7. Accessed 5 November 2021.

References

Aitken, Robin, 2018, *The Noble Liar,* London, Biteback Publishing Ltd.
Alexander, Denis, 2008, *Creation or Evolution: Do we have to choose?,* Oxford, Monarch Books.
Axe, Douglas, 2016, *Undeniable: How Biology Confirms Our Intuition That Life is Designed,* New York, HarperCollins.
Bannister, Andy, 2021, *Do Muslims and Christians Worship the Same God?,* London, Inter Varsity Press.
Barlow, Nora (Ed.), 1958, *The Autobiography of Charles Darwin 1809-1882,* London, Collins.
Barrow, John D., 2003, *From Alpha to Omega: The Constants of Nature,* London, Vintage.
Behe, Michael J., 1996, *Darwin's Black Box: The Biochemical Challenge to Evolution,* New York, FREE PRESS.
Behe, Michael J., 2007, *The Edge of Evolution: The Search for the Imits of Darwinism,* New York, FREE PRESS.
Behe, Michael J., 2019, *Darwin Devolves: The New Science About DNA That Challenges Evolution,* New York, HarperCollins Publishers.
Bergman, Jerry, 2014, *Hitler and the Nazi Darwinian Worldview,* Kitchener, Ontario, Joshua Press Inc.
Berlinski, David, 2009, *The Deniable Darwin,* Seattle, Discovery Institute Press.
Berlinski, David, 2019, *Human Nature,* Seattle, Discovery Institute Press.
Bethell, Tom, 2017, *Darwin's House of Cards: A Journalist's Odyssey through the Darwin Debates,* Seattle, Discovery Institute Press.
Brockman, John (Ed.), 2005, *What We Believe But Cannot Prove,* London, Simon & Schuster UK Ltd.
Brown, Dan, 2018, *Origin,* London, Transworld Publishers.
Bryson, Bill (Ed.), 2010, *Seeing Further: The Story of Science & the Royal Society,* London, HarperCollins.
Burgess, Stuart, 2013, *The Design and Origin of Man: evidence for special creation and over-design,* Leominster, UK, Day One Publications.
Carrier, Richard, 2011, *Why I am not a Christian: Four Conclusive Reasons to Reject the Faith,* Richmond, California, Philosophy Press.
Carter, Robert (Ed.), 2014, *Evolution's Achilles' Heels,* Powder Springs, Georgia, Creation Book Publishers.
Conway Morris, Simon, 2003, *Life's Solution: Inevitable Humans in a Lonely Universe,* Cambridge, Cambridge University Press.
Cox, Brian & Cohen, Andrew, 2014, *Human Universe,* London, HarperCollins.
Coyne, Jerry A., 2010, *Why Evolution Is True,* Oxford University Press.
Crick, Francis, 1988, *What Mad Pursuit: A Personal View of Scientific Discovery,* New York, Basic Books Inc.
Dalrymple, G. Brent, 1991, *The age of the Earth,* California, Stanford University Press.
Darwin, Charles, 1860, *On The Origin of Species By Means of Natural Selection, or the Preservation of Favoured Races in the Struggle for Life,* 2nd ed., edited by Gillian Beer (1996), Oxford, The World's Classics, Oxford University Press.
Darwin, Charles, 1879, *The Descent of Man, and Selection in Relation to Sex,* 2nd ed., edited by James Moore and Adrain Desmond (2004), London, Penguin Books Ltd.

Darwin, Francis (Ed.), 1887, *The Life and Letters of Charles Darwin*, Vol 1, London, John Murray.
Dawkins, Richard, 1989, The *Selfish Gene*, Oxford, Oxford University Press.
Dawkins, Richard, 1991, The *Blind Watchmaker*, London, Penguin Books Ltd.
Dawkins, Richard, 1996, *River Out of Eden: A Darwinian View of Life*, London, Phoenix, Orion Books Ltd.
Dawkins, Richard, 1997, *Climbing Mount Improbable*, London, Penguin Books Ltd.
Dawkins, Richard, 1998, *Unweaving the Rainbow: Science Delusion and the Appetite for Wonder*, Boston, Houghton Mifflin.
Dawkins, Richard, 2004, *A Devil's Chaplain*, London, Phoenix, Orion Books Ltd.
Dawkins, Richard, 2005, *The Ancestor's Tale*, London, Phoenix, Orion Books Ltd.
Dawkins, Richard, 2006, *The God Delusion*, London, Transworld Publishers.
Dawkins, Richard, 2010, *The Greatest Show On Earth: The Evidence For Evolution*, London, Transworld Publishers.
Dembski, William A., 2005, *The Design Inference: Eliminating Chance Through Small Probabilities*, New York, Cambridge University Press.
Dembski, William A. & Wells, Jonathan, 2008, *The Design of Life: Discovering Signs of Intelligence in Biological Systems*, Dallas, The Foundation for Thought and Ethics.
Dennett, Daniel C., 1996, *Darwin's Dangerous Idea: Evolution and the Meanings of Life*, London, Penguin Books.
Denton, Michael, 1985, *Evolution: A Theory in Crisis*, Maryland, Adler & Adler, Publishers, Inc.
Denton, Michael, 1998, *Nature's Destiny: How the Laws of Biology reveal Purpose in the Universe*, New York, The Free Press.
Denton, Michael, 2016, *Evolution: Still a Theory in Crisis*, Seattle, Discovery Institute Press.
Denton, Michael, 2020, *The Miracle of the Cell*, Seattle, Discovery Institute Press.
Denton, Michael, 2022, *The Miracle of Man: The Fine Tuning of Nature for Human Existence*, Seattle, Discovery Institute Press.
Desmond, Adrian, 1997, *Huxley: From Devil's Disciple to Evolution's High Priest*, London, Penguin Books.
Draper, John W., 1873, *History of the Conflict Between Religion and Science*, University of New York.
Eberlin, Marcos, 2019, *Foresight: How the Chemistry of Life Reveals Planning and Purpose*, Seattle, Discovery Institute Press.
Eldredge, Niles, 1982, *The Monkey Business: A Scientist Looks at Creationism*, New York, Washington Square Press.
Eldredge, Niles, 1985, *Time Frames: The Rethinking of Darwinian Evolution and the Theory of Punctuated Equilibria*, New York, Simon & Schuster, Inc.
Flew, Antony & Varghese, Roy A., 2007, *There Is ~~No~~ A God: How the world's most notorious atheist changed his mind*, New York, HarperCollins Publishers.
Fretwell, Thomas, 2019, *Who Am I?: Human Identity and the Gospel in a Confusing World*, 2nd Ed., Leominster, Day One Publications.
Futuyma, Douglas J., 1986, *Evolutionary Biology*, 2nd Ed., Sunderland, Massachusetts, Sinauer Associates, Inc.
Futuyma, Douglas J., 1998, *Evolutionary Biology*, 3rd Ed., Sunderland, Massachusetts, Sinauer Associates, Inc.
Galloway, David J., 2021, *Design Dissected: Is the Design Real?*, Kilmarnock, John Ritchie Ltd.

References

Gauger, Ann; Axe, Douglas; Luskin, Casey, 2012, *Science & Human Origins*, Seattle, Discovery Institute Press.
Gervais, R., 2010, "Why I'm an Atheist", *Wall Street Journal*, 19 December.
Goldacre, Ben, 2009, *Bad Science*, London, Fourth Estate, HarperCollins.
Gonzalez, Guillermo & Richards, Jay W., 2004, *The Privileged Planet: How our Place in the Cosmos is Designed for Discovery*, Lanham, MD, Regnery Publishing.
Gould, Stephen J., 1977, *Ontogeny and Phylogeny*, Cambridge, MA, Harvard University Press.
Gould, Stephen J., 1980, *The Panda's Thumb*, New York, W. W. Norton & Co.
Gould, Stephen J., 1983, *Hen's Teeth and Horse's Toes*, New York, W. W. Norton & Co.
Gould, Stephen J., 1986, *Evolution and the Triumph of Homology: or Why History Matters*, American Scientist 74.
Gould, Stephen J., 1987, *Time's Arrow Time's Cycle: Myth and Metaphor in the Discovery of Geological Time*, 11th printing 2001, Cambridge Massachusetts, Harvard University Press.
Gould, Stephen J., 2000, *Wonderful Life: The Burgess Shale and the Nature of History*, London, Vintage.
Gray, John, 2003, *Straw Dogs: Thoughts on Humans and Other Animals*, London, Granta Publications.
Green, Rod, 2005, *Building the Titanic*, London, Carlton Books Ltd.
Harari, Yuval N., 2015, *Sapiens: A Brief History of Humankind*, London, Vintage, Penguin Random House.
Harari, Yuval N., 2017, *Homo Deus: A Brief History of Tomorrow*, London, Vintage, Penguin Random House.
Harrison, Peter & Roberts, Jon. H. (editors), 2019, *Science without God? Rethinking the History of Scientific Naturalism*, Oxford, Oxford University Press.
Hawking, Stephen & Mlodinow, Leonard, 2011, *The Grand Design: New Answers to the Ultimate Questions of Life*, London, Transworld Publishers.
Hawking, Stephen, 2018, *Brief Answers to the Big Questions*, London, John Murray Publishers.
Hedin, Eric, 2021, *Canceled Science: What Some Atheists Don't Want You to See*, Seattle, Discovery Institute Press.
Holland, Tom, 2019, *Dominion: The Making of the Western Mind*, London, Little, Brown Book Group
Howell, F. Clark, 1965, *Early Man*, New York, Time-Life Books.
Hoyle, Sir Fred & Wickramasinghe, Chandra, 1984, *Evolution from Space*, New York, First Touchstone Edition, Simon & Schuster, Inc.
Johanson, Donald C. & Edey, Maitland A., 1990, *Lucy: The Beginnings of Humankind*, New York, Simon & Schuster Inc.
Johanson, Donald & Shreeve, James, 1989, *Lucy's Child: The Discovery of a Human Ancestor*, New York, Avon Books.
Johanson, Donald C. & Wong, Kate, 2009, *Lucy's Legacy: The Quest for Human Origins*, New York, Crown Publishing Group.
Johnson, Phillip E., 1993, *Darwin on Trial*, 2nd Ed., Washington DC, InterVarsity Press.
Johnson, Phillip E., 2002, *The Right Questions: Truth, Meaning & Public Debate*, Illinois, InterVarsity Press.
Jones, Peter, 2015, *The Other Worldview: Exposing Christianity's Greatest Threat*, Bellingham, WA, Kirkdale Press.
Kahneman, Daniel, 2011, *Thinking, Fast and Slow*, London, Penguin Books.

Kardong, Kenneth V., 2002, *Vertebrates: Comparative Anatomy, Function, Evolution*, 3rd Ed., New York, McGraw-Hill.
Keas, Michael N., 2019, *Unbelievable: 7 Myths About the History and Future of Science and Religion*, Wilmington, ISI Books.
Keller, Timothy, 2008, *The Reason for God: Belief in and age of scepticism*, London, Hodder & Stoughton.
Klinghoffer, David (Ed.), 2015, *Debating Darwin's Doubt*, Seattle, Discovery Institute Press.
Kuhn, Thomas S., 1970, *The Structure of Scientific Revolutions*, Second Edition, Enlarged, London, The University of Chicago Press, Ltd.
Lane, Nick, 2010, *Life Ascending: The Ten Great Inventions of Evolution*, London, Profile Books Ltd.
Latham, Antony, 2005, *The Naked Emperor: Darwinism Exposed*, London, Janus Publishing Company Ltd.
Latham, Antony, 2012, *The Enigma of Consciousness: Reclaiming the Soul*, London, Janus Publishing Company Ltd.
Leakey, Mary D., 1984, *Disclosing the Past*, Garden City, New York, Doubleday and Company Inc.
Leakey, Richard E., 1981, *The Making of Mankind*, New York, Elsevier-Dutton Publishing Company.
Leisola, Matti & Witt, Jonathan, 2018, *Heretic: One Scientist's Journey from Darwin to Design*, Seattle, Discovery Institute Press.
Lennox, John C., 2007, *God's Undertaker: Has Science Buried God?*, Oxford, Lion Hudson.
Lennox, John C., 2011, *Gunning for God: Why the New Atheists are Missing the Target*, Oxford, Lion Hudson.
Lennox, John C., 2017, *Determined to Believe?: The Sovereignty of God, Freedom, Faith, and Human Responsibility*, Oxford, Lion Hudson.
Lennox, John C., 2019, *Can Science Explain Everything?*, Oxford, The Good Book Company.
Lennox, John C., 2020, *2084: Artificial Intelligence and the Future of Humanity*, Grand Rapids, Michigan, Zondervan Reflective.
Lewis, C.S., 1974, *Miracles: A Preliminary Study*, London, Fount Paperbacks. First published 1947.
Lewis, C.S., 1986, *The Problem of Pain*, Glasgow, William Collins Sons & Co. First published 1940.
Lewis, C.S., 2013, *The Abolition of Man*, Milton Keynes, UK, Exciting Classics. First published 1943.
Lyell, Charles, 1830-33, *Principles of Geology*, Penguin Classics (1997 edition).
Lyell, Mrs, 1881, *Life, Letters and Journals of Sir Charles Lyell*, London, John Murray.
Mackean, D.G., 2004, *GCSE Biology*, Third Edition, London, John Murray (Publishers) Ltd.
Mahon, Basil, 2004, *The Man Who Changed Everything: The Life of James Clerk Maxwell*, Chichester, UK, John Wiley & Sons Ltd.
Margulis, Lynn & Sagan, Dorian, 2003, *Acquiring Genomes: A Theory of the Origins of Species*, New York, Basic Books.
Mayr, E., 1963, *Animal Species and Evolution*, Harvard University Press, Cambridge, Mass.
Mazur, Susan, 2009, *The Altenberg 16: An Exposé Of The Evolution Industry*, Berkeley, North Atlantic Books.

References

Meyer, Stephen C., 2009, *Signature in the Cell*: DNA and the Evidence for Intelligent Design, New York, HarperCollins.

Meyer, Stephen C., 2013, *Darwin's Doubt: The Explosive Origin of Animal Life and the Case for Intelligent Design*, New York, HarperCollins Publishers.

Meyer, Stephen C., 2021, *The Return of the God Hypothesis: Three Scientific Discoveries that Reveal the Mind Behind the Universe*, New York, HarperCollins Publishers.

Meyer, Stephen C.; Nelson, Paul A.; Moneymaker, Jonathan; Minnich, Scott; Seelke, Ralph, 2009, *Explore Evolution: The Arguments For and Against Neo-Darwinism*, Melbourne & London, Hill House Publishers, HarperCollins.

Moreland, J.P.; Meyer, Stephen C.; Shaw, Christopher; Gauger, Ann K.; Grudem, Wayne, 2017, *Theistic Evolution: A Scientific, Philosophical and Theological Critique*, Illinois, Crossway.

Nagel, Thomas, 2012, *Mind & Cosmos: Why the Materialist Neo-Darwinian Conception of Nature Is Almost Certainly False*, Oxford, Oxford University Press.

Oard, Michael J., 2004, *The Missoula Flood Controversy*, Creation Research Society Books.

Offit, Paul A., 2017, *Pandora's Lab: Seven Stories of Science Gone Wrong*, Washington, National Geographic Partners.

Orr-Ewing, Amy, 2021, *Where is God in all the Suffering?*, Epsom, The Good Book Company.

Pallen, Mark, 2009, *The Rough Guide to Evolution*, London, Rough Guides Ltd.

Patterson, Colin, 1999, *Evolution (2nd Edition)*, New York, Cornell University Press.

Peterson, Jordan B., 2018, *12 Rules for Life: An Antidote to Chaos*, Canada, Allen Lane.

Pinker, Steven, 2019, *Enlightenment Now: The Case for Reason, Science, Humanism and Progress*, Penguin Random House UK.

Plantinga, Alvin, 2011, *Where the Conflict Really Lies: Science, religion, & Naturalism*, New York, Oxford University Press.

Polanyi, Michael, 1974, *Personal Knowledge: Towards a Post-Critical Philosophy*, The University of Chicago Press, Chicago 60637.

Popkin, Richard H. (Ed), 1998, *David Hume: Dialogues Concerning Natural Religion, Second Edition*, Indianapolis, Hackett Publishing Company, Inc.

Prothero, Donald R.; illustrated by Buell, Carl, 2007, *Evolution: What the Fossils Say and Why it Matters*, New York, Columbia University Press.

Reader, John, 1981, *Missing Links: The hunt for earliest man*, 1st American edition, Boston, Little Brown and Company.

Reader, John, 2011, *Missing Links: In Search of Human Origins*, Oxford, Oxford University Press.

Regis, Ed, 2008, *What it Life? Investigating the Nature of Life in the Age of Synthetic Biology*, New York, Farrar, Straus and Giroux.

Roberts, Alice, 2011, *Evolution: The Human Story*, London, Dorling Kindersley Limited (Penguin).

Roberts, Alice, 2015, *The Incredible Unlikeliness of Being: Evolution and the Making of Us*, London, Quercus Publishing (Heron Books).

Rothery, David A., 2003, *Teach Yourself Geology*, London, Hodder Education, Hodder Headline.

Russell, Bertrand, 1986, *Mysticism and Logic*, London, Unwin Paperbacks.

Saini, Angela, 2020, *Superior: The Return of Race Science*, London, HarperCollins*Publishers*.

Sanford, John. C., 2005, *Genetic Entropy & The Mystery of the Genome*, second edition, New York, Elim Publishing.

Sanford, John, C. & Rupe, Christopher, 2019, *Contested Bones*, FMS Publications.
Sarfati, Jonathan, 2010, *The Greatest Hoax on Earth? Refuting Dawkins on Evolution*, Atlanta, Creation Book Publishers.
Schaeffer, Francis A., 1990, *Trilogy: The God Who Is There, Escape from Reason, He Is There and He Is Not Silent*, Wheaton, Illinois, Crossway Books.
Schwartz, Jeffrey H. (Editor), 2017, *Rethinking Human Evolution*, Cambridge, MA, MIT Press.
Sheldrake, Rupert, 2013, *The Science Delusion*, London, Hodder & Stoughton Ltd.
Simpson, George G., 1967, *The Meaning of Evolution: A Study of the History of Life and of Its Significance for Man*, New Haven, CT, Yale University Press.
Singer, Peter, 2000, *Writings on an Ethical Life*, New York, HarperCollins.
Smith, Wesley J., 2014, *The War on Humans*, Seattle, Discovery Institute Press (Kindle Edition).
Sodera, Vij, 2003, *One Small Speck to Man: the evolution myth*, West Sussex, UK, Vija Sodera Productions.
Spencer, Nick, 2016, *The Evolution of the West: How Christianity has Shaped our Values*, London, SPCK.
Stadler, Rob, 2016, *The Scientific Approach to Evolution: What They Don't Teach You In Biology*, CreateSpace Independent Publishing Platform, North Charleston, South Carolina.
Stanley, Steven, 1979, *Macroevolution: Pattern and Process*, San Francisco, W. H. Freeman and Co.
Stanley, Steven, 1981, *The New Evolutionary Timetable: Fossils, Genes and the Origin of Species*, New York, Basic Books, Inc.
Stark, Rodney, 2014, *How the West Won: The Neglected Story of the Triumph of Modernity*, Wilmington, Delaware, ISI Books.
Strobel, Lee, 1998, *The Case For Christ: A Journalist's Personal Investigation of the Evidence for Jesus*, Grand Rapids, Zondervan.
Sutton, Mike, 2022, *Science Fraud: Darwin's plagiarism of Patrick Matthew's theory*, Great Yarmouth, UK, Curtis Press.
Swift, David, 2002, *Evolution under the microscope*, Stirling, UK, Leighton Academic Press.
Tan, Change L. & Stadler, Rob, 2020, *The Stairway to Life: An Origin-of-Life Reality Check*, Milton Keynes, Lightning Source UK Ltd.
Tattersall, Ian, 1998, *Becoming Human: Evolution and Human Uniqueness*, New York, Harcourt Brace.
Tattersall, Ian & Schwartz, Jeffrey H., 2000, *Extinct Humans*, New York, Westview Press.
Tax, Sol (Ed.), 1960, *Evolution after Darwin: The University of Chicago Centennial*, Vol 3, Chicago, University of Chicago Press.
Thaxton, Charles B., Bradley, Walter L., Olsen, Roger L., 1984, *The Mystery of Life's Origin: Reassessing Current Theories*, Dallas, Lewis and Stanley.
Thaxton, Charles B., Bradley, Walter L., Olsen, Roger L., Tour, J., Meyer, S., Wells, J., Gonzalez, G., Miller, B., Klinghoffer, D., 2020, *The Mystery of Life's Origin: The Continuing Controversy*, Seattle, Discovery Institute Press.
Thomas, Neil, 2021, *Taking Leave of Darwin: A Long Time Agnostic Discovers the Case for Design*, Seattle, Discovery Institute Press.
TInker, Melvin, 2020, *That Hideous Strength: A Deeper Look at How the West Was Lost*, Darlington, Co Durham, Evangelical Press Books.

References

Trueman, Carl R., 2020, *The Rise and Triumph of the Modern Self: Cultural Amnesia, Expressive Individualism and the Road to the Sexual Revolution*, Wheaton, Illinois, Crossway.

Veith, Gene E. Jr., 2020, *Post Christian: A Guide to Contemporary Thought and Culture*, Wheaton, Illinois, Crossway.

Weikart, Richard, 2016, *The Death of Humanity: and the case for life*, Washington DC, Regnery Publishing Inc.

Weikart, Richard, 2022, *Darwinian Racism: How Darwinism Influenced Hitler, Nazism, and White Nationalism*, Seattle, Discovery Institute Press.

Weinberg, Steven, 2019, *Third Thoughts: The Universe We Still Don't Know*, Cambridge, Massachusetts, Harvard University Press.

Wells, Jonathan, 2000, *Icons of Evolution: Science or Myth?: why much of what we teach about evolution is wrong*, Washington DC, Regnery Publishing Inc.

Wells, Jonathan, 2006, *The Politically Incorrect Guide to Darwinism and Intelligent Design*, Washington DC, Regnery Publishing Inc.

Wells, Jonathan, 2011, *The Myth of Junk DNA*, Seattle, Discovery Institute Press.

Wells, Jonathan, 2017, *Zombie Science: More Icons of Evolution*, Seattle, Discovery Institute Press.

West, John G. (Ed.), 2012, *The Magician's Twin: C. S Lewis on Science, Scientism, and Society*, Seattle, Discovery Institute Press.

West, John G., 2015, *Darwin Day in America: How our politics and culture have been dehumanized in the name of science*, Wilmington, Delaware, ISI Books.

White, Andrew, D., 1895, *History of the Warfare of Science With Theology in Christendom*, USA, Astounding Stories (2015), www.astounding-stories.com.

Williams, David, 2020, *Taken Without Consent: How Atheists Have Hijacked Science*, Kindle Direct Publishing.

Wilson, A.N., 2017, *Charles Darwin: Victorian Mythmaker*, London, John Murray Publishers.

Youngson, Robert M., 1998, *Scientific Blunders: A Brief History of How Wrong Scientists Can Sometimes Be*, London, Robinson Publishing.

Credits and permissions

The inclusion of any figures, illustrations, photographs, diagrams, charts, or other types of images in this book should not be construed as an endorsement of the ideas and arguments contained in this book on the part of any copyright holders or creators of those images, other than the author of the book himself.

Front cover image	*Titanic* image: John Parrot / Stocktrek Images via Getty Images, GettyImages-640971129. License No. 2087727018.
Figure P.1	*Titanic* side plan. Image ID: PC4HXP, History and Art Collection / Alamy Stock Photo. License No. OY74667416 .
Figure I.1	Richard Dawkins image, courtesy of David Shankbone [CC BY-SA 3.0], via Wikimedia Commons. Jerry Coyne image from Jeremy Lent's open letter available at https://patternsofmeaning.com/2017/08/10/beyond-reductionism-an-open-letter-in-response-to-jerry-coyne/ Viewed 7th November 2022.
Part 1 header page image	J. Bruce Ismay [Public domain], via Wikimedia Commons.
Figure 1.1	Joseph Priestley image, © The James Clerk Maxwell Foundation, by kind permission.
Figure 1.2	Alfred Wegener, courtesy of Bildindex der Kunst und Architektur [Public domain], via Wikimedia Commons.
Figure 1.3	J Harlen Bretz, courtesy of Dr. Julian Goldsmith [Public domain], via Wikimedia Commons.
Figure 1.4	Egas Moniz, [Public domain], via Wikimedia Commons.
Figure 1.5	Sir Isaac Newton image, © The James Clerk Maxwell Foundation, by kind permission.
Figure 1.6	My wife and my mother-in-law cartoon, W. E. Hill [Public domain], via Wikimedia Commons.
Figures 2.1, 2.2, 2.3, 2.4, 2.5	Copernicus, Halley, Faraday, Babbage, Clerk Maxwell, Galileo and Laplace images, © The James Clerk Maxwell Foundation, by kind permission.
Figure 3.1	Charles Darwin Statue photograph courtesy of Xavier da Costa e Silva [CC BY-SA 4.0], via Wikimedia Commons.
Part 2 header page image	Captain Edward J Smith [Public domain], via Wikimedia Commons.
Figure 4.1	Prokaryote Cell Diagram and Plant Cell Structure, courtesy of Mariana Ruiz Villarreal [Public domain], via Wikimedia Commons.

Figure 4.2	Origin of Life Stages courtesy, of Chiswick Chap [CC BY-SA 4.0], via Wikimedia Commons.
Figure 4.3	Miller-Urey experiment (1953) courtesy, of GYassineMrabetTalk [CC BY-SA 3.0], via Wikimedia Commons.
Figure 4.4 (Left)	Blacksmoker in Atlantic Ocean, courtesy of P. Rona, National Undersea Research Program [Public domain], via Wikimedia Commons.
Figure 4.4 (Right)	Lost City (Hydrothermal Field), National Science Foundation (University of Washington/Woods Hole Oceanographic Institution) [Public Domain], via Wikimedia Commons.
Figure 4.5	International Morse Code, courtesy of Snodgrass and Camp [Public domain], via Wikimedia Commons.
Figure 4.7	Myoglobin image courtesy of Opabinia regalis, [CC BY-SA 3.0], via Wikimedia Commons.
Figure 4.8	Mount Rushmore, courtesy of Thomas Wolf [CC BY-SA 3.0], via Wikimedia Commons.
Figure 5.2	DNA Structure and Bases [Public domain], via Wikimedia Commons. DNA (chemical) Structure, courtesy of A. Obeidat [CC BY-SA-3.0], via Wikimedia Commons.
Figure 5.3	Peptide Synthesis, modified courtesy of Boumphreyfr [CC BY-SA 3.0], via Wikimedia Commons. RNA polymerase, modified courtesy of JWSchmidt [Public domain], via Wikimedia Commons.
Figure 5.4	Monument Valley, courtesy of Moritz Zimmermann [CC BY-SA 3.0], via Wikimedia Commons.
Figure 5.5	(a) Biston betularia (peppered moth), courtesy of Ilia Ustyantsev [CC BY-SA 2.0], via Wikimedia Commons. (b) courtesy of Ben Sale [CC BY-SA 2.0], via Wikimedia Commons.
Figure 5.6	Darwin's Finches, John Gould [Public domain], via Wikimedia Commons.
Figure 5.7	English Bulldog, courtesy of Ultimoribelle [CC BY-SA 4.0], via Wikimedia Commons.
Figure 5.8	Nymph plant-hopper gears from Figure 1(D) of Burrows, M. and Sutton, G., "Interacting Gears Synchronize Propulsive Leg Movements in a Jumping Insect", *Science* 341 (6151), 13 September 2013, pp. 1254-1256. doi: 10.1126/science.1240284. Reprinted with permission from AAAS, license number 5583551027646.
Figure 5.9	Victor-Mousetrap, courtesy of Evan-Amos

Credits and permissions

Figure 5.10	[CC BY 3.0] via Figure 1: Structure of an archetypal flagellum, in Schulz, W. (2021) "An Engineering Perspective on the Bacterial Flagellum: Part 2–Analytic View", *BIO-Complexity* 2021 (2):1-16. doi:10.5048/BIO-C.2021.2.
Figure 5.11	Anatomy of the eye, courtesy of Eloise Keeling *et al.*, "Impaired Cargo Clearance in the Retinal Pigment Epithelium (RPE) Underlies Irreversible Blinding Diseases", Cells 2018, 7(2), [CC BY-SA 4.0] via MDPI, Basel, Switzerland.
Figure 5.12	Adapted from Figure 10.5 of Axe (2016) with author permission. The rhodopsin image is [Public Domain], via Wikimedia Commons.
Figure 6.1	Haeckel's Tree of Life [Public Domain], via Wikimedia Commons.
Figure 6.2	Based on Meyer (2013), p. 141.
Figure 6.4	Trilobite (Paradoxides), courtesy of Dwergenpaartje [CC BY-SA 3.0], via Wikimedia Commons. Marrella reconstruction, courtesy of J. T. Haug *et al.* [CC BY-SA 2.0], via Wikimedia Commons. Opabinia restoration, courtesy of N. Tamura [CC BY-SA 4.0], via Wikimedia Commons. Hallucigenia, courtesy of Qohelet12 [CC BY-SA 4.0], via Wikimedia Commons.
Figure 6.5	Adapted from Figures 2.5b and 2.5c in Meyer (2013).
Figure 6.7	Family tree of the amniotes, from Figure 11.1 in *Evolution: What the Fossils Say and Why it Matters*, by Prothero, Donald R.; illustrated by Buell, Carl. Copyright © 2007 Columbia University Press. Reprinted with permission of Columbia University Press.
Figure 6.9	*Fishapods*, courtesy of D. Souza [CC BY-SA 3.0], via Wikimedia Commons.
Figure 6.10	Adapted from *Fishpods tetrapods*, courtesy of Conty [Public Domain] via Wikimedia Commons.
Figure 6.11	Archaeopteryx, courtesy of H. Raab [CC BY-SA 3.0], via Wikimedia Commons.
Figure 6.13	Evolution of whales from land creatures, from Figure 14.16 in *Evolution: What the Fossils Say and Why it Matters*, by Prothero, Donald R.; illustrated by Buell, Carl. Copyright © 2007 Columbia University Press. Reprinted with permission of Columbia University Press.
Figure 7.1	Homology vertebrates, courtesy of Волков Владислав Петрович [CC BY-SA 4.0], via Wikimedia Commons.

Figure 7.2	Smilodon, modified courtesy of Dantheman9758 [CC BY-SA 3.0], via Wikimedia Commons. Thylacosmilus, modified courtesy of D. Bogdanov [Public domain], via Wikimedia Commons.
Figure 7.3	Haeckel's Drawings, Romanes, G. J.; uploaded to Wikipedia by en:User:Phlebas; authors of the description page: en:User:Phlebas, en:User:SeventyThree, [Public domain], via Wikimedia Commons. Prothero (2007) uses a very similar image in his Figure 4.10, p. 110.
Figure 7.4	Vertebrate Embryos, from Figure 1 of Richardson, M.K. et al., "Haeckel, Embryos and Evolution", *Science* (280), 15 May 1998, pp. 983-984 article. Reprinted with permission from AAAS, license number 5580110374839.
Figure 7.5(a)	The teleost gut formation diagram, also courtesy of David Swift, is taken from Figure 5 in Wallace, K., Pack, M., "Unique and conserved aspects of gut development in zebrafish", *Dev. Biol.*, Mar 1, 2003, 255(1), pp. 12-29. doi: 10.1016/s0012-1606(02)00034-9, Open Access.
Figures 7.5(b), 7.5(c), 7.6, 7.7, 7.8, 7.9	With the kind permission of David Swift, from his website "Evolution under the microscope", viewed 7 July 2023: https://evolutionunderthemicroscope.com/homology10.html; https://evolutionunderthemicroscope.com/homology02.html
Figure 7.10	With the kind permission of David Swift, from his website "Evolution under the microscope", viewed 7 July 2023, https://evolutionunderthemicroscope.com/homology16.html Redrawn from figure 5 in Hamilton, L., "The formation of somites in Xenopus", *J. Embryol. Exp. Morph.*, 1969, 22(2), pp. 253-264.
Figure 7.11	Drosophile normale et bithorax, courtesy of Rachgo20 [CC BY-SA 4.0], via Wikimedia Commons.
Figure 8.1	March of Progress, [Public domain], via Wikimedia Commons.
Figure 8.2	Orangutan: courtesy of Kabir Bakie, [CC BY-SA 2.5], via Wikimedia Commons. Gorilla: courtesy of Anagoria [CC BY 3.0], via Wikimedia Commons. Human silhouette: courtesy of Mette Aumala [CC0 1.0], via Wikimedia Commons. Chimpanzee: courtesy of Hans Hillewaert [CC BY-SA 3.0], via Wikimedia Commons. Bonobo: courtesy of Ltshears [CC BY-SA 3.0], via Wikimedia Commons.
Figure 8.4	Die Familiengruppe der Katarrhinen, from Ernst Haeckel, *Natürliche Schöpfungsgeschichte*, Berlin, 1868: https://archive.org/stream/natrlichesch68haec#page/n3/mode/2up

Credits and permissions

Figure 8.5	Reconstruction of the La Chapelle-aux-Saints Neanderthal by the Czech artist Frantizek Kupka. Image licensed by Science Photo Library. ID 876077.
Figure 8.6	Reconstructed face of Neanderthal child from Anthropologisches Institut, Universität Zürich.
Figure 8.7	Turkana Boy, courtesy of C. Houck [CC BY-SA 2.0], via Wikimedia Commons.
Figure 8.8	*Homo habilis* bone fragments. Image licensed by Science Photo Library. ID 813462.
Figure 8.9	Lucy fossil skeleton reconstruction, courtesy of 120 [CC BY-SA 3.0], via Wikimedia Commons.
Figure 8.10	Anthropoid Feet, adapted from: https://i1.wp.com/www.bigfootencounters.com/images/anthropoid_feet.jpg Laetoli foot impression from Johanson D., "The Paleoanthropology of Hadar, Ethiopia", *Human Palaeontology and Prehistory* 16(2), 2017, pp. 140-154. https://doi.org/10.1016/j.crpv.2016.10.005 Open Archive.
Figure 8.11	*Ardipithecus ramidus* fossils from White T. D., "*Ardipithecus ramidus* and the Paleobiology of Early Hominids", Science 326:5949, 2 October 2009, pp. 64-86: https://science.sciencemag.org/content/326/5949/64.full This image downloaded from Wikipedia where the source page explicitly mentions "Fair Use" as being acceptable, https://en.wikipedia.org/wiki/File:Ardipithecis_Ramidus_skeleton_1994-1996.jpeg
Figure 8.12	*Ardipithecus ramidus* reconstructed skeleton, courtesy of T. Fluegel [CC BY-SA 3.0], via Wikimedia Commons.
Part 3 header page image	Thomas Andrews [CC BY-SA 4.0], via Wikimedia Commons.
Figure 9.1	Antony Flew image [Public domain], via Wikimedia Commons.
Figure 9.2	Günter Bechly modified image, courtesy of Dr. Günter Bechly [CC BY-SA 4.0], via Wikimedia Commons.
Figure 9.3	David Gelernter image, courtesy of Repdan [CC BY-SA 3.0], via Wikimedia Commons.

Figure A.1	Coyne and Dawkins images as per Figure I1. Collins, Miller [Public domain]; Lennox [CC BY-SA 2.0]; Alexander, Cox [CC BY-SA 3.0]; Roberts, Ross, Sarfati [CC BY-SA 4.0]; via Wikimedia Commons. Burgess, Purdom courtesy of *Answers in Genesis*. Behe, Gauger courtesy of *Discovery Institute*. Denton courtesy of *Evolution News*. Haarsma courtesy of *Biologos*. Meyer courtesy of *Focus on the Family*. Rana courtesy of *Reasons to Believe*.
Image on last page	*Titanic* image: John Parrot / Stocktrek Images via Getty Images, GettyImages-640971129. License No. 2087727018.

Index

Page references followed by *fig* indicate the image or caption of a figure.

abiogenesis, 78, 79, 84-85*fig*, 95-96
Aborigines, Australian, 226-227, 233
abortion, 318
Acanthostega, 176,178, 177*figs*
ACLU, 145, 295
Aedes mosquito, 237
affirming the consequent (logical fallacy), 190, 191, 210
Agassiz, Louis, 68, 156, 162, 185
Alberts, Bruce, 83
Aleuts, 237
Alexander, Denis, 308*fig*, 309
allopatric speciation, 159-160
Ambulocetus, 180-182, 181*fig*
American Civil Liberties Union, see ACLU
amino acid, 102*fig*-104
  - translation from DNA/RNA 'alphabet', 118
analogous, see convergent evolution
Andrews, Thomas, 5, 7, 10, 265, 273, 275, 281, 299
Anomalocaris, 165, 168-169
antennapedia, 214
antibiotic resistance, 64-65, 133-134, 152, 268
Archaeopteryx, 175, 178*fig*-179, 185
Ardi, see *Ardipithecus ramidus*
Ardipithecus ramidus, 224, 225*fig*, 245*fig*-247*fig*, 248, 353
Aristotle, 26, 35, 37, 50-51, 96
arthropods, 155, 164-165, 166, 168, 171, 214
artificial selection, 68, 113, 130-132, 148, 152, 214
Astbury, William, 104
Atheistic Evolutionists, 156, 307-309, 308*fig*, 312, 314
Atkins, Peter, 43, 54
atovaquone, 140

Australopithecus afarensis, 224, 225*fig*, 240, 241*fig*, 242*fig*, 243-245, 252
Australopithecus africanus, 225*fig*
Australopithecus/Australopiths, 238-239, 245, 248-249, 261-262, 268
Avida, 125
Axe, Douglas, 107-109, 112, 141, 148, 183, 280, 283, 311

Babbage, Charles, 47, 48*fig*
Bacon, Francis, 41-42, 46
Bacon, Roger, 46
bacterial flagellum, 144*fig*-146, 151
bad design argument, see design
Barlow, George, 129
Basilosaurus, 180-181*fig*, 182
BBC, 42, 79
Beagle, HMS, 69, 126, 156
Bechly, Günter, 204, 279*fig*-280, 283
Begun, David, 247
Behe, Michael, 128, 132, 136-140, 142-146, 148, 152, 183, 269, 277-279, 293, 308*fig*, 311
Berlinski, David, 91, 148, 216, 250, 252, 280
Biblical Creationists/Creationism, 307, 308*fig*, 310, 312-314
Big Bang, 26-27, 30, 32, 37, 97, 106
Biles, Professor, J.H., 11
biogenetic law, 193-195, 197-200, 217
Biologic Institute, 280, 283-284, 311
Biologos, 309
blastula, 201-203*figs*
blind cave fish, 134-136, 152
Blumenbach, Johann Friedrich, 226
Blyth, Edward, 62, 71, 114
Board of Trade guidelines, 10-11, 69
Bohm, David, 97
Boisjoly, Roger, 21
Bondi, Hermann, 26
bonobo, 213, 223*fig*-224, 225*fig*, 250
Born, Max, 31

Bosch, Carl, 20
Boule, Marcelin, 233fig
Boyle, Robert, 47
Bradley, Walter, 89, 92
Brady, Ronald, 193
Brahe, Tycho, 47
brain size/volume, 237-238
Bretz, J. Harlen, 24, 31-32, 275
Briggs, Derek, 165
Britannic, 323
Brocchi, Giambattista, 61
Brown, Dan, 222, 272, 347, 356, 301
Brunel, Isambard Kingdom, 3
Buckland, William, 156
bulldog, 131-132fig, 175
Burgess Shale, 162-169, 191
Burgess, Stuart, 308fig, 310
Bushmen, 236-237

Cairns-Smith, Alexander, 87
Cambrian Explosion, 153, 162-168, 170-172, 185, see also fossil explosions
Cameron, James, 9, 273
Carrier, Richard, 44, 105-106
Carroll, Sean, 291
catastrophist/catastrophism, 24, 156
Cave, A.J.E., 233-234
Challenger, see Space Shuttle
Chambers, Robert, 61
Charles Simonyi Chair, 42
Chemical evolution, 66, 78, 84-85fig, 89, 96-97, 320, see also abiogenesis
Chen, J. Y., 167, 282
Chengjiang explosion, 167, 169, 282, see also fossil explosions
Chernobyl, 21-22, 32, 275
Chicken-and-egg-problem, 120, 114
chimpanzee, 222-223fig, 224, 235, 246-248, 251, 253, 256, 268, 319
chloroquine, 140-142
Chomsky, Noam, 254-255
chordates, 155, 166-167, 171, 191, 212
churnalism, 272
Class, see classification

classification, taxonomic, 128-129, 130, 131, 154, 155, 165, 166, 168, 174, 224, 262
Clerk Maxwell, James, 28, 47, 48fig, 50, 68, 116
cnidaria, 166, 169
Collins, Francis, 2, 122, 308fig, 309
combinatorial problem, 104
Compsognathus, 178
computer simulations, see natural selection
Conflict
 - and war, 317
 - science/religion, 14, 42-51
 - the real conflict, 51-54
continuity/discontinuity, 84, 162, 167, 179, 218, 255, 262-263, 268, 309
 - human/ape: anatomical, 251-253; behavioural, 253-256; genetic, 256-257
convergent evolution, 191-193
coordinated mutations, 142, 207, 258
Copernicus, Nicolaus, 45-46fig, 51
Cox, Brian, 77-81, 286, 307, 308fig
Coyne, Jerry, 13fig, 57, 58, 65, 66, 69, 70, 72, 76, 113, 114, 130, 131, 133, 134, 147, 153, 154, 174-176, 180-182, 184, 193, 199, 211, 222, 223, 237, 288, 297, 298, 307, 308fig, 312, 313
CQD, 99
Craig, William Lane, 43, 326
Crick, Francis, 89, 95, 116, 121, 210, 303, 304, 319
Cunard Line, 3-4
Cuvier, Georges, 156

Dark Ages, 45-47, 327
Darwin and Haeckel's views on
 - Australian Aborigines, 226-227fig
 - black Africans, 226-227fig
 - Terra del Fuegans, 226-227fig
Darwin, Charles, 1, 12, 60fig, 71
 - great naturalist, 59-50fig
 - his contemporary critics, 67-69
 - his contribution, 58-62
 - his core theory, 63

Index

- his "one long argument", 267
- on abiogenesis, 77-78, 85
- on artificial selection, 130
- on complex organ evolution, 143-144
- on conflict and war, 317
- on deep time, 136
- on embryology, 187-188, 197, 203
- on eugenics, 318-319
- on eye evolution, 147
- on fossil 'explosions', 172
- on homology, 189
- on human evolution, 221-222
- on natural selection, 115
- on philosophical materialism, 319
- on transitional fossils, 153-158, 178
- on tree of life, 153-155, 217-218
- on whales, 180
- others had ideas about evolution earlier, 61-62
- racism, 226-227, 261, 318
- today's critics, 276-280, 290-294

Darwin, Erasmus, 61
Darwin-of-the-gaps, 122, 151
Dávalos, Liliana, 211
Davidson, Eric, 203, 213-214
Dawkins, Richard, 2, 13*fig*, 42, 44, 57, 58, 70, 72, 81-84, 97, 112, 113-115, 121-124, 127, 128, 130, 131, 133-137, 147, 150, 151, 156, 166, 167, 180, 185, 192, 198, 199, 209, 210, 222, 254, 256, 258, 278, 281, 286, 307, 308*fig*, 312, 313, 320
Dawson, Charles, 229
de Beer, Sir Gavin, 202-203
Degnan, J., 211, 347
Delisle, Richard, 228, 229, 235, 249
Dennett, Daniel, 44
Denton, Michael, 82, 83, 108, 157, 162, 254, 255, 277, 308*fig*, 311
design
- apparent design, 114, 125
- bad design argument, 150-151

DiCaprio, Leonardo, 9
discontinuity, see continuity
Discovery Institute, 280, 285, 289, 293, 295, 311

disparity (morphological), 166-167, 170, 173, 185, 244, 297, 311
distal-less, 214
diversity (morphological), 162, 165-167, 170-173, 185
DNA
- how its information is used, 118-120
- how it stores information, 116-117
- 'Junk' DNA, 121-123
- origin of, 81, 85-89, 95-96, 120-122
- palindromic DNA, 122-123

Dobzhansky, Theodosius, 63, 161
dogs, 62, 64, 65, 129-132, 136, 152, 175, 224, 231, 272
Domain, see classification
Donoghue, Michael, 211
Dorudon, 181*fig*, 182
Dover trial, see Kitzmiller
Drake Equation, 78-79
Drake, Frank, 78-79
Draper, John William, 44-45, 187-188
Drosophila, see fruit flies
Dubois, Eugène, 234-235

Eberlin, Marcos, 84, 103
echinoderms, 166, 212, 214
E. coli, (*Escherichia coli*), 103-104, 137-139, 141, 144*fig*, 152, 160
Eddington, Arthur, 28
Eden, Murray, 104, 111
Edge Question, 81
Ediacaran fossils, 168
Egnor, Michael, 281-282
Einstein, Albert, 26, 28, 31, 48, 255, 277
Eiseley, L.C., 61-62
Eisenberg, D., 213
Eldredge, Niles, 42, 158-161, 184
Eller, David, 45
embryology/embryonic development
- amphibians, 202*fig*
- birds, 203*fig*
- bony fish, 201*fig*
- cartilaginous fish, 201*fig*
- gills/gill slits, 194-196, 198
- Haeckel's vertebrate drawings, 194*fig*
- humans, 203*fig*

- importance to Darwin, 187-190
- reptiles, 202*fig*
- Richardson's vertebrate photos, 196*fig*
- tailbud stage, 195, 197-198, 201

ENCODE, 121, 257
Endler, John, 127
Enlightenment, 47-48, 275
Eoanthropus dawsoni, see Piltdown Man
Eohippus, 179
Epihippus, 180
Erwin, Douglas, 166
Eskimos, 237
Euclid, 27-28, 30-31
eugenics, 226, 318
Eukaryotic cell/Eukaryota, 83*fig*, 129, 145-146, 169, 171, 224
Eusthenopteron, 176-178, 177*figs*
euthanasia, 318
Ev, 125
Evo-Devo (Evolutionary Developmental biology), 213-216, 291-292
evolution
- definitions used, 66
- different meanings, 64-66
- downhill, 133-136
- edge of, 142
- *Evolution* (definition used), 66
- Extended Evolutionary Synthesis, 290-293, 299
- 'god' arguments for, 69-70, 71
- grand narrative example, 64
- groupthink, 273
- high or low confidence science, 57-59
- human, see human evolution
- link with atheism
- macroevolution (definition used), 66
- microevolution (definition used), 66
- mutations plus natural selection (definition used), 66
- public belief in, 272-275
- quasi-religion, 285-287
- Scientific Dissent from Darwinism, 293
- scientist/academic belief in, 276-280
- universal common descent (definition used), 66

Evolutionary Creationists, 2, 308*fig*, 309, 312, 314-315
evolutionism, 14-15, 270, 317-320
Ewart, Winston, 125
Extended Evolutionary Synthesis, see evolution
extinctions, 153, 174, 180, 259
eye, 147*fig*-149*fig*, 191, 214-215
eyeless, 214

Family, see classification
FANTOM, 121
Faraday Christmas Lectures, 124
Faraday, Michael, 47, 48*fig*, 50
Felidae, 224, 269
Ferguson, Andrew, 283
fetus, 217, 318
Fichte, Gottlieb, 281
finch beaks, 60, 62, 64-66, 75, 126*fig*-129, 152, 268
First Amendment to the US Constitution, 295, 302
Fischer, D., 213
Fitzroy, Rear Admiral Robert, 69
fixity of species, 60-61, 131, 135
Fleet, Frederick, 6, 111, 275
Flew, Antony, 106, 278*fig*-279
flightless birds, 134-136, 152
Flores, 237
Foote, Michael, 169
fossil evidence, 153-185
- 'ice warnings' (interpretation difficulties), 174-176
fossils, sudden appearance (explosions)
- Cambrian (trilobites+), 162-167
- Carboniferous (winged insects), 172
- Cretaceous (angiosperms), 172
- human, 262-263
- odontide (jawed fish+), 172
- Ordovician (marine invertebrates), 172
- Paleocene (mammalian radiation, avian explosion), 172
- Triassic (modern tetrapods, marine and flying reptiles), 172
France, Anatole, 238
Freeman, Walter, 25

free will, 303fig, 319
Friedmann, Alexander, 26
frog, 196, 203, 206-208, 212, 214-215, 273
fruit flies, 129-130, 171, 183, 212, 214-216, 291-292
Futuyma, Douglas, 198-200, 225fig, 243
Fuxianhuia protensa, 168-169

Galápagos Islands, 60, 64-65, 69, 75, 126-128
Galilei, Galileo 35, 45, 47, 67, 71
 – the Galileo affair, 50fig-51
gastrulation, 201-203figs
Gates, Bill, 123
Gauger, Ann, 141, 183, 207, 308fig, 311
Gee, Henry, 229
Gelernter, David, 280fig, 283-284
gene duplication, 121, 141, 213
gene regulatory networks (GRNs), 121, 138, 213-214, 257, 291
Genetic Drift, 292
genetic entropy, 260-261, 263
genetics, birth of, 63
gene trees
 – different genes-different trees, 211-212
Genus, see classification
geological timescale, 162-164, 163fig
Gervais, Ricky, 43-44
Gibbon, Edward, 45
God is dead, 319-320
god-of-the-gaps, 296
Goldacre, Ben, 272-274
Gold, Michael, 276
Goldschmidt, Richard, 161, 196
Gold, Thomas, 26
Gonzalez, Guillermo, 92
gorilla, 223fig-224, 226, 227, 244, 251, 252, 257, 263
Gould, Stephen Jay, 19, 38, 39, 156-161, 165, 168, 170, 274, 318
gradualism, 68, 157, 184
Grant, Peter and Rosemary, 126-127
Grant, Robert Edmond, 61
Gray, Asa, 68

groupthink, see evolution
Guarantee Group, 5, 7, 9
Gunton, Colin, 301
guppies, 127-130
Gura, Trisha, 212
gut formation, 210-203figs

Haarsma, Deborah, 308fig, 309
Haber, Fritz, 20
Haeckel, Ernst, 82, 154fig, 194, 201, 217, 226, 227fig, 233, 234, 274
haemoglobin, 102, 136
Haidt, Jonathan, 275
Haldane, J.B.S., 85, 184, 188, 259
Hall, Brian, 213
Halley, Edmond, 47fig
Hallucigenia, 164fig
Halvorson, Richard T., 287
Handy Man, see *Homo habilis*
Harari, Yuval N., 272, 286, 319
Harland & Wolff, 4, 5, 12, 200
Harris, Sam, 44
Harrison, Peter, 48-49
Harrison, Terry, 247
Hedges, B., 212
Heisenberg, Werner, 31
Helicobacter pylori, 25-26
Hitchens, Christopher, 67
HIV, 140-142
homeobox regulatory genes, 214-215
Hominidae, 223fig-224
hominin(s), 223-225, 228-232, 238-241, 243, 245, 248
Homo erectus, 224, 225fig, 234-239, 249, 261, 262, 268
Homo ergaster, 236
Homo habilis, 224, 225fig, 238-240, 249, 261, 262
homology, 187, 193, 209, 218, 268
 – 'Ice warnings', 190-193
 – what is it? 189-190
Homo neanderthalensis, 225fig, 232, 233fig, 234fig, 238, 249, 262, 268
Homo sapiens, 1, 173, 209, 224, 225fig, 232, 234-238, 240, 241, 243, 244, 248fig, 249, 261, 268

Homo stupidus, 233
horse 'evolution', 179-180
Hou, Xian-Guang, 167
Hox genes, 214, 216, 291
Hoyle, Sir Fred, 26-27, 30, 32, 34-35, 60, 95-98, 108, 111-112, 267
Hubble, Edwin, 26, 58
human evolution
- family tree, 223fig, 225fig
- five "types" of humans (Caucasian, Mongolians, Ethiopians, Americans, Malays), 226
- March of Progress, 221-223, 222fig, 225, 249, 268, 274
- the popular story, 223-225
human fossils
- convincing?, 232-249
- 'ice warnings' and palaeontology, 229-232
- reconstructions, 230-231, 246
- sociology of fossil hunting, 228-229
Human Genome, 98, 99, 121, 136, 268
- difference from chimp's, 256-258
- H. G. Project, 2, 121, 309
Hume, David, 47, 59
Hutton, James, 24, 156
Huxley, Julian, 278
Huxley, Thomas Henry
- bird/dino evolution theory, 178-179
- claim that opposition to evolution was on purely religious grounds, 69, 71
- Darwin's bulldog, 69
- horse evolution connection, 179-180
- Neanderthal and Aborigines, view of, 233
- Oxford debate with Soapy Sam, 67-68, 71, 188
Hyracotherium, 179

Ichthyostega, 176, 177figs
infanticide, 318
information in biomolecules
- as the fundamental problem for neo-Darwinism, 97-98
- definition of, 98-99
- how to quantify it, 99-102

Ingold, Tim, 226
insulin, 102, 104
Intelligent Design, 14, 83, 145, 146, 279, 280, 284, 289, 304, 307, 311-314
- is anti-science?, 298-299
- is/is not science, 294-298
- what is it?, 293-294
intermediate fossil candidates
- dinosaurs to birds, 178-179
- fish to tetrapods, 176-178
- horse 'evolution', 179-180
- whale 'evolution', 180-184
irreducible complexity, 113, 142-146, 151, 179, 216, 295, 296
Ismay, Joseph Bruce, 3-5, 9, 10, 17, 281

Jablonka, Eva, 290-291
Jablonski, David, 290
Jameson, Robert, 61
Java Man, 235
Jenkin, Fleeming, 68
Johanson, Donald, 229, 236, 240-245
Johnny's Child, 239
Johnson, Phillip E., 175, 185, 210
Jones III, Judge John E., 294-298
Jungers, William, 247
Junk DNA, 114, 121-123, 257, 297

Kahneman, Daniel, 271, 273-275
Kauffman, Stuart, 291
Kelvin, Lord, 31, 47, 55, 68
Kennedy, John F., Joseph, Rosemary, 25
Kennewick Man, 230-231
Kepler, Johannes, 47, 50
Kettlewell, Bernard, 126, 127
Kimura, Motoo, 292
Kingdom, see classification
King, William, 233
Kitzmiller versus Dover Area School Board, 145, 294-298
Klein, R.G., 249
Klinghoffer, David, 280
Koestler, Arthur, 269-270
Konrad Lorenz Institute, 290
Kuhn, Thomas, 29-31, 33, 75-76
Kupka, František, 233

Index

Laetoli footprints, 242-244
Lamarck, Jean-Baptiste, 61
Lane, Nick, 81, 86, 87, 89, 96, 97, 130, 147
Laplace, Pierre-Simon, 47, 52
Late Heavy Bombardment, 79
Laughlin, William, 237
Lavoisier, Antoine, 23
Lawton, Graham, 217, 218
Leakey, Jonathan, 239
Leakey, Louis, 238, 239fig, 241
Leakey, Mary, 238, 241, 242fig, 244
Leakey, Richard, 235-236fig, 238, 241, 244
Leisola, Matti, 80, 103, 200, 276, 283, 285, 311-312
Lemaître, Georges, 26
Lennox, John, 32, 49, 308fig, 311
Lenoir, Timothy, 197
Lenski, Richard, 125, 134, 137-139, 152, 160
Lewis, C.S., 49, 282
Lewontin, Richard (Dick), 53-54, 302
Linnaeus, Carolus, aka Carl von Linne, 60-61
Linne, see Linnaeus
Linton, Alan, 134
Lobachevsky, Nicolai, 27
lobotomy, 25, 29, 32
Loftus, John W., 45
Lovejoy, Owen, 236-237, 246-247
Lucy, see *Australopithecus afarensis*
lumpers (of species), 231, 235, 238
Lyell, Charles, 24, 61, 62, 131, 155-157, 293
Lyon, Daniel, 238

malaria, 36, 136, 139, 140, 142
malarial parasite, 136, 139, 140, 142
Maotianshan Shale, 167
March of Progress, see human evolution
Margulis, Lynn, 277, 292
Markkanen, Pertti, 276-277
Marrella, 164fig, 169
Marshall, Barry, 25-26, 32, 275
Martin, Bill, 89

Marx, Karl, 41
materialism, 51-55, 210, 280, 283, 302
 - philosophical, 301-302, 319
 - scientific, 280, 288, 302
mathematical certainty, 10, 75, 112, 142, 185, 258, 265, 289, 299, 300
Matthew, Patrick, 114
Maxwell, see Clerk Maxwell
Mayr, Ernst, 63, 75-76, 161, 230, 255, 317
Mazur, Susan, 290
McAuliffe, Christa, 21
McDonald, Don, 285-286
Meckel-Serres law, 193-194
Medawar, Sir Peter, 43, 104
Mendel, Gregor, 47, 63
Mendel's Accountant, 259-260
Mesohippus, 180
METHINKS IT IS LIKE A WEASEL, 123-124, 258, 274
Meyer, Hermann von, 178
Meyer, Stephen, 33, 84, 162, 166, 169-171, 204, 279-281, 284, 289, 297, 308fig, 311, 314-315
Michelson, Albert, 31, 55
Miller, Brian, 92
Miller, Ken, 114, 121, 145, 308fig, 309
Miller, Stanley, 86
Miller-Urey experiment, 86fig-89, 91, 92, 108, 272, 274
Miohippus, 180
Mivart, Sir George Jackson, 68-69
Modern Synthesis, see neo-Darwinism
molluscs, 155, 166, 191
Molton, Peter, 91
Moniz, Egas, 25fig
Moore, Andrew, 122
Moreland, J.P., 315
Morgan, J.P., 3, 5, 10
Morris, Simon Conway, 165, 191, 218
Morse Code, 99-100fig, 120, 294
Mount Improbable, 113, 115fig-116, 124, 125fig, 128, 132, 139, 143, 144, 151, 152, 159, 267
Mount Rushmore, 110fig, 143, 295
mousetrap, 143fig-144
Müller, Gerd, 290-291

385

Myers, P.Z., 285
myoglobin, 103fig, 104

Nagel, Thomas, 279, 282-283
NASA, 21, 79-80
National Center for Science and Education (NCSE), 285, 295
Natural Genetic Engineering, 292
naturalism (philosophical), 51-54, 287, 291, 301, 319
- methodological naturalism, 52
natural selection
- computer simulations of, 123-125
- Darwin's definition of, 115
- limitations with mathematical certainty, 142
- predicted to have creative power, 113-115
Neanderthal Man, see *Homo neanderthalensis*
Nectocaris, 165
Nelson, Paul, 291
neo-Darwinism, 14, 57, 65, 71, 75, 135, 137, 139, 146, 161, 192, 268, 277, 279, 290, 297, 299, 303, 307, 314
- what is it? 63
neurulation, 201-203figs
New Atheists, 44
Newman, Stuart, 290-291
new proteins for old, 141-142
Newton, Sir Isaac, 27-28fig, 30-31, 46, 47, 50, 52, 255, 277
Niedźwiedzki, Grzegorz, 178
Nilsson, Dan, 147-148
Nutcracker Man, see *Paranthropus bosei*

Ockham, William of, 46
Old Earth Creationists, 308fig, 309-310, 312
Olduvai Gorge, 238
Olsen, Roger, 89, 92
Olympic, RMS, 4
O'Neill, Tim, 45
Oneism, 301-302
ontogeny, 188, 194, 198
Opabinia, 164fig-165

Oparin, Alexander, 85-86
Orangutan, 223fig, 229, 257
Order, see classification
Oreopithecus, 247
Orgel, Leslie, 95, 121
Origin of Species
- full title, 60
- initial objections, 67-69
Orohippus, 179-180
orphan genes, 212-213
Orwell/Orwellian, George, 33, 281
Owen, Sir Richard, 67-68, 255
Oxford Huxley-Wilberforce debate, 67-68, 71, 188, 286fig

Pääbo, Svante, 234
Pakicetus, 180, 181fig, 182
palaeoanthropology (or paleo-anthropology), 222, 229, 240, 244, 261
Pallen, Mark, 114, 193, 224, 240, 248, 249
Panderichthys, 176, 177figs, 178
Panspermia, 95-97
Paranthropus aethiopicus, 225fig
Paranthropus bosei, 225fig, 238-239
Paranthropus robustus, 225fig
Pascal, Blaise, 47
Pasteur, Louis, 47, 96, 238
Patterson, Colin, 232
Pauling, Linus, 190, 211
Paul, the apostle, 304
Pax gene family, 214-216
Peking Man, 235, 237
Pelger, Susanne, 147-148
pentadactyl limb, 189fig, 207-209
Penzias, Arno, 26
peppered moth, 125, 126fig, 127-128
Peptic ulcers, 25-26, 31, 275
permutations, 104-107
Peterson, Jordan, 280-281
Petranek, Stephen, 81
Pettitt, Jonathan, 292
Phlogiston, 22-23, 30, 35, 275
phylogeny, 188, 194, 198-199
Phylum, see classification
Pigliucci, Massimo, 290
Pilbeam, David, 262

Index

Piltdown Man, 229-230
Pinker, Steven, 20, 76, 90-91, 114, 222, 283, 313
Pithecanthropus erectus, 235
Planck, Max, 31, 106
plant-hopper, 142-143fig
Plantinga, Alvin, 52-54, 83-84
Plasmodium falciparum, 136, 139-140
Playfair, John, 24, 156
Plokhy, Seri, 22
Polanyi, Michael, 29, 41, 277, 294
polar bear, 75, 133, 152, 268
Pongidae, 224
Ponginae, 223-224
preformationists, 193
Premack, David, 250, 253-255
Priestley, Joseph, 22-23fig, 30, 32, 35, 275
progress, progression
 - biological/embryological, 188, 199, 204, 227
 - fossil, 154-155, 179
 - human, see human evolution
 - imperialist doctrine of, 226
 - scientific, 19-20, 269-270
 - technological, 227
prokaryotic cell, 83fig, 145-146
proteins
 - how many in simplest cell, 102-103, 108
 - universe build one?, 104-110
 - what are they?, 102-104
Prothero, Donald, 173fig, 174, 179-180, 181fig-182, 194, 195, 199, 285
protist, protistology, 171, 277
Protocell, 85, 92, 94-95
Protorohippus, 179-180
Provine, William, 302-304, 319
Ptolemy, 47, 50-51
Punctuated Equilibria, 153, 159-162, 170
Punk Eek, 159, 160, 170
Purdom, Georgia, 308fig, 310

racism, 228, 318
Raff, Rudolf, 197
Rampassa pygmies, 237
Rana, Fazale, 308fig, 310

Randi, James, 285
Reader, John, 236, 240
recapitulation, see biogenetic law
Regis, Ed, 95
Relativity, 26-28, 31, 48
Richardson, Michael, 195, 196fig, 197-199, 201
Riemann, Georg, 27-28
RNA world, 89, 120
Roberts, Alice, 224, 232, 235, 251, 257, 286, 307, 308fig,
Rokas, A., 211
Roman Catholic Church, 42, 45, 67
Romanes, G.J., 195, 199
Rosenberg, N., 211
Ross, Hugh, 308fig, 309-310
Rothery, David, 81
Rousseau, Jean-Jacques, 45, 47
Royal Society of London, 49, 69, 147, 286, 290
Rupe, Christopher, 231, 244, 246, 258
Ruse, Michael, 32, 287, 319
Russell, Bertrand, 43
Russell, Mike, 88-89

Sabatini, Riccardo, 98
sabre-toothed cat, 191, 192fig
Saini, Angela, 230, 234, 271-272
Salichos, L., 211
Sanford, John, 231, 244, 246, 258, 259, 273
Sanger, Fred, 104
Sarfati, Jonathan, 308fig, 310
Sarton, George, 41
Schaeffer, Francis, 49
Schneider, Thomas, 125
Schrödinger, Erwin, 31
Schroeder, Gerry, 106
Schwartz, Jeffrey H., 235, 240
science
 - conflict with religion, 43-50
 - definitions, 32-33
 - fraud, 38
 - high- and low-confidence, 33-37
 - laws of, 53
 - only source of truth?, 43

387

- peer review, 37-38
- priesthood of, 41-42
Scientific Revolution, 45-47
Scott, Eugenie, 285, 295
Search for Extraterrestrial Intelligence, see SETI
Sedgwick, Adam, 24, 68, 156, 162, 195
Self-organization, 109, 110, 291, 293, 299
Sepkoski, Jack, 166
SETI, 78-79, 81, 295, 296
Shannon, Claude, 100-102, 106, 124
Shapiro, James, 146, 291-292
Sheldrake, Rupert, 37, 38, 41-44
Sherman, Michael, 276
Shubin, Neil, 176-178
sickle-cell anaemia, 136, 139-140
Sinanthropus, 237
Singer, Peter, 318-319
Simpson, George Gaylord, 63, 97, 159, 161, 162
Smith, Captain Edward John (EJ), 3, 5, 9, 10, 73, 174, 228
Smith, John Maynard, 278
Smithsonian National Museum of Natural History, 233, 248fig, 249, 284-285
Smith, William, 162-163
Social Darwinism, 318
Sodera, Vij, 236
SOS, 99-101, 104
Space shuttle, 21, 29, 32
species, see also classification
- biological species concept, 231, 234
- morphological species concept, 231
Spencer, Nick, 47-49, 130
Splitters (of species), 231, 232, 235
Stadler, Rob, 33-37, 52, 58, 72, 79, 81, 112, 156, 190, 197, 230
Stanley, Steven, 158, 162, 184, 232
Stark, Rodney, 45-47, 51
Star Trek, 81, 230
Star Wars, 81
stasis, 157, 159, 160
Steady State theory, 26-27
Steele, Edward, 82, 95, 109
Steiner Trees, 125
Sternberg, Richard, 284

Stewart, Patrick, 230-231
Straus, W.L., 233-234
Sumner, Seirian, 213
Swift, David, 148, 180, 201-209, 214, 276
Symbiogenesis, 292, 299
sympatric speciation, 160
Syvanen, Michael, 212

Tattersall, Ian, 235, 240, 249, 253-254
Teeling, E., 212
Terra del Fuegans, 226
Thalassemia, 136
Thaxton, Charles B., 37, 89, 91, 92
Theistic Evolutionists, see Evolutionary Creationists
Thermodynamic problem, 90-92
Thomas, Dave, 125
Thomson, William, see Kelvin
Thorne, Alan 235
Thylacosmilus, 191, 192fig
Tiktaalik, 166, 177fig-178, 185
Titanic, RMS, 3-5, 6-7fig, 9-12, 19-21, 75, 76, 84, 98-100, 105, 111, 138, 143, 144, 146, 150, 153, 174, 200, 225, 228, 250, 255, 267, 269, 273-275, 281, 299
Titanic, the movie, 9-11, 273, 281, 299
Tompa, Peter, 95
Tour, James, 93-95
transitional fossils, 167-170. See also intermediate fossils
tree-of-life, 153-155, 160, 161fig, 170, 185, 210-211
- assumed (central concept to Darwin), 173-174, 175-176, 189, 209, 217-218
trilobite, 158, 159, 164fig, 166, 168, 169, 171, 174
Turkana Boy, 235-236fig
Twoism, 301
Tyler, Sheena, 203, 218

UCD, see universal common descent
ultrabithorax, 216
uniformitarian, uniformitarianism, 24, 156
universal common descent (UCD), 66, 128, 160, 170fig, 190-193

- evidence from embryonic development, 187, 200-209, 217
- evidence from genetics, 209-217

unsinkable, 9-15, 55, 75, 210, 228, 230, 269, 271, 273, 274, 287, 304
Upright Man, see *Homo erectus*
Urey, Harold, 86*fig*-92, 108, 272, 274

Valentine, James, 166
Valtaoja, Esko, 97
Vasavada, Dr Ashwin, 79-80
Veith, Gene, 320
Vendian fossils, see Ediacaran
vertebrate backbone development
- amphibians, 206-209, 208*fig*
- bony fish, 204*fig*
- cartilaginous fish, 206-207*fig*
- reptile, bird, mammal, 205-206*figs*, 209

Voltaire, 45, 47
von Baer, Karl Ernst, 193-194, 197-199
Voyager, 19

Wächtershäuser, Günter, 87-88
Wagner, Günter P., 209
waiting time problem, 141-142, 258-260, 268
Walcott, Charles D., 162, 165-168, 174
Walker, Alan, 235-236*fig*,
Wallace, Alfred Russel, 62, 227, 255
Waptia, 169
Warren, Robin, 25-26, 32, 275
Watson, James, 89, 116
Wegener, Alfred, 23*fig*, 30, 32, 35, 168, 275,
Wells, Jonathan, 52, 193, 198, 213-216
West, John, 319
whale 'evolution', 180-184
whippo, 180
White, Andrew Dickson, 44
Whitehead, Alfred North, 48
White Star Line, 3, 4, 5, 10, 12, 228, 281
White, Tim, 242*fig*, 243-245*fig*, 246-247
Whittington, Harry, 165, 171
Wickramasinghe, Chandra, 60, 95-98, 108, 111, 112, 267, 282

Wilberforce, Samuel, 67-68, 71, 188, 286*fig*
Wilberforce, William, 67
Williams, David, 301-302
Wilson, A.N., 60, 61, 67-70, 267, 278
Wilson, David Sloan, 290
Wilson, Robert, 26
Winslet, Kate, 9, 281
Wistar Institute, 104, 106, 107
wolf, 130-132, 175, 181, 182, 184
Wolpoff, Milford, 235
Wood, Bernard, 238, 239, 247, 249
Woodward, A. Smith, 229

Xenopus laevis, 206-208*fig*

Young Earth Creationists, see Biblical Creationists

Zallinger, Rudolf, 223
Zhou, Gui-Qing, 167
Zika virus, 237
Zinjanthropus bosei, 238
Zmirak, John, 314
Zuckerkandl, Emile, 190, 211

Are you ready to think the unthinkable, sink the unsinkable?

For since the creation of the world God's invisible qualities – his eternal power and divine nature – have been clearly seen, being understood from what has been made, so that people are without excuse.
Romans 1 v 20

www.ingramcontent.com/pod-product-compliance
Lightning Source LLC
Chambersburg PA
CBHW052130070526
44585CB00017B/1774